and on piano... NICKY HOPKINS

and on piano... NICKY HOPKINS

The Extraordinary Life of Rock's Greatest Session Man

by Julian Dawson

Foreword by Klaus Voormann

Backstage Press
San Francisco

Backstage Press, an imprint of Plus One Press

Book Design by Backstage Press

Cataloging-in-Publication Data available from the publisher

2010913455

First Edition: April, 2011

10 9 8 7 6 5 4 3 2

For Hanne, Robyn, Holly and Clancy

and on piano... NICKY HOPKINS

The Extraordinary Life of
Rock's Greatest Session Man

by Julian Dawson

Contents

Foreword

A small, skinny figure with pallid skin and sensitive features enters the room as though he'd just stepped out of Alice's Wonderland. He sits down at the piano, brushes the keys with his fingers and, with a cheeky smile on his face, proceeds to play "The Teddy Bear's Picnic."

That's the picture that comes to mind when I think of Nicky Hopkins. The well-known children's classic was a Hopkins theme song for years and served as Nicky's stopgap tune during breaks or as a warm-up song, sometimes for the entire rhythm section.

Nicky was the prototype of the true sideman. Quiet and shy, but always a hundred percent focussed when it was time to work. When he wasn't at the piano he would wait patiently, often with his eyes cast down, for his moment to come, but he would laugh out loud whenever John floored us all with another wisecrack.

Nicky never strove to be the centre of attention, but served the giants of pop music with his musical genius: a classical pianist with rock'n'roll fingers.

He played with the elite and his discography is filled with legendary names: The Beatles, The Rolling Stones, The Who, Tom Jones, Dusty Springfield…just the list of names and their songs could fill a book.

We played together often and shared a lot of laughs. Whether on George's "Give Me Love," Harry's "Without You" or John's "Jealous Guy," it was always a joy to work with Nicky, a brilliant player who never forgot the importance of being a good companion and a faithful friend.

And so sideman Klaus looks back wistfully and remembers sideman Nicky: the times we shared with John and George, moments of wonderful insanity with Harry (Nilsson) and Nicky's unforgettable "Teddy Bear's Picnic."

– Klaus Voormann, December 2009

Introduction

'All right friends, you have seen the heavy bands, now you will see morning maniac music. Believe me, yeah, it's a new dawn...the regular guys...and Nicky Hopkins!'

At 8.00 in the morning on August 17th, 1969 in Bethel, New York, Grace Slick introduced Jefferson Airplane to the 500,000 strong crowd before her. Her band had been supposed to play at the very end of the second of "three days of peace and music" but had waited all night to take the stage at the event that took its name from a small artist's colony forty miles away, and went down in history as the Woodstock Festival. Tucked in side-stage behind a grand piano, adding rippling fills to the Airplane's acid-drenched songs, sat the diminutive figure of the one musician Grace mentioned by name: Nicky Hopkins.

Twenty-five years later I found myself in the same town, at one of Woodstock's finest studios, listening to a playback of my own voice accompanied on piano by the same Nicky Hopkins. The situation had come about through a set of coincidences so bizarre and unlikely, I'm convinced to this day that the hand of fate was involved.

It happened like this:

In 1994, I was a singer-songwriter, signed to a worldwide record deal with BMG, and was due to make my eighth album. Pre-production for the new recording began with my producer Stewart Lerman at his home on Manhattan's 14th Street, a process that entailed going through songs I had already written, mapping out arrangements and trying to write more material, before moving up to Dreamland Studios with my band.

One idea as yet unwritten concerned my father, who had died suddenly, though not unexpectedly, days before I was due to leave for the USA. Dad had been an avid classical music buff but, despite having seven sons growing up in the sixties, had successfully avoided listening to pop music. This unfortunately included all my own efforts as a musician. Thinking that he could maybe catch up now on what he'd missed in his lifetime, I was planning to write something for him.

After an intense day's work we were relaxing back at Stewart's apartment, which for him meant a joint and some late-night music. We shared an affection for the very early Steve Miller Band records and on this particular night were listening to *Your Saving Grace*, an album that prominently features Nicky Hopkins on piano and organ. My favourite track was "Baby's House," a nine-minute epic of baroque beauty on which Nicky even received a co-writing credit for his gorgeous keyboard inventions. Neither of us had heard any news of his whereabouts in years.

I wondered out loud, "What ever happened to Nicky Hopkins? Wouldn't it be amazing to have someone like him tracking with us on this record?" This was possibly the first time Nicky's name had ever crossed my lips. I thought no more about it and went back to work.

Two days later, I broke off to play a showcase gig at the South By Southwest Festival in Austin, Texas, as I had a CD currently released on a Texas-based label. The town was milling with record industry types and hopeful bands, all there for the hundreds of shows all over town. My appearance was scheduled at the Cactus Café, a well-known singer-songwriter venue on the university campus, in the shadow of the tower where famously a lone student gunman had picked off passers-by in 1966.

My half-hour show went well and was followed by the first of another six acts scheduled that evening. On came Texas writer/singer Jerry Williams, accompanied on second keyboards by…*Nicky Hopkins!*

After the show I was able to wangle my way in to an "invitations-only" party in a neighbouring room which, by pure luck, was hosted by Ralph Murphy, ASCAP's representative in Nashville. He introduced me to Nicky and his red-headed Scottish wife Moira. With his oversized glasses, long hair and stick-thin frame, he looked more like a slightly pensive but benevolent schoolteacher than a rock star. I explained the coincidence of my recent New York conversation and, being a firm believer in grabbing the moment, asked Nicky if he would consider joining us in the studio. He politely pointed out that he didn't know me, or my music, and asked if I had anything he could listen to before committing himself, so I gave him a recent compilation CD that BMG had put out in Europe.

Fate kicked in again, when it transpired that Nicky had moved that very week from Los Angeles to Nashville, to escape the recent earthquakes. I had spent a lot of time in the country music capital over the years, having recorded two previous albums there, as well as writing regularly with a number of locally based songwriters. I had a flight to Nashville booked next morning, to try and come up with some last-minute gems before going in to record. This gave me a perfect opportunity to follow up my chance meeting with Nicky.

He and Moira were living in a temporary apartment while they looked for a house to buy or rent. Despite nearly twenty years in the States, Nicky had obviously remained very British and even with only necessities unpacked, the place had a distinctly English flavour, with a keyboard set up in one corner, books and Nicky's well-known collection of tins covering every surface and the man himself shuffling about in a pair of comfy slippers.

Over a cup of tea, he said he'd enjoyed my songs, particularly the lyrics, as he himself only wrote music and furthermore that he would be delighted to join us in the studio—for a fee of fifteen hundred dollars per day and first-class flights for himself and his wife. Without for a moment feeling that this was over-priced for someone of his stature, I admitted that this was probably beyond the limits of our budget and, extremely reluctantly, had to decline (a decision I've regretted bitterly ever since).

Before I left, however, I mentioned that I was in town to try and write some more songs for the album and asked if he had any music that needed lyrics. He handed me a cassette with a beautiful piano piece he had recently written and promised that when we could get together again, he would dig out some photos and Rolling Stones stories.

I said my goodbyes, got into my rental car and put the cassette into the player. By the time I arrived at my publisher's office twelve minutes later, I had almost the complete lyrics to a song about my Dad. All I had to do was write them down, an experience I've only had once or twice in thirty years of making songs.

"You're Listening Now" was channeled rather than written. I knew right away that it was one of the better pieces of work I'd ever come up with.

I went back next day and played the completed song for Nicky and Moira. They loved it, so we agreed that I would go and make my album, but come back to Nashville so that we could record our new composition together. I was owed a couple of hours of studio time at the outlying Castle Studio and two weeks later I flew down, picked up Nicky and drove out to Franklin. Surprisingly the impressive Bösendorfer grand piano in the corner of their big room was not to his taste, but we carried on, Nicky playing and me singing live along with him.

One perfect take was ruined when the inexperienced young engineer let the tape run out in the middle (an agonising moment for me at the time), but we soon had a version we both liked, which I took back to Woodstock to finish off. With a Hammond organ (echoes of "Baby's House"), and a second vocal from Curtis Stigers, we had a finished track.

I felt I'd made a great new friend, and Nicky and I agreed to work together again as soon as I came back to Nashville.

I'd been away from home for months and took a break from mixing the album to fly home to London. My Danish wife was pregnant at the time and on arrival I found her in tears on the sofa, having just had the news that her father too had suddenly died.

After the second funeral that year, she was determined to remain at home in Denmark for the birth so, late that summer, I joined her there to await the baby. In the process of selling my flat in London I had put all my worldly goods in storage and only brought the minimum with me. Soon after my arrival, I hooked up the CD player and cassette deck, to copy the now finished album for all the musicians who had taken part.

On a September morning in our tiny one-room apartment, with unseasonably deep snow on the ground outside, the phone rang. It was my brother in England. "Have you seen the paper? Nicky Hopkins has died."

I was completely stunned. I tried to console myself that day by listening over and over to "Baby's House" and calling Nicky's widow and other friends who felt as devastated as I did. Our session together turned out to be his very last recording.

My daughter was born in early October, and the *Travel On* album came out, with a dedication to both fathers and to Nicky in the sleeve notes. I undertook a lengthy tour with my band to support it and found that wherever I played "You're Listening Now," people were immediately asking for the song at the merchandise stand, and there were sometimes rows of people in tears after I'd performed it.

I've now sung "You're Listening Now" hundreds of times, including once at the much-missed Bottom Line in New York, with Nicky's niece in the audience—one of two occasions when *I* couldn't get through it. I've had a man who works in a hospice for the dying tell me that he's played the song for dozens of terminal patients and that it helped them. It seems that not only did we subconsciously write Nicky's own epitaph together, but we also put something in the world that people can use, like a decent pair of shoes.

You're Listening Now

It must have been a silent place, without a soul around
The morning sunlight creeping in, a clock the only sound
I hope you heard a symphony as you left that room behind
Now every note that touches me calls you to mind

The house filled up with music the minute you'd come home
You set a spark that helped me build some fires of my own
But trying to please everybody on earth's
Not an easy thing to do
And all the time I was only trying to please you

It seems to me that dying has set you free somehow
And I know you're out there somewhere
And you're listening now

We said goodbye a long, long time before you had to go
And why that heart stopped beating I'll never know

A strong and silent teacher you let the music talk
I learned to sing in harmony as soon as I could walk
And trying to please everybody on this earth's
Not an easy thing to do
And all the time I was really trying to please you

It seems to me that dying has set you free somehow
And I know you're out there somewhere
And you're listening now
Yes I know you're out there somewhere
And you're listening now

I've been an inveterate record-collector, sleeve-reader and devourer of biographies all my life, and, when I realised that nobody else was likely to write his story, I determined to do it myself. If I had known what I was taking on I might have thought twice.

From my first interview with Carlo Little at his house in Wembley, to my last phone conversation with Yusuf Islam the night before I handed in my manuscript to a publisher, a decade has passed. I've collected photographs and memorabilia and talked to musicians, producers, friends and family about the times they shared with one of the great unsung heroes of rock music history, a man who arguably played on more important records than any other session-player in the world and yet remained, up to his tragically early death, a shadowy and enigmatic figure.

The well-known saying "Nobody said it would be fair," is particularly suited to the music industry. There are as many reasons to take up a music career as there are people to try; some become millionaires, while others end up selling hot dogs outside stadiums where their erstwhile band mates are entertaining fans who pay fortunes to shower their heroes with adulation for a precious hour or two.

A very special few are put in the world with a divine gift of pure music. Lacking a head for business, they are not necessarily the success stories we read about in celebrity magazines, but their spirit and brilliance enrich our lives.

Imagine the voodoo groove of the Rolling Stones' "Sympathy For The Devil" without its driving piano, "Angie" or "She's A Rainbow" without their gorgeous fills; the Beatles' "Revolution" without its perfectly formed solo or the Who's explosive first album without its breakneck keyboard accompaniment. Picture Joe Cocker singing his hit "You Are So Beautiful" alone and a cappella, or try to imagine the strident call-to-arms that is Jefferson Airplane's "Volunteers" without its keyboard riffs. Imagine…well, "Imagine," stripped of its beautiful piano work; Lennon's "Crippled Inside" without the perfectly tailored honky-tonk flourishes or "Jealous Guy" without its haunting and delicate piano decorations. These are just a handful of classic tracks all played by one man's hands.

Nicky Hopkins appeared with so many artists during his life that a complete discography is probably impossible, but a list of his better-known clients would include The Beatles (both together and individually), The Rolling Stones, The Who, The Kinks, David Bowie, Steve Miller, Jefferson Airplane, Quicksilver Messenger Service, Van Morrison, Rod Stewart, Donovan, The Jeff Beck Group, Harry Nilsson, Joe Cocker, The Yardbirds, Alexis Korner, Ella Fitzgerald, The Easybeats…well, you get the picture…

Wherever the centre of the pop/rock universe was at any one time, this Zelig-like individual somehow contrived to be there: in early sixties England at the birth of the British rhythm and blues boom and at the height of the beat explosion that followed the Beatles' meteoric rise; he was an integral part of the music that made "Swinging London" the epicentre of the mid-sixties, before moving to California in time for the blossoming of the west-coast psychedelic movement that sound-tracked the "flower-power" era (including that Woodstock appearance), and on and on to an endless parade of superstar sessions and worldwide tours.

In a media landscape that focuses almost exclusively on the tiny minority of musicians who make headlines or achieve millionaire status, Nicky's career path marks him out as an "Everyman" representing the thousands of background players whose talents are vital to the successes of others.

I've been privileged to get to know many of Nicky's closest friends, to sleep in the same bed at the Cipollina house in Mill Valley that Nicky and his first wife Dolly slept in and to sing "Jealous Guy" and "Give Me Love (Give Me Peace On Earth)" on stage in Berlin and Munich, with Klaus Voormann, who played on the original records with Lennon, George Harrison and Nicky.

Tracing the fifty-year journey of a complex, courageous and intensely private man from wartime London, through life-threatening illness, two marriages and various romances, dizzying ups and downs and, most importantly, the thousands of musical collaborations that led up to his untimely death in Nashville, has been a huge challenge, but with enormous support from Nicky's close family and friends, it's been a path full of revelations. With a player of his calibre, it's a case of "the deeper you go, the deeper it gets."

As Nils Lofgren put it, "Nicky wrote the book on rock'n'roll piano." Now here's a book about how he did it.

It's been quite a trip.

Acknowledgements

With rare exceptions I've found that my interviewees (some now departed), whether speaking face-to-face, down a phone line or in some cases answering questions by e-mail, all thought highly of Nicky and were happy to talk about him. Some contributions were longer than others but all of them were important.

My sincere thanks go out to:

Greg Anton	Martin Carthy MBE	Duane Eddy
PP Arnold	Clem Cattini	Merrell Fankhauser
Mick Avory	Steve Chapman	Herbie Flowers
Cliff Aungier (†)	Blondie Chaplin	Peter Frampton
Long John Baldry (†)	Neil Christian (†)	David Freiberg
Marty Balin	Antonia Cipollina	Girl Freiberg/Julia Brigden
Peter Baron	Joe Cocker	Vince Gill
Eric Bazilian	Ray Cooper	Roy Harper
Martin Belmont	Dave Cousins	Mike Harrison
Cliff Bennett	Alun Davies	David Hayes
Mike Berry	Ray Davies	Dan Healy
Ritchie Blackmore	Spencer Davis	Dick Heckstall-Smith (†)
Pete Brown	Bradley Ditto	Chas Hodges
Rick Brown	Terry Dolan	Chris Jagger
John "Rabbit" Bundrick	Jerry Donahue	John Paul Jones
Sue Bundrick (†)	Greg Douglass	Laurence Juber
Vashti Bunyan	Doug Duffey	Paul Kantner
John Butler	Gary Duncan	Mike Kennedy

Richard Kennedy
Bobby Keys
Al Kooper
Michael Lang
Derek Lawrence
Mike Lease
Chuck Leavell
Albert Lee
Larry Lee
Donovan Leitch
Carlo Little (†)
Bill Lloyd
Nils Lofgren
Reinhold Mack
Jon Mark
Beverley Martyn
Iain Matthews
Scott Matthews
Mike McCartney
Andy McCoy
Kathi McDonald
Michael McDonald
Michael McKean
Ian McLagan
Dennis McNally
Vince Melamed
Robin Millar
Frankie & Annette Miller
Steve Miller
Roger Mingay

Tony Morley
Hugh Murphy (†)
Ralph Murphy
Tony Newman
Chet Nichols
Anne & Billy Nicholls
Helen O'Hara
Andrew Loog Oldham
May Pang
Graham Parker
Richard Perna
Richard Perry
Pamela Polland
Ron Polte
Prairie Prince
Pete Quaife (†)
Keith Richards
Pat Robinson
Tom Rush
Ethan Russell
Scobie Ryder
Brinsley Schwarz
Paul Samwell-Smith
Pete Sears
Harry Shearer
Michael Snow
Leigh Stephens
Cynthia Stewart-Dillane
Rod Stewart
David Sutch (†)

Fred Tackett
Shel Talmy
Mick Taylor
Dave Tedstone
Benmont Tench
Chris Thompson
Richard Thompson
Pete Townshend
Akira Tsukahara
Tyla (Dogs D'Amour)
Joli Valenti
Trevor Veitch
Mike Vickers
Klaus & Christina
  Voormann
Micky Waller (†)
Joe Walsh
David Whitaker
Rick Wills
Bobby Winkelman
Mark Wirtz
Art Wood (†)
Woody & June
  Woodmansey
Bill Wyman
John York
Yusuf Islam (formerly Cat
  Stevens)

Very special thanks to Freda (†), Julia, Dee, Paul & Iris Hopkins, Moira Hopkins, Matthew and Alix Ninfo and Lynda "Dolly" Hopkins for their trust and support.

Further thanks to: Moira Bellas, Manfred Becker, Alan Benson, Bev Bevan, Johnny Black, Deborah Bonham, Vanna Bonta, Geoff Bradford, Trevor Burton, Mike D'Abo, Sherry Daly and Bonnie at Munro Sound, Amelia Davis, John Deaderick, Herb Dodell, Roger Dopson, Pete Dyer for the wonderful pictures, Jean-Luc Epstein, Pete Frame, John Goddard at Village Music in Mill Valley, Gordon Healey, Paul Jones, Nicola Joss at Eel Pie, Ken Kirkman, Denis Knowles, Jeff Knutson, Joni Labaqui, Dave Lang, Carol Lawrence, Gray Levett, Dave Lewis, Mark Lewisohn, Nick Low for the generous loan of interviews he conducted for his fine 2006 BBC Radio 2 portrait of Nicky Hopkins, Jim Marshall, Bernd Matheja, Linda McBride at Konk, Tom McGuinness, Frankie & Annette Miller, Larry Miller, Andy Neill, Gary Nicholson, Angela Nicoletti, Bill Parry at "Holding Together," Paul at Plattenrille in

1. Julian Dawson & Ray Davies

Hamburg, Allan Pepper, Robert Plant, Lord Puttnam of Queensgate CBE, Giselle Rawlins, Kimberley Rew, Ralph Sharp, Roland Schmitt, Ezra Sidran, Mike Smyth at Phonoluxe in Nashville, Andrew Skirrow, Steuart Smith, Mike "Fan Man" Somavilla, Chris Spedding, David Spero, Dominique Tarlé for his support and incredible photographs, Uwe Tessnow at Line Records, Richard Thompson, Rob Townsend, Uli Twelker, Rick Wakeman, Geoff Wall, Bob Weir, Chris Whitten, Dieter Wirth and Ed & Meg Greenberg in Tarrytown, NY, Barry Lewis and Hannah Charlton in London and especially Barry & Holly Tashian in Nashville for their wonderful hospitality.

Special thanks to Jacqueline Smay and Deb Grabien for their editing skills and most especially to Nic Grabien for his tireless work on all aspects of this book. Further thanks to Nick Awde for taking a chance and believing in this project.

Lastly to Karl Maria Hofer and Steffen Missmahl, who gave so much of their time and skills and without whom this book would never have found a home; to my agent Marlene Stringer who helped find it; and to my long-suffering family, who put up with ten years of borderline insanity.

Author's note: Most musicians have one career, but Nicky Hopkins had many. I decided early on that if I wrote his story strictly chronologically, it would simply be an endless list of concert and studio dates. I chose instead to structure the book in such a way that certain parts of Nicky Hopkins' life and work are given their own chapter, so that, for instance, a Beatles or Rolling Stones fan can go straight to the relevant section of the book. I beg the reader's forgiveness for the occasional small anomalies that arise as a result.

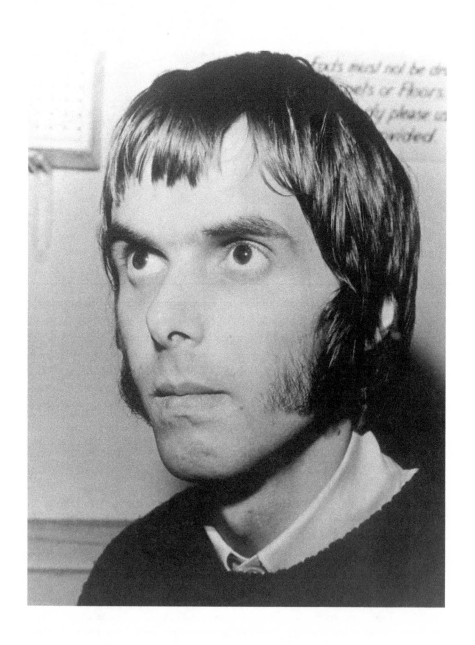

Baby's House
Childhood

'You'd hear this fantastic music coming out of the room. I thought it was a record, but it, it was him.'

— Dee Hopkins

There were better places than London to enter the world on February 24th 1944, but that night, in the suburb of Perivale, Mrs. Freda Hopkins gave birth to her fourth child and second son. She named him Nicholas Christian Hopkins.

The intense onslaught of German bombing that had engulfed the city in 1940-41 had given way to more sporadic attacks, leading in time to a dangerously blasé attitude among the defiant inhabitants. Nicky's older sisters Deidre (known as Dee) and Julia both had clear memories of their very pregnant mother in the last months of 1943.

Julia Hopkins: "We didn't have a shelter dug in the garden so we all used to get under this huge iron table[1], and eat our meals off it as well, because it took up the whole room. Mummy couldn't fit under the table, so she just sat by the side and thought, if it happens, it happens."

While the allies battled their way through Italy, and the German and Russian armies fought brutal winter campaigns on Hitler's Eastern Front, any sense of complacency at home in London was rudely shaken in late January 1944. The series of Luftwaffe bombing raids, later known as "the Little Blitz," pounded the London Docklands, leaving over a thousand dead on the first night alone. The intense bombardment continued unabated until April, with the attacks of Feb-

---

[1] The so-called "Morrison Shelter," a bolt-together steel table with a cage-like construction underneath named after Home Secretary Herbert Morrison

ruary 19th officially listed as "the heaviest raids since 1941." The new baby arrived in the middle of one such air raid.

Julia described him as "a lovely golden-skinned baby with huge brown eyes" and, like many unexpected late arrivals, Nicky was immediately the darling of the Hopkins household.

Details of his family background are hard to come by and even the immediate family members' memories are confused. Nicky's father, Alfred Edward Hopkins, was born in 1901 of partly Welsh ancestry. Julia remembered talk of an aunt who was a musician "who played the piano rather nicely." Alfred didn't like to talk about his father, an alcoholic who disappeared off to Australia, leaving his son to take care of his mother, brother and sister.

Nicky's mother's branch of the family tree is somewhat easier to trace.

Freda Laursen came from a Danish background but was born in England in 1908. Her father, Mogens Christian Laursen was from "peasant stock." When Mogens and his Danish wife (known as Nanny to the grandchildren) moved to England, they initially settled near Birmingham, which they quickly rejected as "so filthy they couldn't keep the curtains clean." The couple then headed south and set up home in Norwood with their three daughters. One married, and for many years successfully ran the "London Apprentice" pub on the Thames in Isleworth.

Julia never met her maternal grandfather but was told by her mother that Mogens had a reputation as a "ladies' man" and that a woman with a child once came to the door, causing great scandal and considerable upset to her grandmother. Julia recalled her as "a sweet little Danish woman who spoke very little English." After her husband's death, Nanny's regular visits to the Hopkins

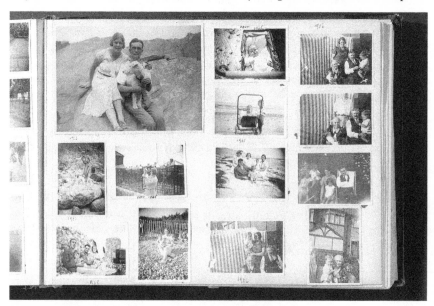

2. Family scrapbook – Freda & Alfred Hopkins

3. Freda & Alfred trading clothes on vacation, 1928

household were popular with the children, not least due to the boiled sweets she brought with her.

On leaving school, Alfred Hopkins trained as an accountant and was confident enough in his future to marry Freda on September 12th, 1931 at All Saint's church in Isleworth, followed by a reception at her sister's pub. Pre-wedding holiday photos showing the young couple swapping outfits, with Alfred splendid in a beret and white dress (looking incidentally the spitting image of his famous son) and Freda in a cap and plus-fours smoking a pipe, testify to a sense of fun early in their relationship that dwindled later with the pressures of work and raising a family.

Alfred Hopkins took up his first job at caterers J. Lyons & Co. in central London, while home was a typical suburban semi-detached house at 38 Jordan Road in Perivale. As soon as the opportunity arose, he moved on to better and more convenient employment at the Arthur Guinness brewery in Park Royal, where he remained for the rest of his working life, eventually became the firm's senior accountant.

The couple's first child Paul arrived in March 1935, followed two years later at the end of May by Dee and in March 1938 by Julia. When war broke out in '39, Alfred remained at work, while his wife and children were evacuated to Abingdon in Oxfordshire. Freda's best friend, whose husband was away in the air force, dreaded having strangers billeted with her and offered shelter to the Hopkins

3

instead, with Alfred coming down only at weekends. With a large RAF base close by, the safety of the arrangement was questionable, but the children enjoyed their exile there, and once back in London, like many wartime kids, they roamed freely and demonstrated a streak of devilment that seems to have been a family trait.

Home life was comfortable without being ostentatious. Even in post-war hard times, Alfred's work provided a solid and prosperous background for his growing family, but his children all remember their father as a severe and remote personality. The combination of his authoritarian bossiness and the stuffy atmosphere of a fifties suburban upbringing prompted all four to leave, not just the family home, but England too as soon as circumstances allowed.

Well-spoken and conservative by nature, though Liberal in his politics, Alfred was said to detest any neighbours who displayed Labour campaign posters in their windows.

Julia Hopkins: "We'd call him 'Mr. Barrett,'[2] which was mean. He was a strange man; I don't think anybody ever got close to him. He'd come in the front door and we'd all rush out the back!

"Because we lived in this big house and were always nicely dressed and very clean, I think that neighbours thought that we were slightly a cut above."

A still sprightly Freda Hopkins, when interviewed aged ninety-two, recalled that when Nicky was due, the late arrival was a surprise and not initially a welcome one:

"I thought I was finished with all that nonsense; I didn't want it (the baby); I was quite happy with what I'd got and I used to chase up and down the hill, thinking that would bring it off."

Her feelings changed as soon as she saw him, but Nicky's mother was convinced that being born during an air raid gave her son a nervous disposition from the start. Despite the other children's self-confessed devotion to their new brother, Julia remembered many childhood incidents that no doubt added considerably to his natural anxiety:

"We had a horrid game when he was tiny, which was to take him in his pram to the top of a hill and let it go—poor Nicky screaming with fear and us all running by the side, yelling with excitement; we were supposed to be taking him out for a gentle airing and a neighbour ratted on us to Mummy…"

Dee remembered the events on Horsenden Hill as revenge for being forced to go to Sunday school, a simple ruse to provide their parents with an hour or two of precious time alone.

Nicky was extremely accident-prone as a child.

Julia: "When he was about two, he pulled the teapot down on himself and his whole stomach area was badly burned. You can see in some of the pictures that there's no muscle, because of all the operations; it was like a very tough and pe-

---

[2] Referring to Elizabeth Barrett-Browning's struggles with her tyrannical father as shown in the film *The Barretts of Wimpole Street*.

culiar membrane of iridescent colours. I remember coming home from school and he was screaming because Mummy was changing the dressings, huge bandages with sticky stuff on. There was no skin left—I can't tell you how dreadful it was."

Listing the accidents that Nicky suffered, it is a miracle he ever made it to adulthood. On a seaside holiday in Dymchurch, he was cut off by the tide while trying to climb a cliff and was rescued in the nick of time by Julia, who dragged her choking and tearful brother out of the sea, though hardly able to swim herself. She remembered a distraught stranger carrying an unconscious Nicky up the garden path, his car having knocked him off his bicycle outside the family home. Dee admitted dropping him as a baby, and Julia has vague memories of a bout with polio.[3]

4. The Hopkins siblings: Paul, Dee, Nicky & Julia

For good measure, Nicky also swallowed a sixpence (childhood friend Anthony Hoskins remembered it as a more indigestible three-penny bit) and, for reasons no one can remember, lost the use of one eye for a time.

Whether resulting from the teapot incident or from his father's internal health issues, Nicky's lifelong struggles with stomach ailments also started early. Since his father's problems eventually landed him in hospital, where he died in 1974, there is a strong likelihood that Nicky inherited his chronic illness; but

[3] An early fifties parents' nightmare, that claimed 20,000 victims every year until vaccines were introduced in 1955.

5. At the beach

despite his own suffering, Alfred made few allowances for his son.

Dee: "Nicky would not eat meat and my father used to get so angry; he'd say, 'Eat it, otherwise you get nothing else!' His stomach couldn't take it, but nobody knew that at the time and he probably didn't know himself why he didn't like it."

During a train ride to a six-week musical summer camp, Nicky was overtaken by such sudden and agonising stomach pains that he had to return home immediately and ended up in hospital for a battery of tests. Though none of the doctors seemed to know what was wrong with him, he had his appendix removed—probably unnecessarily—before he was six years old. The operation had no effect whatsoever on his internal problems.

Freda Hopkins: "I used to think he was fooling about when he didn't want to do things. He would say he wasn't feeling well and I thought he was putting it on."

In addition to his physical problems, an inborn resistance to all forms of authority led to difficulties both at home with his father and with his teachers at school. He first attended Sudbury Primary School in Perrin Road, where a fellow pupil, though not at the time a close friend, was Tony Newman, later to join Nicky in the Jeff Beck Group:

"The school had a huge playground, divided by a white line—girls on one side, boys on the other and I remember Nicky once took his trousers down and mooned the girls in the playground. He had that smile on his face and it was outrageous to see him do that; there was a big to-do about it."

Freda: "He was awfully naughty at school. He never toed the line and was always in trouble for his antics; they used to send for my husband, saying 'We can't do anything with this boy!'"

One school friend remembered an early Hopkins harmonica performance. Nicky's extraordinary talent for music proved to be his salvation.

Freda had studied classical music seriously as a child, and there had always been a piano in the house. She no longer found time to play, but tried to interest her daughter Dee in the instrument. Though she enjoyed playing, Dee preferred sports and swimming. With Nicky it was a different matter; his mother remembered him at age three, mimicking the famous print of the young Mozart:

"There was a funny noise coming out of the living room and he'd got himself on the piano and was trying to play and it sounded as though he was playing a tune."

Though barely able to reach the keys, in a very short time Nicky was able to pick out a melody by ear, with his family as an admiring audience. When he was four, the family moved to a much bigger and more impressive house at 845 Harrow Road, one of several Guinness-owned properties, reserved as a special perk for employees, for which Alfred paid a princely four hundred pounds.

The new house boasted a garden with fruit trees and enough room for a grand piano in the downstairs lounge, a space that was soon given over to Nicky and his music. Julia and her sister thought their brother should have been allowed to take the room over completely. Instead, to their annoyance, Nicky was given a bedroom on his own, albeit a tiny one, while they had to share.

Dee: "He needed it. I'd hear music coming out of the room and thought it was a record that he had on, but it was him playing classical stuff; it was just brilliant."

They watched Nicky's precocious attempts on the piano with a mixture of pride and envy, and it was not long before he began taking lessons from a local teacher, Miss Marguerita Woolnoth. The six-year old prodigy liked his teacher enormously, though Freda had to make sure that he kept up his practice schedule, as Nicky would far rather improvise than play dull but necessary scales. Another gifted local pupil, now a well-known documentary filmmaker, was Alan Benson:

"We were both slightly 'rebellious' and were admired by Miss Woolnoth for our talents, though she disapproved of our enthusiasm for pop and rock. She was very Victorian and both she and her house at 48 Elm Road in Wembley smelt musty in that sort of pot-pourri way. One Saturday each month, we had to give a concert for parents and Nicky and I got 'lumbered' on many occasions; I can clearly see her walnut grand piano with a blanket draped over it and black and white portrait photographs on top.

"Nicky and I won gold medals in the twelve years and under duets section of the Wembley Music and Drama Festival. We played part of a Mozart Symphony arranged for four hands at one piano and I've still got the certificate at home with both our names on."

Mrs. Hopkins' perseverance paid dividends when Nicky's solo performances were also singled out in the local papers:

"Eleven-year-old Nicholas Hopkins played his own composition, 'Processional

6. Wembley Music and Drama Festival First Place Award

March'…The audience so applauded that Nicholas played the march again."

With a sympathetic teacher and the strict but supportive attention of his mother, Nicky progressed rapidly through the classical repertoire. He learned to sight-read and passed all his grade exams, enabling Miss Woolnoth to announce at a similar recital a year later that her star pupil had been awarded a Junior Exhibition at the prestigious Royal Academy Of Music (an honour that his later collaborator and fellow Academician Helen O'Hara confirmed was quite rare and dependent on outstanding ability).

From September 1956, he studied there every Saturday morning, from age twelve to sixteen. Inexplicably, there are no surviving records of his weekly attendances. He was almost certainly a contemporary of eleven-year old Reginald Dwight, another scholarship winner to the Academy in 1958, later better known as Elton John.

Nicky's piano skills were a godsend at school, where he showed little aptitude for any other subjects:

"School was useless. About the only things I was ever good at were music and English, so I used to draw pictures like the *Jamming With Edward* cover."

Nicky's best-known cartoon, immortalised later on the album he recorded with members of the Rolling Stones, was inspired by a math teacher named George Parker, one of the only teachers he remembered fondly:

"He was one of the most amazing characters I've ever met; he used to come in, slam the door, slam his books down on the desk to let you know he was there and then say, 'Good afternoon!' with this big sunny smile, 'Will you sit down please?' We used to say, 'My God, his head's going to fall off one of these days if that smile gets any bigger!'"

The artwork for *Jamming With Edward* was Nicky's only published piece of art. Alongside his musical gifts, however, he showed a natural, untrained talent as a cartoonist. His numerous letters and cards to his family were filled with surreal and childish subject matter, much of it only comprehensible to his brother and sisters. The schoolboy tone, casual racism and occasional touches of cruelty in his

9

7. Cartoon featuring Nicky's father, from a letter to Dee, 1967

writings and drawings are strongly reminiscent of John Lennon's highly popular books from the sixties (*In His Own Write* and *Spaniard In The Works*) and jar somewhat in these more politically correct times.

His main targets seemed to be old ladies with their middle-class pretensions (referred to in Hopkins-speak as "my" ladies and "very kind" and "pleasant") and his Dad's habits and mannerisms, which came in for merciless lampooning. He threw in spoonerisms, rhyming and backwards words and an invented vocabulary, with stream-of-consciousness references to piles of poo, farting dogs, bogeys (boogers), the *Beano* comic, Popeye and other heroes from children's television programmes, that appeared to carry great significance.

To Dee:

"*This is Niggy the Picky writing to you from Olaf's Castle, situated in the wilds and forests of Fartemberg. I am staying with my friend Giant Flemface, in his best dungeon. Ah! Silly bugger! Ever so kind & happy! Woof! When I think of going out to spot the 'my' ladies I have to laugh—must take a trip to Harrod's and see some more!*"

To Paul (on his birthday):

"*And there he goes, boys and girls, moist definitely quacking across the marsh!! How kind! How abso-fucking-lutely lovely! Ahhhhh! I nearly fell over when I found this*

10

card yesterday. Hmmmm—so you're FIFTY-SEVEN are you now? (Heinz Baaked Beans anyone?) Why, you little monkey! Here's one for you—BICKER! I don't know why that came to mind after all these years, but there it was! And hold that spoon properly: it's not a shovel! Dear oh dear oh dear!

"Lots of trafs and special love to the Schnuffie! Birthday bogues,"

Dee Hopkins: "Nicky had a completely wacky, off the wall sense of humour; we'd just look at each other—or Paul and Nicky would—just eye contact and we'd go off into peals of laughter for no reason. We used to carry on like lunatics."

Julia: "He always loved to wear tea cosies; no matter where he was, if he saw a tea cosy he'd put it on his head. Don't ask me why."

But it was his music that made the most impact. Freda told me proudly that the teachers "alighted on his musical talent (and realised) that he could accompany anything."

Julia Hopkins attended several primary school performances and "would get all hot and cold with embarrassment" because she knew her gifted brother would be coming on the stage. "I couldn't bear it, but it was lovely—and of course he was always the star."

Nicky's miseducation continued at the much larger Wembley County Grammar in Stanley Road, where his musical talents continued to flourish, if not his academic skills.

Members of the "Old Alpertonians," who had been Nicky's contemporaries at school, described him variously as "offbeat, eccentric, strange, a misfit, a dropout, oddball and 'not one of us.'" Other pupils remembered Nicky smoking in the bike sheds, smuggling a dog into school, drinking spirits and deliberately wearing odd socks. All acknowledged his brilliance at the piano and one friend commented on his "photographic memory," recalling a poem they were supposed to have learned. Nicky was only reminded of the fact at lunchtime. He asked to see the poem, read it once and recited it perfectly in class.

By coincidence, Anne, the wife of sixties songwriter Billy Nicholls (with whom Nicky would later record), was a contemporary and had clear memories of Nicky:

"He was a year or two above me, but I shared a dinner table with him for a few weeks; he was just an older boy who made fun of the school and the teachers to impress us younger girls; he often played the piano at morning assembly and as the last pupil left the hall, he changed from the traditional classical music to jazz or blues, which made our walk back to the classrooms a much more interesting journey.

"In the last summer term before leaving school, he and his peers organised a lunchtime music club in the woodwork studio, with big speakers situated in the playground, to introduce his fellow pupils to the up and coming music of the time and once there was a Christmas pop concert in the school hall, with the proceeds going to help the people in Hungary after the Russian invasion in October 1956."

The large age gap between Nicky and his siblings made him, from the outset, a solitary child, though—as can be seen from the letters and postcards he sent from all over the world—he maintained close ties with his family. All the Hopkins shared a very distinctive clipped English tone of voice and a special manner of speaking, and their communications, in writing and in person, echo the Brontes at Haworth. Nicky would later forge a particularly close bond with his brother Paul, involving code words, a secret language and their shared surreal sense of humour.

8. Nicky and friends on the railway

Although they doted on their sickly youngest brother, all three of his siblings were preoccupied with their own lives and had their own battles to fight, leaving Nicky at home with his music, his daydreams and his already established passion for collecting.

From an early age he had an exaggerated sense of nostalgia and a devotion to the past. He loved books and anything old: coins, antiques, maps, bus tickets, comics, records, postage stamps, railway memorabilia, photographs of trams and of course tins, as well as vintage comedy, radio plays and films. Unlike most boys his age, however, he showed no interest whatsoever in either playing or following any sport. He remained a dedicated tea drinker all his life.

In the autumn of 1954 he met Anthony Hoskins, who lived in nearby May-bank Avenue and became his closest childhood ally. The two were born within a day of each other and, with a surname only one letter removed from his friend's, Anthony Nicholas Hoskins remains convinced that he and Nicky were destined to be friends for life. Fifty years later, he clearly remembered their first encounter:

"There was a big horse chestnut tree in front of Nicky's house and one day I went round there with my younger sister to knock 'conkers' down; he was fed up with the local kids throwing lumps of wood and other missiles at the tree and came out to tell us to clear off, but for some reason had a sudden change of heart and decided instead to help. I always knew Nicky as Nick and he always called me Ant."

They would take off for the day, accompanied by a large black and tan dog named "Rusty Runters," that belonged to a nearby garage owner, but was always waiting at the garden gate for Nicky to return from school. The trio would roam the neighbouring parks and open spaces, sometimes travelling on buses and trol-leys—and always without a lead.

Anthony Hoskins: "One of our favourite haunts was an area of waste ground we nicknamed 'the Dump,' which provided us with a handy shortcut between our homes and an adventure playground too. Others included Butler's Green, almost opposite Nicky's house, which we called 'the Wreck,' and a hilly area in Elms Lane, christened 'Zulu Land' for reasons I can't recall.

"We would place 78 rpm records, picked up for nothing at local jumble sales, in the branches of trees and throw stones at them until they shattered. The sound of breaking glass was generally music to our ears, so bottles, reject col-oured light bulbs from a local factory—which made a satisfying bang when they smashed—and the windows of empty buildings, were all fair game.

"We struck up an unlikely friendship with an old gentleman who spent most of his daylight hours looking for scrap wood to burn at home, an activity we would cheerfully help him with."

During one school holiday they were at the dump, when a portly local police-man rode past on his bicycle. The two boys waited until he had pedalled past and then chased after him, shouting at Rusty to "get him!" The dog caught up with his moving target, barking loudly all the while, and eventually forced the unfor-tunate bobby to stop. The upshot of this unprovoked attack was a ban on taking Rusty out for the rest of the holidays.

Anthony remembered another occasion when the combination of glass-smashing and canine activities led to disaster:

"We had been smashing bottles on the railway embankment, next to Barham Park in Sudbury, when Rusty cut one of his paws quite badly on the broken glass. He was bleeding profusely and we panicked, convinced he was about to die; so while Nick stayed with the dog, I ran all the way to the fire station and rang the emergency bell on the front door. A kindly fireman answered, and when I blurted out what had happened, called the RSPCA,[4] who immediately sent an ambulance to take the hapless dog to a vet. We told the owner what had happened and Rusty Runters duly recovered, but walked with a limp for a long time afterwards. We never broke glass again!"

The Hopkins family shared a love of pets, with cats being a particular favourite. Nicky had any number of them in his various households during his later life and detailed references to their behaviour were always a regular part of his letters. At one time during his stay in America, he had seven of the creatures, with names such as Pig, Bugger, Floss and Cadabra as well as a large Doberman called Floyd.

On event days such as the soccer Cup Final, the preoccupation with bottles took a more profitable turn, when Nicky and Ant scoured the car parks surrounding Wembley Stadium for discarded fizzy drink bottles, which they collected in sacks and dragged to the nearest sweet shop or café to claim the two penny deposit on each. One irate café owner chased them away, when it became apparent that their offerings came from the bottles stacked outside his own establishment.

Less contentious activities included playing with model trains (Nicky had a Trix set and Anthony a Hornby Dublo), cycling and listening to records; Lonnie Donegan, Buddy Holly, Little Richard and Elvis were favourites and Anthony is still a record collector today. Wembley boasted two record shops, where the top ten hits of the day could be listened to in individual sound booths, and in Sudbury was a newsagent who sold 78s, stacked in enticing piles next to the counter.

They watched films at one of the three local cinemas and television at each other's homes. After one particularly terrifying episode of the popular TV sci-fi thriller, *The Quatermass Experiment*, Anthony had to walk home past the dark trees and bushes in the Hopkins' garden and sprinted at breakneck speed all the way back to his own house.

Cycling trips might include a visit to the former American airbase at South Ruislip to look for cigarette ends to be re-used in homemade roll-ups and, when pocket money allowed, a packet of five Weights or Woodbines, the cheapest and roughest cigarettes available. The two novice smokers would take two each and share the last one by breaking it in half.

When schooldays finally came to an end, their paths diverged, with Nicky busy establishing himself in the music world and Anthony taking a job in public relations. The two remained in contact with letters and occasional phone calls and in 1963, when Nicky went into the Central Middlesex hospital for his longest and most serious period of medical treatment, Anthony was one of his regular visitors. Nicky was discharged just in time to attend his friend's twenty-first birthday party.

Years later Anthony was walking past Nicky's old address and was saddened to see that the building was being demolished. He decided to salvage some of the floorboards and fencing materials and used them in his own newly acquired home in Hayes. He had to leave behind the large and beautiful front door, be-

---

[4] Royal Society For The Prevention Of Cruelty To Animals

9. In the garden at 845 Harrow Road

cause it wouldn't fit anywhere in his house. 845 Harrow Road was replaced in the seventies by a small, unprepossessing block of flats named Katrina Court that still stands today.

In the late eighties, the two friends met up one last time when Nicky accompanied Art Garfunkel at the Royal Albert Hall. He contacted Anthony Hoskins again, inviting him and his wife to attend the show. Armed with a backstage pass, Anthony was able to hear the music and afterwards meet up with Nick and his family and reminisce about their boyhood antics.

In his mid-teens Nicky made friends with another local boy, Bernie Watson, who came from a much simpler working-class background, living in a council house on Douglas Avenue in Wembley. How they met is unclear, but Bernie, who rejoiced under the unfortunate nickname "Bernie Bollock-Brain," played classical guitar, so they had a shared interest in music, as well as a destructive streak and a similarly twisted sense of humour. The two became inseparable friends.

Nicky had a penchant for trashing telephone boxes and his brother Paul vividly remembers him coming home one day carrying a broken mouthpiece with its wires ripped out and dangling. The incident prompted his father to report Nicky to the police and send him to a psychiatrist. Nicky also had a habit of unscrewing the timetables in train carriages and once arrived at school stiff as a scarecrow, a railway sign jammed in the arms of his coat.

Girlfriends do not seem to have been a priority and none of his family remembered signs of any romantic attachments in Nicky's shy teen years, though Freda said that girls used to like him. Apparently all his energies went into music.

The years following World War II were a famously austere and conservative time in Britain and Nicky was ten years old when rationing came to an end on July 4th 1954. Though the Hopkins children had all the financial benefits of a middle class upbringing, the urge to break out of the stifling morality and "greyness" was strong in all of them. Alfred's dour and humourless approach to life dictated the atmosphere in the household. When he was home, enthroned in an armchair with his newspaper, everyone would tiptoe around him, keeping noise to a minimum, avoiding bringing friends home and pretending to be invisible.

10. Nicky and his father, Alfred Hopkins

Anthony Hoskins remembered tea times when Nicky's posture at table would prompt his father to put on his sternest voice and say "Nicholas, stop sagging!" Nicky would respond by growling; his faithful imitations of his Dad kept his friend and his sisters in stitches.

Freda's fun-loving side blossomed the minute her husband was out of the house or asleep upstairs. She could be seen with whichever of the children were home, laughing, listening to the radio and dancing around the kitchen to Frank Sinatra, cranking up the volume whenever a rock'n'roll song made it onto the airwaves.

Julia's ticket out came in 1957. Her striking looks landed her a modeling contract at the prestigious Eileen Ford agency in New York, where she met her future husband and remained for many years:

"Dad wanted me to be a buyer and put me into Woollens Of Knightsbridge to learn the trade. Well, I'd had enough of that. I met a girl called Drina Marsh, who knew Huntington Hartford, a multi-millionaire who owned all the A&P stores in the USA. He had a modeling agency and I was introduced to him at Stephen Ward's place. He spoke to my parents and I really wanted to go to get out of England. It was all very peculiar; the FBI came and interviewed Dad to ask why I wanted to go to America.[5] I went, though I was really a bit too young."

Her older sister Dee's ambitions were less high-flown and she was keen to work in London, but her father wouldn't hear of it and instead found her a job at the Metal Box Company, which supplied trays and tin boxes to Guinness's. Alfred tried in vain to fit square pegs into round holes; Dee, whose great love was the outdoors, was able to break away at nearly seventeen and spent two happy years as a farming student at a Guinness-owned hop farm in the Vale Of Evesham, later becoming involved at a high level in the film world in the USA.

She is convinced that her father did everything he could to encourage his older children to leave the fold as early as possible, simply to regain some peace at home. He facilitated Dee's green card and entry to the USA by opening up a savings account with two hundred and fifty pounds in it (at the time a sizeable sum), as proof for the US embassy. Paul was sent away to be a cadet on a naval training ship.

Nicky's illnesses made him the exception to the family rule, and it would be over ten years before he made his break for independence. In the meantime, like thousands of western teenagers, his life was changed irrevocably by his first encounter with an entirely new kind of music, when Dee brought home Fats Domino's "Ain't That A Shame" and Little Richard's incendiary coupling of "Tutti Frutti" and "Long Tall Sally" on one forty-five. Suddenly classical music seemed slightly less gripping.

Nicky Hopkins: "I remember listening to one song that I really liked; there was nothing special about it except that it was the first time I remember being able to listen and then sitting down at the piano and playing it. That's when I first started to understand music, beyond just having the ability to read it. Rock allowed me to experiment with new styles, but I never lost that classical element in my music. I was twelve when I first heard Little Richard and Jerry Lee Lewis and those records made a fantastic impression on me. I used to turn up my record-player full-blast and drive my old man mad."

While his parents had so far been extremely supportive of their son's musical leanings, when his interests veered towards jazz and rock'n'roll music, his father, in particular, saw absolutely no future in it and predictably wanted him to take up a more serious occupation.

---

[5] Ward was later to become a central figure in the Profumo scandal of 1963, when UK Secretary of State for War John Profumo's affair with Christine Keeler led to his resignation and almost the fall of the government.

Nicky had visions of working for a music publisher in London, but when no vacancy could be found, like both his sisters, his father coerced him into taking a local job in a solicitor's office in Wembley. His only major contribution to the unfortunate firm was to go down into the basement and systematically re-arrange all the files, leaving the entire business in total disarray. Not surprisingly, Nicky lasted just three weeks at his first and only "proper job." When he was discovered one morning asleep at his desk, he was sent home in disgrace.

By this time he was already taking his first steps towards life as a professional musician. He and Bernie had discovered to their delight that they were not the only rock'n'roll fans in Harrow, having met two other local youths keen to make some noise in the world.

The Savages were born.

Flip Flop & Bop Till You Drop
Savage, Rebel Rouser & All-Star

"Someone had to go astray and label the pills
And ride all the way down the motorway that they had yet to build"
      – Kimberley Rew: 'Screaming Lord Sutch' from his CD Great Central Revisited

Exact details of how the original Savages came together depend upon whose account one chooses to take as gospel, but since drummer Carlo Little's version and bassist Rick Brown's overlap, they seem to provide the likeliest scenario.

All four lived within a few hundred yards of each other, with Carlo at 883 Harrow Road and Nicky at 845 and all shared the same passion for then revolutionary performers like Jerry Lee Lewis, Little Richard, Chuck Berry and, of course, Elvis Presley.

Old-school vocalists and crooners such as Rosemary Clooney, Jimmy Young, Slim Whitman, Dickie Valentine and Ruby Murray[6] dominated the British charts of the early fifties. The first shift towards music tailored to "young people"—the word "teenager" had yet to be coined—came in 1955 with the all-conquering re-release of Bill Haley's "Rock Around The Clock." It had first been issued in the USA a year earlier, but it was making a seismic impact through its inclusion in the soundtrack to the hard-hitting film *Blackboard Jungle*.

Little Richard exploded into view in the equally popular Jayne Mansfield vehicle, *The Girl Can't Help It* and by 1957 the previously unchallenged rule of performers like Pat Boone and Doris Day in the UK charts was under attack. Imports arrived from Sun Records, Chess and other pioneer labels. Homegrown

---

[6] Murray was immortalised among musicians as Cockney rhyming slang for an after-show curry!

pretenders like Tommy Steele and most importantly, skiffle messiah Lonnie Donegan—with whom Nicky would later record—began to appear.

Greeted with euphoria by the nation's youth, rock'n'roll music soon spawned dozens of British Elvis clones, many from the London-based impresario Larry Parnes' "stable of stars." Ordinary youths were re-christened with catchy names such as Wilde, Fury and Eager, while the skiffle craze gave birth to thousands of DIY bands all over the country. Sales of guitars, banjos and harmonicas rocketed and many puzzled housewives were left suddenly short of a washboard. As a pianist, Nicky Hopkins passed through the skiffle boom apparently unscathed.

The British media, though initially slow to respond, eventually channeled the new mood into youth-oriented TV shows. Jack Good's *Oh Boy* was launched in 1958, with Cliff Richard performing his influential "Move It" in the first week. Panel-show *Juke Box Jury* followed in the summer of '59.

Nobody expected the new fads to last more than a season or two, and the initial raw energy of rock'n'roll was drastically reduced when its black origins were watered down to make it more palatable to white audiences. With Elvis in the army, Little Richard temporarily lost to religion, Jerry Lee Lewis disgraced in the scandal surrounding his marriage to his thirteen-year old cousin and Buddy Holly, Ritchie Valens and the Big Bopper dying in a tragic plane crash, it seemed for a moment that the music business had returned to its previous diet of ballads and blandness, as if rock'n'roll had never existed.

When twenty-one year old Carlo Little was discharged from his two years of National Service in February 1960, he thought he was the only rock'n'roll fan left in Sudbury and Harrow. Having been "the lad in school who always wanted to drum," he had used his compulsory stay with Her Majesty's forces to improve his percussion skills and sight-reading, joining the Corps of Drums of the City Of London Royal Fusiliers, stationed at the Tower Of London.

After stints in Kenya, Malta and India, his first port of call on his release was his old haunt, the "Cannibal Pot" coffee bar on the Harrow Road (now a pizza outlet), described in glowing terms by fellow local sticksman Tony Newman:

"They had a jukebox, it was threepence a play and it was the real deal; I'd never heard anything like it; you could hear the bass on it and everything! We'd all only had crystal radio sets and would listen to Radio Luxemburg to try and get licks. They'd play three tunes from America on the *Horlicks* show and you'd get an inkling of what rock'n'roll was like. Apart from that, I'd listen to *Two Way Family Favourites* on a Sunday morning, bored out of my gourd, hoping that they'd play some popular song. It was dreadful."[7]

None of Carlo's old pals were around anymore. He consoled himself by putting a few coins in the jukebox, but could find little to please him apart from some Buddy Holly.

---

[7] Nicky's friend Anthony remembered the coffee bar as a haunt for local Teddy Boys, and, despite sporting the requisite suede jackets, tight trousers and luminous socks, the two were far too nervous to go in.

One day, Carlo began chatting to a girl called Gill about the sorry lack of good records and she replied that he would probably get on with her boyfriend. Said party arrived a few moments later, dressed "in a long camel-hair coat, with eighteen-inch-long hair and a pair of flying goggles with no glass in them." This was Carlo's first confrontation with David Sutch, the self-styled "Screaming Lord."

Sutch would have stood out from the crowd in any era, but in 1960 he might as well have come from another planet. He was keeping himself alive with a window-cleaning round, a fairly lucrative undertaking that allowed him to work the hours that suited him and afforded the occasional romantic dalliance with a bored female customer. His mode of transport was a motor scooter, with a trailer to carry his ladder and equipment. The goggles were intended to lend an air of authority, designed to distract any policeman who might have wanted to check his non-existent driving licence and insurance.

Unlike Carlo, Sutch boasted no musical talents or training of any kind, but he was equally devoted to rock'n'roll and absolutely determined to make his mark on the world.

Over a cup of tea, Carlo outlined his plans to buy a drum-kit (for the huge sum of a hundred pounds, with his Dad signing the necessary hire purchase documents) and then start a rock'n'roll band. Sutch immediately offered to help and together they went off in search of further recruits at the local musicians' Mecca: Macari's Music in Wembley.

Ricky Brown was another local boy, still living at home in nearby Sudbury Court Road, and from a similar middle-class background to Nicky Hopkins. In his early teens he spent two years at Selsted, a boarding school in Essex, an attendance cut radically short when he was caught in a compromising position with a girl who worked in the school infirmary.

At Selsted, he had gained some musical experience. Later guitarist-to-the-stars Andy Roberts, two years his junior, remembers him with respect bordering on awe, not just for his perfect haircut, but for his role as a member of the Icebergs, who featured a singer with the unforgettable name of "Flash Sid" Fanshawe. Thus Rick came into the Savages line-up as the only member with any previous group experience.

Carlo knew of Nicky through a nodding acquaintance with his older brother Paul, but it was Bernie Watson who brought him into the fold. In the spring of 1960 the four musicians and their wild-haired mentor met up for a first rehearsal in the back room of the Swan pub, next door to the Cannibal Pot and hired for seven shillings and sixpence.

They began as an entirely instrumental band, with Carlo sitting proudly behind his new black "mother-of-pearl" drum-kit, Bernie and Rick on amplified acoustic guitars and Nicky at an out-of-tune piano with a microphone thrust down the back of it, connected to an amplifier.

Excited by their efforts at recreating some favourite Chuck Berry and Jerry Lee Lewis tunes, the four budding rockers put all they had into making as unholy a racket as possible until one squealing guitar part from Bernie sent David Sutch into such a head-banging frenzy, that his hair exploded out of the confines of his pork-pie hat (with holes drilled in it so his head could breathe) and flew around in the air as he yelled, "Yeah! Fantastic!"

The spectacle was so funny that they all stopped playing and laughed until the tears ran down their cheeks. With calm restored again, Carlo said, "You've got to start singing!" Sutch (correctly) asserted that he couldn't sing, but Carlo persisted and was confident that "a good ear and a sense of timing" qualified him to teach.

For the next three months, the band continued to learn new numbers while the drummer taught Sutch the rudiments of rock'n'roll singing in the front room of his parent's house. Carlo's pupil lacked the most basic ability to hold a note or understand bar structure and rhythm, but by learning parrot-fashion, he acquired a repertoire of about ten songs and came up with the name Screaming Lord Sutch and The Savages.

With carefully chosen numbers like "Great Balls Of Fire," "Roll Over Beethoven" and Bobby Darin's "Bull Moose," Sutch planned to compensate for his shortcomings as a vocalist by having the country's most outrageous stage act. He had already started collecting the stage props that would make him famous, or rather notorious; the more musical developments in the band were left to Nicky and to a lesser extent Bernie, who shared an ability to learn songs almost instantly and grasp the feel of the American originals they all worshiped.

Carlo Little: "Our all-time favourite was 'Flip, Flop & Bop' by Floyd Cramer; Nicky borrowed it for one night and when he came back and played it next day, we fainted, it was so good; same with the guitar. Bernie wanted to be a classical guitarist like Segovia, but Nicky had already done that. It's very rare to have a classically trained person like rock'n'roll, because they think it's beneath them."

Rick Brown referred to Nicky's house as a "small castle," and there was certainly a contrast between the Hopkins' home, where some rehearsals were held, and the others' more humble addresses. Not only could they use the downstairs lounge with its grand piano, but Nicky was also the proud owner of a tape-recorder, at a time when most kids could only afford a "gramophone with changeable needles." Nicky's parents had given up their initial resistance to their son's new career and now supported both him and the band in every way possible, allowing them to play at all hours, paying for an electric keyboard and other band equipment and letting Nicky stay up all night listening to music and making primitive recordings.

Julia Hopkins: "I think Dad was really thrilled that he was doing so well with these boys and realised that the lawyer's office was not the place for Nicky. Later on, Mummy always used to take Nicky's bookings and was very good at it and when he retired, Dad tried to take over. He'd rush to the phone and Mummy would get cross, because people liked talking to her, but I'm not sure that it was quite as easy to talk to Dad who was very officious."

Paul Hopkins: "Father didn't see any future in music, but when Nicky became known he was secretly rather proud, because I found one or two things over the years that he had written down, but never showed anyone."

11. The original Savages with Bernie Watson, Nicky Hopkins, Rick Brown and Carlo Little

Being in a band put paid to Nicky's classical training. His second wife, Moira, remembered him mentioning "a school of music in Devon,"[8] that he had planned to attend but didn't, distracted by his new enterprise.

Rick Brown: "They (his parents) must have been horrified to see us traipsing in, smoking like chimneys and being general layabouts, but they let him carry on."

By the time he was sixteen, Nicky was already a dedicated smoker, usually manufacturing his own cigarettes with a small rolling machine. Despite his constant ill health, it was a habit he would keep up almost to the end of his life.

After a few weeks, the day finally arrived for their first live performance. A

---

[8] Probably Dartington Hall.

group photo was taken in June 1960 (without Sutch), in a youth club building at Lime Hart School in Alperton, where Bernie Watson was a pupil, and which served as another cheap rehearsal room. The picture shows the four aspiring musicians looking absurdly young, with Carlo dapper in a hound's-tooth jacket, the two guitarists proudly clutching their cheap instruments, and Nicky in jacket, shirt and tie in front of the piano and behind a small Vox amp (probably paid for by his parents).

The earliest gigs were unpaid, self-promoted affairs in local halls, with home-made posters stuck on advertising hoardings. Their first professional engagement came when Bob Potter, an established promoter, booked them for a dance in Camberley. Rick Brown described this performance succinctly as "diabolical" and Potter was so furious, that he could be seen "jumping up and down in the wings waving his fists in the air." "I booked a London band and what do I get? This shambles!"

After an equally chaotic second gig at the Clay Pigeon in Eastcote, where Sutch hurled his jacket dramatically skywards, only to leave it dangling from a chandelier, shock set in and the first group was over almost as soon as it had begun.

Undaunted, David Sutch went off to audition at the famous Two Is coffee bar in Soho, a magnet for hopeful pop stars and skifflers, since legend held that Tommy Steele had been discovered there. Sutch was wise enough to know that his vocal performance alone would not see him through, so, with a pair of horns bought at a local junk shop and a Tarzan costume, he arrived as "the Wild Man of Borneo." This secured him not only a contract from Two Is manager Tom Littlewood, but a double page spread in the following weekend's *News Of The World*.

Soon he was off on a national package tour, backed by the already established Vince Taylor's group, the Playboys. Their garish matching shirts and boots, bleached blond hair and hard-hitting approach were way ahead of the other acts around at the time and would prove to be an important influence on later Savages line-ups. When Sutch's arrest for inciting a small riot in Scotland made the papers, he was astute enough to recognise the impact generated by the incident, and immediately enlisted his first publicity agent.

The shell-shocked troops he left behind in Harrow recovered slowly from their disappointing debut and, after lacklustre rehearsals with a girl named Sylvie—who was briefly but unsuccessfully promoted from "groupie" to female vocalist—were approached by a potential manager.

Frank Maher, described by Ricky Brown as "a stuntman and conman," boasted some connections in the music business and spun a good line but, after booking the band to back singer Dickie Pride on a few shows, he failed to convince the more worldly-wise Carlo, who promptly left to join local rivals Dougie Dee and The Strangers on a semi-professional basis, with the additional security of a day job.

Re-christened "The Saxons" and with a replacement drummer named Johnny Jenks and a singer "who'd just come out of prison," Bernie, Rick and Nicky were put to work on the circuit of American military bases, such as Brize Norton and Mildenhall. The gigs provided a reasonable wage and some valuable live experience, but little more. For Rick Brown, now permanently moved from guitar to bass, this proved a lonely time, as Nicky and Bernie Watson were thick as thieves throughout these early years, sharing jokes that band colleagues remember with distaste.

Rick Brown: "Nick had these ridiculous stories about a character he'd seen who had no legs and went about on a tea tray; he was always going on about this and Bernie got roped in; I thought it was absurd, so I was the odd man out."

There were other causes of friction in the Saxons. A naturally modest man, Rick Brown is dismissive of all the music they made in the early years and particularly of his own work. He described his teenage self as "an awful musician and a complete prat as well," and added that "it must have been agony for Nick to listen to my playing." Given the exceptional talents of his two associates, the novice bass-player's more modest progress was considered too slow, and eventually he was unceremoniously ousted from the Saxons.[9]

Lord Sutch, meanwhile, had realised that relying on someone else's musicians to back him would only ever be a short-term solution. He missed the guiding hand and organisational abilities of Carlo Little; in fact, without Carlo, his wayward singing and eccentric timing made it a struggle to keep going.

Back in Harrow, with the drummer's help, Sutch set about forming the "Savages Mark 2," with keyboard-player Andy Wren (who had grown up in the same block of flats as Charlie Watts), and bassist Ken Payne. The group was completed when Chiswick-based guitarist Roger "Scratch" Mingay saw the band's advertisement in the *New Musical Express* and pipped an aspiring fifteen-year-old Ritchie Blackmore to the post of guitarist in the band, at the auditions held at a hotel in Acton.

This was the first Savages line-up to undertake any serious touring. Concert offers came in from all over the country, as Sutch's reputation grew. His stage show had progressed quickly from its shaky beginnings to an impressive, if chaotic, spectacle that left audiences gasping—if they hadn't already fled.

With his horns on for "Bull Moose," appropriate giant footwear for "Blue Suede Shoes," a blazing biscuit tin for "Great Balls Of Fire" and a full-size coffin to step out of on arrival, he blazed a trail across the British landscape. Carlo made a trip up to Carnaby Street and bought the group its own version of the outfits Sutch had seen with Vince Taylor's band:

"There were three shops there and one of them sold orange and purple shirts; I said they'd be good for stage and with black trousers and white boots it looked good—from a distance. A week's wages in them days was about eight quid and we were getting sixteen for half a week's work!"

---

[9] Author's note: Bill Wyman, Keith Richards and Yardbirds' bassist Paul Samwell-Smith spoke extremely highly of Rick's bass-playing and onetime Savage Roger Mingay described him as "simply fantastic."

12. The spectacular Screaming Lord Sutch

Having lost his place in the Saxons, Rick Brown had time on his hands and was back at Carlo Little's house just as Ken Payne left to get married. Rick was drawn, not for the last time, back into the "clutches of Sutch," his stage look further enhanced by having his hair bleached (with the assistance of the faithful Sylvie).

Apart from their intense gigging, this line-up of the Savages had the privilege of accompanying the Screaming Lord on his first ever recording, when Tom Littlewood brought Sutch to the attention of legendary independent producer Joe Meek.

From the chaotic confines of his makeshift studio in a dingy, rented upstairs flat on the Holloway Road in North London, the eccentric maverick had already notched a string of chart successes with artists ranging from John Leyton and Mike Berry, to instrumental groups with fanciful names like "The Blue Men" and "Flee-Rekkers." In 1962 he finally hit pay dirt when the Tornados became the first-ever British group to hit the Number 1 spot in America with "Telstar."

An acetate in Nicky's own collection, labelled in his typically neat handwriting, reveals that the Savages attempted a recording of Chuck Berry's "Roll Over Beethoven," backed with "The Train," as early as March or May 1961, but Nicky's succinct comment: "poor recording," probably explains its non-appearance and there is no information to confirm where the session took place or who was involved.

Sutch was a perfect candidate for Joe Meek's inventive genius. He had already conjured up his most enduring stage persona, appearing as a Victorian stage vil-lain, with white pancake make-up, a top hat and cloak and carrying a large, murderous-looking knife.

The producer was able to conjure up an amazing variety of sounds and effects from his simple equipment and his talents lent themselves particularly well to the horror genre. To capitalise on Sutch's ghoulish stage creation, he followed the blueprint of his own earlier production with the Moontrekkers "Night Of The Vampire" for Sutch's debut disc.

"Til The Following Night" starts with a full forty seconds of howling winds, clanking chains, creaking coffins, gurgling noises and, of course, screaming, before launching into a saxophone-driven rave-up.

Despite the gimmicky production, Sutch's self-penned song, failed to get a chart placing on its release in December '61; the B-side version of "Good Golly Miss Molly," with Roger Mingay's breakneck guitar solo, is by far the better track.

Nicky would have to wait another year before he appeared on a record, but by September, with the Saxons already a memory, both he and Bernie had also re-joined Sutch. This second version of the original band criss-crossed the UK for several months in Sutch's old black gown van, whose high-roofed back—intended for hanging dresses—made an ideal space for piling in amplifiers and instruments. Sutch called the large, unheated van his "horse-box," and the band-members often travelled wrapped in several layers of clothing, with three pairs of socks and polythene bags on their feet for insulation. Carlo was in charge of packing and map reading, while Sutch himself lorded it at the wheel, though still without the benefit of either licence or insurance. Breakdowns were commonplace.

Sutch would think nothing of arriving in a town in his full "wild man" regalia, bearing a giant axe or a club, with which he would chase the unfortunate members of his band up and down the corridors of the local Woolworth's—anything to gain a few column inches and a crowd.

Rick Brown: "I wish I had had a camera in those days. Because there was not so much travel, everywhere had its own character. There were only half a dozen bands touring these village halls and people would go because they didn't have anything else to do. They didn't have televisions or anything and they'd see us, specially being a band from London and thought it was incredible."

Growling, howling and shoving its way through the crowds from the back of the hall to an otherwise empty stage, the band would open with twenty minutes of instrumental fireworks from Bernie and Nicky ("Flip, Flop & Bop" or "Nut Rocker") with bass-player and guitarist shaking their bleached hair-dos in an early version of head-banging. When the band launched into "'Til The Following Night," the audience would be taken unawares as Sutch leapt out from a full-size coffin onstage with his white make-up and butcher's knife, and proceeded to chase their hapless roadie Brian all over the stage, eventually stabbing and apparently disembowelling him or severing his arm. A bloody and lifelike mechanical substitute limb would then wave at the terrified punters.[10]

They were simpler times, and these antics, pre-dating Alice Cooper by almost a decade, were enough to induce hysteria and even fainting fits in the audience. Sutch's theatrical talents, combined with the band's instrumental prowess, soon ensured them headline status and a reputation second to none.

Sometimes the onstage mayhem backfired. Sutch famously set fire to the curtains on his first night at the Star Club in Hamburg. Early Deep Purple member and sometime Savage Nick Simper remembers one show where there was so much water onstage after "Great Balls Of Fire" that Sutch slipped and impaled his head on the spike of the keyboard player's umbrella, resulting in his immediate total collapse. He was stretchered off through a dumbstruck crowd, some of whom weren't sure if it was all just part of the show.

Sutch never missed a photo opportunity and would do anything to get in the papers. A chance meeting with the aptly named Edna Savage was preserved for posterity, with Sutch in his buffalo horns biting the unfortunate songstress's arm. Not all the band members shared their lead singer's exhibitionist leanings and willingness to make an ass of himself for a bit of publicity. In photos they often appear to be uncomfortable extras in Sutch's mad theatrics and onstage. Nicky and Bernie shied away from the lunacy, but more than made up for their static stage poses with instrumental bravura.

This set a pattern that would define the rest of Nicky's professional life. He harboured little ambition for personal fame and, unlike Sutch, would never be comfortable in the spotlight or when leadership was demanded of him. His Piscean character traits: musicality, skill in interpreting the thoughts of others,

---

[10] Brian was nicknamed "Cannonball," and was often prevailed upon to appear in women's clothing

good humour, an amazing memory, the ability to adapt quickly to different circumstances and an almost complete lack of a competitive streak or jealousy (professional or otherwise), became invaluable in his role as sideman.

Rick Brown: "Although Nick was musically so much further advanced than the rest of us, in rehearsals he'd never say anything unless somebody asked him and he still wouldn't say much; if you asked him to play something, he'd play it straight away but he never said, 'Why don't you do this or you do that.'"

On tour, Nicky had his own problems to cope with. In the early days he carried his own microphones and was forced to make do with whatever instruments the venues offered. Rick Brown recalled him coping with some appalling situations with great astonishing dexterity:

"Some of the pianos hadn't been tuned for years and he had to play a semitone out of tune or in a different key altogether from us; he took to bringing his own tuning equipment along to try and get them somewhere near pitch."

Despite his weak disposition, no one remembers Nicky suffering unduly on the road.

Carlo: "He was never ill while we were away, but we never drank in pubs or anything; it was always a coffee bar or café: sausage, egg and chips, grease and all that sort of thing, which he didn't mind, because he never got it at home and it was relief to be part of a gang. We played in nearly every town in Britain; Sutch paid us four quid a night, you paid a pound for your digs and still had a bit of money when you came home. I was older than the rest of them and had to pay my Mum; they probably didn't."

Sandwiched in between gigs, a second visit to Holloway Road produced Nicky and Bernie's first appearance on record, Sutch's single, "Jack The Ripper" / "Don't You Just Know It," another horror milestone that sadly still failed to ignite the pop charts when it was finally released over a year later.

The second era of the original Savages ended after they played one of several double shows with Cliff Bennett and the Rebel Rousers in Chesterfield. The highly respected Bennett's set-list at the time consisted largely of Jerry Lee Lewis covers, with sax-player Sid Phillips covering the pianist's role. While Cliff's band were bowled over by Nicky Hopkins' and Bernie Watson's instrumental virtuosity, Nicky was equally taken with the rival band's more serious musicianship and piano-heavy repertoire.

He apparently felt no great allegiance to his present employer, as he quietly offered his services if an opening were to come up in the Rebel Rousers. Two weeks later, when Sid Phillips left (another marriage victim), it did. Nicky agreed to join, but insisted that his sidekick Bernie be included, a condition to which Cliff Bennett reluctantly agreed.

The dynamic duo exchanged one-nighters and Sutch's "horse-box" for a Thames van and Cliff's regular weekly round of mostly suburban clubs. Musically, Nicky was an undoubted asset, stunning audiences everywhere and even winning the ultimate stamp of approval when he met his idol Jerry Lee Lewis at a

13. Nicky with Jerry Lee Lewis

Wimbledon Theatre show and received the comment, "Goddammit, that boy can really pound that keyboard!"

Nicky Hopkins: "Cliff Bennett could sing exactly like Lewis and I had learned all the piano bits. We went up to Birmingham to see Jerry Lee and stopped at the Blue Boar services on the way and in walked Lewis; we went to his gig, met him afterwards and I had my photo taken with him; then I took the photo and I got it signed in London. He still remembered me years later when I ran into him at Steve Paul's Scene Club in '69, with Jeff Beck."

Nicky kept the precious autographed snapshot in his personal scrapbook.

On a package tour of Granada Theatres, the Bennett band members were told that apart from their own spot, they would be backing yodeller Frank Ifield, who

14. Nicky with Delbert "Delton" McClinton and Bruce Channel

duly arrived at the first date carrying reams of his sheet music. When he counted off the first number at rehearsals, not surprisingly, total silence ensued, as no one except Nicky could read music. After several embarrassing false starts, they owned up to the furious singing star and eventually improvised five country numbers that luckily went down a storm.

Cliff Bennett became quite emotional recalling another night during Nicky's brief stint as a Rebel Rouser, at Burton's Club in Uxbridge:

"At the end of the evening we were packing up and they had a lovely black Bechstein piano on stage, because there was ballroom dancing at the place as well. Nicky came out when he'd put away all his stuff, sat down at the piano and played Chopin's 'Nocturne in E Flat' and was so into it, he was unaware that

15. The Rebel Rousers with Nicky and Bernie

people stopped sweeping (mimics gasping disbelief). That's my favourite piece of music anyway, but talk about fill up! When he finished, the whole place cheered and he went all embarrassed; 'I didn't know anyone was listening.' Listening? It was so brilliant even the clock stopped. I'll never forget that."

In July 1962, pianist and Star Club talent scout Roy Young was over from Germany, and saw the band play at the Top Rank in Reading. He was impressed enough to book them for the usual lengthy season in Hamburg, giving Nicky his first professional trip abroad.

31

16. On piano with the Rebel Rousers at the Star Club

Nicky's uncanny knack for impersonating Jerry Lee Lewis made him (and thus the band) an immediate hit with the German audiences and prompted Star Club owner Manfred Weissleder to offer an immediate re-booking. When Cliff returned some months later with a brass section and no Nicky Hopkins, Weissleder sent an outraged letter of complaint to Bennett's manager Bob Alexander:

Dear Bob,

I just found out today that there have been personnel changes in the Rebel Rousers with whom we have a contract for 30.12. Apparently the Liedgytarrist and pianist will not be with the band anymore.

We regret this greatly, being of the opinion that exactly these two musicians contributed a large part to the quality and uniqueness of the band. The Liedgytarrist could be described as an outstanding performer and the piano-player too was way above the average.

It is therefore extremely important to us that the band returns with the line-up we know and like and we are unwilling to accept any drop in standards.

We very much hope that it is possible to put together the old version for our engagement, so that we can still work together effectively.

Please let us know as soon as possible…

The considerably older Cliff Bennett promised Nicky's parents that he would look out for their son, who was already spared from carrying the heavy equipment at gigs. Once in Germany, the bandleader kept a fatherly eye on his youngest charges, who anyway showed no signs of interest in the wilder side of life on the Reeperbahn, opting instead to head back to their rooms at the Hotel Pacific when not on stage. Nicky's sole recollection of Hamburg to his second wife Moira concerned the important topic of food:

"They used to go down the Seamen's Mission to get egg and chips, because that's all they could afford, and I remember Nicky telling me he learned to ask for it in German; it was called "Ei und Kartoffel." He was really proud that he could remember."

Back home in September, Nicky made it onto vinyl again on the B-side of Cliff Bennett's "My Old Standby," another session produced by Joe Meek. Just as on the first Lord Sutch release—on which he hadn't even played—Nicky meticulously listed all the players' names in his neat handwriting on the cover of his personal copy of the single.

Bennett's parting of the ways with his two star players, after a comparatively short stint as Rebel Rousers, had nothing to do with music and everything to do with the inseparable young duo's attitude and behaviour, in particular that of Bernie Watson. Cliff echoed Rick Brown's distaste for the duo's snickering attitude to disabled people:

"I shouldn't be saying this, but they were too weird—Nicky as well; they used to say, 'Oh look, there's a bus-full of "lick-the-window people"' and I'd say, 'You two are sick bastards.' They had a scrapbook of people with disabilities and they'd be laughing at the back of the van. Maybe geniuses have their drawbacks."

Bernie's petulant personality, both on and off stage, caused the final rift. He would play fantastic instrumentals, but when the audience duly applauded, would swear at them as being too ignorant to tell good from bad. He carried a Spanish guitar with him and would sit in the dressing room playing classical music until just before show time, threatening on more than one occasion not to show up for the next gig at all. One day Cliff Bennett's patience finally gave out:

"I told him we were on in a minute and he said, 'Oh, fuck, have I got to go and play all that fucking shit?' and I said, 'I tell you what, you don't have to. Why don't you fuck off!' He went, 'Yeah I'll do that.' Nicky said, 'No, you don't want to do that, because if he goes, I go,' and I said, 'Nicky, if that's it, you go too, because I can't deal with it.' There's no way in the world I wanted to let Nicky go, but I couldn't deal with the other guy, he was a lunatic. I said to him, 'Why do you want to hang out with this tosser?'"

Nicky's loyalty, misplaced or not, cost him his place in the Rebel Rousers, and he would never return full-time to the Savages either.[11] The time he'd served in two pioneering British bands had cemented his reputation as an up and coming name to watch. At the tender age of eighteen he was already a seasoned professional.

When Bernie Watson went for the guitarist's job with Mike Berry's Outlaws, he returned a favour and refused to join without Nicky. Joe Meek stalwart Chas Hodges, himself no slouch as a keyboard player, recalled Nicky's shadowy presence at the audition:

---

[11] Rick Brown suggested that Nicky was glad of the excuse to leave Bennett, whom he had never liked anyway.

"Nick sauntered in and didn't look like a wild rock'n'roller at all—you know that later on Jim Sullivan's nickname for him on sessions was 'the living dead.' He sat down at the piano and I asked him which player he liked best; he said Jerry Lee Lewis and offered to play 'I Could Never Be Ashamed Of You,' a song that has a particularly difficult solo. When Nicky played it note for note, we decided on the spot that we should ask them both to join."

Though they declined the offer, Nicky did eventually end up on a Mike Berry track, when John Burgess later produced the cheerfully rolling "Somebody Stole My Gal" for EMI. Nicky's piano solo is introduced by Mike's shout of "Take It, Fingers!"

Nicky's growing reputation led to his first two sessions as a guest musician rather than a band member, one for singer Neil Christian and one for Casey Jones & The Engineers' "One Way Ticket," which also featured a very young Eric Clapton on guitar. Both singles were released on Columbia in 1963. At Neil's recording, Nicky came up against the old guard in the form of producer Norrie Paramor.

Neil Christian: "We got about thirty-six bars into the number and Norrie Paramor shouts out, 'No, no, no that's all wrong. I don't know what the piano player's playing, but it's not on my musical sheet;' I said, 'Oh, isn't it? We'll go over and see;' I said to Nick, 'Play what's written.' So he did, and Norrie still says, 'That's not what's written.' Nicky says, 'You play it then!' He played it, and Nicky was right and Norrie Paramor was wrong. He didn't apologise or anything, which I thought was bad."

Nicky's unassuming personality and somewhat childlike habits are remembered by most of his ex-band mates, but there were times when glimpses of another side of him showed through. When occasion demanded, he could be witheringly sarcastic and he displayed an explosive temper when aroused, though seldom remaining angry for long. Roger Mingay, who only shared a stage with him on one or two Savages shows, vividly remembers one such night:

"He was on the right-hand side of the stage, hidden behind this huge grand piano; I was busking my way through because I didn't know any of the numbers and at the end of the night, we were packing up and this terrible old 'jobsworth' caretaker came up and started all the usual crap about 'Come on, you've got to get out now, I've got to close this hall up.' It sticks in my mind because Nick was usually so quiet; he just sat behind the piano going, 'Fuck off, fuck off, just fuck off, fuck off, fuck off!'"

The early sixties group scene in London was small and very incestuous, with band members coming and going and frequent personnel changes. Bearing in mind that most of the players were still in their teens, it was no surprise that before long there was another falling-out in the Sutch camp, probably based on a financial dispute, which left all four of the original Savages once again at a loose end.

Rick Brown attended a session-night at South Harrow Memorial Hall, organised by pioneering jazz/bluesman Ken Colyer. After sitting in for a few numbers, he was approached by the imposing figure of Cyril "Squirrel" Davies:

"I didn't know him from Adam really and he was raving about leaving Alexis Korner and wanting to form the first blues band in the country with electric bass and would I be interested? So I said 'Yeah, and as it happens, I know a drummer, a guitarist and a pianist' and that was it; I got them in."

By trade a panel-beater and by nature quick-tempered and moody, Davies had become a key figure in the parallel universe of the nascent folk and blues scene in London, playing a gritty and uncompromising version of American blues on a Grimshaw 12-string guitar and an especially authentic sounding harmonica. His colleague Long John Baldry recalled Cyril's taste for expensive cigars, "not cheap old shit like Alexis would smoke, but the full Cuban deal" and good whisky as opposed to the pints of beer drunk by everybody else.

17. Cyril Davies

With fellow blues fanatic Alexis Korner—another graduate of jazz pioneer Chris Barber's early R&B experiments and a key figure in the development of the English group scene—Cyril had started the London Skiffle Centre at the Roundhouse in 1955 and later the weekly "Blues & Barrelhouse" club in Soho. The two joined forces in the influential Alexis Korner's Blues Incorporated and on March 17th, 1962, opened their own R&B club in the basement of the ABC tearooms in Ealing, West London. Long John Baldry, who sang with the band from the very first night, remembered the speed with which the word spread:

18. The Cyril Davies All-Stars

"All these other people started filtering in: Paul Jones and Zoot Money up from Portsmouth; Mick Jagger came up the second or third week; Keith Richards was a very shy person then and had to be persuaded to get up on stage.

"Then it started taking off. (West End promoter) Harold Pendleton came down and said, 'I can put this on at the Marquee,' because the capacity there was six or seven hundred people as opposed to the two hundred odd in the tearoom. Within a week of the move, the Marquee was jam-packed every Thursday night."

The famously irascible Cyril Davies soon fell out with his partner, but insisted on keeping the Marquee residency, forcing Alexis to move on to the rival Flamingo Club. Speculation as to Cyril's next move was rife in the R&B scene.

Keith Richards: "There's a big buzz around the club scene at the time; you know, 'What's Cyril doing?' and finally he unveils the Cyril Davies All-Stars, which, of all people, is Screaming Lord Sutch's band. It so happened that Sutch actually had the best, most together rock'n'roll or rhythm & blues band in England."

Cyril was looking for a hard-hitting blues sound and, after a few adjustments, found his perfect team in the ex-Savages.

Rick Brown: "Cyril came from the jazz scene, then he suddenly got Carlo on drums and had to keep him in his place a bit. On the other hand, Carlo was a lot better for him than some of those limp-wristed jazzers that he might have had; he had the real blues punch that people understood and of course Nick was perfect for that stuff."

David Sutch appears to have given his blessing to the wholesale theft of his backing group; he continued using them on selected dates when available and was a regular visitor to Cyril's live gigs. Their personalities and approaches could hardly have been more different. Playing the blues was a world away from Sutch's manic version of rock'n'roll, and Cyril was a highly opinionated purist and a man who didn't suffer fools gladly.

Carlo Little: "Cyril said, 'You're all on wages; I've got you covered, I've got you covered and I've got you covered, so no monkey business, otherwise you're out.' We'd never heard anything like it; we just wanted to play. He was a very frustrated man."

A young Martin Carthy, now a leading figure in the British folk revival, was already performing as a guitarist and singer in the acoustic clubs around London, before the split that separated folk music from R&B, and remembers seeing the band for the first time:

"I thought it was quite radical because it was electric. Cyril was following the likes of Muddy Waters and at that time, electricity was considered the son of Satan. He was very much the pure unstrained, unrestricted goods."

John Baldry: "Cyril was fairly loose in allowing people to spread their wings. As long as the material fell loosely into the blues format, he was quite happy. I did quite a few Ray Charles numbers such as 'Leave My Woman Alone' and the old Hank Snow song 'I'm Movin' On,' so it didn't all have to be Chicago and Muddy Waters."

Luckily the standard of musicianship of Cyril's new recruits was more than up to the challenge. The band was soon gigging regularly, with residencies on Tuesdays at the Railway Hotel in Wealdstone, Wednesdays at the Piccadilly Club in Soho and Thursdays at the Marquee, where they played to capacity crowds of eight hundred and more.

Photographer and harmonica-player Pete Dyer took pictures at the Marquee, from behind Nicky's offstage grand piano, that show open-mouthed young fans such as Keith Richards, Brian Jones and Jimmy Page in the audience, all still sporting short hair, collars and ties and cardigans and anoraks. The newly formed "Rollin' Stones" became one of

> BOXING NIGHT AT THE PICCADILLY
> WITH
> CYRIL DAVIES R & B ALL-STARS
> PLUS
> ★ THE ROLLIN' STONES ★
> COME EARLY, PLEASE! 7.30 p.m. : 5/-

the All-Stars occasional support bands, with bassist Bill Wyman watching the headliner's performance in considerable awe:

"The first time I ever saw Nicky was in the Marquee and they did a Chuck Berry thing, 'Deep Feeling,' which was fantastic. I used to try to emulate Ricky Fenson the bass-player, because he really swung. He was the first player I heard who really beat it out."

19. Nicky at the Marquee Club piano, with a young Jimmy Page looking on

Paul Samwell-Smith, a founding member of the Yardbirds, was another fan, but learned to be wary of the quick-tempered Davies:

"The reason I played bass was because of Ricky Fenson (a stage name chosen by Brown as a blend of Fender and Gibson). The way he went up the fretboard, playing high octaves on the bass and then bouncing down again, made my hair stand on end! The Yardbirds actually went to see Cyril in Croydon; he had the Saturday or Sunday gig and we asked the pub landlord if we could come along on a Tuesday or Wednesday; Cyril came up to us and got quite angry because he said we were poaching his territory. He was dangerous—a not very well man."

It was during this era that Nicky acquired the nickname "Diamond Tiaras," which was later adopted by the Rolling Stones.

Keith Richards: "That goes back to Cyril Davies; he would yell into the microphone when he wanted a piano solo, 'Come on, Diamond Tiaras,' and it stuck, because Nicky played that brilliant Otis Spann stuff, you know, the really high trills... 'Diamond Tiaras, Nicky, Diamond Tiaras.'"

Carlo Little remembered that Nicky's classical training was curiously helpful when Cyril brought in a record of Big Maceo Merriweather's tour-de-force "Chicago Breakdown":

"It was an A and B-side all in one and was so long that Nicky couldn't memorise it, so he wrote it down on manuscript; it was at least four folds and hundreds of dots and notes! We played it when Cyril went off stage and it was seven or

38

eight minutes long, like the record, but with bass, drums and guitar as well; guys used to come up and say, 'That's the first time I've ever heard that played live, and it's note for note!' We'd call 'Chicago Breakdown' and Nicky'd say 'Hang on a minute' and all this paper would be on the piano. He would do it, say 'Thank you' and that was it; he wasn't puffed up."

Nicky Hopkins: "I was more knocked out by Big Maceo than any other pianist except perhaps Albert Ammons. That is a record that Cyril turned me on to; I stayed up many a night actually transcribing the entire thing."

During his time with Cyril, Nicky also solved the thorny problem of bad on-stage pianos. Relief from broken-down uprights came with the purchase of a Cembalet—a stand-alone electric keyboard launched by the Hohner company in 1959—which John Baldry described as "a short-scale thing, with typical 1950s legs that screwed on to the case of the instrument and sounded even more bell-like than a Fender Rhodes."

Inspired by the sound of Ray Charles' "What'd I Say,"[12] Nicky carried the keyboard with him as a "safety net" to gigs, though, with its wobbly legs (as Carlo observed), "on a dodgy stage it would start walking on its own and crash and crumble into a million pieces." It was soon immortalised on the band's first and best single.

The exploding popularity of rhythm and blues music in general, and its top London practitioners in particular, inevitably led to record company interest. For his first outing with the All-Stars, Cyril had offers from both Decca and Pye. He opted for the latter's brand new "International R&B" label imprint. The band went in to Pye Studios with producer Peter Knight to record "Country Line Special" backed with "Chicago Calling," their two most popular numbers and traditionally the climax of their concert dates.

Both were faithful renditions of the band's live sound and captured all the excitement they generated at shows, with Nicky's frantic and driving electric piano (on the A-side) and acoustic (on the B-side) prominent in the mix. Ten years later, he still referred to the record as his most important to date.

---

[12] In fact, played on a Wurlitzer

Carlo Little: "Every time it came to the harmonica solo, I did a drum roll, hit the big cymbal and went mad, 'cause I thought I was back with Sutch; I got faster, it lifted and of course everyone had to follow the drummer 'cause I'm the time-keeper. The producer said, 'Leave it, that's great, listen to the excitement.'"

Not everyone present agreed. Carlo remembered British orchestra leader Ted Heath, who was in the studio at the time, describing their efforts (after about thirteen takes) as "a load of rubbish!"

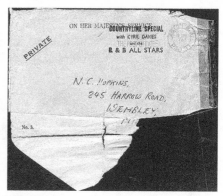

Released in April 1963, Cyril's single can claim to be the first great British R&B record, and possibly the first credible recorded blues played by white people at all.[13] Opening with a defiant blast from Cyril's harmonica, the track captured all the energy of the American originals, and yet came from the heart of London.

Ray Davies of the Kinks first became aware of Nicky's playing on "Country Line Special" and commented that, although the piece is a harmonica instrumental, it's the piano that really drives the track: "It's the unsung British R&B classic. To me it said this can be done in Britain; we don't need to go to America to get players."

A surviving envelope from the British taxman to Nicky's Harrow Road address, dated the month of the record's release, proudly features a band stamp promoting the single. With support from the music press, more live work than they could cope with, full houses at their shows and a semi-successful single under their belts, spring 1963 must have been an exciting time for the All-Stars.

Nicky was still living at home during all the months he spent touring, and during this period he began to spend a lot of time with his brother Paul, drinking late night cups of tea and chatting after a show somewhere in the provinces.

Paul Hopkins: "I was working near St. Paul's and used to come home between three or four o'clock in the morning and, as often as not, Nicky would be coming in around that time too and my mother used to wait up for us. We'd sit around the kitchen table—of course my father didn't like that at all; I think he was a bit jealous—and that's where the closeness started. A nine-year difference counts a lot when you're young, but when you're over twenty and going on thirty, it doesn't matter anymore and we really started having fun. In the daytime we'd have the afternoons to ourselves and used to watch silly programmes on the television. Popeye and Bluto was one of our favourites: 'Bluto' became 'Otulb,' because everything was backwards you see, and Popeye was always the 'little runt.'"[14]

---

[13] His earlier album collaboration with Alexis Korner, *R&B Live From The Marquee* came out in 1962, but didn't carry the same punch or have the same influence.

[14] Similarly, Nicky mostly referred to Paul as "Draeb" on account of his naval-style beard.

On the road, the All-Stars were now augmented by Long John Baldry. He had joined the ranks as additional vocalist after a stint in Germany, opting for Cyril's band over Alexis Korner's literally on the toss of a coin. They were beginning to travel further afield.

John Baldry: "We used to travel up to the northern provinces and do all-nighters at the Twisted Wheel (a famous Manchester club). We even went up to Scotland, and because Cyril's original profession had been as a panel-beater, we

20. The Velvettes

got a good deal with Timpson's coaches and didn't have to put up with a draughty van; he would hire a coach with a good driver and we'd go in style.

"It was before all the motorways had been developed in England, so going up to Manchester or Liverpool was a day's safari; you had to leave at six in the morning to get there on time."

They needed the extra seats on the coach, because, heavily under the influence of Ray Charles, Cyril decided to have his own "Raelettes" and found three South African girls who'd come to London with a successful Zulu musical show named *King Kong*.

John Baldry: "There was Peggy Phango, Mumsie Tobeni and Patience Gwabe. She had a connection to Dr. Stephen Ward and all that Christine Keeler thing and because of Patience's involvement with whatever she was moonlighting on, we were getting visits from MI5 and MI6 down at the Marquee, at its old building, below the Academy Cinema on Oxford Circus."

Though the girls were entirely unschooled in the gospel tradition and had a negligible command of English, Cyril trained them from scratch to sing their vocal parts phonetically and christened them "the Velvettes." Things were definitely on the up, until at the end of May disaster struck.

A small article in the June 1st 1963 issue of *New Record Mirror* states that Cyril Davies and his band had been working on a pilot show for ABC television add-

21. Cyril and Nicky

ing that "Cyril's pianist, Nick Hopkins, was rushed to hospital last week with internal trouble and is on the critically ill list." Since he had successfully kept any troubles he experienced to himself while on tour, this turn of events took the band completely by surprise. Rick Brown said Nicky "kept smoking like a chimney and didn't really care about his health."

Understandably, given his frail appearance, some reports described his sudden hospitalisation as the result of simple exhaustion, but the episode was to be Nicky's longest and most dangerous bout with stomach-related illness and would take the nineteen year-old out of circulation and into a medical nightmare for more than a year and a half.

While Nicky languished in hospital Cyril Davies carried on, unsentimentally drafting in Keith Scott as a replacement pianist, The band continued using Nicky's keyboard for their weekly TV residency as house-band on the pioneering folk music TV programme, *Hullabaloo*, and at dozens more gigs played up and down the country.

Insiders had known that Cyril too suffered from recurrent pains and illness, but to the outside world, the shock was complete when shortly after New Year, the hard-drinking, hard-living Davies died suddenly aged only thirty-two, of "pleurisy resulting from leukaemia." He had been taken into hospital at six in the evening and was dead within five hours.

John Baldry: "Cyril had a very healthy date-sheet right through '63 and when he died, it was expected and it wasn't. At our Eel Pie Island residency[15] we were walking back over the footbridge when he said, 'You know, I've got a funny feeling that this is the last time I'll ever cross this bridge,' so I'd known he was ill since about October or November of '63, but I didn't realise how serious it was 'til he ended up in hospital just after Christmas and then died on January 7th 1964."

Nicky Hopkins saw his ex-boss a week before he died, when Cyril came to see him in hospital, "looking really well." When he got the message, he didn't believe it. "He was only thirty-two, though I was surprised to hear that, because he looked so much older."

With Cyril's untimely death the UK Rhythm and Blues scene lost one of its most vibrant personalities and, at the time, its finest harmonica player. "Country Line Special" remains a milestone in British music, and assures Cyril Davies his place in history. The remnants of his "All-Stars," re-named "The Hoochie-Coochie Men," continued as a backing band for Long John Baldry. They were soon augmented by a fledgling singer and harmonica player named Roderick Stewart, who had been a regular audience member at the Marquee and, according to legend, was spotted by Baldry, playing blues harp on a railway platform in Twickenham while "waiting for a train."

Nicky was left fighting for his life in his hospital bed, having spent the first three years of his professional life in three of the UK's most influential groups. It would be several years before he ventured back out on the road with a band.

---

[15] Referring to their regular weekly gig at The Eel Pie Hotel, located on Eel Pie Island in the Thames, near Twickenham.

Wing And A Prayer
Hospitalisation

"He's the only patient whose name I remember. When you think of all the patients I've nursed over the years, he obviously made a big impression on me."

— *Nurse Sylvia Currie*

For those who believe in astrology, Nicky's tendency to sickliness in childhood and digestive complaints fulfill the Piscean blueprint to the letter. Later in life, a frequently poor diet and intermittent reliance on pills and alcohol accentuated his problems, but despite the physical handicaps he was born with and which dogged him all his life, he possessed immense inner strength and courage. He dealt with hardships without complaint, often hiding his pain behind a smile and a joke, a Hopkins family trait.

Nicky's niece Alix Ninfo: "They were all like that; my grandmother was very stoical too and was quite ill on and off—as was my grandfather, but you'd never have known."

Anyone from the fifties or sixties who can remember having to go into a British hospital as a child (back in the dark ages before it was understood that kids generally benefit from the presence of their parents and frequent visits by their friends and family), will testify to the total sense of abandonment felt when left in a large room, full of total strangers suffering from a variety of medical disorders, under the stern eye of a dark-blue uniformed matron, apparently unsympathetic to any symptoms of boredom, hunger pangs, fear or homesickness that assailed those in her charge.

The rigidly enforced discipline, primitive amenities and dark Victorian corridors were more reminiscent of prison than a place of healing. At least the run-of-the-mill children's complaints such as appendix or tonsil removal generally meant a short sentence.

When Nicky entered King Edward's Hospital, Park Royal in May 1963, he was destined to stay bed-ridden for the next nineteen months.

It was an unimaginable ordeal for a nineteen-year-old, especially coming so abruptly after the intense and exciting schedule he'd become used to. He was admitted as an emergency after an internal rupture prompted by a fall at home. His mother had vague but distressing memories of the events leading up to Nicky's hospitalisation:

"He fell down some stairs and was crying out in terrible agony, but when he went into hospital, they couldn't find anything wrong with him; it was awful to see him; he must have ruptured something, because they took so much of his intestine that he had very little left at all and used to get terrible cramps."

Another round of tests sought to establish the cause of his suffering, but in the early sixties, understanding of the complexities of bowel disorders was in its infancy. Surgery tended to be exploratory and the results were unpredictable.[16]

The symptoms that recurred throughout Nicky's life eventually led doctors to conclude that he suffered from Crohn's disease. Named after gastroenterologist Burrill Bernard Crohn in 1932, it remains to this day an illness about which many theories abound, though none have to date been proven.

The most generally agreed upon explanation is that, with a Crohn's sufferer, the body's immune system mistakes bacteria, other substances and even food as foreign bodies and responds by attacking the invaders. The resulting white blood cells accumulate in the lining of the intestine, producing chronic inflammation, which in turn can lead to swelling, scar tissue and ultimately to severe blockages of the intestine itself.

Treatments include drugs, dietary supplements and surgery, but there is still no known cure. Flare-ups can recur at various times over a person's lifetime, but the changeable pattern of the disease makes it extremely difficult to know if and when a treatment has actually helped. Certain however, is that up to three quarters of Crohn's patients will need surgery at some point in their lives.

Possible complications to the disease (including arthritis, lower back pain, skin problems, inflammation of the eyes, kidney stones, gallstones and other diseases

---

[16] Now known as the Central Middlesex, the hospital is still in service today, but all attempts by this author to access information or medical records foundered on a double dilemma: the length of time that has passed since Nicky was a patient and the strict confidentiality that made it impossible for even his family to gain access to his records.

of the liver) underline the misery and physical hardships common to many sufferers. No special diet programme has proved effective in preventing the onset or
recurrences of the disease, but doctors agree that following a nutritional diet and
avoiding foods that seem to aggravate the symptoms are well advised. The "sausage, egg and chips, grease and all that sort of thing" referred to by Carlo Little as
an on the road regime with Lord Sutch probably didn't qualify as a nutritional
diet.

Although all the signs seemed consistent with it, Freda Hopkins remained to
the end of her life unconvinced that the diagnosis of Crohn's was correct. Julia
was equally sceptical, although, recalling her father's digestive problems, she
agreed that a strong element of heredity was definitely present; more recently,
her daughter Alix, who has lived almost all her life in the USA, was diagnosed
with Ehlers-Danlos Syndrome, a connective tissue disorder with symptoms extremely reminiscent of Nicky's condition, though not necessitating the
devastating surgeries he was forced to undergo.

Alix Ninfo: "It's more obvious now that Nicky was suffering from some sort of
complication from Ehlers-Danlos Syndrome—as is my mother. It's almost like
Crohn's disease could be a precursor—the generation before. Some of the things
that you get when you have Ehlers-Danlos are similar; there's a weakness of the
veins and people are very thin, have see-through skin, long fingers and double-
jointedness; it's a combination of things."

One medical reference book lists all the above traits along with a tendency in
sufferers to have "large eyes, a thin nose, lobe-less ears and thin scalp hair"—an
exact description of Nicky Hopkins.

Understanding of both diseases has progressed in the intervening years, yet
both are still the source of considerable discussion and controversy. It is unlikely
that we will ever know exactly what was at the root of Nicky Hopkins' lifelong
medical problems, but certainly in 1963 doctors remained at a loss to diagnose
his condition. At Park Royal, they decided on a major operation to remove almost all Nicky's intestine, leaving the already weakened patient in a coma and
sufficiently in danger for a member of his family to recall crying and wishing he
would die, to spare him such pain and misery. For some time he wasn't expected
to live, but against all expectations, he came round and started on his long, up-
hill journey to recovery.

The major surgery he had undergone would have been hard for anyone, com-
bining not only enormous pain, but also all the discomfort and indignity of
having his digestive functions disrupted. In Nicky's case, the burns he had suffered as a child further complicated proceedings. His doctors were insistent that
his wounds heal from the inside out and, with almost no skin on his stomach,
this process took an incredibly long time. He had to wait until he was healed
before even the comparative convenience of a colostomy bag was available to
him.

Paul Hopkins: "They were very concerned about the wound closing up and it
wouldn't. They found a new method, which they used on him and it worked,

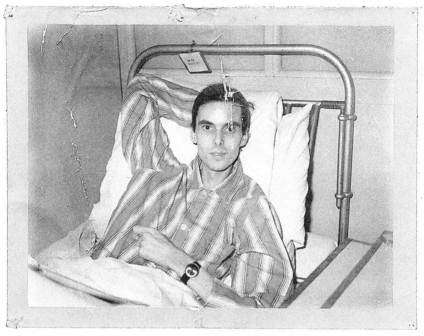

22. At King Edward's Hospital

slowly but surely; he was like a skeleton—a real cadaver! I've never seen anyone look like that."

Despite all these trials, Nicky appears to have kept up his spirits to an amazing degree and throughout his ordeal was seldom heard to complain. Keith Richards, with whom Nicky was later to make so much great music, and himself a walking miracle of survival, recognised his own instincts in Nicky:

"He had so many things wrong with him and was so complicatedly ill, that it's amazing his frame put up with what it did. He shouldn't actually have been alive. Other people would have just given up the ghost, but underneath there was a very, very strong guy there."

As a long-term patient, Nicky had his own room at the hospital, with French windows looking out to the gardens. His courage and resilience made him popular with the nurses, one of whom, Sylvia Currie, was on Nicky's ward and contacted this author after hearing a BBC radio-broadcast in 2008:

"He is the only patient whose name I remember, and I continued nursing until nine years ago. I think it was because we were very much the same age and we got on as friends. In those days it was more formal than it is now; I wouldn't have called him Nicky or Nicholas for a start, I would have called him Mr. Hopkins.

"I trained at the Central Mid. so I was there for roughly four and a half years; he used to call me 'Strawberry Norbury,' because that was my surname then and he'd tease me because I was going out with 'fellas.' We had to put a really thick zinc paste on to protect his skin and when I went out for a date one night with a new bloke, I was having dinner and had my elbow on the table. Right up my fore-arm was this big streak of zinc paste that I obviously hadn't reached with the soap."

Despite their closeness, Sylvia didn't recall any romantic element in their friendship:

"He was very quiet; I can't remember anything except his sense of humour and that he was extremely patient; it was very strict in those days and you were trained not to think of patients in that way, but looking back now, if you remember somebody that long, even as a friend, then they were attractive to you. When you think of all the other patients I've nursed over the years, he obviously made a big impression."

His family, of course, were regular visitors, with Paul coming in the afternoons, after his night's work as a printer in the City of London, to relieve his mother from her almost daily visits, and Nicky's sisters both making trips home from the USA to come and see him in person. The three of them shared all too clear memories of Nicky's deathlike appearance and of the atrocious smell in his room, resulting from his open wounds and drainage. Paul described him as "a pitiful sight in those days," while Dee's first visit was made when Nicky was still unconscious:

"He was in a coma and had been for some time; the matron said, 'Thank goodness you're here.' I just sat there and talked to him and he came round."

Conspicuous by their absence during his long ordeal, were Nicky's ex-band mates and musician friends. Musicians often seem to feel that serious illness or death may in some way be infectious, and keep well out of the way while someone is ill, saving all the tears and emotional outpourings for the funeral or tribute concert. Carlo Little and Bernie Watson did appear once or twice, though Nicky's mother remembered that one of Carlo's visits was to borrow a piece of equipment—possibly the vital keyboard:

"I asked Nicky if I could loan it to him and he said it was all right, but he (Carlo) never even wrote to say thank you; I was very hurt; it would have been nice if he'd at least acknowledged it; Nicky was so upset."

Although still extremely weak and often plagued by terrible cramps, initial fears for his survival gradually receded, and the battered patient's biggest enemy became boredom. Nicky's scrapbooks reveal that he kept up his habit of cutting out references to his recent band's activities, even for events he was unable to attend; this doubtless emphasised the helpless position he found himself in, and of course he missed playing the piano terribly.

Singer Roy Harper passed on a touching recollection of Nicky and his illness, as told to him by Jimmy Page, who remembered Nicky saying that as he lay on his back, he pictured himself playing actual piano pieces in his mind.

There was in fact an upright instrument in the nurses' home close by, but since male visitors were strictly forbidden at all times, Nicky was refused permission to play it. This caused his family considerable anguish; they couldn't see the harm in it and never forgave the hospital authorities for their decision. They argued that the positive effects of having an instrument to hand would have far outweighed any further risks to his health, but the doctors were adamant. Eventually his exasperated mother organised the purchase of a "silent keyboard," a replica designed for practicing purposes, but hardly a substitute for the real thing.

Lighter moments were few and far between. When Paul came to visit, he found the sight of Nicky lying flat on his back with a gaping hole in his stomach so pitiful, that to cheer him up he used to put him in a wheelchair, take him outside and "whizz round the gardens" to the consternation of the ward staff.

Time dragged on. Nicky was still bed-ridden when Christmas came around. New Year 1964 must have seemed a bleak prospect, with little sign of recovery and the untimely death of his erstwhile boss in early January dashing any hopes of returning to his band.

23. A family visit

Quite apart from the appalling physical deprivations he was coping with, the mental stress must have been extraordinary. Nowadays any patient facing long-term hospitalisation would be offered social services and psychiatric support, but in the sixties such care was unavailable, and Nicky's search for spiritual comfort led him instead to religion.

During the next year, two of his nurses, one of them named Jenni (who made a strong enough impression on him to be immortalised later in Nicky's composition of the same name), introduced their vulnerable patient to the Baptist faith. Nicky was a willing convert. Sylvia Currie thinks that Jenni was a staff nurse on the ward throughout Nicky's stay, whereas Sylvia herself was only there for the last six months. She believes the girl went off to South Africa.

Though the Hopkins household had never been regular churchgoers, apart from the children's Sunday School visits, Nicky took his new faith very seriously. He studied the scriptures almost obsessively, as evidenced by the pages of under-lined passages and handwritten notes that he added in the margins of the leather-bound Bible his mother gave him for his twenty-first birthday (the February after he finally left hospital).

It was not until Christmas Eve, 1964 that he was finally able to re-enter the outside world.

Sylvia Currie: "I must have been off the day he left, because I went back in and said, 'Where's Mr. Hopkins?' and they told me he'd been discharged. That's when I found out that he was classically trained, because when he left, the con-sultant got him and most of the staff and went to the hospital chapel where he played classical music for them."

In the almost two years he had spent at King Edward's, and after—by his own calculation—fourteen operations, Nicky now returned to a world that had moved forward at an astonishing pace, particularly in music. When he entered hospital in May 1963, the Beatles were a comparatively new success story with their third single "From Me To You" just arriving in the charts. By the time he came home at the end of the next year, they had conquered America and were a worldwide phenomenon, with their first film already under their belts and yet another number one single and album with "I Feel Fine" and *Beatles for Sale*.

24. Nicky's bible

Having pioneered the concept of a touring rock band with Lord Sutch, often taking rock'n'roll to the provinces for the first time, Nicky came out to a completely different landscape. The influence of the Beatles had spawned a national explosion of beat groups that dwarfed even the earlier skiffle craze that followed Lonnie Donegan's success.

The rhythm and blues boom which Nicky had spearheaded with the Cyril Davies All-Stars was no longer only London-based. The charts were full of British pretenders such as Them and the Animals, while his erstwhile support band at the Marquee, the Rolling Stones, had moved on from fumbling beginnings in a Denmark Street demo studio to an established chart band with hit singles to their credit. The Sixties, as it is now remembered, had truly arrived.

Alongside events in the outside world, the many months he spent recovering spanned what would have been a critical time in any teenager's life. His sister Dee, for one, felt that his incarceration had a huge influence on his future relationships, particularly with the opposite sex, reinforcing his natural shyness and a certain introspection already instilled in his childhood through his father's strict and rigid rules at home.

The figure that left Park Royal was such a shadow of his former self that his friends didn't recognise him at first. Long John Baldry recalled, "He looked like a stick insect—parchment skin stretched over bones."

Curiously, even though it was Christmas time when Nicky came home, none of his family recall there being any kind of party or celebration, though they certainly had much to be grateful for. Perhaps Nicky's haggard appearance and weakness made a party seem inappropriate. Whatever the reason, the prime concern now was to build up his strength again. Apart from occasional visits to local venues to see his friends' bands play, he spent his first weeks of freedom recuperating at home.

On July 11th, 1965 he was officially baptised at the Duke Street Baptist Church in Richmond, with the Reverend John L. Bird presiding; the ceremony included full underwater immersion and there may have been another, earlier ceremony, as Dee swore she remembered him being carried straight from his sick bed to the church:

"He was taken from the hospital in white robes and baptised; he was getting better at that point, but it still amazes me, because he was actually dunked under the water. They slide back the floor and you go in backwards."

Spiritually strengthened he may have been, but it was obvious that in his present condition, his previous 'on the road' lifestyle was no longer an option. There had to be a better way to remain in music and still be able to make a living. A phone call from Carlo Little provided Nicky Hopkins with the answer he was looking for.

All Day...

The London Years – Part 1

"I had a goal, which was to be the busiest studio guy in London, and I quickly achieved that."

– Nicky Hopkins

Despite Nicky's recording experiences prior to his illness, he hardly qualified as a session musician. Like many of his contemporaries, however, one successful engagement soon led to another and with the outstanding reputation gained through his previous live activities, once he entered the studio world, he hit the ground running.

Opinions differ as to Nicky's first ever studio job on his release from hospital. Singer Neil Christian swore he remembered persuading Nicky to play a session, when he was still in his pyjamas and dressing gown at his parents' house, recovering from his illness:

"We were at Abbey Road with Jimmy Page on guitar, Carlo Little on drums and my bass player and we needed a raving piano, so I suggested Nicky. Carlo said 'No chance, 'cause he's just had an operation,' but I said I'd go down and see him and brought him two hundred cigarettes. He came shuffling in, laughed when I showed him the ciggies, but said he didn't think he'd be able to make it. He was bent double, so I said, 'We'll get an ambulance for you and lay on everything;' he did the session and it sort of brought him round. After that he was on the road to recovery and his Mum phoned me up a couple of months after and thanked me for getting him out of the rut he was in; he was on a real downer at the time."

Forty years after the event, people can be forgiven for lapses of memory; in fact, Nicky's typically neat, handwritten notes on his own copy of "A Little Bit Of Someone Else" / "Get A Load Of This," date this session to March 1963, before he entered hospital, though he may well have been at home in pyjamas and dressing-gown.

Both Nicky and Carlo agreed that it was the drummer who first called him in January 1965. The booking involved Jeff Beck (who Nicky remembered "standing in the corner trying to look like Mick Jagger"), Jon Mark on electric and acoustic guitar, Cliff Barton on bass and Carlo, of course, on drums. When the keyboard player failed to arrive, Carlo tried the Hopkins house.

Nicky Hopkins (in conversation with Charlie Gillett, May 1981): "Jimmy Page was producing with Glyn Johns engineering and from that I got an incredible amount of work, especially from Glyn, who introduced me to Shel Talmy. The next thing I did was about a month later and it was (The Who's) 'Anyway, Anyhow, Anywhere.'"

Carlo: "He obviously couldn't go out on the road and we got a session backing this singer called Andy Anderson at one of the studios in London.[17] We did this song in three or four takes and there was two hours left of the session, so Page said, 'Do you want to have a blow together?' I started a rhythm, somebody joined in and we carried on 'til the three hours was up, got our money and that was it. Six months later they put all that out on an album! He shouldn't have done that, but Jimmy Page was always one step ahead of everyone—a bit cute, you know."

If indeed this was Nicky's first proper session, it was an early lesson in the dubious morals of the record industry. The various blues jams recorded that day were sold to Immediate Records and have since been issued half a dozen times or more, under a variety of headings, but always with Jimmy Page's name entered as author of the songs—even on Nicky's feature number "Piano Boogie," an action even Nicky later described as "a bit rank." Years later, Carlo was to take him to court to challenge the songwriting credits. Page, by then a multi-millionaire, took full advantage of his superior financial and legal power to defend his claims to the hilt, ceding neither credit nor a penny of royalties to the hapless musicians.

American entrepreneur Shel Talmy was already a successful independent producer, and Nicky's contact with him led to bookings for a lengthy client list that included the Easybeats, David Bowie, the Who, the Kinks and a host of other acts, known and unknown. In 1966 he even helped Nicky to record his first solo album.

The session world was another part of the British cultural landscape that had emerged from post-war gloom blinking into the bright sunshine of the early sixties. Most studios had been record company-related undertakings like EMI's Abbey Road complex, run by in-house producers, "Artist and Repertoire" men and a team of white lab-coated technicians and "balancing engineers" working to strict "clock-in" schedules, recording pop vocalists, classical orchestras, spoken-word comedy, jazz and "light music."

---

[17] The artist was almost certainly bass player and singer Arvid Anderson, now living in Switzerland, but whoever he was, his song was apparently never released

Like so many other areas of fashion and culture, the established rules of recording music had been challenged and then overthrown by the arrival of rock'n'roll and beat music, spearheaded in particular by the huge success of the Beatles. Andrew Loog Oldham was one of a new breed of manager/producers:

"Sessions in those early days were very different from how the recording process works today. EMI had Abbey Road, Decca had West Hampstead, Phillips had Stanhope Place, west of Marble Arch and Pye were located the other side of the Arch off Great Cumberland Place, below Lew Grade's ATV House. As for the independents, the main three were Lansdowne, IBC and Olympic, which was then located off Gloucester Place."

The players who populated this twilight world had been dance band members, "trad." jazz refugees or trained classical musicians, capable of sight-reading the most complicated music scores but ill-equipped to play with any conviction the new rhythms that were now in demand. Most felt that the raw rock'n'roll brought in by Elvis Presley and his cohorts would only be a passing fad and were generally contemptuous of the new style and its practitioners. Drummer Clem Cattini, who, by his own account, played on forty-three number one singles in his session career, clearly remembers one "old jazzer" named Frank Clarke, the bass player on one of his first ever studio jobs, referring to "this rock'n'roll shit," while being quite incapable of actually playing it well.

Thankfully, a new generation of younger talent was waiting in the wings. Some, like Cattini, had served their apprenticeship in early rock'n'roll formations and skiffle bands; others like Carlo Little and bass-player Herbie Flowers came straight out of national service and the armed forces, where stints in regimental marching bands had given them great timing and a thorough grounding in reading music.

Nicky Hopkins was a comparative latecomer to the scene, but he arrived uniquely equipped, having not only served his time in three pioneering groups, but having been classically trained. Producer Derek Lawrence was one early convert:

"The first thing that impressed me was that he could play Floyd Cramer's 'Last Date' and was the only bloke in London who could; I can remember thinking 'If he can play that, he can play anything.'"

Musician and arranger Mike Vickers, who exchanged a popstar lifestyle with Manfred Mann for a career behind the scenes, was another:

"There are people who read music and don't make things up and people who make things up and don't read music, so when you put them together it's a powerful thing. Nicky could play whatever you put in front of him; it's a rarity to have somebody who could do that as perfectly as all the other session players but have that endless inventiveness, flexibility and above all feel.

"You can't actually notate the subtle variations of a free guitar or keyboard track. If you try and put it in front of a session musician, it's going to sound awful; you rely on them to supply what you want, which is a sympathetic role. He was supreme at that."

John Paul Jones was one of the younger breed who, before finding fame with Led Zeppelin, hit the studios at the same time as Nicky:

"Being of the same generation, we got on well together; everybody else was so much older. Only me, Nicky and Jimmy Page were of that age; Jim Sullivan was the next one up, but in the really early days there was only the three of us. It was nice to be in a young rhythm section and infinitely better than working."

Guitar hero (and one-time Savage) Ritchie Blackmore recalled the general panic that would often break out if a producer suddenly wanted to change the key of a song. It would be down to Nicky to hastily write out new chord charts for self-taught talents such as Blackmore and Page. Other keyboard players, such as the Small Faces' Ian McLagan, were simply envious:

"Years later I mentioned to Nicky that I had an idea for a song in the middle of the night and wrote down what I thought was the melody. He was amazed that I couldn't read or write music, but it never occurred to me to learn, so that you could write down an idea that you or anybody could play the next day."

Herbie Flowers, one of the era's busiest bass players, painted an eloquent picture of a typically traditional session, before the gradual shift in the London marketplace from manufactured solo singers to successful bands:

"Half the time we were booked to do things that were written out note for note and you had to play exactly what was in front of you. It was all done in one go—the strings on one side of the studio, with screens up, the rhythm section on the other side, playing quite quietly, with the drummer in what was like a homemade dug-out air-raid shelter, so that you couldn't hear too much spill. Guitar players had their amplifiers in little chicken huts; it was like Hampton Court Maze—loads of people in the studio, but you can only see the tops of their heads bobbing up and down.'

Nicky Hopkins quickly made his mark as a pianist who could come up with the goods, irrespective of the task put in front of him. His natural concentration and quiet demeanour meant that he was largely unaffected by the pressures familiar to any musician who enters the recording realm. Herbie Flowers again:

"There'd be a big orchestra and Dusty Springfield, Shirley Bassey or Tom Jones and you had three hours to lay down six tracks, so there was a lot of pressure when the red light went on. It was positive stress, but still very stressful, so the way to cope would be to be a bit over the top, smoke forty fags a day and not give a toss for anyone."

Andrew Loog Oldham: "Nicky was a young recruit in a barrack room of hardened musicians and tried to remain anonymous; at the end of the take, he'd cross his legs, hunch his shoulders—what there were of them—and give you a quiet but slightly distraught 'Is that all right, Andrew?'"

Once his credentials were established, Nicky joined a small elite of musicians who, until it became common practice for bands to write and perform their own songs, were responsible for playing on most of the hit records that graced the charts. Yusuf Islam, then known as Cat Stevens, was one of the young performers faced with the daunting sight of a full band and orchestra, all waiting to play his latest batch of songs:

"It was sometimes a bit lonely being the only self-taught musician in a room full of seasoned professionals, but very exciting—and occasionally disappointing—to hear the transformation of my song, from its simple beginnings to a fully orchestrated hit recording.

"I remember Nicky Hopkins and John Paul Jones playing next to each other and it was nice to have other people my own age in the studio. Nicky played on some of my biggest hits: the jangly harpsichord on 'Matthew And Son' for instance, but some of my favourite performances of his, were on my darker, more soulful numbers like 'Image Of Hell' where I was under the influence of Ray Charles. He was there for 'Granny,' 'Bad Night' and 'I'm Gonna Get Me A Gun' and I think it's him taking the organ solo on 'Blackness Of The Night.' I remember his incredibly long, thin hands dancing all over the keyboard.

"I never saw him outside of the sessions, because we moved in totally different circles and anyway there was always that pressure to get all the tracks done, or you could end up paying a lot of money in overtime."

Yusuf had another experience in common with Nicky, when he lost two years to a bout with tuberculosis, which had a predictably disastrous effect on his career as a pop star. When he returned with a different and ultimately even more successful version of himself as an acoustic guitar wielding singer-songwriter, he no longer thought of involving Nicky: "It never occurred to me because in my mind he belonged with everything else to that earlier time."

Mike Vickers: "It was a golden era for Abbey Road and many other studios in London, but EMI seemed to be central to it, putting out a massive number of singles every week and recording vast amounts of stuff. So if you were a session player, as Nicky was, or an arranger, as I was, we were there all the time."

Days were generally structured into three blocks of time—ten o'clock till one, two till five and seven till ten, with each session paid at a Musician's Union approved rate.

Herbie Flowers: "You'd see the same people over and over because we worked as units—Clem Cattini, Alan Parker, Joe Moretti, Big Jim Sullivan—I used to see more of Barry Morgan the drummer than I did of my family, for probably fifteen years. You had to work a lot of hours. The going rate when I first started was four pounds ten shillings a session, then it became six and then nine pounds, which was a reasonable wage; but it couldn't have been that reasonable, because we lived in a tiny house and I was working my butt off, like all of us were and only had a Morris Minor!"

Musicians were mostly booked either by company based or freelance "fixers," who were often musicians themselves, but astute enough to make an extra living as a contact point between the players and the employers.

Jon Mark: "I did lots of sessions with Nicky, because I was also a booker for Philips-Fontana; they'd call me and my wife would book the musicians; of course, they were always my mates and the best players."

Legendary characters such as Charlie Katz, Sidney Sax and Laurie Gold, EMI's in-house booker, held enormous power, and their favourites became the "first-call" musicians. For those skilled enough or lucky enough to be constantly in demand, life became a hectic round of dashing from studio to studio.

Andrew Loog Oldham: "My fixer was Charlie Katz, who would give you your regular crew or mention 'new boys,' which is how John Paul Jones, Jimmy Page and Nicky came into my life. Charlie would say, 'Andrew, Reg is not available on Tuesday, he's doing an Alma Cogan session over at EMI, but I've got this new lad, Nicky Hopkins—quiet, reads, but a lovely young boy. Why don't you try him?'"

Mike Vickers: "Morning, afternoon and evening: pack up, get across town through the rush hour, park again and in the meantime try to get something to eat that's going to keep you going. I know it would be harder today, but it was blinking hard enough then!"

Clem Cattini recalled halcyon days when he could park outside Chappell's in Bond Street, get his kit upstairs to the studio and leave the car there. Then parking meters came in, initially only costing sixpence an hour, so it was easy to get a meter and never a problem to feed it. In present day London you might pay as much for the parking as you would earn for a session. Nicky Hopkins was untroubled by these concerns, as he relied on taxis and trains and had keyboards waiting for him on arrival, but drummers and percussionists often employed full-time help to transport their equipment.

It was a period when innovation ruled in every area and at every level of the music business. Some changes were spontaneous, while others needed to be helped along. When records started to sell not just thousands but millions of copies, company producers like George Martin became dissatisfied with their salaried existence and the lack of reward for their successes. Following in the footsteps of earlier mavericks like Joe Meek, Martin set up independently with colleagues Ron Richards, John Burgess and Peter Sullivan as AIR London, though he continued to work freelance with his most famous EMI clients such as the Beatles, thus receiving valuable royalty points on his productions, instead of a meagre weekly wage.

The technical advances resulting from the experimental climate of the times have been well documented elsewhere; brilliant engineers (and later producers) such as Geoff Emerick, Alan Parsons and Gus Dudgeon were constantly forced by their clients' extravagant demands and expanding imaginations to push the envelope further and further in the studio. This led to techniques such as multitracking, the close miking of instruments and amplifiers, direct injection of guitars into the mixing board, phasing, flanging and automatic double-tracking.

The hired musicians had a hand in many of these advances. They were inspired by the depth and the intensity of sound they heard on records from America, made in Hollywood by such talents as Phil Spector or in Detroit at Berry Gordy's Motown production line. Many felt that home grown productions paled by comparison and worked hard to analyse and learn from U.S. imports.

Clem Cattini kept a detailed log of the sessions he played and recalled a two week period in February 1968, when he and Nicky worked together all day in various studio situations, went straight from the last session of the day to join John Paul Jones and Alan Parker at the Talk Of The Town nightclub to back Lulu in cabaret and got up next day to start all over again. German producer Mark Wirtz booked both musicians constantly and recalls Cattini as a pro-active organiser and a leader in fighting for a better deal for players.

As the popularity of a few of the "star" players grew, they used their newly acquired power to confront some of the practices and pay structures. Cattini once persuaded like-minded colleagues such as Nicky and John Paul Jones to join him in a month-long strike to raise the porterage (equipment transport) fee to two pounds instead of the ten shillings that had been paid for years.

Herbie Flowers: "There was an outcry when suddenly percussion players, who had to carry xylophones, vibraphones, conga drums, bongos, tambourines—you name it—a Volkswagen van full of stuff, suddenly said, 'We're going to actually charge more than ten shillings (fifty pence) for the porterage.' There was absolute uproar from the fixers."

Mark Wirtz: "It was a war. They would lie to us; I would call Sid Sax and say, 'I want Nicky and I want Clem,' and was told that Nicky couldn't make it, as he was already booked. Of course he wasn't. They would try and get kickbacks and backhanders from some of the guys. It was very corrupt. It was only when the producers and record companies said, 'Why isn't Cattini on this session?' that the fixers were forced to back down and agree to the raise the rate."

Despite his support for the porterage strike, such confrontational behaviour was far from Nicky Hopkins' usual style. The anonymous atmosphere of the studio suited his temperament perfectly and his friends and peers universally describe him as quiet and unobtrusive when at work, though with a deadpan sense of humour when caught in the right mood, and with a wonderful ability to defuse a tense situation with an impromptu rendition of the "Teddy Bears' Picnic" or some TV comedy theme.

Mike Vickers: "He used to be called 'the skeleton,' but he took it very well and everybody loved him. I don't think I ever saw him being difficult, obstinate, touchy or grumpy, all of which things I could throw at almost all the other session musicians I ever encountered."

Cat Stevens' guitarist Alun Davies, who with Jon Mark formed the short-lived group Sweet Thursday with Nicky, described him in the session era as "cocoa and malted milk biscuits." Clem Cattini confirmed that the two of them were united in abstaining from drink and drugs and remembered saying to Nicky, "It's you and me against the world," because of his fantastic timekeeping.

Nicky Hopkins (*What's New Boston*, September 1979): "I'd get home and go

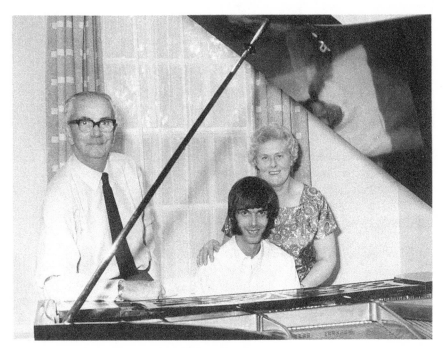

25. Proud parents

to bed and have fifteen minutes' sleep. I was doing all this on the natch, no drugs, no nothing; I didn't drink then; I didn't even like to take an aspirin."

In today's media landscape, which thrives on and even promotes the "sex, drugs and rock'n'roll" aspects of the music business, these qualities may seem uncontroversial and "unsexy." In the high-pressure, businesslike confines of a studio session, however, Nicky's ability to produce an inspired and rock-steady performance every time without fail was invaluable, and soon made him the most sought after piano player on the scene.

Surprisingly, throughout the period from 1965 to 1968 that he worked in London, Nicky continued living at his parents' house in Harrow, with his mother taking his bookings.

"I used to start at ten in the morning, go through to about eleven at night and then be going to Stones sessions, which would start whenever I got there and often go to about four or maybe eight a.m. in the morning, which meant some-times I didn't get any sleep."

With this hectic schedule continuing for months on end, it seems incongruous that Nicky remained a homebody in a time when other young people were doing all they could to break away from parental control. His mother could be accused of overcompensating in her attentions to her son, but Nicky's frailty warranted special care and the convenience of staying in a familiar environment, where the right kind of food was available and where his clothes were not only washed but bought for him by his mother, tipped the balance. He had his own room, his piano, his tape recorders, his collections of comics, coins, records and other weird and wonderful objects and no rent to pay, though his sister was emphatic that money was never his motivation or priority.

Dee Hopkins: "He used to come home and just throw it on the side in his room. If Mum needed something he'd say, 'Help yourself.' There was money all over the mantelshelf in the bedroom; he never spent anything; he didn't buy clothes. She'd say, 'You really do need some new underwear, you know.' 'Oh well, OK Mum, you do it.'"

Buried among the surreal nonsense in his letters, a cosy, humdrum home life is revealed, more reminiscent of boyhood than adulthood, with cats, cups of tea and biscuits and favourite television shows, a peaceful existence marred only by constant tension with his strait-laced father.

November 1967, to Dee:

"We've just been watching 'I Spy' on TV. (Dad went to bed before it started). Mum is making lovely mugs of tea. Lily has just wandered out for her saucer of milk before she goes out for the night (with a little hot water in the milk to take the chill off it!) Mum is getting her some biscuits, she's wandered in here & is sitting on the mat by the boiler, waiting for it, as she prefers to eat her biscuits there and NOT in the kitchen! As you can guess I'm sitting by the hatch at the breakfast-room table. I can just see Chi-Chi's tail as she sits on the floor. Now Mum has let her out! Ah! So kind!

"Do you remember an old annual we used to have—THE KNOCKOUT FUN BOOK for 1945? Well, I put an advert in Exchange & Mart, which is a magazine consisting entirely of adverts, and that cost 11/2d. I got one reply and he had a copy of the book for 7/6d. So I got it for under a £1 all in! Oh, it is funny! So much better than all the crappy annuals out now, with the exception of the Rupert annual which is exactly the same as it used to be and just as good. It hasn't gone all modern or anything. The pictures, colours, printing, and even the style of type and the format of the pages are just the same! Long live Rupert!

"I still can't talk to the old man. Every time I come out to the breakfast room he looks at me. I can feel his eyes watching. He never looks quickly—always a long look following you as you move. I know all he wants is a smile in return but it's IMPOSSI-BLE! So I get annoyed. Probably I get annoyed because I can't do it! He still doesn't know where he went wrong! He used to laugh at us just the same—ridiculing laughter. Now I know why I grew up so self-conscious. If he could ever go back in time and start all over again, as I'm sure he'd love to, he would make EXACTLY the same mistakes again!"

The cosy portrait of domestic bliss dates from when Nicky was twenty-three years old. His contemporaries in the pop world would have been spending their nights out on the town in clubs and discotheques, chasing the opposite sex and living in their own flats in the fashionable areas of London, a lifestyle Nicky could easily have afforded.

Instead he chose to spend what little downtime he had with his books, his tapes and his piano, and didn't leave home until he was twenty-five years old. There is a theory that the meticulous categorising of data and obsessive collecting are sub-conscious efforts to impose order on an otherwise chaotic world, and reading Nicky's neatly handwritten filing systems suggests that he was a perfect example of the type.

His working day would begin with breakfast and a taxi ride to his first session and continue on from there, until he returned, usually the same evening—though it would often be breakfast time again before he made it back home.

...And All Of The Night
The London Years – Part 2

Happiness At A Recording Session Is:
- ❖ *Finding that the top few notes on the piano aren't a semitone sharp*
- ❖ *Getting a part with just chord-symbols and no dots*
- ❖ *A paper cup of coffee and a wooden spoon*
- ❖ *A cigarette thrown from the other side of the room*
- ❖ *Knowing the song beforehand and making out you're a great 'reader'*
- ❖ *Losing your place and finding it again*
- ❖ *Realising they stopped for someone else's mistake and didn't hear yours*
- ❖ *Hearing that what you played can ACTUALLY BE HEARD on the playback*
- ❖ *When you get money instead of a cheque*
- ❖ *When you've got time to kill and get asked to do overtime*
- ❖ *A solo*

– Nicky Hopkins (from his diaries).

Any attempt to accurately list all the sessions that Nicky played on in the sixties is impossible. Such records as were kept have mostly either been lost or destroyed.

Nicky Hopkins: "From about '67 to '68 it was really machine-like; I didn't even know whom I was working for half the time. Anthony Newley was at one session; Sammy Davis Junior was at another; maybe those two were for a movie

soundtrack or maybe they were singles; I don't know. I don't even know if they ever came out!"

Nicky had become the pianist of choice, for old guard producers such as Norrie Paramor and Ivor Raymonde and the newer breed that included George Martin, Shel Talmy, Mark Wirtz, Derek Lawrence, Simon Napier-Bell, John Schroeder and Andrew Oldham. He was making definite though uncredited contributions to records by mainstream artists such as Dusty Springfield (who gave Nicky a beautiful gold inscribed Parker biro, which he used all his life), Marianne Faithfull, Peter and Gordon, Paul Jones and Del Shannon, as well as probable but unconfirmed appearances with others such as Tom Jones and Engelbert Humperdinck.

Shel Talmy's run of chart successes enabled him to start his own Planet label at the end of 1965. Though it lasted just a year and produced only one bona fide hit, if there was a piano on one of his twenty-two releases, it was almost always Nicky Hopkins playing it.

Shel Talmy: "I used Nicky for years on everything that needed a keyboard because he always added something; his ability to play the right thing at the right time is not something you can teach."

Derek Lawrence turned down EMI's offer to become a staff producer "for £15.00 per week and luncheon vouchers" and instead struck a deal that guaranteed him £50.00 cash and one per cent of any individual record he produced:

"I used to do three a week! Most of them were crap, but I got all the boys in. If you worked for EMI, they had a guy who paid everybody, who used to come down with a little board with names on and envelopes with their session fees in and sometimes we used to put bogus names in and send the guys round twice."

Nicky played on many of these sessions too, which appeared under a variety of group names: Soul Survival or the Ritchie Blackmore Orchestra. Some, such as the Outlaws' "Don't Cry" / "Only For You" and the imaginatively named The Sessions ("Let Me In" / "Bouncing Bass"), were never intended for UK release, being licensed exclusively to America.

Mark Wirtz, who became one of the era's busiest arrangers and producers, also booked Nicky regularly in London and even took him abroad, when he used his

German contacts to produce a few projects for EMI Electrola in Cologne. After one bad experience using local musicians,[18] the producer insisted on bringing in a complete team of UK players for future productions. Two that Nicky played on were issued under fictitious names, one as "The Rock-A-Fellas," while the aforementioned Hammond album was christened "The Nick Hopkins Caravan." Wirtz described the (now extremely rare) results as "only having curiosity value":

"It was 'in and out' and most of the stuff was done live; they had a very nice studio—that Germanic, pristine sound with no punch to it. We would fly in first thing in the morning, work all day, stay the night and get back to London the next day with a bunch of money in our pockets; they paid us cash in Deutschmarks. We had a good time, it was fun and nobody outside of Germany even knew about those records back then."

Despite his early skirmish with Norrie Paramor, Nicky also became one of his regulars and one notable booking at Abbey Road was for the Scaffold single, "Lily The Pink" and its B-side "Buttons Of Your Mind." The session also featured

---

[18] *Hammond On The Rocks,* featuring Nicky—accompanied by German jazz drummer Charlie Antolini—struggling manfully through a repertoire that includes sludgy versions of "Peter Gunn," "Great Balls Of Fire" and various other unimaginative rock 'n' roll cover versions; as musicians would say, "it cooks like a salad!"

a very young Andy Roberts on guitar, who came down from Liverpool while still a law student and stayed overnight at Paul McCartney's house in nearby St. John's Wood. Andy was able to draw a clear picture of the studio layout at Abbey Road, with Norrie Paramor upstairs in the control room, Mike Vickers on a ros-

trum in the centre, Clem Cattini and his drum kit hidden away behind baffles in the corner, Herbie Flowers to Andy's left, and Nicky off to his right playing 'tack' piano on the A-side and harpsichord on the flip.

Given his classical training, it is surprising that it didn't occur to Nicky to add arranging to his list of skills, as Mike Vickers and John Paul Jones did. He obviously already had more than enough work to keep him busy.

Probably the hippest of the younger producers was Andrew Loog Oldham. After enormous success with the Rolling Stones and Marianne Faithfull, he fulfilled the dream of owning and running his own label. With his partner Tony Calder, he formed Immediate Records, with its slogan "Happy To Be A Part Of The Industry Of Human Happiness." Modelled on the blueprints of legendary American successes such as Motown and New York's Brill Building, his later office in New Oxford Street became a legendary hangout for musicians, designers, scenesters and hangers-on of all descriptions. Immediate was a lifestyle, not just a label.

Andrew Oldham had no musical training, or indeed any schooling in the finer points of recording, but he had enormous energy and a fantastic talent for publicity; it was his idea, for instance, to transform the mundane John Baldwin into the more charismatic sounding John Paul Jones, arguing that, for his ventures into film music, the name would look more spectacular in widescreen.

Above all, Oldham had a God-given instinct for what sixties youth wanted. His early productions with the Rolling Stones were rough and ready affairs, low on sonic quality and high on attitude, but he quickly realised that the most important step for them, was to follow the Beatles' example and write and record original material. Supposedly he locked Mick Jagger and Keith Richards in a room and refused to let them out until they had written their first songs, thus establishing a lifelong songwriting partnership second only to Lennon and McCartney.

Marianne Faithfull was one of the first artists to benefit from a Jagger/Richards co-write when Oldham took her into the charts with "As Tears Go By," but his fast-paced lifestyle meant that when her follow-up flopped, he lost interest in producing her any further. In twenty-year old Jennifer Vashti Bunyan he found an alluring replacement for the posh-spoken Marianne and wasted no time in recording her (as simply "Vashti"), on "Some Things Just Stick In Your Mind," another Jagger/Richards number. Vashti recalls Nicky at her first recording session:

"When I turned up at the studio it was crammed with musicians and I just couldn't believe my eyes and ears; there were so many instruments there: violins, violas, three French horns, trombones, two bass guitars (6 string and 4 string), all the percussion—and there was Nicky. I've still got all the original parts that David Whitaker wrote for the session and the piano is the only one that isn't written out in great, great detail; it just had the basic chords written on the page and the rest was left to Nicky to improvise. He played this fantastic honky-tonk type piano and all the other session musicians were amazed that he did it off the top of his head. I remember a great deal of respect for Nicky from all the people there, some of whom wouldn't seem to have had a respectful bone in their body. I remember him very fondly though he was incredibly shy and I was incredibly shy and I'm sure we didn't speak a word to each other."

To Vashti's great relief she was able to add her double-tracked vocals later, though still under the intimidating gaze of Andrew Oldham, Mick Jagger and an engineer.

Vashti's reticence, a bit of bad luck and Andrew's unreliability meant that her first single failed to repeat the instant success of her blonde-haired predecessor,

but she remained at Immediate long enough to record one more unreleased single of her own, contribute vocals to the duo Twice As Much (with Nicky on keyboards) and attend recording dates with PP Arnold and others.

Pat Arnold was equally shy and even younger when she arrived in London, but, unlike Vashti, was used to singing live in the studio, having sung backing vocals on the seminal "River Deep Mountain High":

"I met Nicky right about when I arrived in England with Ike and Tina Turner. I was doing a lot of stuff with Mick Jagger and he was Mick's right hand piano man. Mick would swoop down to the hotel, pick me up in his Aston Martin and we would go into Pye Studios on off-days. Nicky played on all those tracks. He used to read a lot of comic books. I'm not going to say that I knew him that well, because in those days you didn't really know anybody personally, but I remember him playing grand piano and he was jamming! Where did he learn to play like that?"

After the inevitable business split from the increasingly savvy and self-reliant Rolling Stones, Andrew Loog Oldham continued to indulge his fondness for full-on production, in imitation of his Los Angeles idols, Phil Spector, Jack Nitzsche and Brian Wilson. In its brief life, Immediate had a roster of artists that included Chris Farlowe, The Small Faces, Billy Nicholls, Duncan Browne and the aforementioned Twice As Much and PP Arnold. Sometimes Oldham dispensed with the artist altogether and recorded as the "Andrew Oldham Orchestra." Nicky Hopkins played with them all.

Andrew Oldham gave his own postscript to those times:

"Every young man of nineteen should have an orchestra; it does wonders for your confidence. If I had self-confidence it was because I had a love and a muse—music and records—and it wasn't nerve-wracking to have an orchestra waiting on you; on many occasions it was as good as and sometimes better than sex.

"Woody Allen once said that cocaine was God's way of telling you that you had too much money. With me it was Immediate Records. I had a group of friends and workers, and results that set standards that are still enjoyed today; it was all a weave of wants, dreams and possibility—the songs, the sound, the play-ers and the moment—and Nicky was a part of that team and of those wonderful days when we did not seem able to be wrong."

Indeed, wherever Nicky turned up, his speed and versatility, combined with his ability to notate songs instantly, left other musicians gasping. Mike Harrison,

later of Spooky Tooth, met him with his earlier line-up, the V.I.P.s. Producer Guy Stevens told him:

"I've got this guy who's going to play the solo of a lifetime on this track ('In A Dream'). Nicky arrived, played and left almost without speaking!"

Mike Lease, whose trio The Pyramid featured a pre-Fairport Convention Iain Matthews (then known as Ian Macdonald), was another satisfied Hopkins customer. He remembered an unusual five-day marathon session with producer Denny Cordell, for folk-blues singer Beverley Kutner (who later be-came Beverley Martyn when she married singer-guitarist John Martyn in 1969). The unlikely line-up included regulars Jimmy Page, John Paul Jones and Nicky Hopkins, joined by Pen-tangle guitarist John Renbourn and Lease himself on Hammond organ. The resulting single, "Happy New Year" / "Where The Good Times Are," was the first ever release on the Deram label. Beverley remembers Nicky's special contribution:

"They all got on so well—it was magic; the feel and the sound of those ses-sions was brilliant and they were so far ahead of their time. 'Happy New Year' was a Randy New-man demo from Schroeder Music and Nicky transformed the piano part for the record; he was like a mouse, with a long, black coat—and shy, just like Nick Drake."

As Tin Pan Alley and beat music gradually mu-tated into Swinging London and psychedelia, situations that were a stretch for some in the session fraternity would occasionally arise. Shel Talmy, who moved increasingly away from pop and into acoustic music with bands like Pentangle, made two albums with folkie Roy Harper, known for his lengthy, meandering and extremely wordy songs. Talmy brought in his usual favourites for the album *Folkjokeopus* but the usually unflappable Clem Cattini was flummoxed by Harper's curious time signatures and weird song structures.

Roy Harper: "It was the length of them and the fact that you had to keep in mind that it was going to change after ten minutes. I remember Clem sitting there waiting for me to finish one particular passage before he came in and he dropped a drumstick and we very nearly called, but didn't."

Nicky had no such problems.

Roy Harper: "Nicky was there, sat at the piano and smiled briefly; he was the best; he very rarely did anything like smiling, but quietly asked you what you expected him to do; whether you wanted it played fortissimo or whether there were crescendos in it, whether there were soft passages. He was very attentive to detail and also the quickest of any musician I ever met; you only needed to play it to him once and he had it, so he was very, very easy to work with.

"With Shel I had to fight my corner; it wasn't easy because he was really coming from Tin Pan Alley and I was coming from Jack Kerouac and we were meeting head on, but Nicky could understand and was much more in tune with the youth of his age than Shel was—a very sympathetic guy."

Another curious project that came out under different guises in different territories, is best known under the title *No Introduction Necessary*. It was marketed with the focus firmly on Jimmy Page's involvement.

Recorded at Olympic and produced by Glyn Johns, the session featured Nicky in distinguished company: top guitarists Jimmy Page, Big Jim Sullivan and Albert Lee, the ubiquitous Clem Cattini on drums and background singer and conga player Gerry Temple (real name Keith De Groot) as nominal lead vocalist, on an album of Jerry Lee Lewis-style rock'n'roll. Unusually, Nicky Hopkins was also credited as arranger and even took a leaf out of Jimmy Page's book and gave himself a writer's credits on "One Long Kiss" and the raving six-minute jam session "Burn Up." Since all concerned were working as hired hands and the line-up never played live, it was just another day's work in the studio. [19]

_____

[19] The author has a wonderful and rare French LP version of the same recording, with slight variations in the track listing, titled *Burn Up*.

Just as producers' dissatisfaction with their salaried existence led to a points system that awarded them a percentage of a record's earnings, some in the musician's fraternity became jaded with the endless succession of anonymous recording dates, and tired of seeing their contributions to hit records, for which they had been paid a pittance, taken for granted by record companies. Young, good-looking but often talent-free performers ended up miming all over the world to music they had no hand in creating, sometimes becoming fabulously wealthy in the process. Mike Vickers was philosophical about the session players' role:

"If you freelance, you have to accept that you will end up doing a huge variety of stuff, some of which you don't really care for; you're committed because you won't get work if you don't take things on, so it definitely becomes a compromise. You trade being in a name band and having huge success for being busy and getting a fee. Also, the arranger or musician is not the songwriter and even if you're an incredibly skilled professional, it doesn't mean you can actually write even one decent song."

Some players, like Herbie Flowers, managed to work successfully in both worlds:

"When I worked on recordings by people like Bowie, I was working for them, so I had no comment about any of it; it's like asking a bus-driver what he thinks of the bus. 'It's a bus, innit and the roads are a bit bumpy.'"

"I had no time for Lou Reed, for instance, or the miserable stuff that I played on; I only ever met him for three days, he hated *Transformer* and so did I. To this day when people say, 'Oh, you played on "Walk On The Wild Side," my comment is, 'Yes, but only once!'"

Herbie established two groups in his career, made up exclusively of studio colleagues and both Blue Mink and later Sky went on to have hits of their own.

Jon Mark, who shared a flair for business with Jimmy Page, formed a production company with him, Page/Mark Music, when they were both in London. He distinctly remembers the moment when he realised that Page was moving on:

"Jackie De Shannon came over and took him with her to America and after he got back, he told me he was going to form the 'biggest, loudest rock'n'roll band in history,' called Led Zeppelin. I said, 'Jimmy, you don't stand a hope in hell; let's just carry on with what we're doing.' Later on, when I was with John Mayall, Johnny Almond and I went to a nightclub after a gig and 'Whole Lotta Love' came on. I couldn't believe it! Jimmy had done exactly what he said."

To John Paul Jones joining Led Zeppelin seemed risky but necessary, as he really wanted to be part of the band scene and to play music under his own terms:

"The sessions were a great schooling and I'm really glad I did them, but I was burning out on two or three sessions a day, six or seven days a week as well as doing thirty or forty arrangements a month; it was insane."

Nicky Hopkins joined at least two band projects during his session years, though with nothing like the same level of success as his two former colleagues.

Formed in 1968, Poet and the One Man Band featured Albert Lee, Tony Colton and Ray Smith, alongside the tried and true rhythm section of Pat Donaldson and Barry Morgan and…Nicky Hopkins.

Nicky had crossed paths with Albert in the early years, when Lee joined the backing vocalists on Lord Sutch's "Jack The Ripper" at Joe Meek's, as well as on records with Chris Farlowe's Thunderbirds and on various Derek Lawrence productions. The "Poet" project stemmed from the Colton/Smith writing partnership and was intended as an outlet for their more unusual material. Studio magazine *Beat Instrumental* picked out Albert Lee and "Micky" Hopkins as the best known of the participants.

Despite some positive reviews, their one officially released album failed to make waves and there was neither enough impetus nor money to tempt the two busiest session players in the line-up away from their London-based work. Nicky and Barry Morgan left without ever playing live with them. Guitarist Jerry Donahue, who joined the band after being brought in to arrange vocals on that first album, remembers how hard it was to find another piano player who measured up to Nicky:

"When we were looking for keyboard players, there wasn't anybody that came near; they brought in Mike O'Neill, who used to be "Nero" in Nero and The Gladiators and he was good; it's just that Nicky's style of playing was so unique."

Sweet Thursday was a more genuine attempt to a start a band. Derek Lawrence, who had produced Deep Purple's first three albums, financed the 1968 recording and offered a connection to US based record company Tetragrammaton, a label started with backing from comedian Bill Cosby.

Linchpin of the group was Jon Mark, who brought in his old friend Alun Davies, jazz bassist Brian Odgers, drummer Harvey Burns and young producer Hugh Murphy[20], whom Jon knew from when he had worked in Shel Talmy's office:

"I was a songwriter and wanted to get the songs out there. Alun had the thump and the pizzazz, I was more laid-back and we thought, 'We need a piano player.' I called Nicky up and said, 'I've just started a band called Sweet Thursday, do you want to be part of it?' and he went, 'If it's you Jon, yeah.' The name came from the Steinbeck novels and we all wanted to go to Cannery Row and live like they did; Nicky and I used to talk about the idea of going to America; it was always uppermost in our minds: the land of milk and honey."

Despite the crazy schedules they all faced as session-players, they still found time for the band.

Alun Davies: "It was pretty scattered, but we got dead studio time and managed to fit it in. It was important that it was a group project and was seen like that; Jon never wanted to hog the limelight; it was very democratic and we had a common interest in emerging roots-based music. When we were half way through making the album, *Music From Big Pink* (the immensely influential first album by The Band) came out and utterly changed the mixing of what we'd al-

---

[20] later to find fame with Gerry Rafferty's "Baker Street"

ready done; we were all excited by the idea of being released by an American label and it was heady stuff for us."

Both musicians remember Nicky being as enthused as anyone in the band, and an album and single were completed, best described as US-influenced folk-rock. A cover photo was shot by the Thames at night, with equal prominence given to each member. But though all were looking forward to taking the line-up out on tour, particularly to the USA, Sweet Thursday never actually played a live gig.

Jon Mark: "Tetragrammaton was L.A. based and had Jo Bergman[21] running the London office. We wanted to get the album out and start to tour, but the company was all big egos and power plays and nobody could get anything going; Jo did a really good job, because she tried to get us gigs, but it just never came together and the guys were like all musicians. I was the bandleader and had to

sell them on doing gigs for free, which was really hard. 'Hey man, where's the money? I've got to pay the rent, are you crazy?'"

The album went on to cult status in the USA and was re-issued a number of times over the years, though it could never be described as a success ("not as far as my doormat knows" – Alun Davies). The various members would have to wait to fulfil their ambitions to travel: Jon Mark with John Mayall and his own Mark-Almond group, Alun Davies and Harvey Burns with Cat Stevens and Nicky Hopkins with the Jeff Beck Group. Brian Odgers apparently continued working in London. Nicky was last to join and first to leave.

Nicky's personality did not lend itself to bitterness or to union style industrial action. As one of the most in-demand musicians on the scene, he was kept too busy and paid too well to think much about making improvements to his lot as a session man. It was only after his later experiences in America, where top studio players were routinely paid double and even triple scale, that he realised things could be better. He'd been able to buy himself luxuries such as a grand piano for use at home, which he proudly described in a letter to his sister Dee:

"It's a second-hand black Bechstein, 6ft. 6ins. long and it's marvellous. I got it from Camden Town for £180!! What you might call a real bargain! It sounds so different from the upright piano. Chi-Chi mustn't go in there because she might like to sharpen her claws on the piano legs! I've had all the old scuffed and scratched polish taken off and completely redone, which cost £20 extra, and now it looks like new! No cups of tea get put on top of this piano!'

He could afford to travel to New York to visit his sisters and to lead a peace-

---

[21] later spokeswoman for the Rolling Stones

ful, settled existence at home. He had
appeared on countless records, both
good and bad, a very high percentage
of which are now considered the classic songs of the era. A random trawl
through the music papers of the time
reveals that hardly a week went by
without a release from one of Nicky's
satisfied customers and sometimes
several at once, a pattern later repeated in America in publications like
Rolling Stone magazine.

In later interviews, Nicky summed
up his years as a session man:

"It's quite secure, except you don't get paid if you're off sick, but you don't
have to depend on the success of a record to keep you going; the funniest sensa-
tion is working with someone who's currently a hot name and then three months
later he's faded out and there you are, still banging away.

"There were a lot of good times and I enjoyed it because I'd never done it before; it improved my reading ability and gave me an insight as to what I'd
eventually do; you learn from everything: from straight sessions to film tracks to
commercials for dog food."

The very randomness of the session life eventually caused a certain indifference and cynicism to creep in. Nicky recalled one soundtrack session for a film
called *Joanna*, where, among the hundred and ten musicians in the studio, the
American producer had booked no less than five keyboard players at once:

"Three harpsichords, a piano and an organ...I didn't feel like playing, so I sat
underneath the harpsichord and read *Melody Maker* for the entire morning, just
to see if anyone would twig—and no one ever did!"

It was definitely time to move on.

Session Man
The Who and The Kinks

'He reads the dots and plays each line, and always finishes on time, no overtime, no favours done…He's not paid to think, just play…'
– Ray Davies 'Session Man' from the Kinks album 'Face To Face'

As soon as Nicky Hopkins was in with Shel Talmy, the Kinks and the Who became two of his earliest clients. At first glance, the two bands had a lot in common. Both moved from the same blues and R&B based roots to writing their own material, and both had a songwriter on board more than capable of keeping up with the insatiable demand for the classy pop material necessary to stay on top in the fast-paced singles market of 1965: a time when every group was only as good as its last "forty-five."

By the time Nicky met them in early 1965, both groups had already landed their first hits; The Kinks were ahead of the game, with "You Really Got Me" topping the charts in August the previous year, followed in October by "All Day And All Of The Night" and in January '65 by their second Number One, "Tired Of Waiting For You."

The Who's first release (under that name) came out the same day as the latter single, with several reviewers noting an unhealthy similarity between "I Can't Explain" and the Kinks' style. The common factor was their hit-hungry producer, who stuck closely to the same blueprint that had helped the Kinks to succeed.[22]

Though "I Can't Explain" already carried elements that would become trademarks of the Who's sound, Pete Townshend himself admitted to adapting the

---

[22] Talmy had also, to his considerable advantage, successfully persuaded both bands to record his copyrighted song "Bald Headed Woman"

Kinks formula in a bid to impress Shel Talmy as a potential producer.

Nicky Hopkins didn't play on any of these earlier recordings, but once brought into the fold, he became a firm fixture for both groups. With his American mentor at the helm, Nicky's function initially was largely the same in both situations.

Given that both bands were established and close-knit units, the arrival of an outside player could have been a source of friction, but Shel Talmy had already introduced keyboards, backing vocals and an extra rhythm guitar to the Who's first recording and, like his Kinks counterpart, Pete Townshend had been a big Cyril Davies fan.

Pete Townshend: "I knew of Nicky from 'Country Line Special,' which I had once persuaded Roger to learn; we actually played that tune. Nicky fitted in beautifully; it's hard to explain how strange I found it to see someone write down chord names as I played them; I can do it myself now, but at the time I'd never seen any-

26. Townshend, Talmy and Moon, with Nicky in the doorway

one do it. As a result, Nicky learned tunes in minutes, without prepared chord charts or rehearsal; what he then did was immediately spontaneous. He didn't look the part, but he played the blues—maybe a bit too quickly, but it was blues."

Shel Talmy: "I suppose if I'd tried to sell another guitarist (laughs), I would have gotten a lot of hassle. Nicky pretty much stayed out of the way and brought something unique to the recording without angering anybody else."

Nicky's almost supernatural ability to play with bands, particularly guitar bands, without ever getting in the way of either bass-players or guitarists is commented on again and again throughout his career. Pete Townshend actually welcomed his presence, as he felt that the live impact of his three-piece line-up was diminished in the cold confines of the studio, and benefited from support.

In early April, with Nicky on board, the Who managed to squeeze three days of recording at IBC in Portland Place into their crowded concert schedule. They cut about a dozen cover songs culled from their soul-based live set and one original composition. Pete and Roger Daltrey's "Anyway Anyhow Anywhere" was destined to be their second single release.

Nicky's first appearance on record with the Who was swiftly picked as the theme tune to *Ready, Steady, Go,* one of the most popular music shows on British television at the time and second only to the BBC's *Top Of The Pops* in importance. This exposure and the group's growing live presence helped the single to a respectable No. 10 in the hit parade, almost certainly Nicky's first showing on any chart. The impact of his piano contribution, however, brought problems when the band went to Bristol to mime the track on TWW's *Discs A Go-Go* TV show in June, and the producer initially insisted the pianist from the record should be present.

The Who's schedule didn't allow them to make it back into the studio until October, by which time Townshend, encouraged by his managers, had accumulated his first batch of really good original material.

Various authors have gone to great lengths to describe Nicky's role on the subsequent *My Generation* LP, but one listen is worth pages of print. Suffice it to say that coming in as a pianist to a band that has been described as being "three lead instruments all trying to solo at once" presented challenges that Nicky effortlessly mastered. His subtle "comping" fattens up Townshend's chords, while his bluesy Johnnie Johnson/Floyd Cramer style riffing in the upper register provides a miraculous middle ground between Keith Moon's thrashing drums, the stop-start sparseness of the slashing guitar accents and John Entwistle's rumbling bass. When present, the piano is generally placed lower in the mix than the electric guitar, but  by jumping from mid-range to the higher registers and occasionally moving from riffs to solid chords, Nicky helps build the intensity of several tracks in a dramatic fashion.

As so often, he shines on the more familiar blues-based material such as James Brown's "Please, Please, Please" or "I'm A Man," where his channelling of Otis Spann provides a backdrop to the lead guitarist's explosive soloing. But his contributions to Townshend's own songs—highlights being "Anyway Anyhow Anywhere," "A Legal Matter" and "It's Not True"—are like a master-class in rock piano accompaniment. Though never loud enough to dominate proceedings, his revved-up Mose Allison-style riffing provides a vital element that would leave a yawning gap if removed.

Despite his enormous part in creating its sound, Nicky's only credit on his first full album was as co-writer of the "The Ox," the frantic instrumental that closes side two, where his timing was put to the test mid-track, when the other three suddenly dropped out, leaving him on his own for several bars, but with an unfaltering grip on the tempo.

Nicky Hopkins: "That was just a one-off. There were five minutes left on the clock at the end of one session and Shel just said, 'OK boys, play!' I wish we'd had time to re-do it actually; I had no idea they were going to break and didn't know if I was supposed to keep playing or what!"

Shel Talmy: "It was just a jam, I mean, hell, I should probably have had (a credit) on it as well! Everybody got a piece of it—and quite right too."

In interviews over the years Nicky remembered the Who at that time, with typical understatement, as "having trouble getting on with each other." Nevertheless, he always referred to the album *My Generation* as a personal highlight in his playing career and to the Who as one of his all-time favourite clients, and it is curious that after such an immediately successful first collaboration, he didn't work with them again for several years.

Having signed up the band with Shel Talmy in a mad rush to get them recorded at all, the Who's managers Kit Lambert and Chris Stamp only afterwards realised what a hideous contract they had agreed to. The group's percentage was so low that the lion's share of royalties went to the producer, not the band. After their first three singles had all charted, with "My Generation" (without Nicky) falling just shy of the Number One spot and their debut album going into the top ten on its pre-Christmas release, band and management were desperate for a way out. In addition, both Talmy and engineer Glyn Johns strongly resented Kit Lambert's presence in the studio and influence on Pete Townshend. Something had to give.

Deciding that attack was the best means of defence, they produced their next single themselves and released it, not on Decca's Brunswick label but through Robert Stigwood's new Reaction imprint, distributed by Polydor, knowing full well that this would provoke a legal confrontation with their erstwhile producer.

The details of the ensuing dispute are well-documented, with Shel Talmy refusing point-blank to relinquish control of his cash-cow and eventually securing a settlement that ensured him a production royalty on any Who recordings released within the next five years. Though the action successfully freed the band from the onerous terms of their contract, the financial implications proved to be a deciding factor in the subsequent development of the Who's career, forcing them for years to earn the greater part of their income through live appearances rather than album sales. One of Talmy's tactics was to shadow each new independent release by the Who with another Brunswick single extracted from the first LP, starting appropriately with "A Legal Matter" and finishing up with "La La La Lies." This caused confusion for fans and media alike, though none of the older songs seriously threatened the amazing run of hits conjured up by Pete Townshend in 1966 and '67.

One casualty of the split was Nicky Hopkins. When asked why Nicky wasn't invited to play on subsequent recordings, Townshend insisted that it was because he began to play keyboards himself, but it seems more likely, in the atmosphere of acrimony following their break with Talmy, that "the baby went out with the bath water" and that Nicky, who came in with Shel, left with him too.

In the meantime, he had plenty of other clients, not least among them the Kinks.

Ray Davies' awareness of Nicky Hopkins also dated back to the Cyril Davies band, whom he remembered seeing live, supporting Sonny Boy Williamson.

Nicky's first Kinks appearance came in October 1965, when he and drummer Clem Cattini were brought in to Pye Studios for the sessions that resulted in *The*

Kinks Kontroversy album and its accompanying single release "Till The End Of The Day," released within a week of each other in November.[23]

Initially, Nicky's role in the Kinks set-up was similar to that with the Who, though if anything his contributions were even more subliminal. At this stage in their development the two bands were quite similar, with very up-front electric guitars carrying most of the songs. Talmy again used Nicky's piano mostly to boost the rhythm section, but mixed it even lower than on *My Generation*. Neither drummer Mick Avory nor bass player Pete Quaife remembered the studio set-up at Pye with much affection:

Mick Avory: "There were two studios: Number 1 to fit orchestras, and 2, which was smaller. They were a bit box-like with all those slats of wood around the place and we'd sit down together playing live, because things weren't so structured then. Later on recording changed and everything was built up from the bass and drums, but during those days it was a band playing together."

Pete Quaife: "We'd be down in the dungeon in Number 1 and it was a lot of stairs to go back up to daylight; I didn't like it down there because I'm really claustrophobic and we'd be there at two o'clock in the morning with all the doors locked."

Ray Davies remembered his first contact with Nicky:

"We never phoned him personally; it was always done by management; musicians just seemed to turn up and no extravagant plans were needed, not like today, where everyone seems to have a million things to do. He was very friendly, and very quiet. I think that's why he worked so well with other musicians, because he blended in and you always knew he'd get it right in a couple of takes."

Sometimes just playing fat left-hand chords and sometimes reprising the tinkling Johnnie Johnson-style backdrop he had provided for the Who, Nicky got the opportunity to step forward and solo on only two songs, "I'm On An Island" and "It's Too Late."

---

[23] This contradicts Doug Hinman's otherwise brilliant day-by-day account of the Kinks' activities, *All Day And All Of The Night*. A 1964 session, mentioned in his book and supposedly including Nicky Hopkins, must have featured another player, as it was recorded while Nicky was still languishing in hospital.

Both Ray's brother Dave Davies and Avory remembered Nicky fitting instantly into the band and indeed, in the early years, he was only prevented by ill health from accepting an offer to tour with the Kinks as well as record.

The Who had started life with a contentious gang mentality, and in their pilled-up state were not averse to the occasional punch-up. The Kinks were an even more volatile and dysfunctional "family;" strife, both on and offstage, continued throughout the band's career, particularly between Ray and his flamboyant younger brother.

It had not taken long for Townshend to bridle at Shel Talmy's dictatorial approach, and in Ray Davies the producer found an equally opinionated and contrary adversary. It became common practice for the Kinks to re-record certain songs a number of times until their leader was satisfied, with the result that several singles appeared without a Shel Talmy credit. Bassist Pete Quaife remembered some of the more painful moments:

"He (Ray) is a control freak. This wasn't obvious in the beginning, but it slowly came to the surface, until in the end he had us all standing around in the studio, while he listened to a tambourine. We said, if that's all he was going to do, then we might as well go, but he insisted we stay, so we'd sit there for five hours listening to a bloody tambourine. We had fun occasionally but for the most part there was just tension. Nicky saved Ray's arse on a lot of occasions, with the construction of the numbers and so on."

The band's confidence in and respect for Nicky's playing seems to have spared him from the worst of the studio infighting and he managed to keep his head down when words (or objects) were flying. As Ray Davies' songwriting became more ambitious and his self-confidence grew, Nicky's role changed. The following year, he was asked to add more varied colours to the next Kinks album, *Face To Face*. The subject matter of the songs had expanded considerably and where the previous LP still had room for rave-ups like "Milk Cow Blues," the fourteen original songs on the newer record included witty and critical pieces such as "Party Line," "House In The Country," "Holiday In Waikiki" and the immortal "Sunny Afternoon."

Though his piano is unmistakable on several tracks and on "Sunny Afternoon" he also played melodica, Nicky's first ever musician's credit, on the rear sleeve of the album, is limited to the succinct legend: "Harpsichord – Nick Hopkins."

Dave Davies: "When we went into Pye Studios they had a big harpsichord and he sat down at it. We said, 'Oh God, we've got to use this.' The sound seemed to lend itself to the type of songs we were starting to write and record."

"Session Man" is one of the most celebrated tracks to feature the instrument and has gone down in rock history as being written specifically for the man who played it. Years later, Ray Davies said he "half-wrote" the song for Nicky, although its lyrics are not entirely complimentary and make accusations that could hardly be aimed at Nicky. Brother Dave disputed the dedication altogether:

"There were certain session men around that weren't very nice people and if you listen to the words of "Session Man," they're a bit cynical. Some of them used to look down their noses but say nothing about taking the money; Nicky was not like that. He was a real lovable, easy guy."

In a 1973 interview Nicky made it clear who he thought the song's targets were:

"The Kinks were using various straight musicians at the time, like clarinet, sax, trombone and string players and they really were a hard lot to get on with. If the parts weren't written out for them, they'd grumble, they wouldn't go into overtime without getting paid and they'd talk about things like gardening between takes!"

Ray Davies finally put the question to rest in a written reply to this author:

"I didn't actually write 'Session Man' for Nicky, or with him in mind and he made no comment when he played on the track, but responded instantly when I asked him to put something classical sounding on the front. Come to think of it, he did play the rest of the track a bit aggressively, so the lyric content may have had some effect on him."

Like Pete Townshend, Ray was a capable piano player and there are a number of instances on Kinks recordings where the keyboard parts are so simple that it is hard to determine who is playing them.

Ray Davies: "I remember 'Sunny Afternoon' vividly because I was playing piano in a typical songwriter's stabbing style and Shel Talmy said, 'Copy what Ray does.' The next morning we went in and did two or three takes and Nicky had it pat; other musicians would have been insulted, but Nicky seemed to get inside my style and played exactly as I would have; he would play beneath himself to accommodate the style of others. No ego—perhaps that was his secret?'

In November 1966, a brief holiday in New York meant that Nicky missed the next single "Dead End Street," after which he wrote to his sister Dee:

"I've done quite a lot of work since I've been back— nine sessions so far, so things aren't so bad. The Kinks'

record was rush-released and is already out. Someone else did the piano part, but I'm quite flattered as it sounds like me! Hmm, copied eh?! I wasn't going to bugger up my holiday for them or anybody! The new Kinks LP, which I was on, is now out over here, and I hear that this time I did get credit on it—I bet it's in the smallest print possible!"

Though absent on "Dead End Street" and its flipside "Big Black Smoke," Nicky's close association with the Kinks continued in 1967 with follow-up, the jaunty and satirical "Mr. Pleasant," which featured him prominently in full honky-tonk mode and lent itself so well to piano that Nicky recorded his own instrumental version of the song in this same year, with one of his own titles as a B-side.

The Kinks' run of singles continued with "Waterloo Sunset," a timeless classic that underwent several attempts in the studio. Nicky was present during initial efforts, but was left out of proceedings when Ray went back in to Pye, without Shel Talmy, to record the version finally used. Nicky had to be content with his presence (on piano and harpsichord respectively) on its different UK and American B-Sides.

The growing importance of his role in the Kinks' music was underlined by regular invitations from the band to accompany them on BBC live broadcasts, several of which performances survived to appear much later on a fascinating CD compilation. They provide a wonderful glimpse of the band's live power, stripped of studio enhancement and recorded under extreme pressure.

Pete Quaife: "We went in, set up and they'd say, 'Right, this is number one. Go!' and we did virtually every single one in one take."

Even when absent on the original records, Nicky was called upon on these occasions to guest on such songs as "Waterloo Sunset" or "Harry Rag" and was featured on piano, organ and Mellotron, freeing up Ray Davies, who was increasingly playing acoustic guitar on his own compositions.

Brother Dave had also begun to write for the band and sang lead on his own hit "Death Of A Clown" and on several songs on the next album, *Something Else By The Kinks*. Nicky contributed a rickety "tack" piano introduction to "Death Of A Clown" on record and reprised his part live at the BBC in August, when he and Dave delivered a stunning duet version of "Spider" John Koerners's "Good Luck Child," (re-titled "Good Luck Charm"). This acoustic guitar and piano romp with its eccentric timing is rhythmically so tight and so perfect that it almost defies belief, but such radio excursions were considered purely promotional, and the real work continued in the studio.

Something Else By The Kinks, which came out in September 1967 in the UK, was another fine collection of Davies originals (three of them Dave's) and is, if anything, even broader in scope than its predecessor. Nicky plays on all but four of the thirteen songs, mostly on piano, but with a few organ tracks and one on the harpsichord. This time his sleeve credit was reduced (along with two Pye studio engineers) to the even more spartan composite, "Our thanks to macirishdavenickykeith."

The subject matter and overall feel of the record was massively out of step with the times and Ray's "gallery of brilliant musical portraits" of British suburban life, though rightly considered ground-breaking now, made little headway in the psychedelic freak-out year of *Sgt. Pepper's Lonely Hearts Club Band* and *Their Satanic Majesties Request*. The album failed to make a dent in the British charts and managed only a fleeting appearance in America.

Undeterred, the Kinks leader followed up with the incredible mini-symphony 'Autumn Almanac,' featuring a distinctive Mellotron part. A lack of accurate studio information makes it difficult to be sure whose hands were on the keys, but the result put the group comfortably back in the top ten. Subsequent singles on which Nicky certainly played, "Wonderboy" and Dave's "Susannah's Still Alive," were both flops.

Up to now Nicky's relationship with the group, and most importantly its leader, had remained cordial, though he almost never socialised with the band outside the confines of the studio. Ray summed up his somewhat unsentimental attitude:

"Session players are, for the most part, anonymous shadows behind the stars. They do their job for a fee and then leave, rarely seeing their names on the records. Their playing never stands out, but if you take them out of the mix, the track doesn't sound the same. You only miss them when they are not there…Nicky and I were hardly bosom buddies. We socialised only on coffee breaks and in between takes."

Mick Avory: "He wasn't a drinker; we used to have a break at Pye Studios and go down the pub, but he didn't socialise a lot—probably because of his health."

Whether it was his health or simply the demands of his session schedule that sent him home at the end of a day's work, rather than to clubs like the Ad Lib or Cromwellian, frequented by many group members, all Nicky's clients commented on the clear line between the studio and the outside. Even bands like the Kinks that booked him over a period of months or even years, only recall seeing him at work, though Mick Avory remembered giving him a lift home on a number of occasions.

Although Ray Davies was experiencing similar tensions to the Who with his producer, his relationship with Shel Talmy had held up so far. The group's next release would prove to be the first one credited solely to Raymond Douglas Davies as producer and the last with Nicky Hopkins on keyboards. This time it was Nicky who terminated the relationship.

The upcoming album was preceded in June 1968 by another wonderful single release, "Days," on which Nicky took the honours on piano and Mellotron. Ray Davies referred to this song as having "an air of finality about it" and suggested it was written with the feeling that it might be the last record he'd ever make.

Ray Davies: "It has that strange emotion to it; it was obvious I was saying

81

goodbye, not only to a house, but to a way of life, a time, an inspiration; Nicky's part gave 'Days' a mysterious religious quality, without being sentimental."

The Kinks Are The Village Green Preservation Society, released in November, was a logical continuation of the direction in which Ray Davies was taking the Kinks, though even more at odds with the contemporary scene. While the single

scraped the top ten in England, the album many consider to be the group's finest, failed to chart anywhere and disappeared without trace.

The loosely linked but immensely varied songs almost all feature piano, organ or Mellotron parts. Some are simple enough to again make it difficult to determine exactly who is playing. Others, such as "Big Sky," "Sitting By The Riverside," "Village Green" or "People Take Pictures Of Each Other" are distinctively "Hopkins."

Pete Quaife: "I think you can hear how much better all the songs are; they're much more imaginative and that's because we were given permission to start coming up with our own ideas—including Nicky. 'Phenomenal Cat,' (hums piano part) that was pure Nicky."

Ray's reputation as a perfectionist presented few problems to Nicky, whose combination of intuitive brilliance and easygoing compliance meant that he could almost always come up with whatever part was demanded. The songwriter's equally famous financial tightness, however, was a recurring cause of strife. Clem Cattini, who filled in for Mick Avory on a couple of live dates when the drummer was taken ill, remembered the aftermath of a Kinks rehearsal:

"Ray asked if I fancied an Indian (meal) and since there were two restaurants within walking distance, one to the left and one to the right, he sent Dave on ahead to see which one was cheaper. After we ate I had to pay my own three shillings and sixpence towards the bill!"

Session musicians ply their trade without accolades or audience applause, but those at the level Nicky had by now established himself could at least expect a credit for their contributions. A mention on an album sleeve was often the only visible reward available

A glance at Nicky's "cuttings book" reveals how focused he was on his various achievements and on press reports of his activities. When the new Kinks album was released with the legend "I am Raymond Douglas Davies – guitarist, keyboard player and singer" and no mention of the name Hopkins, it was a slight, intentional or not, that he took to heart. Ray joined Jeff Beck as one of the very few artists Nicky regularly bad-mouthed in interviews over the years. An American journalist in July 1969 was taken aback by Nicky's vehement reaction on being asked whether he still worked with the Kinks:

"No! I'm a bit uptight about that. I did about seventy per cent of the work on the *Village Green* album and not only did they leave me off the credits, but they put Ray Davies down on keyboard. I was so mad; I'm just not into the Kinks. They don't mean anything to me whatsoever. Ray Davies is such a mixed-up person. He's unbelievable!"

He was still seething in 1973:

"After the *Village Green* LP, I stopped working with them. They didn't pay me for the sessions and I did a lot of TV work with them as well. I'm really pissed off. I'll never work with him again. They're greedy bastards. Ray Davies is so tight his arse squeaks when he walks. He used to come to sessions with five shillings in his pocket, which is less than a dollar.'"

Mick Avory had no recollection of any falling-out taking place, but pointed out:

"A lot of things went on I was unaware of. It was usually Ray that called the tune and he didn't really explain what was happening. People came and went and you never knew why."

Ray said they stopped working with Nicky simply because they "couldn't seem to find him;" (by this time he was already off and touring with the Jeff Beck Group). Whatever caused the breakdown, *Village Green* was his last recording with the Kinks. A relationship that had produced a wonderful body of work ended in acrimony, though typically Ray Davies failed to see any reason for the pianist's change of attitude:

"The last time I spoke to Nicky was in 1988, when I called about the possibility of working together again. He said, 'Just let me know the time and I'll turn up,' but his voice was distant and lacked commitment."

In the circumstances, not surprising.

At the time of Nicky's death, Ray seemed to have plenty of positive memories of working with him and paid eloquent tribute in the various English newspapers that honoured Nicky with an obituary. Journalist Pete Frame also remembered attending a live show shortly after Nicky's untimely passing, where Ray Davies sang a song in his memory. In 2007 Ray had this to say:

"It's always a shock when somebody you know dies and I dedicated 'Too Much On My Mind' to Nicky because what he played was in such contrast to the mood of the song. It worked perfectly. I wanted him to play on a grand piano but we'd just recorded 'Session Man,' so he was sitting at the harpsichord and he said, 'Do you mind if we stick with the harpsichord, because it might sound good.' I don't know to this day if he was just too tired to get up and walk to the piano. When I work with new musicians, I say to every drummer, 'Can you play like Al Jackson?'; to every guitar player, 'Can you play like Steve Cropper?'; and to every keyboard player, 'Can you play like Nicky Hopkins?' He was that good."

Nicky's lengthy hiatus from the Who's recordings finally came to an end in May 1968 when, shortly before he left the London session scene for good, he was invited in to play on the curious "Dogs" single. Not surprisingly, with its cheerful "cockernee" vocals and lyrics extolling greyhound racing, it was a flop.

In the intervening years, the band had been regulars in the British and (slightly less often) in the American charts, with a string of brilliant Townshend compositions.

27. Pete Townshend

After an abortive attempt to capture their leader's latest concept *Lifehouse* on tape in New York—with an increasingly drug-fuelled Kit Lambert disrupting rather than producing the sessions—the Who returned in some disarray to England and started anew with the sober and disciplined Glyn Johns at the helm. Sessions began in May 1971 at Mick Jagger's Stargroves home, but soon moved to Olympic Studios and a call went out—possibly at Glyn Johns' suggestion—to Nicky Hopkins. He features on just two of the eight songs that make up the slimmed down *Who's Next*, but is right up in the mix in the complex and beautiful "The Song Is Over" that ends Side One of the original LP and "Getting In Tune," that opens the second side.

From its stately opening and delicate piano chords and the enormous sound of the ever-modulating choruses—with Roger Daltrey's inhumanly high vocals—to the tinkling arpeggios that introduce Pete Townshend's plaintive voice on the bridge and powerful chords that carry the "Pure And Easy" segment towards the end, the six minutes plus of "Song Is Over" is without doubt a high point both in Nicky's work as a session man and the Who's recorded output.

John "Rabbit" Bundrick, who has now held the position as the Who's keyboard player for more than a quarter of a century, found live performances of the song a challenge he dreaded:

"I hated playing that song—too many damn chords, and anyway how can anyone follow Nicky Hopkins on that?"

"Getting In Tune" also begins with Daltrey singing over solo piano before reaching full strength. Nicky carries the first minute of the tune almost on his own, before Townshend's entry on guitar; the song's finale is a piano-driven build-up reminiscent of "Salt Of The Earth" from the Stones' *Beggars Banquet*. Nicky's ever more intricate figures over Keith Moon's manic drumming manage to keep up the intensity to the very end. Nicky is the last sound heard as the track fades..."just banging on my old piano" indeed!

Pete Townshend: "Rabbit and Nicky are similar in that they really, truly *listen* to what they are about to play on. They play only the notes that are in the chord, which is important with guitar, which obviously only has a few notes in each chord. Pianists with ten fingers can create harmonic chaos or totally destroy the simple modality of a three-chord guitar trick with chords with no third or fourth. Nicky and Rabbit have never caused me to say, 'Listen, that's very cool what you are playing, but I'm only playing two notes here, E and A.'"

Townshend's songwriting had taken enormous leaps forward in the years since Nicky's early appearance with the Who. The role demanded of him now was completely different from the group's first album. Both parties had experienced a similar learning curve and *Who's Next* found them at their peak.

Later compilations and CD bonus tracks, well documented in specialist books on the Who's history, revealed previously unreleased songs such as "Too Much Of Anything" and the single "Let's See Action" from the same year, prominently featuring Nicky. Pete Townshend showed his appre-ciation by offering Nicky a permanent place in his band, if and when he ever chose to commit again to one group. Indecision and myriad other commitments made this another flattering invitation Nicky refused, but his contributions helped make *Who's Next* arguably the best album the Who ever did. While unavailable for a few years, once back in the fold, he was to work on three more projects with various members of the band.

Nicky was one of a group of musicians—including Chris Stainton, Eric Clapton and Ron Wood—who were brought into Ramport in 1974 to re-record the *Tommy* opera, after its previous incarnations as an album, a stage musical and a ballet score. This time it was for Ken Russell's extravagant film version, which involved all four members of the Who—though not necessarily playing together, Keith Moon being in particularly poor shape at the time.

Nicky remembers working with Stainton, and the confusion that occasionally arose over who had actually worked on Townshend's earlier project, *Quadrophenia*:

Nicky Hopkins: "Chris and I look so alike that I've had people think it was me. We finally met during the *Tommy* soundtrack in '74 at the studio and of course we'd heard about each other and it was like looking in the mirror. We both stopped and froze and looked at each other—both skinny, long hair, same facial features—very, very strange."

Since the film was to feature a purely musical soundtrack without dialogue, Pete Townshend had reluctantly taken on the task of re-recording his most popular work, enlisting his bass player's help in producing the tracks. Nicky's unique combination of skills made him another particularly important ally in the process.

Pete Townshend: "He was in a second wind when we worked on the Ken Russell film score and was really useful in helping me to deal with Ken's desire to embellish and lengthen the tracks so he had time to fit in his storyline. Nicky's playing on 'Christmas' is particularly constructive and sensitive. He ended up taking an active part in the composition as well. I'd be wandering around trying to do everything at once, saying, 'I want it to go from here to here—oh, make up something to go in there' and nine times out of ten he'd get something that worked."

Townshend rightly singled out that one track for praise when interviewed thirty years later, as it is a wonderful example of Nicky Hopkins' talents. In fact, Nicky's unmistakable signature is all over the film soundtrack. Nicky's pivotal contributions, however, only gained him a misspelt musician's credit and "special thanks for help with arrangements," rather than an obviously well-deserved composer's credit. One hopes that he was at least financially rewarded for his efforts.

Nicky is also present on *Odds & Sods*—the mixed bag of Who out-takes compiled that year by John Entwistle—and by late '74 he was living back in England and available to join the various combinations of star names, including Entwistle and Keith Moon, on the soundtrack album of the comic-book based science-fiction musical, *Flash Fearless versus The Zorg Women Parts 5 & 6*.

Guitarist Mike Kennedy, who played on Nicky's solo album *No More Changes* from the same era, was also booked for the occasionally chaotic *Flash Fearless* recordings:

"Directly after the session I played on, Tony Newman and John Entwistle totally destroyed the drum set we had just used on the song, 'Trapped.' I saw them smashing the drums and got the hell out of the room with my Fender Broadcaster and AC30 fast!"

Nicky's last appearance on a bona fide Who album came in spring 1975 when the re-energised group again enlisted Glyn Johns as producer for *The Who By Numbers*. Arguably more of a Pete Townshend solo album than a vintage Who release, the overall tone is one of disillusion and melancholy, with "Blue Red & Grey," for instance, almost a solo performance, with Pete on ukulele.

The sprightly "Slip Kid," which opens proceedings, is one of the album's standouts, and one of only two tracks that definitely feature Nicky, though, just as with the Kinks, there are several songs where it is hard to decide whether it is Nicky or Townshend who is playing. On side two he guests on the elegiac and almost folky "They're All In Love," where his playing perfectly underscores a beautiful melody and an unusually gentle vocal performance by Roger Daltrey of Townshend's bittersweet words.

Apart from occasional re-releases of earlier performances as the inevitable extra tracks on CD, this was to be Nicky's swansong with the Who. Through the inclusion of "Anyway Anyhow Anywhere," he made it onto what is arguably the band's best album, *Meaty Beaty Big & Bouncy*, a tremendous compilation of their singles.

In stark contrast to the acrimony that ended his working relationship with the Kinks, Nicky always had a soft spot for the Who and rightly considered the work he did with them as among his very best. He singled them out for praise in numerous interviews over the years when the inevitable question came, which of his hundreds of sessions were his favourites:

"They're great to work with; they're so funny all the time, not just onstage, but anywhere. Moon and Townshend are unbelievable. Keith pulls the most bizarre things at the most unexpected times…but he had perfect timing. He'd do these amazing fills all around the kit and you'd think, 'There's no way he'll be back at the on-beat by the next bar,' but somehow he was. He'd always hit it."

"They were all shit-hot musicians—a great drummer, a great bass guitarist, a great guitarist and of course Pete was a brilliant songwriter. They were probably my favourite band to play with."

There is ample proof that the appreciation was mutual and when Nicky died, Pete Townshend was among those who contributed to a lengthy obituary in the English *Independent* newspaper:

"Nicky was a great talent. His work on the first Who album was spectacular. He played on the Who's definitive album *Who's Next* and later worked alongside me when I was music director on Ken Russell's film of *Tommy*. He is gone but his wonderful playing will live on and I'm proud that so much of his work will be heard as part of my own."

Satanic Majesties Request
The Rolling Stones – Part 1

"They used to phone him in the middle of the night and he'd hire a taxi and go up to London. I used to get so cross. It was nothing to them, was it? But he'd come home exhausted."

– Freda Hopkins

Although Nicky Hopkins' acquaintance with the Rolling Stones went back to the early days with Cyril Davies, he did not actually work with the group until 1966.

Bill Wyman: "We played four times in the Marquee supporting Cyril and then left that R&B club scene and went into ballrooms, theatres and package tours, so I didn't see him for years and years."

It was Brian Jones who, on Jimmy Page's recommendation, brought Nicky in to IBC Studios in September 1966 for the soundtrack of Volker Schlöndorff's German language "film noir," *Mord und Totschlag (A Degree Of Murder)*. The music, composed, arranged, produced and largely played by the multi-talented Jones, remains the most memorable aspect of the film, which featured future Stones siren Anita Pallenberg. Nicky's prominent role in the recordings prompted an invitation to join the Stones in November at Olympic Studios for two tracks of their album *Between The Buttons*, with mentor Andrew Loog Oldham in the producer's chair and the ubiquitous Glyn Johns engineering.

After their massively successful run of early singles, the group was in an experimental, if slightly directionless, state of mind. They were attempting to follow a path to an English "music hall" style, already trodden far more successfully by Ray Davies and the Kinks. Neither "Cool Calm And Collected," with its faux upper class vocal and the unlikely combination of dulcimer, kazoo and Nicky's barrelhouse piano, nor "Something Happened To Me Yesterday," with brass, tuba and Mick Jagger's spoken parody of the English TV Police drama *Dixon Of Dock Green*, qualify as high points in the group's achievements, but they were Nicky's introduction to the Rolling Stones' inner circle.

Andrew Loog Oldham: "This was only the second album that Mick and Keith had composed 'en totale' and the overdubbing in England—Nicky and the horns etc.—was an important element to quite a British album, whose basic tracks had been cut at RCA in Hollywood."

Nicky Hopkins: "I know they'd been impressed with the Who's records, because I can remember running into Mick in a restaurant in Soho and he complimented me on my playing on 'Anyway, Anyhow, Anywhere.'"

Group memories are vague about who originally brought Nicky in. Glyn Johns said he was responsible, having already used him on so many other sessions (a claim Bill Wyman supported), while Keith Richards thought it must have been pianist and roadie Ian Stewart:

"I think it was sort of everybody's idea, probably Stu's as well. You know what it's like with musicians, usually everybody's playing somewhere else and it was basically availability; somebody bumped into Nicky and said 'Yeah, let's get Nicky in.' Stu liked his straight-up blues sequences; if you started throwing minor chords in he would say, 'These are Chinese chords, you'd better get Nicky' (laughs)."

Bill Wyman: "If Stu didn't like some of the chords, he'd play the rest of it and just leave those out!"

Sessions at Olympic continued without Nicky, since American arranger, mover and shaker Jack Nitzsche, who had been a key part of the group's U.S. based recordings, was still around for the taping of tracks such as "Ruby Tuesday" and the controversial "Let's Spend The Night Together." In February 1967, however, Nicky was back at the piano.

The Stones were going through one of their most difficult (and well-documented) periods. Serious cracks were appearing in their relationship with manager Andrew Oldham, while Brian Jones, the driving force in the formation of the group, was drifting increasingly away both from the band and from reality, and had appeared regularly in court on a series of drug offences. There were complicated upheavals in their love lives, with both Brian and Keith involved with Anita Pallenberg, while Jagger made the headlines with Marianne Faithfull. Events came to a head with the famous drugs raid at Redlands, Keith's Sussex home, which led to Keith Richards and Mick Jagger becoming fixtures on the front pages of the English tabloids, and briefly going to jail.

The close scrutiny from both the law and the media inevitably distracted the band from their musical plans, and the sessions for their next album, the *Sgt. Pepper* inspired *Their Satanic Majesties Request* sometimes featured only the ever-reliable Bill Wyman and Charlie Watts. Tired of waiting for his band-mates to show, Wyman began work on a song of his own, "In Another Land."

Bill Wyman: "I did that with Nicky, Charlie and two of the Small Faces (Steve Marriott and Ronnie Lane)."

The dirge-like track was given a rare thumbs-up by the beleaguered writing team of Jagger and Richards and after further work, found a place on the Rolling Stones' most psychedelic, and, some would argue, least successful album. Bootleg recordings testify to the interminable hours of experimentation that started off the song-writing process; despite the poor quality of much of the material, Nicky Hopkins emerged as a linchpin of the sessions, being responsible, incidentally, for the first and last sounds heard on the record.

Bill Wyman: "All Stones stuff came from jamming in the studios. A riff or a few lyrics would be built on, sometimes for days and days, but you could always say, ''Ere Nicky, can you try something completely different, something much more off the wall' and he'd do it. He wasn't bogged down in a particular way of playing like I might have been; if I couldn't get some bass line idea out of my head then someone else, like Keith, would try, just to get a different feel, but Nicky could change totally from one style to another."

Keith Richards: "You could give him a song and, with a couple of passes, he'd almost immediately develop it into something. He was so easy to work with and he could hang! We'd do sessions for fifteen hours—sometimes two days and he'd still be there."

English guitar icon Richard Thompson, who was recording next door at Olympic with Fairport Convention, remembers peeking in on a Stones session and being shocked to find the larger studio in almost complete darkness and Keith Richards doing take after take to nail just one guitar part. Nicky became accustomed to lengthy periods of waiting.

Freda Hopkins: "They used to phone him in the middle of the night and he'd hire a taxi and go up to London. I used to get so cross. It was nothing to them, was it? But he'd come home exhausted."

Nicky's friend Jon Mark knew the Stones through his role as accompanist to Marianne Faithfull:

"I was booked on all the sessions with Glyn Johns and so was Nicky. We would turn up there at six o'clock and Glyn would say, 'They're not here yet, why don't you guys go over to the pub.' We would have a few pints of beer and come back at eight; they still weren't there. Nip back to the pub and come back at nine; still not there. We'd hang in and then perhaps one of them would turn up, sometimes three, but it would be twelve or one o'clock in the morning. Occasionally they'd come early and would have ordered a whole dinner; caterers would bring food into the recording studio, laid out on large trestles and we'd all eat. It was money for nothing. We were just waiting to be told what to do!"

Satanic Majesties' extravagant record sleeve only credits Nicky Hopkins with piano, but in fact he contributed keyboard parts to every track: sometimes eerie and dissonant piano chords, occasional organ and harpsichord parts, a bluesy style on "The Lantern" (anticipating the sound of *Beggars Banquet*), an increasingly tuneless "pub piano" on the final track "On With The Show" and a subliminal tinkling on "Citadel." The spirit of the album is perhaps best captured by the loud snoring which concludes Bill Wyman's song and the demonstrative inclusion of "Where's that joint?" at the opening of the chaotic and ominously titled "Sing This All Together (See What Happens)."

Nicky's most memorable moment is on side two's opener "She's A Rainbow," where his distinctive neo-classical piano intros and beautiful soloing over John

Paul Jones' string arrangements make for one of the album's few genuine highlights. Nicky's distinctive parts carry the proceedings, in an early example of a song where a co-writer's credit alongside Jagger/Richards would have been appropriate.

Nicky recorded the equally trippy "We Love You," the Stones' defiant reply to the English judiciary, during the same set of sessions and had his first professional encounter with members of the Beatles, when John Lennon and Paul McCartney guested as backing vocalists in a show of solidarity, just as Mick and Keith had contributed to "All You Need Is Love." "We Love You," issued as a single in August 1967, opens dramatically with the sound of footsteps and the clanging of prison doors, but apart from Brian Jones's Mellotron parts, the key musical element of the song is Nicky's dark and percussive piano riff. Nicky later recalled the origins of the song to *Contemporary Keyboard* magazine:

"The piano riff that starts the song was an idea I'd had in my head for about three weeks, and it fit beautifully."

Keith Richards cheerfully acknowledged Nicky's pivotal role in the creation of "We Love You," though apparently without seeing any discrepancy between the pianist's huge contribution and his total lack of a credit:

"Probably that's the best example. We just had a very, very basic thing and Mick and I think we're going to jail, so our minds weren't totally concentrated; but yeah, that was Nicky's riff all the way through. Without that piano it wouldn't have happened."

Chuck Leavell has been the band's keyboard player for over twenty years and boasts at least one co-writer's credit on a Stones song. He remembered finding plenty to talk about when he first met Nicky and explained his own attitude to the Jagger/Richards songwriting monopoly:

"We did commiserate together a little bit. Obviously, Nicky had credits that were probably due to him. Even though he may not have written the chordal structure to some of those songs, by virtue of the fact that he influenced them so heavily and made them what they were, to me says he should have had some kind of credit; maybe not fifty per cent of the song, but ten or twenty…But the Stones just don't dole that out very easily. We both agreed that, at the end of the day, it's not a bad thing to have your name associated with the Rolling Stones, and the contributions we made are there for anybody to hear. I think Nicky probably had more exposure with the Stones than I do these days. He had his picture on some of the album covers and in those early videos, there's a few camera shots his way. Those are issues that I fight all the time."

Long-term Stones saxophonist Bobby Keys explained: "Of course, in order for Jagger to accept anything that anybody else thought of, you'd have to make him believe that it was his idea to begin with. I'd say, 'Mick are you gonna put some horns on this track?' 'Oh no, we don't need horns on this.' We'd listen and then say 'Hey man, you remember that idea you had about horns? Man, that was a great idea.' Nicky would do the same. If you are going to put this in print, wait till this next tour is over will you (laughs), Jagger's a vengeful sonofabitch!"

Bill Wyman: "The Stones never gave directions to any musician. They just came up with an idea or riff and everybody just added their bits and messed about with it and after a while it would come to fruition and become a song. Nicky had a lot of input in the studio, as we all did, but the songs always ended up Jagger/Richards of course."

Whether or not Nicky Hopkins was given his due for his musical input and the endless hours he spent in the studio with the Stones, the fact remains that, in a matter of a few weeks and months, Nicky had become an essential part of the band's recording set-up, whether the red light was on or not. Apart from his contributions to their "serious work," both Keith Richards and Bill Wyman paid tribute to Nicky's wonderful ability to defuse a tense situation and keep those present entertained with his inexhaustible supply of TV themes and children's songs or his deliberately wonky versions of famous pieces.

Keith Richards: "When we were working and for some reason something was wrong in the studio—down time, you know—and everybody's, 'Oh, take a break,' I would hang with him and Nicky would stay at the piano and start to play what he called 'wrong music.' He would play a song almost perfectly, but every now and again just make it go right off and we'd all crack up. 'Play some more wrong music!' (laughs)."

Nicky's appearances depended upon what Keith described as a fairly haphazard booking policy:

"Usually Nicky would turn up if he was around. If you tried to find him, you'd discover he was a thousand miles away, but otherwise he'd stroll into the studio or (there would be) a quick phone call and he'd say, 'I'm in town,' or you'd simply bump into him.

"I had a car crash once up in the north of London and turned over my Bentley. The only thing to do was to go into this house. I'd crashed through the fence and my car had come steaming to a halt on this lovely lawn, in the middle of the rose bushes and I'm going, 'Oh my God, what am I going to do now?' Out come this couple from the front door and they go, 'Hello Keith.' It was Mr. and Mrs. Hopkins (laughs)! Of all the houses I could have crashed into in London it was the friendliest one…'I'm sorry, I'm just dropping in; there's a steaming pink Bentley in your lawn!'"[24]

Nicky made a brief but significant cameo appearance on the next single, 1968's "Jumpin' Jack Flash," which signalled a welcome return to the band's true strengths and a turnaround in their fortunes.

Chuck Leavell: "That organ bit at the end…Oh man! I wish Nicky were still around. I'd ask him how in the hell he got that great organ sound. Distorted, whacked-out, really straight; it sounds like it's not even running through the Leslie, and it probably wasn't; it was probably direct input. And the way it builds at the end…'

Years later Nicky told journalist Peter Rodman (*Bone Magazine*, 1994) somewhat wistfully that he "wished he could just play with the faders one time" on classics like "Jumpin' Jack Flash," where some of his best work was barely audible. "Most engineers have guitar player's ears. 'Oh, the piano is *so* difficult to mix! We'll turn it down so you can just *feel* it there, but you can't really hear it!'"

Nicky came into his own on the next album, *Beggars Banquet*. In contrast to the previous record, this time he was on his favourite instrument, the grand piano, in a stripped-down context where he could really shine.

Nicky Hopkins: "Brian Jones was in very bad shape. He was OK on the sessions for *Satanic Majesties* but on *Beggars Banquet*, he'd come in with his guitar and half an hour later he'd keel over and be out cold. There's a lot of very prominent piano on that album and that's the reason—essentially they were short one guitarist."

With Oldham no longer part of the team, the role of "producer" was taken over by the inspiring and musically much more capable Jimmy Miller. The switch ushered in a magical era for the band, where their music dominated the *Zeitgeist* in much the same way that the Beatles had previously with *Revolver* or *Sgt. Pepper's Lonely Hearts Club Band*.

Guitarist Mick Taylor, who was yet to become part of the circus, commented later on the importance of Jimmy Miller's influence:

"The Stones wouldn't have made those albums without Jimmy Miller, Glyn Johns and Nicky being

---

[24] This obviously favourite anecdote appears in different forms in both Dominic Tarlé's book *Exile* and Michael Cooper's *Blinds And Shutters*, (both published by the wonderful Genesis Books) and in a highly embellished version in "Spanish Tony" Sanchez' *Up And Down With The Rolling Stones*.

patient enough to sit there all those hours, until they made up their minds whether they'd got a decent take. Sometimes, by the time you'd done fifteen takes, you'd have to go right back to the beginning to reconstruct the song you were trying to record. Jimmy would say, 'Take a break,' and it needed somebody like that.

"When I joined them, he was very good and forceful in the studio, but like a lot of other people, he got sucked into the self-destructive lifestyle and became a casualty. It's a shame, because he was a really good producer and the Stones did benefit a lot from his input. I don't think fans and some writers know how much influence he had."

Both in politics and in their private lives, times had taken a much darker turn and now it was Jagger and Richards who were writing the songs to match. Returning to familiar R&B and blues roots and a simpler style of production, the Rolling Stones began what many critics and fans consider the finest album of their career, and one of the sixties' seminal recordings. Nicky makes his presence felt right from the outset of "Sympathy For The Devil." His spare but effective chords mesh perfectly with Keith Richards' stinging lead guitar lines, and help the wild voodoo percussion track drive the song to its menacing ending.

Jean Luc Godard's film *One Plus One* (later re-named *Sympathy For The Devil* without Godard's consent and described succinctly by Keith Richards as "a big intellectual wank") offers a unique insight into the Stones' working methods. It follows the progress of the title song from its almost folky genesis with Jagger, Jones and Richards jamming on acoustic guitars, to its manic final incarnation. Even in the studio, the Stones are all decked out in their rock'n'roll gypsy finery, while Nicky is odd-man-out with his shorter hair, sideburns and neat jacket, shirt and cufflinks.

Everybody present smokes incessantly between takes and Nicky has a bottle of Coke balanced on the organ he is initially playing on the song. Despite the presence of crew-members, cameramen, studio lights and all the paraphernalia necessary for shooting a film (and with their more illegal habits no doubt cleaned up for the cameras), *One Plus One* gives a pretty accurate glimpse of life in the studio.

After a number of tame run-throughs (with Jagger commenting, "It's a bit dead!"), the breakthrough comes with the re-arranged line-up of Rocky Dijon on congas, Keith on bass and Nicky back where he belongs, on grand piano. It is fascinating to watch him at work, with his shoulders hunched, an impassive expression on his face, and still as a statue except for his long fingers, playing effortlessly fluid runs on the keys; a sharp contrast to Jagger's gurning features at the microphone. As so often with the Stones, although Nicky obviously plays a part as important as anyone else, he receives not a mention in the film credits.

Benmont Tench, of Tom Petty's Heartbreakers, sought to define Nicky's role:

"He was my favourite piano player. Jack Nitzsche wasn't nearly as rhythmic a pianist as Nicky was, but when they played with the Stones they had a similar thing going. Nicky could drive the whole thing; like a drummer; his time and rhythm were fantastically precise, but he was never cold. There's something lyrical and warm and beautiful about him and he knew when to leave a hole and what range of the piano to play. That the same guy could take over the whole track on 'Sympathy' and then play as delicately as he does on 'No Expectations,' on the same record, is terrific."

The importance of Nicky's piano part on "Sympathy For The Devil" was borne out in 2003, when three different dance specialists remixed the song for the Stones' *Forty Licks* collection. Every single one used Nicky's piano prominently in their new versions.

One of his greatest champions was producer Richard Perry:

"I still listen to 'Sympathy For The Devil' with great wonderment. I think that that was definitely his finest work. He had many fine recordings, but that was one of the only songs in the Stones repertoire when they let the piano be the lead instrument throughout."

Like Keith Richards, Chuck Leavell singled out "Sympathy" as an all-time favourite Hopkins performance:

"When you go back to me playing in bands in Alabama, it was a big wake-up call. 'You mean a piano can play rhythmically in a song like this and have that big a role on a record?' He used the sevenths brilliantly. I've often talked about his melodic contributions, but Nicky could get funky!"

The first track fades into the acoustic strumming and down-home slide of "No Expectations," another Hopkins master-class. Chuck Leavell described Nicky's entrance in verse three, with beautiful Floyd Cramer-style embellishments, as "putting a smile on the song." He starts in the lower registers, then rises, before finally going up a full octave for some quintessential "Diamond Tiaras" to take the song home.

Nicky referred more than once to the album's last track, the piano showcase "Salt Of The Earth," as his favourite on *Beggars Banquet*. It begins with Keith's acoustic guitar and wonderfully strangled lead vocal, with Nicky waiting for Jagger's entry in verse two, getting stronger as the band picks up the intensity. By the time the gospel-tinged vocals of the Watts Street Choir join in, the track is already motoring along at a tremendous pace. Charlie Watts' thunderous drum-roll heralds in one of the most thrilling outros in the Stones' catalogue.[25]

Being forced to burn the candle at both ends, keeping up his daytime session schedule and his nocturnal Stones commitments, led Nicky Hopkins to abandon the London studios to go back on tour. In interviews throughout his life, he consistently picked *Beggars Banquet* as one of his personal favourite recordings, because, for once, his piano was mixed right up with the other instruments.

---

[25] Author's Note: I remember sitting in a school common room at my over-privileged boarding school, with my friend Toby Buxton, listening to "Salt Of The Earth" over and over again on a Dansette record player. Though the intricacies of the lyrics were beyond my grasp, it still encapsulated all the feelings of isolation and aggression that plagued my teenage existence and gave me the kind of rush I could later only achieve with illegal substances.

Rolling Stone magazine heralded the Stones' new work as "the great comeback of their career" and made special reference to "Nicky Hopkins, a young Englishman who has played on several of the Stones' records, but really excels in the new album, the cover of which reads, quite rightly, 'We are deeply indebted to Nicky Hopkins...'"

Blues De Luxe
The Jeff Beck Group

"I get a kick out of playing live, the audience reaction thing is new to me."
– Nicky Hopkins

Both Mickie Most and the notorious Peter Grant, who together made up Jeff Beck's management company RAK, subsequently claimed to have produced the guitarist's first album *Truth*.

The group, with Rod Stewart on vocals, Ron Wood on bass and Mickey Waller on drums, convened at Abbey Road on 14th May 1968, and with just three days to complete a record, called on session stalwarts John Paul Jones and Nicky Hopkins to help out on organ and piano. It was a return visit for both musicians, as Nicky had made a brief appearance on "I've Been Drinking," the B-side of Beck's ill-advised instrumental version of "Love Is Blue," and both had contributed to a version of "Beck's Bolero," recorded as a one-off with Keith Moon and Jimmy Page in 1966, but included on the new album.

John Paul Jones had wisely accepted Jimmy Page's invitation to join his "New Yardbirds." Nicky had declined the offer, convinced that, with that monicker, no good could possibly come of it. In a Nashville café, Robert Plant recalled Nicky being asked to join the new band on two separate occasions. One of those followed the "Beck's Bolero" session, when someone suggested taking the impromptu line-up on tour. That prompted Keith Moon's much reported comment that they would go down "like a lead zeppelin."

Nicky was still freelancing as a hired hand and his most prominent contribution to *Truth* was the exemplary piano on the lengthy "Blues De Luxe," an ordinary studio recording, overdubbed with extravagant audience applause from a sound effects album, to give the impression of a live atmosphere. Beck later conceded that they may have "overdone it a bit" with the crowd noise, but the track is one of the album's highlights and a quintessential example of Nicky's mastery of the Chicago Blues idiom.

The finished record was rush-released in July, to capitalise on the breakthrough in the USA that followed the Beck Group's sensational June debut at the Fillmore East in New York as openers for the Grateful Dead.[26]

Jeff Beck had already built a healthy trans-Atlantic reputation through previous visits with the Yardbirds, and was perfectly placed to fulfil the demand for a heavy band fronted by a guitar-hero. Influential *New York Times* critic Robert Shelton's statement, in a glowing review, that the Beck Group had upstaged the headliners, ensured a certain notoriety wherever they appeared in the States. Peter Grant made sure that early copies of *Truth* were sent ahead, together with the review, to other promoters and DJs, and the rest of the tour proved to be a triumphant trawl through the USA's premier rock venues. The U.K. audience had to wait until October to hear the new Beck opus.

After this taste of stateside success, Beck decided he wanted to recreate the full sound of his album on stage, and called Nicky Hopkins for advice on a potential keyboard-player for the live group. He was as surprised as the rest of the pop scene, when London's top keyboard player offered to take the job himself, a decision Nicky put down to restlessness and his disillusionment with the endless grind of the session scene:

"I had been doing session work for so long, he assumed that I didn't want to travel. He asked me if I knew a piano player who played like me and would go on tour with him. I told him 'Yes, me!'"

In conversation with *Rolling Stone* in their May 17, 1969 issue, he added, "The last twelve months before Jeff were chaotic. I worked from 10.00 in the morning to 10.00 at night and then all night with the Stones and this went on week after week."

He had been invited to tour abroad by several other bands, but with studio bookings stacked up three or four months ahead, Nicky had always had to decline. He decided to draw a line in September 1968 and to take the next offer of a U.S. tour that came along. Jeff Beck's call came at exactly the right time.

---

[26] Third on the bill were the Seventh Sons, featuring Buzzy Linhart, with whom Nicky would record in the mid-eighties. Since he would also go on to work with Jerry Garcia and Bob Weir of the Dead, this bill represents a preview Hopkins "treble."

The news was noted in all the important music papers, *Disc & Music Echo*, *Melody Maker*, *Cashbox* and *Rolling Stone*:

"Nicky Hopkins, the fantastic young English pianist, who has been featured on many excellent records out of London, has joined the Jeff Beck Group and will be appearing with them on a U.S. tour beginning in October. With him as an additional member, this may bring the Beck group's live show up to par with their record."

He made his onstage debut with Beck on August 10th at the U.K.'s annual National Jazz & Blues Festival, held that year at Kempton Park Racecourse, not far from Nicky's home territory in Harrow. Not long after this baptism, Nicky joined the band full time, flying in to New York in for their second Fillmore appearance—this time as headliners—on the weekend of October 18th/19th. *Billboard* magazine heaped praise on the band's performance and gave particular attention to the newest member:

28. On stage with the Jeff Beck Group

"The big addition was Nicky Hopkins, one of England's top studio pianists. While some groups have lost by expanding their membership, this one has not. Hopkins' pianistic brilliance was a match for Beck's guitar."

Nicky was delighted to be back on stage and initially Beck was clearly glad to have him on board. He regularly sang Nicky's praises in interviews, both for his playing and for helping him with his song-writing, conveying ideas "in a musical way," that he was incapable of expressing on his own to the other musicians.

A bootleg recording from the band's three-day stint at the Boston Tea Party confirms that Nicky had quickly found his place in the group's sound and was already prominently featured in their performances, especially on the blues numbers. Beck demonstrates the full palette of his guitar pyrotechnics and the audience response is ecstatic. Nicky introduces "Rock Me Baby" on his own, while his "showcase" number is an instrumental version of Goffin and King's "(You Make Me Feel Like A) Natural Woman," that seems out of context amongst the heavy riffing going on around him. The *Harvard Crimson* reported that the group had "entered a period of maturity and taken on a new dimension" and added that "if Jeff Beck did not have Nicky Hopkins, he would have to invent him."

For his part, Nicky told a reporter that he found the band's mix of rock and blues suited him perfectly, that accompanying a great player like Jeff allowed him freedom to experiment, and that live music and the audience's reaction was a new pleasure. He had been pleasantly surprised to find that his name was familiar to so many fans in America, from album credits he had received during the previous years.

Onstage he was up against considerable difficulties. Amplification for the piano had not moved on at all since his touring days with Screaming Lord Sutch, and with the primitive contact microphones available at the time, Nicky was often forced to face sideways or even away from the audience, to keep him as far as possible from the deafening amplifiers and from potential feedback. This did wonders for his reputation as an enigmatic and mysterious figure.

Despite his experiences with Sutch's extrovert brand of "showbiz," the combination of Nicky's physical frailty, introverted personality and years spent in the invisible world of sessions and studios, meant that his onstage contributions were confined to musical highlights rather than the crowd-pleasing antics and sparring of the front men. In the liner notes to the re-issued CD of *Beck-Ola*, Jeff Beck recalled one night when Ronnie Wood purposely dropped ash from his cigarette on Nicky's shoulder and supposedly found it still there at the end of the show.

Nils Lofgren, who later went on to work with Nicky on his own and other projects, first crossed paths with him on the Jeff Beck tours:

"I used to follow around the *Truth* band when I was just a teenager; I was always trying to get backstage and that's where I bumped into Nicky; it was a fabulous band, very rambunctious and reckless, not unlike the Faces, but with a much more serious leader steering them. Jeff just turned Nicky loose and let him do his thing; I don't know what they were using in the mid-sixties to amplify an upright piano, but it sounded great and was amazing to watch. Peter Grant was always trying to throw me out when I was trying to get a few minutes with my heroes of the moment. It was a spectacular, loose, powerful bunch of players and Nicky made the instrument his own and really did write the book on rock'n'roll piano playing at a very early age."

Not for the last time in a group setting, Nicky made a mark that won many new fans but alienated others. Opinions were divided, even inside the group.

Mickey Waller: "I wasn't too pleased—nothing to do with Nicky, but I thought we had a good thing going and with Nicky we had to bring the volume down onstage. I'd have much preferred it with just us four. Nicky and I didn't get on too well on that tour. I annoyed him in some way—but we made up."

With his arrival, instrumental workouts like "Mother's Old Rice Pudding" became even more stretched out, featuring snatches of the Stones' "Satisfaction" from the bass and "We Love You" from the piano. Despite audience approval, however, performances on this second tour were hit-and-miss affairs.

When drummer Tony Newman later joined the group, he commented that in his eight months with the band, they only rehearsed twice. As the tour continued, Beck's unpredictable mood swings became another problem.

After a successful first night at L.A.'s Shrine Exposition Hall, Jeff Beck, Nicky and Rod Stewart were all invited by the members of the outlandish groupie act, Girls Together Outrageously (aka the G.T.O.s) to get together at their cabin and meet their producer Frank Zappa. The visit resulted in Beck's participation on three tracks of the girls' album *Permanent Damage*, while Nicky and Rod (nicknamed Rodney Rooster by the wild hostesses) had to be content with a cameo on the track  "Shock Treatment." Miss Pamela (Des Barres) and her friends entertained the Beck group throughout their week's stay at the Sunset Marquis. In her book *I'm With The Band*, Pamela recalled passing the time, not in the usual rock'n'roll pursuits, but in watching soccer on television.

Unleashed for the first time into the world of rock'n'roll touring, Nicky was not immune to the available temptations, though he was a slow starter compared to Rod Stewart and Ronnie Wood. Stewart remembered him having a liaison with a "bit of crumpet" in Sausalito, but while a contemporary magazine feature during the group's San Francisco visit showed the spiky-haired duo entertaining groupies in a bar, Mickey Waller and Nicky were pictured riding the cable cars.

Apart from snippets in his letters home, Nicky's activities on this first tour are not otherwise reported, but he put an extra day in San Francisco to good use, visiting the Jefferson Airplane's legendary Fulton Street mansion and loading up with all their albums, in anticipation of future collaborations.

Off-stage socialising with the star was the exception rather than the rule. Jeff Beck's moodiness caused a natural divide, accentuated by his management's policy of booking him separately into five star hotels, leaving the rest of the band sharing rooms in third-rate accommodation and feeling distinctly second-class.

Rod Stewart: "It was grim in that they made it very hard for us to get paid. I remember Woody and I having to scrounge around Peter and Mickie Most's office to see an accountant—funnily enough his name was Derek Nibb—who would make us and Nicky wait five or six hours to get paid; I think he got some sadistic pleasure out of it; but we had fun, the three of us, and Ronnie and I were always close mates. Jeff was so well looked after and the band was totally ignored; that's where the ill feeling came from."

Nicky's first professional visit to the USA ran from October to December

29. Nicky and Rod Stewart

1968. The morning after his return to the U.K., without even a day off to re-cover, he pitched into the Rolling Stones' *Rock And Roll Circus* extravaganza, taped not far from his birthplace in Wembley.

After the excitement of the tour, it was a comedown for Nicky to return to playing just occasional club dates back in Britain. The overwhelming onstage volume remained a constant irritation, but there were other and worse tensions in the ranks and in early February, they culminated in the volatile leader sud-denly firing both Ron Wood and Mickey Waller.

Over a pint near Olympic Studios in Barnes, the drummer was still not sure why he was sacked, but said he had been convinced at the time that it was an attempt on Beck's part to avoid having to go back on the road in America, an experience he had not enjoyed. Rumours indicated that it was Nicky who wanted Waller out, while Beck had problems with Wood, possibly threatened by his talents as a guitarist, even though he played bass in the band.

Rod Stewart: "I don't think we'll ever hear the truth of what happened. Some people say Jeff was jealous of the relationship between Ronnie and I."

In February 1969, Beck, Stewart and Hopkins flew out for another assault on North America, with drummer Tony Newman and what soon proved to be a totally inappropriate replacement bass player. After two disastrous dates, at Rod Stewart's insistence, a panic call back to the UK soon had Ronnie Wood on a plane and back in the group, though this time very much on his own financial terms: reputedly a huge (for the times) £2,000 per week!

Beck was certainly heavily under the influence of his managers, who made no secret of the fact that it was the star they were interested in, not the group. New drummer Tony Newman successfully encouraged his band mates to make a stand:

"I called a strike at the Schaefer Beer Festival. I was always the bad guy. We were getting something ridiculous like a hundred and twenty-five quid a week and I pointed out (to Peter Grant) that there were twenty-five thousand people at these concerts…and we were top of the bill! He refused to pay any more, so I

30. The shortest-lived lineup of the Jeff Beck Group

said, 'We ain't going to the Schaefer Beer Festival unless someone writes us a cheque for five thousand dollars!' and sure enough the lawyer showed up with five grand apiece."

Reunited for the first time since school days, Nicky Hopkins and Tony Newman shared rooms and a lunatic sense of humour that made life on tour more bearable. Tony also reported Nicky's first brushes with the drug culture:

"I'd sit next to him on planes and we'd find pictures of cats in the in-flight magazine and pretend to stroke them, while making purring sounds and we'd get stoned together. In New York this famous artist wanted us to go over to his studio. He had some outrageous dope and we got so out of it, we all became submarines; Nicky and I had coats on and put the sleeves up as periscopes and walked down Broadway at rush hour; we had to talk through the sleeves 'for security reasons.' We all got so paranoid that we locked ourselves in our rooms. We met Ronnie at breakfast and he had drawn a grotesque picture of what he was feeling while tripping in his room. We were a real mess."

Nicky's health bore up surprisingly well to the stresses of life on the road. Rod Stewart remembered him as "a bit of a worrier" and as "always looking like he was going to fall apart." "When he played the piano, I told him he looked like a pair of tights on a clothes line on a windy day."

Tony Newman: "Nicky had to have a light on at night, because he couldn't sleep in the dark. In retrospect, I think that most of us that grew up in the Second World War air raids, had some degree of post-traumatic stress from our mother's womb; I'm sure that that amount of adrenalin and fear pumping through you does something."

Between the clashes with management, the struggles over fair wages, and the beginnings of drug use by band members, the Jeff Beck Group's February tour seemed to be under a bad star from the beginning. The general sense of dissatisfaction sometimes reached boiling point, as Tony Newman, now a Nashville resident, recalled:

"They booked us in this Jewish resort with an additional afternoon show. Of course it wasn't to our liking, so we all got pissed in between the shows, got on stage and were fucking about because we didn't like being at a holiday camp. I got off the drums and started dancing all round the tables and the next thing I know, Beck's got a fire extinguisher and he's fired it on the audience. Then a riot broke out and we were all thrown into the limos to head back to New York. The road manager's eyes were like saucers and he was just terrified. There was big trouble over it; I was put up as the instigator and one of the kids got hurt by the fire extinguisher foam. It was very unprofessional."

Such unpredictable antics seriously damaged the group's standing with promoters, fans and the ever-powerful American Musicians Union.[27] The tour was abruptly cut short when Beck decided overnight to go home, leaving his hapless companions stranded.

Nicky: "I woke up one morning in New York and Beck was back in England;

he had flown back overnight without telling anyone, and he did that twice. It didn't show at first, but he was impossible to work with."

Nicky had particularly been looking forward to the tour reaching the West Coast again. When everything ended so abruptly, he decided to go there anyway, having heard through the grapevine that the Jefferson Airplane were looking for him to play piano on their new record, *Volunteers*.

---

[27] Similar transgressions had cost the Kinks their US market at the height of their popularity and it took them years to recover.

He spent a week with the band in the newly established Wally Heider studios in San Francisco, and found himself having to acclimatise to a much looser approach to recording than he was used to. Conversely, his speed and precision astonished the Airplane members; Paul Kantner remembered them liking each piano pass so much that they attempted one mix using three at once. The level of respect for Nicky in America was notably higher, and his efforts earned him not just a credit on the album sleeve, but a photo as well. Nicky arrived back in the U.K. having left his mark on one of the sixties' most significant albums and determined to return to California as soon as possible.

Back in London, he found the Jeff Beck Group in a state of disarray. A reputation for unreliability is easily earned but hard to shake, and traces of the disastrous tour were still evident when they went back in the studio, to record a follow-up to *Truth*. Four days at De Lane Lea in central London found group morale at a low ebb and Nicky Hopkins dashing back and forth to Olympic Studios, to work parallel with the Rolling Stones.

Beck-Ola ended up, perhaps not surprisingly, as a patchy affair, with two improvised Elvis Presley covers and tracks that sounded more like heavy-metal jam sessions than songs. Nicky shared three co-writing credits and provided the elegant instrumental "Girl From Mill Valley," his first in a series of highly distinctive

piano compositions, on which Beck gracefully opted to provide little more than rhythm guitar and fills. One interviewer commented, on first hearing, that he kept expecting Aretha Franklin to come in at any minute, and Beck would later dismiss it as "sounding like a backing track," but the piece became an instant favourite with fans.

Nicky once said that "Girl From Mill Valley," was "about nobody," but rumours circulating at the time said that he composed it for Girl Freiberg (Nicky's "bit of crumpet from Sausalito"), the wife of Quicksilver Messenger Service bass player David Freiberg. Now living under her married name of Julia Brigden, Girl revealed the full story in a transatlantic phone call:

"My husband and I were split up and I was living at my Mom's house in Sausalito, with my daughter Jessica. I have a friend, Catherine James, who was a very beautiful girl; all the guys liked her and for a minute, she was Ronnie Wood's girlfriend; she came to town and introduced me to Nicky.

"Nicky really liked me and I liked him: he was a decent, sensitive guy but very innocent and naïve; he'd had a very sheltered life, but he was sweet and I could tell he had a big crush on me; I kind of took advantage of that. I wouldn't sleep with him or anything, but he invited me to go to England with him and I went. I'm sure he was hoping for more. I was so excited about going over there, so it was really hard to say no. I met his Mom and Dad, who were very nice and I think that they were very excited for him that he had a girl in his life. I had the feeling that maybe he hadn't had much of a social life."

After ten days in England, she returned to Mill Valley and didn't see Nicky again until he came back to record with the Steve Miller Band.

"I remember when that record came out with 'Girl From Mill Valley,' we were at somebody's house and they came bounding down the stairs and said, 'You won't believe it Girl, but Nicky wrote a song about you on a Jeff Beck record.' Then Nicky came in and was mad because he'd wanted to tell me about it. I was so flattered and surprised.'[28]

Nicky's keyboard parts on the rest of the album range from classy melodic interludes in "Rice Pudding" to flashy and frenetic riffing on "Jailhouse Rock." The "heavy" feel of *Beck-Ola* is "of its time." To these ears, the acoustic piano never sits easily among the bombastic guitar sounds that dominate the album, but David Bowie drummer Woody Woodmansey, who later became close friends with Nicky, recalled how impressed he and Mick Ronson were on hearing Nicky with Jeff Beck:

"We hated keyboard players; it was a guitar thing in those days and keyboards made it softer and muddied it up; you never knew where to put them. 'Listen to this keyboard player. What's his name? Nicky Hopkins?' He's the only one who communicated to guitarists, drummers and real rockers."

A third Jeff Beck tour of the States lasted less than ten days. The damage had been done and this time reviewers were less than enthusiastic. In his book recalling the Fillmore East era, Richard Kostelanetz reviewed Beck's May 3rd show in damning terms: the concert was disappointing, Beck scarcely in control of his musicians, arrangements often sloppy and the musicians ill at ease with one another. Even Nicky Hopkins was apparently a disappointment.

It was clear by now that the spark was gone from the Beck group, and on their return to London, their last joint task was to back Donovan—another Mickie Most client—on a handful of tracks recorded at Advision Studios. This unplanned and totally improvised session was the producer's idea and the two songs that appeared on Don's album *Barabajagal* were an unexpected success, both artistically and commercially. Whatever bad blood there was in the band was apparently put on hold and Donovan later described the recording as "the most incredible session of my life":

"The drummer was setting up and not one of the band had heard the song, as Mickie wanted a fresh recording, but Tony Newman was actually playing the pattern. 'Have you heard the song?' I asked. ''Aven't 'eard a bloody thing!' This was a good omen. Nicky came in, sat down at the piano and opened a comic book on the music stand—*Silver Surfer* it was; Mickie said to me 'Play Nicky the song,' so I did and Nicky looked at me and said, 'Got it.' Of course, he had—all two chords. We cut the track as a long jam but what a track!"

---

[28] Hopkins aficionado Dave Lang revealed that "Girl From Mill Valley" found a home much later, as the sponsor identification theme for the PBS radio show, *America's Test Kitchen*.

31. Donovan

After this briefly harmonious interlude, the final straw for Nicky Hopkins came after one argument too many. Years later he remembered June 4th 1969 with great clarity as the day he left the Jeff Beck Group. He wasn't idle for long, as work continued across town for the Rolling Stones' *Let It Bleed* album.

Nicky Hopkins: "About two days later Ronnie Wood quit, then I think either Tony or Rod was next. It broke up within about a week."

Nicky would appear with Jeff Beck one more time, on record at least, when the guitarist was added to an already existing track for Nicky's old employer Screaming Lord Sutch, on his *Lord Sutch & Heavy Friends* album. The leftover "Gutty Guitar" featured Carlo Little, Ricky Brown and Nicky Hopkins—most of the original Savages. Despite the presence of Beck, Jimmy Page and other star guests, the LP, once voted the worst of all time, was little more than a curiosity and flopped dismally, with its aerial cover photo of the self-styled Lord and his Union Jack Rolls Royce its most memorable aspect. In 1973 Nicky told *Music Week* that when he was given a copy of the album, he listened briefly and then hurled it at the wall.

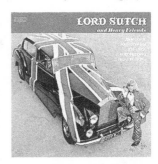

Beck-Ola came out after Nicky's departure to a surprisingly positive response, with *Rolling Stone* writer Ben Gerson giving a glowing review in the August issue:

"The group benefits from the addition of Nicky Hopkins, the most perfect of rock pianists (although his playing is sometimes overshadowed by the electrical sturm und drang around him.)"

Other reactions were mixed, but, unlike its predecessor, *Beck-Ola* charted both sides of the Atlantic.

32. On stage at Woodstock with the Jefferson Airplane

August 1969 found Nicky back on American soil, and onstage with his new friends the Jefferson Airplane in upstate New York:

"They asked if I could come and do an open-air festival in the east and said it would be about three days; I sort of liked the idea so I said, 'Yeah, I'll come along.' I went with them and it turned out to be Woodstock."

Nicky's sister Dee remembers him telling her excitedly that he'd flown in on a helicopter, but neither Paul Kantner nor Marty Balin were able to recall a single thing about their guest pianist or any other aspect of their Woodstock experience, possibly related to Paul's confession that by the time they got onstage at 7.00 in the morning, he was coming down from his third acid trip! Nicky's appearance was preserved for posterity, on camera and through Grace Slick's introduction, included on the soundtrack album and in the director's cut of the festival movie.

Nicky must have stayed more or less straight as, many years later, he was still able to describe his memories of the experience to a reporter from the *Nashville Banner*:

"We were behind schedule, because every act ran longer than its allotted time. By the time the Airplane took the stage, the sun was shining brightly. I didn't know what I felt and I still don't. There was a kind of awe and wonder that that many people could come to hear this music and when our turn finally came, there was no problem with fatigue; it was impossible to be tired; there was such a buzz; the adrenaline rush was tremendous. I've never experienced anything like it ever again."

The Airplane's performance is as rough and ready as that of any of the bands over that legendary weekend, suffering particularly from having to come on directly after an explosive performance by Nicky's old comrades, The Who. Nicky had again shown his uncanny ability to be in the right place at the right time—unlike his recent ex-boss Jeff Beck, who had cancelled his slot advertised for the same day. The historic weekend wound up with a TV taping the following day on the Dick Cavett show, with the band and their guest pianist performing the title song from *Volunteers*.

Later in his career, Nicky was to play many times with both Rod Stewart and Ron Wood; his only lasting falling-out was with Jeff Beck, one of the only musicians approached for this book who declined to contribute. In the light of Nicky's comments on touring and recording with him, this seems hardly surprising:

"We were having arguments about money, weren't getting paid for the tours and there were always excuses. We'd get together to discuss artist royalties and agree to split them, but Mickie (Most) didn't like that. He thought Beck should have it all, or at least double what anybody else had. He said, 'Listen, nobody's going up to see anybody but Jeff. You think people are paying to see Nicky Hopkins, Ronnie Wood or Rod Stewart? Don't be crazy!' It completely confused Beck. He's a bit schizoid to begin with; half of him wanted to be a star and the other half wanted to be a garage mechanic. You could never tell which half would be in his head at any one time."

Soon after leaving, legal proceedings were insti-
gated on Nicky's behalf against Beck, though
subsequently abandoned. In a lawyer's letter dated
October 9th 1972, Nicky agreed not to pursue litiga-
tion as he was currently working "with musicians
associated with Jeff Beck" and foresaw further difficulties if he pursued his claim. Beck himself
remained unrepentant and in a 1973 interview re-
wrote history and cheerfully admitted that he still
owed money to his one-time keyboard player:

"It's too late now. He won't get no money out of
me. He was nothing but a shit-stirrer in the group,
causing trouble all the time. When he joined, things
started to fall apart. He started putting ideas into the
heads of the other members."

Nicky and his second wife Moira met Ronnie
Wood in the eighties:

"Anything that happened during the Beck band
was buried and when we were backstage at a Stones'
concert at Wembley, Ronnie was so happy to see
Nicky. He was bouncing up and down. 'You've got to
come and stay in Ireland with us' and 'You've got to
come to my party. Go and see such and such and
make sure that you come tonight...' but once they
went on stage, we were left with the security people
and nothing happened."

Unhappy and unprofitable as the Jeff Beck Group
experience ultimately proved to be, it helped open
up the USA to Nicky. With his studio reputation
preceding him, he was able to take full advantage of
the new opportunities that came his way and soon
moved to California and on to a new and exciting
phase in his life.

Brave New World
Mill Valley And Beyond

"There was this terrible rumour going around that the whole of California was going to fall into the sea in 1969. I thought if I go back to England, I'll never see it again. So I decided to stay in California and go with it."
— Nicky Hopkins

A chance meeting at Olympic Studios in the spring of 1969 with Glyn Johns, who had already played such a pivotal role in establishing Nicky's career in England, now gave him his passport to the West Coast. Having fallen in love with both the climate and music scene in San Francisco during the Jeff Beck tours, Nicky Hopkins wasted no time in exchanging the damp grey of London for the sunshine and good vibes of California.

Glyn was in the last stages of mixing the Steve Miller Band album *Brave New World* and asked Nicky to overdub a piano track that same night on an unfinished song, just prior to its completion. Nicky's beautiful part on "Kow Kow" came so late in the proceedings that cover art had already been completed and he was initially only credited on the record label but not the sleeve (alongside Paul McCartney, who guested on "My Dark Hour" under the pseudonym Paul Ramon).

Steve Miller: "Glyn brought Nicky in and introduced him to us; we heard him play and he instantly improved everything we did, so it was a very good connection."

So good that in mid-June, just ten days after quitting the Jeff Beck Group, Nicky was on a plane to San Francisco to play on Miller's next album *Your Saving Grace*, with Glyn Johns again producing, at the "state-of-the-art" Wally Heider Studios, where Nicky had already cut tracks with the Jefferson Airplane. By today's standards, the idea of recording a follow-up so soon is hard to imagine, but Miller recalls making his first four albums all in the space of eighteen months!

Nicky's classical training perfectly suited Steve Miller's romantic, almost baroque melodies. In sharp contrast to the raucous blues-rock of the Beck band's output, it's the ballads on *Your Saving Grace* that bring out the best in Nicky; whether on piano, Hammond organ or harpsichord, he adds touches of sheer beauty and atmosphere to the songs.

Steve Miller: "There was just an instant bonding between Nicky, me and the band; it was like running into a brother. You didn't have to say anything; you just listened and went, 'Wow! Look what he did to this simple little tune.' He played just the right amount and was always inspirational to play with."

On "Baby's House," his contribution on both piano and organ was such that Steve Miller gave him the well-deserved accolade of a co-writing credit. The track anticipates Eric Clapton's "Layla" by a year but shares a similar structure, with the main song followed by a lengthy instrumental coda, which Miller confirmed was "pretty much Nicky's work." Rolling Stone's Ed Leimbacher, in his December 1969 review of the album, singled out the performance:

"Hopkins' keyboarding seems like a capsule history of techniques from high-church chorale organ to ricky-tick rock'n'roll. His touch is gentle and immaculate as he just goes on and on, playing umpteen styles at once. Play "Baby's House" for somebody you love!"

Nicky was always a meticulous timekeeper. Listening with modern ears, apart from his inventive keyboard parts, his greatest achievement with the Miller band was managing to mesh in with some extremely wayward drum tracks. When I asked Miller if he and Glyn Johns were aware of the shortcomings in his rhythm section, he laughed:

"Our drummer was like the heartbeat of the band, but he was a lousy drummer too; the guy could not keep good time and that always made it very, very difficult to record; he was one of my best friends and it was that 'all for one and one for all' kind of thing that bands start out with; eventually it got to where it drove me nuts and I had to change my band around. When I go back and listen, I'm always amazed at how good the tracks feel and how sloppily they're played."

Steve Miller bassist Bobby Winkelman remembered the band's unusual dynamics in the studio:

"I've got to give Glyn Johns credit for a lot of help with tambourine on the earlier stuff that he did, because he pulled it in to feeling like it was in time; Glyn saved a lot of those tracks. When Steve and Tim (Davis) could play to Nicky,

Tim might be out, but at least Steve and Nicky weren't; he had an incredible sense of time."

Despite Miller's obvious fondness for Nicky, he only recalled playing a handful of live dates together, while Nicky, for his part, insisted he only ever recorded with Steve.

Steve Miller: "We played a few gigs in San Francisco, but he never really came out on the road with us, because he was really not in good shape. I remember being surprised that he had come over (to America), because he'd had so many health problems. We called him 'The Mummy' because he was so thin, but we were still disappointed that he joined Quicksilver and not us."

His three-week stint with Miller also introduced Nicky to a woman who was to play a pivotal role in his life for many years, often to the consternation of those around him, New Jersey-born Lynda Louise Van Orden, also known as "Dolly."[29] Steve Miller described her at the time as "the girlfriend from hell":

"We met her in Mill Valley when she briefly went out with one of the guys in my band and we went, 'Holy shit! Look out!' Then she picked up on Nicky and pretty much ran his life for a while—it was like *Spinal Tap*. You couldn't really deal with Nicky because you had to deal with her and she was treating him badly—it was awful."

Dolly Hopkins: "My then boyfriend John Hunt (who later did the cover for *The Tin Man Was A Dreamer*) and I were working in New York and met some of the musicians from Spanky & Our Gang. They needed a roadie and she needed an assistant, so we took the jobs and landed up in L.A. Spanky was doing a gig with Steve Miller, before Miller was really known, and we met him when her band was taking a break from recording and touring. Miller asked John if he could come to San Francisco to help out with some gigs; he got the OK from Spanky and I went up later. We were at Miller's house in Sausalito one day when this tall, skinny English guy appeared at the door asking if Steve was home. That's when I first met Nicky."

Miller Band guitarist Greg Douglass was another who had reservations concerning Dolly: "I believe she was born in New York. If I can be blunt, I'm instantly suspicious of anybody who affects an accent that's not where they're from; she spoke with a stone English accent—it's like somebody from Brooklyn trying to sound like they're from Nashville."

Nicky gained a travelling companion, a lover, a business secretary and a safety net all in one and it was only when the couple's partying lifestyle later escalated into full-on substance abuse, that cracks began to show in their relationship and things went rapidly downhill.

Nicky appeared on one more Steve Miller Band album, the 1970 release *Number 5*, surprisingly recorded mostly in Nashville, at the legendary but very basic Cinderella Studios.

---

[29] This was Nicky's pet name for his first wife and she will be referred to as Dolly for the purposes of this book

Steve Miller: "We had been recording at Heider's and I was having trouble working with Glyn and with my band; there was a party going on and nothing was getting done; one day I walked into the studio and found a piano that had been rented two weeks earlier and nobody had played it; the rent was actually

more than the piano would cost and I just said 'OK that's it, these sessions are over!' It was out of control and Glyn and I were reaching a point where I really wanted to be free to do what I wanted, not what he wanted me to do, so we were kind of at odds."

The three tracks that feature Nicky were left over from the earlier California sessions. "Never Kill Another Man," which closes the album, is another Hopkins highlight and his swansong with Steve Miller, who confessed that afterwards he was "on the road three hundred nights a year and I didn't see much of anybody" and lost touch with Nicky.

Miller provided a strange postscript to their collaboration when compiling his self-chosen box set in the 1990s. Inexplicably (and to the dismay of diehard fans) he cut "Baby's House" down to little more than two minutes. Asked why, he laughed and explained:

"Everybody gave me a rash about that; this is a *bad* decision! It was late at night and I just went, 'You know I just like it this way.' 'OK, you're the boss...'"

Thirty-five years later Miller eloquently summed up Nicky's playing:

"It had a lot of church feeling, was very romantic and very moving. You couldn't help but love what he did; it was his natural gift. When we met Nicky, he was a 'studio cat,' but our approach was completely different. There was a very rigid 'pop music' thing happening in London and we were more freeform and more about experimentation and blues; so I think when we met Nicky, it was a mutual admiration society. He loved the freedom of what we were doing, and what we brought to Nicky, was to say, 'You are so good' and to get him out of that session world and give him a chance to express himself."

His sessions with the Jefferson Airplane and Steve Miller provided Nicky with a top-level entry into the San Francisco scene; his next involvement would last significantly longer and anchor him in the idyllic setting of Mill Valley for some time. Seduced by the warm weather, he refused to go back to London, even for the Rolling Stones' Hyde Park Concert on July 5th, the decision that Dolly insists cost him a permanent place in the group.

Nicky Hopkins: "There was this terrible rumour going around that the whole of California was going to fall into the sea in 1969. I fell in love with Mill Valley and San Francisco and I thought. 'If I go back to England, this is all going to fall into the sea and I'll never see it again,' so I decided to stay and go with it."

As early as 1966 Quicksilver Messenger Service had established themselves as one of the leading bands in the Bay Area psychedelic scene and became regular fixtures on the ballroom scene and at numerous local free concerts. Led by the twin-guitar sound of incendiary lead-player John Cipollina and driving rhythm guitarist Gary Duncan, both veterans of local rock and R&B bands, the four-piece line-up (completed by bass player and vocalist David Freiberg and drummer Greg "Lumo" Elmore) signed to Capitol Records in October '67. The band's reputation was built on its adventurous improvisations and blend of rock'n'roll with a hippieish spontaneity that stemmed from Freiberg's background as a "folkie," in the same coffeehouse scene that had nurtured David Crosby, Jerry Garcia and the Airplane.

Quicksilver was one of the last of the Bay Area bands to sign with a major label in the industry feeding frenzy that followed the Monterey Pop Festival and the media's discovery of the Haight-Ashbury scene. Their deal with Capitol Records was groundbreaking, not only for financial reasons, but for the almost complete control that the group negotiated for itself. After a tentative and eclectic debut album, their second effort *Happy Trails*, instantly became one of the benchmark albums of its time, from a band totally in sync with its audience.

Gary Duncan: "…LSD and pot. I took LSD every day for four or five years straight—every day! I did speed every day. Nobody knew I was doing it, they just thought I was crazy. I did so much that I never really came down from it. I don't sleep much; I'm up all the time and it's all right, I figure I've got plenty of time to sleep when I'm dead, you know."

Befitting their legend as primarily a live band, *Happy Trails* was mostly recorded at the Fillmores, East and West. Leading off with the acid-drenched intensity of the band's lengthy dissection of Bo Diddley's "Who Do you Love," it established the band internationally as flag-wavers for the LSD-fuelled times, on a par with the Jefferson Airplane and Grateful Dead.

It was a shock to the system then, when writer, vocalist and second guitarist all-in-one, Gary Duncan, frustrated at the stagnation and lack of progress shown by his fellow musicians and burned out by his excessive lifestyle, suddenly announced his departure on New Year's Eve 1968, only weeks after the concerts captured on the new release.

With Duncan having rejoined founder member Dino Valenti in search of new adventures and a new band, the remnants of Quicksilver initially tried performing as a trio, but soon realised that they badly needed another player, particularly with a new studio album on the agenda. Manager Ron Polte recalled their relief when they found their new recruit, after word filtered through of Nicky Hopkins' arrival in town:

"We were looking for six months or more and auditioned a few people, but no one fit. Nicky was so versatile, it was perfect. His playing on Beggars Banquet had flipped us all out and I really wanted to meet the guy."

Contact was established via Girl Freiberg and Nicky returned to Wally Heider's, to try out on Cipollina and Nick Gravenites' song "Joseph's Coat," making an instant impression on John Cipollina. Pete Frame recounts John's comments in a *Melody Maker* article:

"He listened to it once, making a few notes on a piece of paper and then went straight over to the piano, taped his jottings in front of him and played it first take! It was just astonishing. So he joined the group and we felt a real resurgence."

Nicky found a kindred spirit in John and lifelong friends in the Cipollina family. Having decided to stay, he initially alternated as houseguest between Miller and Cipollina, though spending most time with John. The two had a lot in common, sharing similarly offbeat personalities, an unmistakeable physical

33. Quicksilver at John Cipollina's King Street house

resemblance, a common history of illness and fragile health and, once living together, a common drift into substance abuse.

Ron Polte: "What they wanted to do in life was get in trouble. They were like twins."

David Freiberg: "They were born exactly six months apart—actually astrological opposites, yet they were so close to being the same. I don't think either one of them ever threw away a matchbook—they collected everything."

Antonia Cipollina: "They both had a sweet tooth and didn't have the best eating habits. When they were young, they thought that fast food was the answer—coca-cola and lots of sugar in your coffee!"

It was through her friendship with Cipollina that singer Kathi McDonald met Nicky:

"They'd stay up till four in the morning writing songs and playing checkers and chess—kindred spirits; Nicky didn't laugh all that much, but he would shriek with laughter when he and John were together. They were nuts."

Nicky's recent membership in the Jeff Beck Group and his insider status with English rock royalty turned a few heads locally, and he and John shared more than just their lifestyles. Dolly Hopkins revealed that early on, Nicky had a brief affair with John's wife Jan, entirely with the blessing of the "almost asexual" Cipollina, a story confirmed by John's sister Antonia:

"That's true. I don't know how deep they went. I remember them holding hands and walking around but they didn't live together or anything. Jan was like a fawn: very pretty, very lean and tall, but very childlike. Men (wanted) to be a father figure to her."

Nicky's more serious dalliance with David Freiberg's wife almost derailed proceedings before they'd begun, as Polte observed:

"He had a problem with David because of his wife and that kept them apart even though they played music together. We were in John's living room one evening, when David was in the studio mixing and they got on the phone and made up; by the time the conversation was over, Nicky was happy and the next day we invited him to join the band and he accepted."

Once settled in America, Nicky wasted no time in catching up on the hedonistic attractions of the music scene. His rock-star credentials allowed him to make up for the two vital years he'd lost during his late teens and he became quite a ladies' man, taking advantage of the spirit of the times to be involved in several affairs at once.

As a typical Pisces, his most striking feature was his deep-set and expressive eyes (a friend described his 'mischievous eyes that would twinkle') and many women friends called them beautiful. He had the Neptune adult's distinctive gaunt frame, fine, silky hair, translucent skin, elegant hands, long fingers and masses of charm. Over and over again, he

is described by colleagues as gentle and extremely sensitive, not only as a musician, but to atmospheres and other people's feelings, all of which definitely made Nicky very attractive to a certain kind of woman.

One relationship began when a hippie hitchhiker named Deborah accepted a ride from sound engineer Dan Healy, who took her to John Cipollina's house. The moment Nicky came out of the guest room, "exuding the mystique of the English rock musician," Deborah decided he should meet her best friend, Barbara, as the two "shared a poetic angst and were both brooding beauties." She played Cupid, and Barb still has the scribbled note her friend passed to her about Nicky.

Barbara Holden: "My mother was English and was also a pianist, trained at the London College Of Music; and in San Francisco you didn't have too many

34. With Barbara Holden

parents that were from England. I had no idea who he was, what he did, or what his background was, but on New Year's Eve, '69 going into '70, the Airplane were playing with Quicksilver, the Sons Of Champlin and Hot Tuna at Winterland. I was on LSD and at some point towards the end of the evening, Nicky and I met and, for me anyway, it was love at first sight and that night, Nicky gave me the little piece of paper…with his number.

"We started seeing each other and were together for the next six months; John and Jan slept in this brass bed that was in an alcove upstairs and Nicky and

I had a twin bed in the side room; we both were thin then and none of us were very good cooks. We used to have bowls of cereal—that was our big meal. Nicky and I would go up to John's parents' house on Shady Lane for dinner and Nicky and John's mum would play four-handed piano.

"I was living a double life, trying to balance what my mother thought I was up to and staying with Nicky. We went on the first trip to Hawaii, when Quicksilver played at Diamond Head, and took a helicopter from the heliport in Sausalito; my mother hadn't even met Nicky at that point, so she had to come out to the

35. Hawaii

airport in San Francisco. Her eighteen-year-old daughter is going off to Hawaii and she knew that if she said no, I'd go anyway, but she liked Nicky because he was a pianist, he was English and he was a gentleman.

"I was actually very innocent when we met and after we broke up, he told me that he'd had an attraction and maybe even a fling with Jan and also with Girl Freiberg; it didn't matter except I'd been hanging around with both of them in Hawaii and didn't know. The next trip none of the old ladies were allowed to go. I only know what Nicky told me; I have postcards from that trip and everything was still fine and when he got back, after the recording, we broke up.

"Dolly, whom he later married, was living with an old friend of Nicky's and he and I were invited to dinner at their house in San Francisco; she'd made roast beef and Yorkshire pudding and in those days I couldn't cook to save myself; I'd only just left high school six months earlier. I was eighteen and Nicky was twenty-five. He was my first love and I really didn't know how to handle it. I saw John Cipollina's dad after we broke up and Gino said, 'I'm really sorry that you guys broke up, but Dolly is a woman and you're a girl,' and that was the truth. Dolly went over to Hawaii and that's where Nicky's relationship with Dolly started."

Barbara had fond memories of her time with Nicky: taking his picture outside Grauman's Chinese Theatre, meeting Rod Stewart at the Fillmore, with a backstage pass Nicky had organised for her, or taking organic psilocybin together on a beach in Hawaii. He had been absorbed into the familial atmosphere of Marin County:

"A group of us from Quicksilver, the Dead and the Airplane went to see *Hair* in San Francisco and Nicky had a cowboy hat on. There were some people sitting behind us and this rather slight-looking man said something to Nicky; I don't know if Nicky was trying to smoke or if it was his cowboy hat, but he turned around and said, 'Who are you? The Fire Marshal or something?' The man stood up thinking, 'Well, I can take you' and suddenly there was a whole row of people standing up: 'Do you have something to say to Nicky?'"

Universally remembered as a quiet tea-drinker in London (even surviving his nights with the Rolling Stones intact), Nicky had his first LSD experience in the studio when he was dosed, courtesy of his new band-mates, "But," said David Freiberg, "he could still play perfectly."

It is not surprising that the sudden exposure to the "real world" Nicky experienced as soon as he arrived in America left him adrift in the uncharted seas of sex, drugs and rock'n'roll. He had a lot of catching up to do and no instruction manual.

Opinions vary as to the prevalence of drugs and drink in the scene surrounding Quicksilver. Barbara Holden, who remained friends with John Cipollina, didn't remember cocaine being around and was surprised by what she later heard about Nicky, since when they were together they smoked pot but didn't even drink a lot. Ron Polte, who travelled with the band, was another with no recollection of Nicky appearing to live a particularly wild lifestyle:

"He took care of himself, slept nights and ate good; I didn't live with him, but I could tell by how he acted on the road, at the motels and at the dinner table and it was easy to see he was living pretty normally."

Behind closed doors however, things were changing.

Kathi McDonald: "It wasn't really an alcohol thing. There was a lot of playing of music—Coca-Cola, cigarettes, cocaine and a *lot* of weed. When cocaine came in, people stopped jamming and started getting paranoid."

Antonia Cipollina: "John did not drink—he never did. Yeah, they did coke—good cocaine though, the hot shit! And pot was everybody's drug of choice. Even when I knew Nicky was high, he was always polite to me. He said 'Shi-Shi (Antonia's pet-name), I would never show that side to you; I always respected you; but with people I didn't respect, I didn't care how I acted.'"

Jon Mark had also left London and had been making inroads in the USA, through his stint with John Mayall and later with his own band Mark-Almond. He met Nicky at an airport in February 1970, on the way to a huge festival in the Midwest at which both their bands were billed, and was shocked at the transformation in his friend:

"The naïve, childlike person had changed. He'd gone to America and suddenly this whole thing had jolted him. He had always had bad problems with his health, but I noticed that he was even gaunter. Our paths crossed lots of times as we criss-crossed America and I have to say I noticed a degeneration in Nicky; he was getting further and further out there."

The December 1969 Capitol Records promo sheet that accompanied *Shady Grove* (the first album Nicky made with Quicksilver) perfectly captures the times and the spirit of the "tie-dye" community that had adopted him:

"And they live with the trees, and with friends and with their environment and with their times. They live with themselves and ask much in the way of human decency and intelligence. They live without forfeiting human values – they express their values in their music. They bring the message of contemporary, concerned, honest men. They are a messenger service. They are the Quicksilver Messenger Service…They live in and around Mill Valley, which is very greenery (sic) and flowery and lovely and lush with talent and foliage and good vibes."

(L-R) Nicky Hopkins; Gregory Elmore; John Cipollina;(front) David Freiberg

QUICKSILVER MESSENGER SERVICE

Capitol

John Cipollina's father, a local realtor who sold houses to all the stars that were making big money, helped Nicky buy his own place in Mill Valley. He was now a full-fledged member of a band again, and the combination of Nicky's classical background and studio discipline made its mark on the more laid-back and untrained Californian musicians and radically changed the sound of Quicksilver. Rolling Stone noted in its May 1970 review of the album:

"For those of you accustomed to Happy Trails, *(this) will come as something of a shock. The absorption of Nicky Hopkins and the departure of Gary Duncan has changed the sound and thrust…entirely…The Quicksilver on* Shady Grove *has had its collective head turned around by Nicky Hopkins. The result is a more precise, more lyrical, more textured Quicksilver…Echoes of the old Quicksilver…do crop up quite often. The title cut, after a classical-tempoed Hopkins introduction, settles down into that old familiar Bo Diddley beat… The rest take some getting used to. They are muted, delicate and Hop-*

kins-infiltrated. He switches from piano to celeste to harpsichord to organ on 'Flute Song,'
'Too Far' and 'Flashing Lonesome,' all the time forcing the exploding essence of Quicksil-
ver to focus on such matters as melody, tone and lyrics. It takes a few listenings to adjust
to this switch and absorb Hopkins' keyboard mastery...in a way they have become the
'straight men' for the facile Hopkins. Fine music is still the result—but that rock'n'roll,
free-form jamming quality seems to have been sacrificed."

Apart from his many fine keyboard parts, Nicky is also credited for his first recorded appearance as a dog, barking an intro to Cipollina's "Three Or Four Feet
From Home"! David Freiberg was far from happy with the new album, but knew
that Nicky had saved the group from what could have been a total disaster. Dan
Healy, who was a close friend of the Grateful Dead,
knew Quicksilver, before and after Hopkins, and
remembered some hostility to their new direction:

"Whenever you try anything different, there's certain to be followers that are going to complain
because you've deviated from what they grew up
with. I saw it as a sort of hybrid Quicksilver and I
liked it myself, I thought we were going places. Nicky
was such a monster musician. John and Nicky both
had the most morbid senses of humour. They would
sit and talk about wanting to see perverted sights and stuff and within a half hour,
we'd all be laughing so hard, that tears would be streaming down our faces. To give
an example: they wanted to find an unborn foetus and have it cast inside of a clear
plastic bowling ball and go to the ladies' afternoon bowling with it!"

An undisputed highlight of *Shady Grove* is "Edward The Mad Shirt-Grinder,"
the funky nine-minute mini-symphony that is still the best known of Nicky's
piano instrumentals and whose genesis, to the amazement of his new band colleagues, took place on the spot in the studio. Its composer's only explanation for
the title was, "I tell you, it was strong grass."

David Freiberg: "I was overdubbing a bass track and all of a sudden Nicky put
his hand to his head and got this huge smile on his face; he ran and got a bunch
of music paper and started scribbling like crazy. I don't know whether my bass
overdub inspired him, but he wrote out the whole thing and it was just a joy. We
always kept a two-track going, just for all the little 'doodads' he played in between."

"Edward" was an instant favourite, with *Rolling Stone* giving it deserved attention:

"It is stunning in its complexity and satisfies the need for a wide-open instrumental.
Hopkins overwhelms on piano, but the supporting guitar/bass/drums should not be
slighted. Hopkins fans should buy this album for this cut alone."

Neither a new style nor Nicky's influence helped the album to sell noticeably
better or worse than its predecessor and there were only a handful of concerts to
promote it.

The new line-up made its debut at a free show in Golden Gate Park, followed by an open-air event in Mill Valley. A contemporary live review in *Women's Wear Daily* (!), described Nicky in florid terms as "brooding over the keyboard in his corner of the stage, pouring out rainbows of sound, feinting, flaunting and volleying with John Cipollina's solid-as-ever guitar," while the influential Ralph Gleason complimented him as "an amazing and original pianist with a personal driving style that gets the kind of scream in the treble I have heard previously only from Albert Ammons."

Despite Nicky's skills, it became evident that the absent Gary Duncan had provided much of the focus and driving force behind Quicksilver. David Freiberg said he couldn't play without him, and by year's end Duncan was back, bringing his running partner Dino Valenti with him, though the circumstances of his return are not entirely clear. Nicky claimed that he had disappeared to L.A for a week, without telling anybody and came back to find that they were in the band.

The 1969 traditional New Year's Eve concert found Gary back on stage with Dino, exactly a year after his departure, turning Quicksilver overnight into a sextet. The two wasted no time in throwing their weight around, informing all concerned that the album made in their absence sucked but that with their help the band could do much better. Gary Duncan didn't even know who Nicky Hopkins was, but greeted his presence with enthusiasm:

"An electric guitar has no overtones to sing with, but if you've got a piano, all of a sudden the rainbow shows up; I was very happy to see him; good session-players know how to add what's needed without inflicting themselves on the music. That's a sign of somebody that has 'carriage,' as Miles Davis would call it."

The six-piece Quicksilver Messenger Service toured heavily in the early part of 1970, with dates in Hawaii, California and Texas and two or three visits to New York.

Dan Healy: "When Dino and Gary came back, a lot of stuff changed politically in the band. It was one of those 'too hot to handle' situations that eventually got top-heavy and toppled over. There was a period of time there, right after *Shady Grove*, when we went out and did tours. That band would have really made it, had there been no outside things—and Nicky was the catalyst that made it work."

British band Brinsley Schwarz ended up on a bill with Van Morrison and Quicksilver in April 1970 for their disastrous and over-hyped U.S. launch at the Fillmore in New York. Guitarist Brinsley recognised Nicky from a session in London back in 1967, when he played on two singles for their earlier incarnation Kippington Lodge.

Nicky's radical influence on Shady Grove had received a mostly positive response but it was now the fast-talking Valenti who dominated, taking the lion's share of the writing credits on the next two albums and being responsible for the contentious decision to take the band and its entourage back to Hawaii to record. It would later become common practice for bands to seek inspiration and a fresh perspective by recording in exotic foreign locations, but in 1970, Quicksilver had neither the equipment nor the organisation to pull it off.

David Freiberg: "I thought it was a really silly idea. There are no studios there, but they said, 'We're going to build our own studio!' Actually the only reason we went was so Dino and Gary could get away from their mainland girlfriends."

Nicky went along with the plan, but shared Freiberg's reluctance and later described the scene that greeted them in disparaging terms:

"Dino had a real gift of the gab and would be able to talk any one of us around his little finger. We were all living on top of each other and the personality clashes were just so bad. We were on the far side of Oahu, about as far away as you can get from Honolulu, and then it was five and a half miles through private sugar cane fields to get to what was once a boy scout's lodge."

Dan Healy: "One of those turn-of-the-twentieth-century industrial revolution families had a daughter who was a Quicksilver freak and her family owned Opaelua Lodge, a colonial-style mansion made of redwood, shipped over from the north-west coast of Oregon. It was up on the very top of the mountain, in the north end of Hawaii, over-looking Pearl Harbour and it was just unbelievable. We built the studio, broke it up into pieces, put it into shipping crates and took it over."

Gary Duncan: "It was right on the edge of a cliff, with no electricity, just gaslights, and we put in a Caterpillar generator that ran twenty-four hours a day, wired the house up and built a studio inside of it. What a waste of money! On the hill underneath the house, the military had built these radio bunkers: three levels of cement rooms under the ground, with a manhole going down that they had kept the radios in so they wouldn't get bombed. They'd been empty for a long time and they were spooky. We made echo chambers out of them, with speakers and a microphone. At night you could turn the microphone up and you'd hear all these critters running around and if you walked outside the house at night you could hear the music coming up out of the ground—it was magical!"

Though he liked the natural beauty of Hawaii, Nicky still struggled despite the group's efforts to accommodate their star member's needs, particularly because he hated bugs and creepy-crawlies.

Freiberg: "Here he was in Hawaii, beautiful sun and everything, and he'd pull the shades down in his room and keep it dark all the time. There were three or four bedrooms; we gave Nicky the master bedroom, to keep him happy."

Dolly Hopkins: "He gaffa-taped up all the cracks in the window frames, put down the blinds and stayed in his room eating candy bars, sitting in bed and drinking tea."

Dan Healy: "You know about the suitcases full of candy bars he would hide under the bed, right?"

It was three weeks before a note of music could be recorded, while various problems related to the electrical power and studio set-up were ironed out. When they finally did begin working, Nicky hated the crowds of up to a hundred hangers-on Valenti had invited in, apparently to give himself the adrenalin of a live audience while performing. Unfortunately the same freaks and groupies would crash there for the night and Nicky remembered having to pick his way through the inert bodies of total strangers each morning in search of breakfast.

Most of the visitors were girls, collected on regular expeditions to jam after-hours at a nightclub called the Red Noodle in Waikiki. Some stayed in the house and some in tepees put up outside the building, becoming a growing source of tension between the more voracious of the Quicksilver musicians. Nicky had other preoccupations. His close friend and one-time Mill Valley neighbour, David Hayes, passed on one story as told to him firsthand by John Cipollina, starring Nicky as an early precursor of Basil Fawlty:

"It was miles of dirt road to get to the house but Nicky didn't drive—he never drove. He noticed that everybody had a car but him, so he mentioned it. They said, 'But Nicky, you don't drive.' 'I don't care, I want a car!' So they got him a rental and it sat there for days and days until he finally got up the nerve to drive it and off he went. A little while later John and Greg had to go to the store for something and a few miles down the road they came across Nicky and his car on a precipice at the side of the of the road, half hanging over the cliff; Nicky was beating it with a big stick; they stopped and said, 'Nicky are you all right?' and he went, 'Yeah, yeah, everything's fine.'"

Ron Polte: "I think it was the jack handle, but he took it out on the car."

Women and recording problems were not the only causes of dissent. The rough playbacks they would listen to at the end of each night sounded fine, but because Dino Valenti's self-belief and steamroller tactics extended to the mixing process as well, he took advantage of the power vacuum and assumed responsibility for finishing off the tracks back at Capitol Studios and, in Nicky's opinion, ruined them in the process.

Nicky Hopkins: "He screwed up the sounds. He took a lot of the bottom end out and added far too much echo on the instruments as well as on his voice and the mix was shitty as well. It was a real shame because they sounded great untouched."

Ron Polte: "The music that we had all envisioned for the next year or two disappeared when Dino moved in; he was so heavily affiliated with Gary and David that it was hard to oppose anything and the stuff we worked on was mostly his. A democracy turned into a dictatorship."

The tensions that arose in Hawaii led to the inevitable but premature break-up of the group, and Nicky Hopkins was first to go. At one point, the ever-confrontational Valenti is reputed to have drawn a line in the sand, forcing those present to decide on the spot whether they would stay or go. It was an easy choice for Nicky and by the end of June he was back in California and out of the band. When Valenti's aggressive behaviour led to him waving loaded guns around in the studio, Cipollina, Dan Healy and Ron Polte soon followed.

Julia Brigden: "Dino Valenti was such an asshole: a charismatic, talented guy, but also a real difficult person; I think he was jealous of Nicky. The fact that Nicky was really a star made him very nervous and I don't think there was room for more than one star with Dino around. Too bad, because he exploded that band one piece at a time."

Dan Healy: "He was a tyrant and we no longer wanted to participate. I hesitate to be real candid about it, but he was extremely vicious, especially to the women. He would walk in the studio and just start flipping on somebody, which is not conducive to creativity, and Nicky was very sensitive to that stuff; he could sniff a vibe right out of the air. Because of his accomplishments, he was not prone to want to put up with it and I can't say that I blame him. Nicky Hopkins did not need to take crap from anybody about anything."

The sessions limped on and ultimately provided enough tracks for almost two albums, all of 1970's *Just For Love* and half of *What About Me*, released the following year. Neither album is a favourite with Quicksilver aficionados. Buried among the many mediocre compositions on *What About Me*, mostly attributed to Jesse Oris Farrow (Valenti's pseudonym for publishing purposes), is "Spindrifter," another elegant addition to the list of Hopkins originals, which stands out both in style and quality from the rest of the album. The reflective melody is played almost solo and, bar a rhythm section accompaniment, has as little to do with Quicksilver's other music as "Girl From Mill Valley" had to do with the Jeff Beck Group's proto-metal.[30]

Gary Duncan: "That was just him and his overdubbed piano parts and if anyone else had played with him, it wouldn't have been nearly as good; I wanted to leave it alone because it was beautiful."

---

[30] Nicky received an unexpected windfall when L.A. arranger/producer and "Wrecking Crew" member Al De Lory—best-known for Beach Boys sessions and for his orchestrations on hits such as Glen Campbell's "Wichita Lineman"—recorded "Spindrifter" as a single on one of his occasional excursions as a bandleader. Nicky's publishing on the track is assigned, in typically Pythonesque style, to "Snarley Grumble Music," a name he had first used on the cover of *Shady Grove*.

After barely a year, his latest group membership was already history. The complicated comings and goings of the personnel in Quicksilver necessitated the drafting of a special contract amendment with Capitol around the time Nicky left, listing the different line-ups (designated "Units 1, 2 and 3"), when they began and ended and to whom royalties should be paid (Nicky's share was to be sent c/o Ron Polte).

Nicky went on to collaborate with John Cipollina, his closest Quicksilver associate, on numerous projects in the next few years and became a stalwart of the

scene in and around San Francisco. He made one more record with the full Quicksilver line-up, when the group reconvened for an inauspicious reunion album in 1975 (Valenti, Duncan and Elmore having kept a touring version on the road during the intervening years). Gary Duncan candidly confessed that the motivation was "to make money, pure and simple" and Nicky appears on just two tracks of Solid Silver, the remaining keyboard duties being taken by fellow Englishman Pete Sears and by Michael Lewis. He declined to take part in the touring that followed.

Dan Healy: "Live, we got up to ten or twelve thousand-seater halls and when Nicky would play solos, you could almost hear jaws hitting the floor. There would be moments, during 'Edward The Mad Shirt Grinder' when I would look around the room and all the jabbering and milling around would stop and the entire audience was paying perfect attention to what was going on."

When John Cipollina died in 1989 aged only forty-five, although Nicky was on the other side of the world at the time touring with Art Garfunkel, he rearranged everything to rush back and guest on four songs with local band Terry and The Pirates (including Quicksilver's "Pride Of Man"), at a tribute show for his fallen comrade.

Antonia Cipollina: "It didn't surprise me at all when Nicky called from Australia and said he had arranged to be there. He was just in time to get his white coat on and go out on stage and, after not being with these guys for twenty years, it was as if he'd been playing with Terry (Dolan) all along. I think there was one rehearsal and he didn't even make that, because he flew in the night of the actual tribute."

In retrospect, the collapse of Quicksilver Messenger Service can be attributed to the usual conflicts of personality common to most rock bands, amplified by the intense atmosphere of constant drug use that was a mark of the times. In a conversation recorded later, Nicky delivered a surprisingly harsh verdict on the band:

36. California Cowboy

"I recall people coming backstage at Winterland to tell us how great we all were, and everyone in the band being so wiped out they were a semitone off, either way, through the whole set. It was so awful it made me want to puke. It was very strange, because it really wasn't my sort of music and I joined them for totally the wrong reasons; I'd fallen in love with San Francisco and was smoking grass all day long. Music was way down the list of reasons to stay with them."

Gary Duncan was convinced that choice of drugs was a major dividing factor in the band and insisted that pot was not the only item on the menu:

"They (Cipollina and Hopkins) did cocaine and that's another ballgame; I've never met anybody yet that can do anything on coke; they think they can, they talk about doing stuff, but they never do; people that take crank (amphetamine) usually get in trouble, but they do *do* things; but there's something about the aura around cocaine, I don't know what it is—and they were both sick to start with."

When asked if he had tried to bring any benign influence to bear on Nicky's escalating drug use, Gary replied:

"The only time I ever said anything to him about it was when he was still fucked up, before he went to L.A. I loaned him a thousand dollars—well, gave him a thousand dollars, because he was broke, and I said, 'Nicky, do me a favour. Please stop drinking and taking coke, because it's killing you; you ain't healthy enough to do it; I can and it ain't gonna hurt me, because I've got extra life, but you don't.' He knew what I was saying, because he got clean. The next time I met him was quite a while later at the Fillmore, where he looked the healthiest I ever saw him.

"He knew that he wasn't going to live to be an old man. I would imagine that anybody who's been through that kind of physical trauma, pretty much knows that. I think we did one big nationwide tour when Nicky was in the group, but the conditions were good because we had money; we flew first class and had good hotels and limousines, so we were taken care of. But going on the road later on, when you've got a lower budget and you've got to carry your own shit gets tough and I don't know if he could have handled it; I mean he wasn't going to be moving no pianos! But all in all, in my life, he was a very memorable person. A unique person."

Though his stay with Quicksilver had ended in similar disagreements to the Jeff Beck Group, Nicky was determined not to return to the soulless grind of London sessions. He opted to remain in Mill Valley, in the house he had bought in July 1970. Being currently unemployed, the thorny question of how to remain in the USA needed to be addressed.

Dolly made a poor impression on most of Nicky's musician friends and acquaintances, being variously referred to as "the girlfriend from hell," a groupie and a vampire; one musician believed she was a practicing witch, a statement to which Bobby Keys scornfully added, "Yeah, a self-proclaimed witch who didn't know the difference between a full moon and a new moon!" Whatever the rest of the world may have thought, the ever-fragile state of Nicky's health made having a partner who was free to travel with and care for him almost a necessity. His lack of experience left him wide open to what many perceived as Dolly's agenda of finding herself a bona fide English rock star to help leave behind her roots in Teaneck, New Jersey and become not just a rock star's wife, but eventually even a writer, manager and performer in her own right.

In the aftermath of leaving Quicksilver, Nicky stayed home, composing at the piano and planning his next move. Recurrent pains in his back led to a doctor's examination, X rays and an emergency hospitalisation in San Francisco, where a combination of kidney infection, jaundice and a blood clot, led to the removal of one of his kidneys and a stretch in intensive care, when doctors once again almost gave up hope of his survival. Bizarrely, among the stream of visitors who called in at the hospital, were fans wanting to make home movies of Nicky in his sick bed. Dolly was only twenty-one at the time and offered up prayers at his bedside. Either her spiritual efforts or the doctors' attentions were successful enough for Nicky to be back in action by the end of 1970—a miracle cure, according to her.

During the following twelve months he was offered full-time membership of the Who and a place in John Lennon's Plastic Ono Band and, despite the frostiness following his non-appearance at their mammoth Hyde Park show, Nicky remained a regular fixture with the Rolling Stones. It was clear that for the foreseeable future he was going to be living a transatlantic lifestyle. To secure his status in America, Nicky took a common route and suggested formalising his relationship with his live-in girlfriend. Dolly remembered the exact words of Nicky's less than romantic marriage proposal:

"Do you want to marry me? I need a green card."

She accepted. Ron Polte, despite having misgivings about the marriage, assisted the process by finding Nicky a good immigration lawyer and serving as official witness at the civil wedding in San Rafael on October 29th, 1970, with Dolly resplendent in hot pants. Ron was not the only one who foresaw trouble ahead.

Antonia Cipollina: "Nicky liked nice things; he had gorgeous rugs and, when he wasn't working, he was home and liked to keep things organised and know where they were. Dolly was a hardcore biker type, and I recall late night phone calls from Nicky, asking my father to come over and help him, because she was trying to hurt him and tearing up the house, drunk and crazy; Dad would go over there and break up a fight, get them separated and get Nicky out of there. She was very volatile, especially when she drank."

37. Nicky & Dolly Hopkins

Dolly Hopkins contacted this author from her then home in Arkansas, where she was living as a born-again Christian. She warned me not to portray Nicky as some kind of saint: "Trust me, all the good in him went into his music," a comment whose harshness angered Mick Taylor:

"You could say the same thing about Mozart, for God's sake, or about most musicians. They're all difficult!"

Nicky Hopkins' time with Quicksilver may not have produced a great volume of memorable music, but he had made his presence felt in the USA, and at the same time added significantly to his reputation back in the UK. The continuing demand for his skills soon necessitated a second home, and he and Dolly decided on a semi-detached house in Epsom as a base for his English activities. The house was a good size, though not palatial, and came with its own housekeeper.

A green card application entails a period of waiting outside the USA for official approval, so Nicky found himself back in England, with only a grand piano, a Fender amplifier and his American partner for company. His West Coast activities had generated considerable interest and he gave a number of interviews to the English music papers, in which he extolled his home in California, but, in a talking to *Disc & Music Echo* in December 1971, he was dismissive of the looseness he had initially found so liberating:

"The music scene over there doesn't interest me at all. Bands here take their music so much more seriously, and there is such a heavy drug scene over there, it gets out of hand.

"In San Francisco, it's almost as if the music becomes secondary. You're supposed to start work in a studio at seven, nothing happens for four hours, then everybody gets loaded and nothing gets done."

These are curious words from someone who had sat through so many Rolling Stones sessions and was himself not immune to temptation, but after the clock-watching discipline of the London studios, perhaps understandable. The financial aspect of recording in the USA, however, received full approval:

"If they can pay eight-five dollars for a three-hour session in the States, why can't they here?"

However poorly paid the work may sometimes have been, Nicky's familiarity with the reigning superstars of the time had helped him build up a bulging address book, an immensely valuable asset and vital to his next venture—a long-overdue second solo album.

All Down The Line
The Rolling Stones – Part 2

"When I finally meet my maker, Marty, I'm afraid I'm in for a bit of a spanking."

– Keith Richards *(overheard by Vince Gill in conversation with Marty Stuart in a Nashville studio)*.

38. Nicky (upper right) with the all-star cast of the *Rock And Roll Circus*

When the Jeff Beck Group's tour ended in December 1968, Nicky immediately flew home for a seriously jet-lagged get-together for the taping of the Rolling Stones' over-ambitious *Rock And Roll Circus*. It had been some months and thousands of miles of American highway since he had last worked with them on *Beggars Banquet*, and he now found himself at Intertel Studios, with the Stones' remote truck dutifully capturing the proceedings.

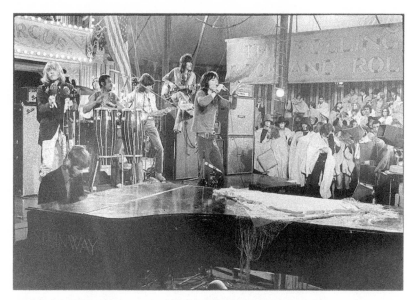

39. Performing at the *Rock And Roll Circus*

Nicky's main recollection to his sister Julia of the *Circus* was his refusal to wear the ponchos and silly hats that all those present were asked to put on. Having missed the rehearsals at the Londonderry Hotel, he somehow managed to stay awake throughout the chaotic sequence of supporting bands, until the Stones finally took the stage at one o'clock in the morning. Dominic Tarlé's evocative photographs and the "Salt Of The Earth" finale show that Nicky did reluctantly agree to put on his fancy dress costume. Though prominent throughout the Stones' segment, when the film was eventually released in 1996, guess whose name was left off the credits?

In February '69, studio work resumed for what would become *Let It Bleed*. For obvious reasons, being a full-time member of Jeff Beck's touring line-up meant Nicky was no longer always available to the Stones. But he did manage to break away long enough to appear on four of the tracks that make up the next of the band's indisputably great albums. The same sessions also produced the tracks which ended up on *Jamming With Edward*, which some have suggested was the Stones' way of repaying Nicky for unaccredited writing contributions he had made on previous albums.

Mick Jagger's lyric flirtations with drug references, near-the-knuckle sexuality and the darker side of existence came to the fore in songs such as the brooding "Gimme Shelter,"[31] the title track "Let It Bleed," the strutting "Live With Me," and especially "Midnight Rambler." The band was at the peak of its powers, with new recruit Mick Taylor stepping in for the first time in place of the mostly absent Brian Jones.

If "Salt Of The Earth" made a perfect closer to *Beggars Banquet*, "Gimme Shelter" is one of rock music's all-time great openers. Nicky's piano emerges ghostlike out of the dense stew of Keith's bubbling guitars, and Merry Clayton's incredible guest vocal adds to the overall sense of tension and foreboding.

After two keyboard-free tracks, "Live With Me" starts out with Leon Russell at the piano.

Bill Wyman: "Ian Stewart came into the studio with the first Delaney & Bonnie album and said, 'You've got to hear this, Nicky' and played a track ("The Ghetto," featuring Russell) to him and said, 'Isn't it fantastic?' Nicky listened to it, went out and played the whole song by himself on the piano. Stu said, 'That's what I don't like about Nicky.'"

Leon had been introduced to the Stones when Delaney & Bonnie came through London. He was invited into the studio to lay down his signature piano licks and flamboyant glissandos on "Live With Me," as well as arranging the track's horn parts (a first appearance on a Stones track for the

---

[31] Recorded late in the sessions as a response to the events of the infamous December 6, 1969 concert at Altamont, California.

long-serving Bobby Keys). Nicky's far more intricate and precise sixteenth notes entry provides a great contrast.

In a Nashville barroom, Bobby Keys recalled his first meeting with Nicky, and his complete puzzlement at Nicky's strait-laced demeanour:

"Nicky was in San Francisco at the time (October '69) and he came down to the studios in Los Angeles to do some piano overdubs. We were both pretty young back then and he was very, very English—not your usual rock'n'roll type. Back then everybody was taking acid every day and smoking joints, and Nicky didn't do any of that; he drank tea—no booze or nothing. I thought, 'How does this guy exist in this culture?' When everybody around him was engulfed in confusion, he'd be sitting there with his head down—just like Linus, man, in the *Peanuts* cartoon; he didn't seem to be affected."

Nicky delivers one of the most elegant and perfectly conceived performances of his career on *Let It Bleed's* quietest track, "You Got The Silver." Keith Richards' love song to Anita Pallenberg was his first outing as sole lead vocalist and his heartfelt singing, acoustic slide and guitar tracks are perfectly underpinned by Nicky's understated organ and gentle piano. Over the years Nicky often referred to the song as one of his top five favourite performances, a sentiment echoed by Keith and others:

"Oh, it's always hard with favourites...but 'Silver' is up there..."

Chuck Leavell: "The organ in that starts out so subtle and easy and then as the song goes on, not only the volume, but the intensity and even the chord structure intensifies."

Benmont Tench: "He finds the range, the perfect tone and the perfect settings; I guess he didn't play much organ, but he played the hell out of it on 'You Got The Silver' and leaves a lot of room between the notes."

"Monkey Man," which follows, is more typical of the Stones' usual swagger and the intro is carried by the double-act of Nicky's piano and Bill Wyman's simple but effective vibes, heralding in Keith Richards' fantastically assured riffing and the crack of Charlie's snare. Nicky's echoey replies, inventive as ever, carry the song's elongated instrumental break until Jagger's almost puking re-entry with 'I'm a monkey!'—every parent's nightmare and a triumph of rock'n'roll.

New York scenester Al Kooper had actually arrived in London looking for a holiday from his endless U.S. studio commitments. Instead, he ended up with the Rolling Stones, playing organ, piano and French horn and helping to arrange the album's last track, "You Can't Always Get What You Want":

"I have Nicky to thank, because I was in England and he was in the United States. They called me because he wasn't there. I miss him. He was a great one."

With Kooper, Leon Russell and Stu all credited with keyboard appearances, Nicky still comes out ahead for the number of tracks he played on *Let It Bleed* and every one is a classic. The possibility of making any further contributions was removed by his departure from the Jeff Beck Group in early June '69 and subsequent disappearance to California.

When Brian Jones died on July 3rd, just two days before the Stones were due to play an enormous open-air show in London's Hyde Park, the band decided to go ahead with the gig as a memorial to their wayward founding member. Despite a flurry of phone calls from the Stones' office, begging Nicky to come back for the event, he stayed right where he was, claiming illness. He remained convinced for the rest of his life that his refusal to return to London, for what would have been his first live appearance with the Stones, cost him a permanent place in the group.

His first wife Dolly remembered "a lot of pissed-off phone calls from Keith," because Nicky decided not to do Hyde Park. "The Stones pretty much thought they had exclusive rights to him at the time, because they had asked him to join the band so many times and he kept saying no."

The answer to the thorny question of whether Nicky was ever formally invited to join the Rolling Stones depends on whose opinion one believes. Bill Wyman firmly denied it, while Keith was not a hundred per cent sure:

"I think it probably was mooted around but I'm not sure if it was actually offered to Nicky as such—Screaming Lord Sutch (laughs), if you'll pardon the pun. That's a bit blurry, but it was close. Obviously it didn't happen and I can't really remember why, but at the same time I know we wouldn't have turned him down."

Both Nicky's mother and brother Paul were both equally sure that he was offered a full time position and in his 1994 *Bone Magazine* interview with Peter Rodman, Nicky offered this nugget:

"We never really got into details about it. I had discussed it with Mick and Keith and I wanted to be (a member), and it really only got as far as, 'Oh, you want to join up with us Nicky? I s'pose you'll *want* a lot!'"

It remains impossible to confirm the truth, but whatever went down around the Hyde Park concert, there were no long-term hard feelings. When Nicky arrived back in England in February '71, he received a call from Mick Jagger, who had been trying unsuccessfully to reach him in California, with an invitation to go on the road.

Before his first Stones tour, Nicky made one fleeting appearance on *Sticky Fingers*, playing piano on the weighty "Sway." He was no longer as prominent in the

mix as on the two previous records, and fights for attention with Paul Buckmaster's string arrangement and Mick Taylor's lead guitar. However, with recording taking place not just at Olympic, but at Jagger's Stargroves home and the Muscle Shoals studio in Alabama, piano duties on the rest of the album were shared among no less than seven different players, most notably Billy Preston.

Sticky Fingers ushered in a new phase in the band's existence. It was the first release on their own label and the leering and unforgettable "tongue and lips" label logo and Andy Warhol's cover art displayed a new air of self-confidence and a celebration by the Stones of their own myth.

After their disastrous financial dealings with the notorious Allen Klein, the Stones' affairs were in disarray. Their new mentor Prince Rupert zu Loewenstein advised them to avoid paying their huge tax debts in England by going into exile for at least a year. France was decided upon as being nearest to home and they bid goodbye to Britain with a concert blitz through the provinces In March 1971. With Nicky alternating with Stu on piano and with the horn section of Bobby Keys and Jim Price, the band previewed some of the new, as yet unreleased *Sticky Fingers*. A show in Leeds was broadcast live by the BBC and the brief tour concluded with a sadly shambolic concert, filmed, for old times' sake at London's

40. Nicky (and Dolly) backstage, 1971

tiny Marquee Club for U.S. television, with Nicky, as usual, audible but completely invisible.

The chaos in the Stones camp was not just financial. Keith Richards' increasingly drug-fuelled lifestyle had become the element upon which all the band's arrangements depended. Nicky's first experience of travelling with the band was a catalogue of Keith-related delays and missed flights, with wives (Jagger accompanied by his soon-to-be-wife Bianca) and hangers-on such as Keith's running buddy Gram Parsons along for the ride. It was only an endlessly patient and resourceful production team that held whole edifice together.

After his stay in the U.S. there had been a marked change in Nicky's behav-

41. On the band bus, 1971 UK tour

iour. Though he still lagged far behind the excesses of Keith and his cronies, it is a miracle that he held out against the all-pervasive drug use around the Stones for as long as he did. Many sixties musicians, influenced by their experiences in Hamburg or by all-nighters at Mod venues like the Flamingo, coped with their punishing schedules by reaching for speed-induced energy. Mike Harrison, who met Nicky with his pre-Spooky Tooth band the VIPs, recalled departing for a month to Germany with a bag of five hundred "Black Bombers" acquired through the same notorious "Dr. Robert" of Harley Street who was immortalised by John Lennon on *Revolver*.

Bobby Keys noticed a gradual change in Nicky:

"I was on the wilder side of the line and he was on the more conservative side and slowly our two paths began to converge. I guess that first tour with the Stones was the first extended period of time that we spent in close proximity to each other; we would always try to get Nicky to smoke a joint, but he stayed completely away from that stuff and then I began to notice that he'd have a little drink every now and then and I thought 'Well that's cool, the guy's coming round.' You could fill up that downtime with some awfully expensive things—and not just money-wise; it took a heavy toll."

Keith Richards: "Nicky was a very quiet guy in many ways, but there was a manic side to him. Lurking underneath a very quiet studious persona was this quite wicked little devil and after he started to live in America—you know, it's quite different to living in Harrow. I think he got pretty wild out in California from what I hear."

Bill Wyman: "He didn't rave it up too much. He hung around Charlie a bit and me because we were much more easy-going and normal, if you like. He didn't indulge too much in the excesses—not that I know of."

In 1989, Nicky's own recollections to Australian journalist Bryan Patterson (*Sunday Express*) were quite different:

"It was while working with the Stones; I'm not blaming anybody; it was the way it was. In 1965, when I started doing session work, there were hardly any drugs around; I think Pete Townshend was one of the first persons I ever saw fire up a joint on a recording session; I didn't know what he was doing, but by 1967, when I started working with the Stones, drugs were around a lot and I felt quite left out because I was the only one not doing it."

Rolling Stone journalist Robert Greenfield's description of a long-haired and moustachioed Nicky onstage in Newcastle, "cigarette dangling out of the corner of his mouth, two bottles of whiskey on the piano, honky-tonking it all the way" confirmed that the "cup of tea and a biscuit" Hopkins was a thing of the past. Nicky's frail health meant that Dolly was his constant companion, which caused considerable dissent in the Stones' camp, especially as she involved herself in business matters.

Bill Wyman: "She wasn't very popular; I found her a pain in the arse actually, but he wouldn't go anywhere without her, so we finally agreed and put up with it, because of his talent. He said, 'The only way I'm coming on tour is if I bring Dolly,' so you had to bring Dolly."

42. Mick Jagger holds court, 1971 UK tour

The Stones left the UK on April 15, 1971 for their year in tax exile, and would not return as a unit for a decade. Meanwhile, Nicky and Dolly were two of

43. At Mick Jagger's wedding

the select group of rock royalty flown from London, on a specially chartered Dan-Air flight, to attend Mick Jagger's nightmarish nuptials in the south of France. After the newlyweds escaped the unseemly scrum of fans and photographers at the church, Nicky joined an extensive cast of celebrities, including various Stones members, Paul McCartney and Ringo Starr, Eric Clapton, Stephen Stills, PP Arnold, Terry Reid, David Lindley and Faces Ronnie Wood and Kenney Jones, for a jam session that lasted well into the early hours, with the bridegroom himself playing harmonica and singing backing vocals.

After the wedding, Mick's understandable preoccupation with his new bride meant that he was often in Paris socialising, rather than giving attention to the Stones' affairs. His absences combined with Keith Richards' unpredictable lifestyle made preparations for recording another album particularly difficult. Eventually, with the band members quartered in various nearby addresses, the centre of operations became, by default, the Villa Nellcôte, Keith Richards' palatial pied-à-terre in Villefranche-sur-Mer near Nice, which he shared with Anita Pallenberg and a floating cast of sometimes thirty or more visitors.

The new location brought its own share of problems: the myriad distractions available to wealthy young musicians on the Côte d'Azur, one of the hottest French summers on record, levels of humidity that played havoc with their equipment and made tuning guitars a nightmare, power cuts and equipment failures and a cramped basement totally unsuited to recording. One huge advantage, however, was that whatever his condition, the errant guitarist was at least always present. Charlie Watts eloquently described "working on Keith time":

"You have to remember that when Keith was in his drug period, the time was his. You could get somewhere at a particular time, but Keith wouldn't be there. You could make a record but he wouldn't be on it."

Mick Taylor: "Our work totally revolved around Keith's sleeping and waking schedule. On tour he had to get to the next gig; he wasn't always in great shape, not that anybody slated him for that, we just kind of accepted it, but Mick used to get furious with him. Maybe it's just my lack of foresight, but I really didn't think the band would stay together; the dynamics seemed so fragile and there were so many people that were becoming affected by it."

Having none of the financial pressures that faced the Stones, Nicky Hopkins didn't join the rest of the band until later in the summer. He had, in the meantime, recorded landmark albums in England with the Who and John Lennon and contributed to records for his colleagues Jim Price (at Jagger's Stargroves) and Bobby Keys (at Nicky's "second home," Olympic Studios).

Nicky was never much of a fan of "abroad" and particularly disliked France and the French, so the sessions at Nellcôte were a lengthy trial from start to finish—from July to November—with only very occasional breaks. Dolly Hopkins recalled some of the charming domestic details at Nellcôte:

"Keith would be downstairs with Marlon and the baby would be peeing and shitting everywhere on the floor. When I suggested that taking him to the toilet might be a good idea, Keith replied, 'He'll find it eventually when he's old enough.'"

Though officially quartered with the horn players, Nicky stayed much of the time with Bill Wyman and his family, where life was slower-paced. Bobby Keys loved the new location:

"The French Riviera was a wonderful place to record—Villa De Vigne was the name of the house that Nicky, Jim Price and I shared. It was so big that we hardly saw each other; I don't remember a lot about that whole period of time; Keith and I got to be very good friends—we were both born same day, same month, same year, within a few minutes of each other—and we entertained our-

selves (laughs) in the downtime, so to speak. You're either Keith's friend or Mick's and I started out being Mick's friend, but found it was a hell of a lot more fun being Keith's. And Keith is a lot better friend. Jagger's kind of phony!'

Mick Taylor: "The schedule was much looser than anything I'd been used to. I would imagine it was quite frustrating for somebody like Nicky, but when you're paid as a session musician, you have to sit there and suffer in silence."

In a *Zoo World* interview a year later, Nicky's summary of the *Exile On Main Street* sessions was that "it took four months and was enormously boring!"

Robin Millar, whose sister Rose was married to Mick Taylor, later became a well-known producer, and as a junior member of the team was given the unenviable task of capturing the disjointed basement sessions on the Stones' mobile recording truck. He has unusually clear memories of the four months he spent at Nellcôte and of Nicky's part in the proceedings:

"I had come across Nicky Hopkins when I hung around as an innocent teenager at Olympic or Advision. Through my connections with Mick Taylor, I was able to get into the inner sanctums, but until *Exile* I certainly didn't know Nicky as a person and I think other people that worked with Nicky would agree that getting to know him wasn't something that was likely to happen casually in a studio canteen. He was a person who spoke happily when spoken to but rarely volunteered.

"*Exile On Main Street* we look at now as a project, because it has a name and a history, but it was a ragbag of sessions. There are really only four songs and the rest of it is a series of jams and half-put-together pieces, some of which were started in London, so there was a lot of stuff already on tape that was being salvaged. The recording set-up itself, down in the basement of Keith Richards'

44. With Keith Richards at Villa Nellcôte

house, was a nightmare scenario because it was a series of corridors; it wasn't like there was a big studio with everyone in it; I can only remember 'Tumbling Dice' and perhaps one other track as being, 'Set up the bass, drums, keyboards, guitars, guide vocal—everyone—one, two, three, four, play!'

"Half the time you couldn't see Nicky because he'd either be playing the electric keyboard or the piano, which was actually upstairs; everything was done via tie lines and headphones and there weren't any two-way cameras or anything, so you really didn't see him a lot of the time.

"At the beginning it was hard to assess whether Nicky was shy or whether he was diffident; I realised that it was a mixture of two strong factors. One was professionalism; he very much was there to play the piano, being booked by the day, by the week or by the month and would play as required. He would always focus when it was time to do a take, but really wasn't participating or joining in the general banter.

"He wasn't into partying; they would take any excuse to go off on the Harley-Davidsons and Nicky would be hanging around or sitting on a sofa reading a book or a magazine. He was there to do a job."[32]

Mick Taylor: "It was very hard for Nicky because he was in a room on his own. In a proper studio you'd have the piano miked up or a bit of separation, but there was one very small room where Bill, Charlie, Keith and I sat and Mick did his vocals in a toilet. Bobby and Jim were down the corridor somewhere, so everybody was communicating by headphones and there were power cuts; it was a shambles."

Robin Millar: "There were very rarely more than one or two members even there at the same time, so a lot of what Nicky did, would have been done in the afternoon, sometimes just with Jimmy Miller, with Charlie, with Bill—sometimes just with Keith. There weren't many opportunities really for a normal band-type interaction. Jagger was often away because Bianca was pregnant. When they were together, the sessions would go on for thirty hours, forty hours…"

The full members were at least compensated for their time and discomfort by the promise of shared royalties and band income, but the Stones' session men were certainly never overpaid. When this author mentioned Nicky's tiny fee for playing on the Beatles "Revolution" to Keith Richards, he laughed:

"I think we were a bit more generous! We didn't do it by the hour, we did it on a sessions (basis) for how many days and we'd just sort of come to an agreement, you know; it was just sorted."

Nicky didn't necessarily share Keith's opinion and Mick Taylor confirmed that any financial matters would have to have been discussed with Mick Jagger:

"I used to observe things going on and I remember especially in the South of France, when Nicky was trying to renegotiate his session fee, which probably wasn't very much, because they used to pay their musicians notoriously minimal wages; I thought it was good actually, for somebody as good as him to be pushing for a bit more money, because there's no such thing as down time when you're a session musician; you're hired to play and when you don't, you are still using up your time.

"I've only played with one really famous rock band and that's the Stones, but I've played with people like Bob Dylan and sometimes it's a strange paradox; as much as they admire the musician they've hired, they cannot seem to get out of the session musician mentality when it comes to paying them; it's almost as if they think, 'These guys should feel honoured to be playing with me,' and some

---

[32] During the only significant break in proceedings in France, rather than relax or take a well-deserved holiday, Nicky kept up his breakneck pace and flew back to San Francisco to work with singer Pamela Polland.

people might think like that, but not somebody like Nicky. I don't think he was willing to accept minimal pay for maximum hours and input."

Despite the hurdles they faced in its creation, the Rolling Stones somehow managed to piece together another fine album. Although almost universally panned on its original release, *Exile* is now considered one of their very best.

From Keith's classic riffing on the opener "Rocks Off," which sets the tone for the whole album, to the last notes of the loping mid-paced "Soul Survivor," Nicky is an integral part of all but a handful of the tracks on *Exile*. Whether laying low in the gloriously ramshackle backing track for the single release, "Tumbling Dice" or taking centre stage for the intro and accompaniment to "Loving Cup;" whether

45. Session man

playing fast and furious on rockers "Rip This Joint" and "Turd On The Run;" playing classic country licks on "Torn And Frayed" or bluesy and loose on the Mick Taylor inspired "Ventilator Blues," Nicky draws on all his skills. Together with Bobby Keys' ripping saxophone breaks and Mick Taylor's soulful lead guitar, he provides the perfect accompaniment to the album's inspired sound, even if Messrs. Jagger and Richards may have taken his talents for granted.

Robin Millar: "Nicky was obviously a more advanced musician, and the Stones lapped up that extra layer of musical adventure. They really did go through a very productive and inventive period, but I don't think that the band, what with one thing and a lot of the other, were in a position to value anything at all; I don't think they valued Nicky Hopkins, I don't think they valued money, I don't think they valued success, I don't think they valued their own bodies, I don't think they valued one another; I don't think they were in the position to appreciate their wives, girlfriends, their own children—nothing. I think if you asked them all now, they do value one another and they value what's left of their bodies desperately; they cherish their simple rock'n'roll roots and would be happy to acknowledge the extra musical dimension that Nicky, Mick Taylor, Bobby Keys and Jim Price did give their work."

The drift towards a more drink and drug-fuelled lifestyle, which had begun in California, accelerated during Nicky's tenure as a touring member of the Rolling Stones and even more during the endless recording sessions. As West Coast vocal powerhouse Kathi McDonald—brought in on backing vocals when *Exile* was being mixed in America—said: "You can't out-Keith Keith and don't ever try, unless you have a death wish or you're fond of jail."

Robin Millar: "If you weren't taking drugs down there, you were the only one who wasn't, so what would you do all day and whom would you have a meaningful conversation with? Marshall Chess was head of the record label, master of ceremonies and supplier of whatever was required; you're expected to sit at a keyboard and make a meaningful contribution twenty-eight hours after you've started and if someone offers you something, you're going to take it because the option of saying, 'To hell with you lot, I'm going to bed,' probably didn't seem viable."

Nicky's sister Julia believed that he started to drink and take drugs because he hated being on stage, especially with the Stones, terrified at how close the audience was; "It was a bit like agoraphobia. He was a session pianist that probably should never have left home."

Mick Taylor took advantage of some down time to learn to play piano:

"It was a golden opportunity; I taught myself by listening to Nicky and by having a piano at my disposal in the studio to tinkle around on. One night at Nellcôte, Nicky, Jimmy Miller, Keith Richards and I were playing a very un-Stones-like instrumental track that was just a little riff; it's on one of their studio bootleg albums and it's really quite beautiful; it's called 'Separately.' It said 'co-written with Keith Richards,' but one could also say it was co-written by Nicky Hopkins, because there's a very distinctive piano phrase in it."

Though Nicky had already worked in the studio with many high-profile clients, there is no doubt that the visibility accorded him as the "sixth Stone" helped enormously in advancing his own plans (or rather perhaps Dolly's) for a solo career. After four months in France, in December 1971 he returned to the USA to continue preparations for his upcoming solo album at home in Mill Valley, though henceforward he would be splitting his time between California and his new address in the U.K. First there was the small matter of a Rolling Stones tour of the USA to be dealt with, and by the time Nicky reconnected with the band, he had his own record deal with CBS under wraps.

On June 3, 1972, after final rehearsals at the Warner Brothers Studios soundstage in Los Angeles, the first Stones tour of the USA since Altamont—and their longest excursion yet—commenced in Vancouver, with the same line-up as the previous year's British dates.

Nicky referred to the trek as "the most memorable musical tour since Joshua played the trumpet," and indeed the scale and expectations had grown enormously. Along with the equally rampaging Led Zeppelin, the Stones helped break the traditional mould for touring in the USA. Demand for tickets was often ten times the availability, and when the touring party came to town, it seemed like the band was, for that moment, the centre of the music universe. (Mick Taylor noted ruefully, "Well they've always thought they were the centre of the universe.")

46. Nicky and Dolly on the STP plane, 1972

To be carrying one of the prized, countersigned STP laminate passes, meant membership in that summer's most exclusive club and Nicky—with Dolly along to support him—was on the inside, travelling under the pseudonym Tony Lock and with a personal request for a bottle of Johnnie Walker with Coke on each and every rider. A full-page photo in the tour's black and white programme shows him, pale as a ghost in his aeroplane seat, cigarette in hand, glowering at the camera with Dolly in the background.

Nicky had his own piece in the tour programme:

**THE ROLLING STONES
AMERICAN TOUR 1972**

"Inside The Tour Machine 1972

"If any one rock musician could insure his hands for millions of dollars, it would have to be Nicky Hopkins. His distinct piano style has been in demand with just about every major group on both sides of the Atlantic and he finally performs live with the Stones for this tour.

"Both the Beatles and the Stones had been using Hopkins on recording dates for quite a while before he decided to start performing live. His piano can be heard on the Stones' Beggars Banquet LP, especially "Street Fighting Man." He toured America and Europe with the Jeff Beck Group a few years ago and since then has appeared with Quicksilver Messenger Service and the Jefferson Airplane.

"Nicky is a quiet type who sits perfectly still as his fingers sensitively probe the keyboard. He looks like a gaunt statue with a perpetual impish grin. Because he can fit unobtrusively into any musical setting, he is the ultimate backing musician."

Nicky began the tour in poor health, as further complications from his earlier hospitalisation had necessitated treatment for a collapsed lung and a gall bladder operation, less than two weeks before the marathon run of dates. Trying to gain an impression of how he fared while travelling is difficult, since attention was then, as now, entirely focussed on the star members of the band.

The Stones commissioned their own tour documentary, the charmingly titled *Cocksucker Blues*, which for obvious reasons was never commercially released. Robert Franks' home-movie styled narrative depicts graphic scenes of sex in hotel room and "mile-high" in the band's own chartered jet, while various band members, groupies and hangers-on are caught on camera smoking, snorting and injecting a smorgasbord of illegal substances. Chief party animals Bobby Keys and Keith Richards indulge their audience with the ultimate rock-star cliché activity of throwing a television from a hotel balcony and, surrounded by staff and security, the main characters display a bulletproof contempt for conventional behaviour, akin to diplomats or travelling royalty. Though some of the wilder scenes filmed are obviously staged for maximum 'shockability,' the fact remains that the behaviour depicted had become commonplace for the Stones entourage.

Nicky Hopkins makes only fleeting appearances in the film, chatting backstage to Keith or following the rest of the band Spinal Tap-like along endless corridors in search of the stage. He is notably absent in notorious scenes such as an in-flight orgy, when two girls are passed around by the road crew, to a percussion accompaniment from some of the musicians. Onstage, Nicky's piano is tucked in behind the horn section and he can be seen, the eternal cigarette dangling from his lips, pumping out riffs during a wild medley of "Uptight" and "Satisfaction," when the Stones invite opening act Stevie Wonder and his entire band back to join them for an encore.

The on-tour atmosphere was brilliantly captured in print in Robert Greenfield's book *S.T.P., A Journey Through America with the Rolling Stones*. He described Nicky as "an arrow-thin young man, with the overlong hair and thick sideburns of a typical British rock star with a face that would be ghoulish, were it not for the kindness in his eyes," while Truman Capote, who was also initially invited to join the tour as an official observer, but didn't last the course, declared dramatically that Nicky had "the mark of death on him."

When the Stones cavalcade hit New York, Nicky's eight-year-old niece Alix had a glimpse of her famous uncle:

"I remember going to see them at the St. Regis Hotel and they were in a room with the biggest bed I'd ever seen. Dolly had four-inch sparkling platform shoes, a velvet blazer and the coolest pair of jeans I'd ever seen, with a dragon all done in sequins, wrapped around her leg like a tattoo. Nicky had his hair long, a flowery shirt and a very tight-cut velvet blazer; they looked very Biba-esque."

The fifty-show schedule was gruelling enough without the additional damage that the constant all-night partying wreaked on the wilder members of the entourage. For Nicky Hopkins, whose health was fragile at the best of times, on-tour boredom soon became a dangerous factor:

"The actual playing at night made it all worth it, although especially towards the end, I did sometimes find myself on automatic, playing the same leads and the same runs. I started smoking grass and hash, then used heroin and cocaine. I also did a lot of tranquilisers, sleeping pills, some uppers, LSD—and of course a lot of drinking."

I asked three members of the Stones what memories they had of Nicky during the legendary tour. Keith Richards rather sweetly failed to remember him being there at all:

"I was never on the road with him, and that's when you really find out about a guy (laughs); he had so many things wrong with him he shouldn't actually have been alive; it's amazing what he put up with; you didn't think about it, because when you were with him, it wasn't obvious, but you didn't feel that you'd want to put him through a whole Stones tour…"

Mick Taylor: "I don't have any memories of Nicky taking part in the general craziness that the rest of us may have got involved in. I remember seeing his stomach once and it was like a patchwork quilt."

Bill Wyman's recollections were mostly of more mundane activities: "He used to hang out in our room with Dolly, and I went and stayed with him for a weekend up in Mill Valley. He showed me his collections and we'd go out and search junk shops for old twenties or thirties newspapers, magazines and comics—and the four of us went to see the paddle steamers in New Orleans."

Greenfield's book gives by far the best account of that '72 American tour, describing in lurid detail the protagonists' gradual descent into infighting, debauchery and excess. By the last concerts at New York's Madison Square Garden, the burnt-out army was glad to be done with their mammoth run and separated to recover, considerably richer but not in the best of health. Annie Leibovitz's end-of-tour group photograph shows the entire touring party in matching football jerseys; Nicky is typically one of the only participants to shun the uniform and wear his own clothes.

Fortunately, while Robert Frank's cameras were capturing the mayhem backstage, another team was shooting concert footage. The two Texas shows filmed were by no means the best of the tour, but the succinctly named *Ladies & Gentlemen, The Rolling Stones* immortalised an unstoppable band on peak form. In a mid-eighties interview, Nicky made a wry but trenchant observation of his part in the film:

"I think you can see a left hand appearing now and again; a very minimal appearance—more in sound than vision!"

47. Backstage, 1972

48. Munich, 1974

No Expectations
The Rolling Stones – Part 3

"If you've got any ego at all, you'll never be catered to by the Rolling Stones."

– Glyn Johns

Despite his solo commitments, Nicky couldn't turn down a Stones invitation to record again, this time in Jamaica, in late November 1972. Dogged by tax problems and their previous drug busts, Keith Richards, a confirmed reggae fan, decided that the band would benefit from the vibes at the ramshackle Dynamic Sound Studios in Kingston. Nicky's passport shows him arriving in late November and leaving December 9th, returning to Jamaica on Christmas Day and back to the USA on New Year's Eve.

In a Christmas card sent to his brother Paul from England, Nicky looked back on the months since the marathon tour of America ended and obviously found

49. Postcard from Jamaica

the Caribbean and its inhabitants even less attractive than France and the French:

"I have started my first album, (first official one that is!) for U.S. Columbia and am pretty busy writing and recording it. We've been here since September, when I spent two weeks in the studio starting on my album, two weeks on George Harrison's next album, a few more bits on mine and then went to Jamaica to record with the Stones, who at present are exiled from Britain, France and the States."

He was more explicit in a particularly outspoken interview for *Rock Magazine* the following year:

"Personally I didn't like Jamaica at all. After having been to Hawaii and hearing everyone rave about how much more beautiful Jamaica is, it was a real disappointment. Kingston itself is just a slum!"

Mick Taylor, who had recently guested on Nicky's solo record, was equally unenthusiastic:

"I didn't like going to Jamaica; it was considered a nice idea to go somewhere different, soak up the atmosphere and hope that the studio and the people there would have some kind of influence on the music; but wherever the Stones went, it was always the same way of working—in fact it got worse. As the seventies progressed, things got slower and slower and slower! I used to complain about it for a few years and then I kind of accepted Charlie Watts' and Bill Wyman's philosophy that that was the way it had always been with Mick and Keith and it would always remain that way."

Rolling Stone magazine described the band as working "sundown to sunup, seven days a week," quoting insider Marshall Chess for information on the hardships of island life:

"Nobody has had any time to go sightseeing or shopping and their only relaxation has been a few late afternoons by the pool at the Terra Nova hotel. Finding something to eat has been a problem. We usually get up too late for lunch and too early for dinner and when we return from the studio, it's too early for breakfast."

The appropriately named *Goat's Head Soup* is not one of the great Rolling Stones albums. The songs are longer and lack focus, showing the effects of Keith Richards' ongoing battles with heroin and the consequent fragmentation of his writing partnership with Jagger.

Nicky Hopkins can be heard on exactly half the tracks: On the album's opener, "Dancing With Mr. D," he is almost buried in the mix, though given a little more room to shine towards the end, but with "Coming Down Again" and "Angie," Nicky makes a major contribution to two of the most elegant ballads in the entire Stones' repertoire. The former begins with a typically stately intro, the piano supporting Keith's vocal all the way through, while "Angie" achieves a perfect balance between the piano, the picked acoustic guitar and the lush strings—another Hopkins lesson in eloquent accompaniment and a performance that Chuck Leavell was later happy to adopt:

"I don't think you try to change something that has historic value. I certainly tried to learn Nicky's parts in 'Angie' and recreate them as best as possible with my own input. It's an honour to play them, and while I don't do them exactly the way Nicky did, I try to do them properly; he was the one that came up with those parts and I want to be sure that the beauty of them is carried on."

Nicky can also be heard on "Winter," and "Can You Hear The Music."

Nicky's photograph on the inner sleeve (Dominic Tarlé's shot taken at Mick's wedding in the south of France), is dwarfed by an extravagant live shot of Billy Preston, who, having popped up on just one track of *Exile*, could boast two appearances on the new record. In deference to Nicky's new status as a solo artist, his appearance is listed as "courtesy of CBS Records."

Dates for a January tour of the Far East had already been announced in October 1972. It began with a one-off charity show (with a hefty $100 ticket price) at the Los Angeles Forum, an event suggested by Mick's wife Bianca to benefit victims of the recent earthquake in Nicaragua. It's unclear whether Nicky or only Ian Stewart played the show; Nicky was in the country, but working his own album at the time.

Two shows in Honolulu were followed by an unexpected and financially damaging ten-day gap, when the Japanese government refused an entry visa to Mick Jagger, due to a 1967 marijuana offence in Britain. A Hong Kong show and six sold-out concerts at Tokyo's Budokan were cancelled and Nicky spent this forced break dashing from Hawaii back to his own mixing sessions with David Briggs at Wally Heider's. The Stones' schedule picked up again with a brief stopover in Sydney to meet TV and newspaper journalists, before a one-day visit to New Zealand.

Nicky was now established enough in the Stones camp to take part in the pre-tour press activities in Australia and be featured in band photographs. He was able to put a word in for his upcoming solo release, as well as field questions on his past clients and all things Stones related, before flying off to Auckland, where the band played for 35,000 fans. Opening with "Brown Sugar," the band played a flawless, high-energy set with Mick Taylor and Nicky the standout musicians—and with a special mention in the press for Jagger's much-photographed sequinned denim jacket. Nicky's sense of humour took a practical turn.

Bill Wyman: "When we were touring in the '70s, Nicky always used to be over on the side, often with his back to the band, so he had wing mirrors fitted on the grand piano, like on a car, so he could see what was happening. He invented it, got them set up and then showed us and we thought it was hilarious. I don't think anyone's ever done that before or since. We all used to pull faces at him."

On February 24th, 1973, Nicky spent his twenty-ninth birthday onstage in Perth. A bootleg recording reveals that after a suitable introduction from Mick, an impromptu version of "Happy Birthday" was added to the usual set-list and

Nicky received glowing reports in the local papers, one drawing attention to his "taste and delicacy throughout":

"Off to Mick's right sits an unobtrusive but musically dynamic presence: it's Nicky Hopkins, out of the spotlight, almost out of sight, but definitely not out of sound, doing

what he does best, playing brilliant and exuberant piano, adding a distinctive musicality to a group that would seem to need nothing more than their own sweet selves."

That he had now become a celebrity in his own right, was confirmed by a curious *Rolling Stone* magazine item at the time concerning a Nicky Hopkins imposter:

"...who's been making the rounds of recording studios, reserving time and ordering equipment. The charlatan keyboardist reportedly speaks in a London accent that occasionally lapses into a mid-western twang. Apparently, he has some trouble finding 'C' on a keyboard, so if anyone impersonating the Stones sessioneer and former Quicksilver Messenger Service man comes your way, ask him to reprise a lick from 'Edward The Mad Shirt Grinder.' That'll get him every time."

The ex-pat familiarity and faded colonialism of Australia obviously agreed with Nicky and he spent most of his days off shopping for collectables and curios, often accompanied by Bill Wyman. His visit down under nearly ended in disaster during the band's two-day stint in Sydney, as Nicky described in a birthday card to his brother:

"We both really liked Australia and neither of us expected to! People were nice, lots of things to see, old buildings, trains and cheap prices at antique stores. Two days before we left, we went on a boat cruise round Sydney harbour from 6pm-9pm. It was dark and raining when we got back to the dock, and who slipped between the boat and dock into the water? Ah well, could have been worse – Dolly and our bodyguard (!) caught me, so I only got my legs wet!"

He survived to fly back to the USA the day after the last show on February 27th and, after a run of U.S. radio interviews for his newly-released *The Tin Man Was A Dreamer* album, was back in London at the end of May, overdubbing tracks for *Goat's Head Soup*.

The Stones' release was supported by nearly thirty European shows in September and October, taking in the U.K., Austria, West Germany, Switzerland, Denmark, Sweden, Holland and Belgium. Nicky was suddenly no longer in the touring party and his keyboard duties were shared between Ian Stewart and opening act, Billy Preston. What was no doubt intended as a temporary absence, due to conflicts between his Stones commitments and the demands of his new solo career, in fact became permanent and Billy Preston was waiting in the wings, eager to replace him.

Preston epitomised the showbiz description "not being backward in coming forward" and went to far greater lengths than Nicky ever did to ingratiate himself into the Stones' circle, as he previously had with the Beatles.

Robin Millar: "Billy Preston was ambitious, personable, but in a more sycophantic way; he would often be at Mick or Keith's house entertaining everyone at the piano and being very 'Darling, darling' to Bianca and so on. I was probably equally intent on being engaging to that crowd, because I realised the value of being part of it; If you were a musician like Nicky, it was the best scene you could be in, because it was loose, instinctive rock'n'roll, it paid very well, you got to travel, you played to packed houses, you had a great time and there was a lot of kudos from being attached to them. You'd have to have been a fool not to have your nose put out of joint, if you saw a new kid on the block like Billy Preston, coming to steal your thunder."

Bill Wyman: "Nicky was kind of replaced by Billy. He'd still come back to do sessions with us, but we stuck with Billy because he had a more soulful thing going; there was all that disco shit going on in those days and they were getting on that bandwagon a bit with the songs."

Bobby Keys: "When I went back to working with the Stones, I wondered why they never hired Nicky to come back and I asked Keith about it; he just said that Nicky was unavailable at the time when they needed him, so they had to move on, which I always thought was a shame, because he added so much; not that Mac wasn't good or Ian Stewart or Chuck Leavell, but Nicky just had a special thing about him."

How much regret Nicky felt at the time is open to conjecture. He had his hands full with his own record contract and an abundance of top-level sessions, but having contributed so much to so many of their best records, he did feel let down by the Stones, a band that famously always rolled on, regardless of who fell by the wayside. In an interview he recorded during Joe Cocker's 1977 tour of Australia, Nicky was asked why he had left the Stones and let slip that "there would be six spotlights for the stage; 'Sorry Nicky, we haven't got one for you.'"

Mick Taylor followed soon after, to save himself from being drawn further into habits that threatened to destroy him; apart from brief guest appearances, neither of them would ever play live with the band again.

Fired up from the run of shows, the Stones went straight back into the studio, less than a month after the last date in Berlin. The band had visited Munich several times during the tour, and liked the town enough to use Musicland Studios in the Arabella Complex for their next two albums. Another important attraction was German model Uschi Obermaier, who was courted fiercely for weeks by both Mick and Keith. With Jimmy Miller also succumbing to the darker temptations of life with the Stones (soon to be followed by Andy Johns, who survived to tell the tale), the sessions for *It's Only Rock 'N' Roll* were self-produced by the two band leaders under their new moniker as the Glimmer Twins. The songwriting is showing signs of becoming formulaic and so to an extent is Nicky's piano accompaniment.

As on *Goat's Head Soup*, Nicky Hopkins plays on exactly half the ten tracks, and again seems to have been called in whenever the acoustic guitars were taken out of their cases.

The album's standout is, without doubt, the six and a half minutes of "Time Waits For No One," which combines a memorable chorus and Mick Taylor's almost Santana-like guitar riffs. Nicky takes a back seat until his dramatic, harp-like arpeggios lead into a brief but effective solo interlude, before the guitar re-enters for the last notes Mick Taylor would deliver as a member of the Rolling Stones.

In a postcard to his Mum dated March 2nd, 1974, Nicky was obviously more comfortable in a less exotic location:

"We are in Munich until Monday (4th), recording with the Stones <u>again!</u> It's certainly the nicest German city I've been to. I've taken loads of slides, bought lots of records and done a broadcast for A.F.N.[33] Also got my photo in the local Munich paper."

50. Munich

In the photos he refers to, he looks haggard and unwell, and his radio inter-

---

[33] The American Forces Network radio.

view was a listless and unfocussed affair. The picture chosen by the *Münchener Abendzeitung* shows Nicky, camera in hand, taking pictures of his perennial favourite, a passing tram.

On May 12th, Nicky's father died and he returned home for the funeral, posing for pictures with his brother and sisters in one of the rare moments they all gathered in one place. By this time he was well into the darkest period of his life, with the ruinous combination of an addiction to painkillers and excessive drinking affecting both his personal life and his working life as a musician.

51. Paul, Julia, Dee and Nicky, at their father's funeral

In the studio with the Stones, it was all change. For the upcoming *Black and Blue* album, the brass section that had helped make the early seventies tours and albums so distinctive was gone, and with Mick Taylor having announced his official departure, the December 1974 sessions served as an audition for a potential replacement. Even by Stones standards, they were unusually stressful.

Bill Wyman's diaries paint a chaotic picture of the band, already one man down, with Keith and Nicky both failing to turn up on the first night, with only Bill, Mick and Charlie present on the second night, partly due to Nicky's collapse from an accidental overdose in a hotel corridor. Keith eventually showed late on the third night and work finally began.

Producer Reinhold Mack was their engineer at Musicland:

"They had different guitarists to try out, so it was a little tense. Mick & Keith stayed in suites at the Hilton, near the Englischen Garten, while most of the lesser ranks stayed on the two hotel floors at the Arabella, with convenient service elevator access to the 1st basement floor, where the Studio was located. I remember Nicky Hopkins doing some string arrangements on an Elka synth."

With his alpha position at the keyboards now lost to Billy Preston, the sum of Nicky's contributions to the resulting album consist of a shared piano part with Jagger on "Fool To Cry" and organ on the stilted, poor man's reggae of "Cherry Oh Baby," while on "Memory Motel," Jagger inexplicably plays a poor imitation of Nicky on the piano.

Black And Blue is the first of the Stones albums on which, instead of setting an agenda for the world to follow, they adapted themselves to fit in with fashions that had little to do with their history or their talents, and everything to do with keeping up with trends. (Witness Jagger's falsetto vocals, the wahwah guitars and the spartan, bass-drum heavy mixes. Munich was, after all, the home of the "Disco Machine.") Some would argue that the quality of the Rolling Stones' output deteriorated with the disappearance of the players that accompanied their classic era, but there were many other factors that played a part. At the time, and without apparently a trace of regret, Mick Jagger gave his explanation for Nicky's departure:

"Well, he's just finished his album and he's going to go on a tour on his own. He's going to do his own thing from now on, so I guess we'll use other keyboard players. Nicky's often busy."

A glance at Nicky's seventies discography confirms that he was certainly busy enough, but though outwardly there appeared to be no hard feelings on either side, his contact with the Stones from then on was limited to occasional meetings when they found themselves in the same place at the same time. Chuck Leavell's first question to Ian Stewart when he joined the band was why Nicky wasn't still with them:

"Stu was very candid about it and said, 'Well you know, Nicky has health problems.' He said the band was very afraid that he could go out on a long tour, get ill and have to drop out—and that became a reality that Nicky acknowledged."

The backstage visit the Stones paid on Nicky's first-ever U.S. date with his own band in the summer of 1975, caught him at rock bottom, both physically and mentally.

It was a full three years later that Nicky made a well-received impromptu appearance with Bobby Keys at two Stones shows in Anaheim, on July 24th and in Oakland on 26th (Mick Jagger's birthday). The shows were described in the press as "probably ... their worst Southern California appearance in a decade," though to Nicky, "The Stones seemed the same as they always were, except they had a better sound system!"

Some Girls, recorded in Paris the same year, brought Nicky's unbroken run of appearances on Rolling Stones albums—begun in 1966—to an end. He would be credited on both of their next two records, but only on leftovers from earlier sessions. (On 1980's *Emotional Rescue* he played on both "Send It To Me" and "Indian Girl," recording his parts just before mixing took place).

Nicky Hopkins: "At the end of January (1979) I went to New York to do an album with Graham Parker, and while I was there, I ran into Mick and overdubbed on some tracks for the forthcoming Stones album. I think the ones that went onto *Tattoo You* are a lot better than the ones on *Emotional Rescue*."

The patchy *Tattoo You* would be his final credit on a regular Rolling Stones release, with Nicky evident on "Tops," (rescued from the '73 Jamaica sessions) and most probably on "No Use In Crying."

In later years, as life became more difficult for Nicky, his friends and family often wondered why the Stones had treated him so shabbily (though producer Tony Visconti mentioned in a BBC interview that Nicky's fees "rocketed" after he played with the Stones. Nicky himself remained philosophical and loyal to his erstwhile employers, when discussing his time with the band, but couldn't always disguise his disappointment that things had not worked out differently.

Nicky Hopkins (from a January 1986 interview at Lulu's Club): "We just drifted apart. It's no more than that. I'm living in L.A. and they don't record in L.A.—they're usually in Paris."

(From a July 1989 interview in Australia's *Sunday Press*): "In those days, I really felt I was at the centre of something important. The music was exciting and it was nice to be part of the band and still be anonymous. I remember walking down a street in Los Angeles with Mick Jagger and he was yelled at by all these rednecks driving past. I suppose it was understandable because he was wearing bright yellow pants and carrying a handbag!"

Freda Hopkins: "I used to get so cross with them because they didn't realise his worth. He should have got a lot more money, but they were so mean, and Nicky, I think, didn't ask. He was very retiring—that used to annoy me. He didn't really put himself forward enough. He talked about it occasionally and didn't bear them any malice, but he was upset about it. He said, 'I would like to have joined the Stones.'"

One musician, who chose to remain nameless, voiced rumours that had always surrounded the Stones camp:

"You know he was rather embittered at that whole experience. The Stones would throw studio parties and invite the best musicians they could, and anything you could imagine would be present. At a certain point they'd be jamming and Mick Jagger would give a signal to the engineers to start recording. These parties could last for days and then, when everyone was exhausted, Mick and Keith would disappear with the tapes and they would re-surface later as Jagger/Richards compositions.

"Keith knew that things Nicky had come up with on the piano were the chord progressions to some of their hits and that they should have compensated him somehow, or at least acknowledged him. It did give him that notoriety, but he also felt that he had been used and that they were using other musicians to fuel their songwriting machine. The idea was, 'Well, you got to hang out with us, man! That's your payment,' and maybe for everyone else that was great, but I think Nicky had too much class for that. 'Well you guys got to hang out with me too!'"

Nicky stayed more closely in touch with some members of the band than others and there were occasional Hopkins sightings at the Stones' live gigs. In an interview with Stuart Colman in May 1981, he mentioned a low-key session with Ian Stewart's boogie side-project Rocket 88 at the Pied Bull in London's Islington:

"It's the first time I've sat in with a band for ages; it was packed solid and I haven't sweated so much on stage for years. It was George Green, Bob Hall and Stu playing piano and I sat in for two numbers. I didn't even know if I'd remember how to play that stuff but it all came back."

There were studio opportunities too. Bill Wyman called in Nicky's talents on a number of occasions: in 1969, for his production of The End's *Introspection* album; in the mid-seventies for his solo album *Stone Alone* and in the late eighties for an all-star charity concert in Southampton, in aid of the Kampuchea appeal. After Wyman left the Stones, in his new role as band-leader of the Rhythm Kings, he cut five blues songs in one afternoon with Nicky and Andy Fairweather-Low, at least two of which ended up released as bonus tracks on a compilation CD.

Nicky played just once for Mick Taylor's replacement Ron Wood, on his album *1234* in 1981, probably the most chaotic solo project of Ronnie's career. In his autobiography *All The Rage*, "the other keyboard player," Ian McLagan, recalled the sessions at Ronnie's Mandeville Canyon home in Los Angeles as "a waste of great talent," with Woody and Mac making repeated visits to the bathroom for another hit on the freebase pipe while Charlie Watts and Nicky Hopkins waited patiently in the makeshift studio. Producer Andy Johns had the unenviable task of turning the resulting music, recorded in a bathroom and a garage, into a finished record. Nicky's contract agreement with Ronnie reveals that he at least came out of the experience $7,000 better off.

Ian McLagan: "It wasn't good, but Nicky played so beautiful, and it was the only time I actually recorded with him at the same time, playing B3 to his piano."

Chuck Leavell first had a piano player's get-together in the early '80s:

"I grew up in Tuscaloosa, Alabama and started my useful career playing in small bands. It seemed like every time I heard something that caught my ear, or that I thought was really cool, I'd go to the record store, look at the credits and Nicky's name was on it. I thought, 'God, who is this guy?'"

"We played Wembley Stadium and Ronnie Wood came up to me and said, 'Nicky Hopkins is here. Do you want to meet him?' and I was like, 'God, I don't know if I could survive that,' because he was just a hero to me.

"Ronnie introduced us and I did the 'I am not worthy' thing, and we instantly hit it off and became friends. Within a day or two, he called me and the two of us had lunch; he reminisced about his experiences with the Stones and I told him what was going on at that point in time and we shared some stories.

"Nicky and I stayed in touch, writing letters in the old fashioned way, before e-mail and all that. He always seemed to me an upbeat person. He was facing challenges as a great musician trying to do well, which I'm sure he did, but not to the degree that he would have liked or that I think he deserved. He was such a brilliant player."

Bobby Keys would play with Nicky in a number of different situations over the ensuing years and in 1994 was surprised to find Nicky in Tennessee:

"I ran into him in a bookstore here in Nashville and I couldn't believe my eyes. We were on Elliston Place and I said, 'Hey, is that you?' We found out we were both living here and we played a little bit together, with another fellow from Oklahoma, Jimmy Markham and some guys from round here."

Mick Taylor also stayed in contact and as two ex-pats in Los Angeles, later brought Nicky into a promising band project:

"I was putting a three-piece together with (drummer) Bruce Gary, and a bass player called James Jamerson Jnr. It sounded really good, so we thought we'd add keyboards and have Blondie Chaplin do a bit of singing, plus he writes songs, to do some local stuff in and around Los Angeles. Nicky played keyboards, but we only ever did one gig, somewhere in Hollywood. Why it didn't go any further, I don't know.

"We put together another band for a gig in Florida as well, with Nicky and Bobby Keys; it was some promoter's idea to book us for three nights at a place called Charcoals."

With the band billed as the "Tumbling Dice," these shows, in Kendall, Florida, commenced April 29th, 1992 (the same day that Rodney King's beating by the L.A.P.D. led to city-wide riots in Los Angeles) and were preserved on a bootleg recording, revealing a set-list that showcased each musician's most famous recordings ("Hideaway" for Taylor, "Mercy, Mercy, Mercy" for Bobby Keys, the inevitable "Edward" for Nicky, and with a dip into their collective past with the Rolling Stones for "You Gotta Move" and "Can't You Hear Me Knocking").

'92.4.29/5.1/5.2   Florida Three Gigs

Rolling Stones

TUMBLING DICE
Mick Taylor
Bobby Keys   Nicky Hopkins

These brief groupings did not do much more than help pay the rent, and Nicky's second wife Moira and his sister both remembered him, later in his life, contacting the Stones office to suggest that he might rejoin them for an upcoming tour.

Dee Hopkins: "He desperately wanted to. He loved the Stones. He enjoyed being with them, playing with them and, even though he was straight as a die at that point, evidently there was a big discussion about it and the office got back to him and said, 'The boys say it would be terrible if something happened while you were on tour. We don't think you're really strong enough to do this.' He was heartbroken."

Moira also remembered a backstage meeting when Charlie Watts asked Nicky if he was doing all right, at a time when finances and health issues were both far from their best. Though a cash transfer would have helped his situation immeasurably, Nicky was too proud to ask for help. When he was hit by yet another life-threatening medical crisis in 1993, with crippling American hospital fees requiring immediate settlement, the Rolling Stones management redeemed itself and discreetly paid the most urgent bills on Nicky's behalf.

It was obvious from my conversations with the various group members that there was enormous affection for their ex-keyboard player and that they all held Nicky in high esteem. The Rolling Stones brand is nevertheless a steamroller that never stops, and no one has time or energy to spend on those not immediately necessary to the band's survival and ongoing interests.

To his considerable annoyance, Nicky was dogged for the rest of his life by fans wanting to know "what Mick Jagger is *really* like" and other Stones-related revelations. Moira remembered one backstage situation when Nicky declared that the next person to ask him a question about Mick, would be set on fire. Sure enough, a candidate arrived, and he took out his lighter and set fire to the unsuspecting man's coat!

When Nicky died, the Rolling Stones were in the middle of another mammoth trawl through the USA, on their *Voodoo Lounge* tour and played the following day in Raleigh, North Carolina. Moira received flowers from the Stones' office, with a sympathy note attached:

> "*To Diamond Tiaras. A good friend, sadly missed.*"
> – The Rolling Stones, Mick, Keith, Charlie, Ronnie and Bill.

There were also individual messages from the four full members of the band:

> "*Nicky was a quirky and original piano player, whose trills and runs rolled like the sea and sparkled like 'Diamond Tiaras.' He faced the world with all its ups and downs with his own sense of humour, which shone through his playing and he will be sorely missed by all his friends.*"
> – Mick & Jerry Jagger

"The most difficult of times – words run out. Nicky was a very rare guy –
all that heart, – all that talent. Another goodbye to another good friend –
I'm so sorry. Everytime we play a song that Nicky played on, we all look at
each other and give it a bit more – Condolences."

– Keith & Patti Richards

"I've known and loved Nicky as a person and a musician since we were
both young boys in London. Over the years we've played some long songs
together, (the prettiest piano player I've had the pleasure to accompany),
and now no more, only memories. We'll all miss him."

– Charlie & Shirley Watts

"Nicky will be sorely missed – he was a true treasure…but now it's you
who must be strong. He fought illness the majority of his life and did fantastically well to survive as long as he did. Please don't worry about anything.
We are all here to help you and his surviving loved ones. We will miss
Nicky – God bless him. Once again, be strong – we love you."

– Ronnie & Jo Wood

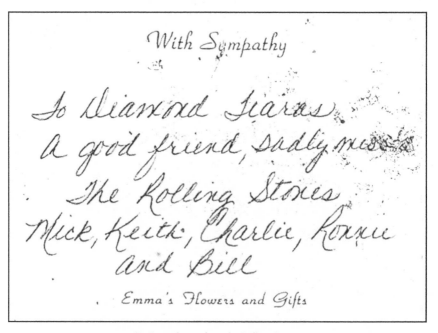

52. Funeral note from the Rolling Stones

Chuck Leavell sent a note for Nashville resident Bobby Keys to read out loud at the funeral:

> "I loved Nicky's playing so much and I cherished the fact that he cared to return my letters and stay in communication with me. Oftentimes, when I'm hired to play a session for artist X, Y or Z and somebody counts the song off, it pops right into my head: 'What would Nicky play?' I'm not ashamed of that in the least."

The sentiments expressed were no doubt genuine and heartfelt, but did not hold up for long in the pressured lifestyles of the Rolling Stones. The next time Moira Hopkins called the band's office to arrange for a backstage pass to a Rolling Stones show, a voice at the end of the 'phone told her that 'those days are over.' She still attended, but not only did she not meet up with the band, she even had to buy her ticket to see the show!

"It's Only Rock'n'Roll…"

Revolution
The Beatles – Individually & Collectively

"John loved Nicky – this part I know! The things he did on 'Imagine' – I mean that's pure Nicky Hopkins."

– Bobby Keys

With his constant visits to Abbey Road in the mid-sixties, Nicky Hopkins must have had at least a nodding acquaintance with the four Beatles. Paul McCartney certainly met him as occasional producer of his brother Mike's group The Scaffold, but Nicky didn't join the exalted ranks of those actually invited to

record with the Fabs until 1968, when he played the perfectly formed solo on John Lennon's song "Revolution," the B-side of "Hey Jude."

Why it took the group such a long time to utilise his talents is open to guesswork. Previous keyboard parts had been played either by the Beatles themselves or by producer George Martin; seeing Nicky working at first hand with the Rolling Stones seems to have prompted the decision.

In an interview for the Westwood One Radio Series *The Lost Lennon Tapes*, Nicky recalled that first meeting:

"Paul and John came to the studio to sing background vocals[34]—the first time I met John—and this led to being invited to play on 'Revolution' the following year. There were rumours of the two bands not getting along too well; it didn't

---

[34] The two Beatles sang on "We Love You" and "Sing This All Together" from *Their Satanic Majesties Request*

exist, in fact it was totally the opposite, with Paul and John coming down to help out their mates."

Lennon had supervised the recording of a more up-tempo version of his song in hopes of persuading his band mates that it should be a single in its own right. The extreme distortion on Lennon's electric guitar, achieved by plugging the instrument directly into the mixing desk, initially caused considerable furore among the powers-that-be at Abbey Road. The Beatles had left a hole in the arrangement for an as yet unidentified instrumental. Having decided it should be piano and that Nicky Hopkins should play it, EMI's in-house booker, Laurie Gold, called him for the afternoon of July 11th. Nicky was sufficiently used to the company of superstars to be unfazed by the Beatles and got the job done in a short time and with minimal fuss, uncharacteristically using a Wurlitzer electric piano.

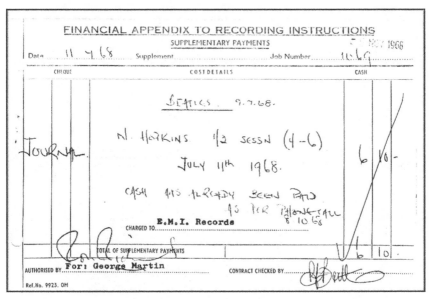

53. Nicky's paystub for the "Revolution" session

Nicky Hopkins: "There weren't really any instructions, except where they wanted the piano to start and I basically just played some blues stuff and we did it in one take. I'd have preferred to do it again, but they were fine with that. I remember I was surprised at the amount of distortion; it was John's rough side coming out and it sounded wonderful. I quickly got tuned into hearing it that way and it still holds up great—a wonderful record!"

For his small part in Beatles history, Nicky was paid a standard sixties session fee of exactly six pounds and ten shillings, as noted in an EMI accounts memo from November that year. Meanwhile the single was distinguished by being the first release on the newly formed Apple Records and quickly went to Number One on both sides of the Atlantic when it hit the shops at the end of August.

In an unfortunate postscript, Beatle fans all over the world were incensed when "Revolution," one of the flagship protest songs of the sixties, was given to Nike in 1987, with full approval from Yoko Ono, for use in a running shoe commercial. In 1994, Nicky noted ruefully to Nashville journalist Peter Rodman: "I think somebody's finally sending me a gold record for that one—about 25 years late."

Though the financial rewards may not have been life-changing and his brief appearance would remain his only real session on a Beatles record,[35] it gave him immense kudos and led to numerous sessions with all four individual Beatles, on their own and other peoples' productions, after their break-up.

Years later, he asked Lennon why, during the group's heyday, he'd only ever had the one call; John replied, "We just thought you were too busy, with the Rolling Stones and all."

With their own label to play with, all four Beatles dove in a flurry of recording activity. George Harrison was first to call Nicky, inviting him to join an all-star cast at Trident Studios later in 1968, with Ringo on drums, Paul on bass, and both George and Eric Clapton playing guitar, for George's first Apple production with their old Liverpool and Hamburg crony Jackie Lomax. *Is This What You Want?* was one of the first gatherings of the elite group of musicians that would, in various combinations, grace some of the best albums of the era. Nicky Hopkins is unmistakeable on George's own song "Sour Milk Sea."

It was unfortunate timing that no sooner had Nicky made the Beatles' acquaintance, than he left London to tour with Jeff Beck and subsequently disappeared to California. When he eventually resurfaced, after his stint with Quicksilver Messenger Service, the Beatles as a group were already in the ground, with the somewhat lacklustre *Let It Be* as a headstone. Nicky missed out on all their first solo releases, but John Lennon booked his services in early June 1971, for his one-off project, the Elastic Oz Band, whose only single, "God Save Us" / "Do The Oz," he produced in support of the beleaguered Oz magazine's obscenity trial fund.

Though seldom mentioned in discographies and despite conflicting reports of its genesis—British journalist Charles Shaar Murray, who reputedly played acoustic guitar on the record, swore he remembered a keyboard player named Diane at the sessions—it is undoubtedly Nicky's signature piano licks on both sides of the single, with Bill Elliott (later signed to Apple as half of Splinter) on the A-side, while John is unmistakable on the flip.

Billy Preston, who joined the Beatles for their last performance on the roof above the Apple offices, had played the only guest piano on Lennon's raw debut

---

[35] Rumours that he also appeared on "Ob-La-Di, Ob-La-Da" are unfounded, though he can claim a presence on the *The Beatles*—aka the "White Album"—due to the inclusion of a few seconds of piano at the beginning of the surreal "Revolution No. 9"

album, *Plastic Ono Band*. But it was Nicky who was called to John's Tittenhurst Park home in Ascot[36], the third week of June 1971 to join the select group of players he had chosen to record what would become his best-loved and most iconic album, *Imagine*.

Bassist Klaus Voormann described Tittenhurst as a particularly conducive place to work; though the rooms were far from large and the constant stream of visitors sometimes distracting, the rolling gardens with their exotic trees and plants and the "Zen-like" vibe in the house itself, made recording mostly a pleasure. The sessions, which usually began around midday and ended in the evenings, got later and later as the days went by, with downtime often spent round the kitchen table, where the family atmosphere of tea breaks, jokes and communal meals visibly helped John relax.

Nicky had already, by any standards, had an intense year. His passport confirms that he left the UK on June 10th to spend two weeks at home in Mill Valley and did not return until June 28th, when he and Dolly joined George Harrison, Voormann and the other musicians. In an e-mail from Arkansas, his ex-wife Dolly set the scene from her perspective (though confusing the exact dates, as Nicky didn't leave to record with the Stones in France until after the *Imagine* sessions):

"Yoko disliked him. She said that 'his numbers are wrong' and that 'he's water under the bridge,' but Lennon loved Nicky's playing. He had been trying to reach Nicky for a long time before they finally connected, because he wanted him to tour with the Plastic Ono Band, but we were at Keith's house in the south of France and Nicky never got the messages John said he left for him. Nicky was pissed!

"On one of the breaks from recording *Exile*, Nicky finally got in touch with John and we went to see him in Ascot. Yoko pretty much dominated that whole meeting, as she did everything else to do with John's life and music. John wanted Nicky to play the acoustic piano on the song 'Imagine,' but she said NO, so he ended up playing electric instead. She handed out sheet music for the musicians to follow and, needless to say, Nicky, George, Klaus and the rest said a few choice words about that. I went off to play pool with John's bodyguard. I know there was a lot of discord and tension during all John's sessions because of Yoko's dominance. Whether anyone likes to hear it or not, the fact is Yoko ran John!"

The more reticent Klaus Voormann had no such outspoken comments to offer and managed to avoid mentioning Nicky at all in his autobiography. When prompted, he did remember Nicky giving between-takes renditions of "The Teddy Bears' Picnic" during the recordings. Bobby Keys was less tight-lipped and apparently equally unpopular with certain parties:

---

[36] John's in-home recording studio at Tittenhurst is generally referred to as "Ascot Sound Studios."

"I was living in the property adjacent to John and Yoko's out in Ascot. At this time Yoko was very much against drugs and she was really keeping him isolated. I would sneak over to John's house with a little hash or something every now and again and have a smoke. Yoko never caught us, but she knew something was afoot and she didn't like me one little bit. Yoko was not fun to be around, but John loved Nicky—this part I know! He really respected his musicianship; the things he did on *Imagine* man, I mean that's pure Nicky Hopkins.'

John and Yoko's personal assistant May Pang attended many of Lennon's recordings and summed up his attitude in the studio:

"John gave his musicians free rein, but if he didn't like something, he definitely would tell you; he would give them a chord and let them choose how they wanted to build from it: 'This is how the song goes. Go for it!' But if John felt strongly about something, that wall came down and what Yoko said was out."

In his German autobiography, Klaus Voormann, who shared so many sessions with Nicky Hopkins, gave insight into the pitfalls of being sideman to a superstar:

"Sometimes he (John) gave me the feeling that he owned me, as if I was sitting home waiting for him to need me. Of course it wasn't like that, because I had to make a living like everyone else. The Plastic Ono Band wasn't a typical group with equal partners, with everyone getting his share. It was John and Yoko's band and the remaining musicians were paid wages for gigs and sessions just like any other players. I couldn't live off that, so I had to finance my then 'not too shabby' lifestyle by other means. Outsiders have a false impression, thinking that anyone taking part in these legendary songs and concerts must be swimming in money like the stars. Quite wrong!"

Luckily for future fans, the Lennons decided to have the *Imagine* sessions filmed for posterity, and in the 1999 documentary *Gimme Some Truth* we are granted an insider's view of the informal atmosphere, as work on the album progressed. While the two ex-Beatles and Phil Spector are obviously comfortable with the presence of the cameras, others, particularly Nicky Hopkins, appear extremely uneasy at the intrusion into their private world.

The film opens with John teaching "Imagine" to Nicky and discussing whether to play the song four handed at one piano, or on two instruments. It is Voormann who first suggests that John should move to the familiar white grand piano. Dolly Hopkins perches next to her husband on a sofa in the background. Every step of the proceedings is enveloped in a cloud of cigarette smoke, with almost all the participants puffing away constantly.

After various attempts at accompanying John on the title song, once playing a full octave above, in the end Nicky only provides subliminal echoes of John's piano on the final version that opens side one of the album. By contrast he is out front and in full honky-tonk mode for the deceptively sprightly "Crippled Inside," with Lennon's cry of "Take it, cousin!" leading into Nicky's excellent solo.

"Jealous Guy," which follows, may be the high point of the album and is certainly one of Nicky's finest performances. His majestic introduction sets the mood perfectly and the sensitivity of his accompaniment underpins but never overwhelms the vulnerability of Lennon's lyrics and vocal—a masterpiece!

The mood shifts briefly for the gentle "Oh My Love," until 'How Do You Sleep', the album's most controversial track, shatters the peaceful moment. *Oz* magazine's Felix Dennis visited during the sessions and remembers some of the musicians being extremely uneasy with the song's bitter lyrics, though John and Yoko, who co-authored it, seem to have taken a childish delight in their provocative diatribe.

In another sequence from the film, Nicky takes his place at the electric piano again for the vitriolic hate message to McCartney (referred to by John as "the nasty one"), and Lennon smirks like a mischievous schoolboy as he unveils the lyrics to George Harrison. As he shows the chords to Nicky, he says he hears the sound of BB King's "The Thrill Is Gone" in his head. Basic tracks go down with the musicians playing together behind Lennon's excellent and often improvised guide vocal: "How do you sleep, yer cunt!"

Yoko is a constant presence throughout and is not shy of offering her opinions, not just to John, but also to the engineers, to a surprisingly patient Phil Spector and especially to the musicians. One promising take is halted when Yoko whispers her dissatisfaction to her husband, who responds immediately, telling the band it is too loose, to stop improvising and to "keep it solid." Nicky works hard to hide his disgruntled expression as Yoko, the self-proclaimed arbiter of good taste, takes him to task at his own instrument.

Early out-takes of "How Do You Sleep" illustrate the collaborative work methods favoured by the ex-Beatle, with the song developing with every pass and the heavy reggae-ish riff that characterises the choruses growing in intensity as the musicians pick up on one another. Lennon demonstrates on guitar the way he hears the accents and, after discussions with Spector in the control room, instructs everybody to do it, as well as suggesting a fade-out over Nicky's piano solo. The input from the players is evident throughout, with different solos from George and Nicky each time and the track coming together after a few takes to its final familiar version.

"How Do You Sleep" again lists two pianos, with Nicky's role purely supportive. The album finishes with the bouncy "Oh Yoko," where, apart from Lennon's brief bursts of Dylanesque harmonica, Nicky's piano is the only soloing instrument over a bed of strummed acoustic guitars.

Whatever circumstances led to its creation, the music on *Imagine* is undeniably strong and Nicky contributed hugely, with all his various skills, to the finished product. His piano parts and Harrison's distinctive slide guitar, over the simple, dry bass lines of the underrated Voormann, are the bedrock of the album's sound—and all recorded in a week.

Nicky's personal copy of the LP has a typically neat, handwritten list of the musician credits on the back of the poster that came with the album, with his own contributions highlighted proudly in red. The small matter of being paid for the sessions was overlooked at the time.

After such a positive studio experience, Lennon's plans for a first solo tour were announced in the press. His only post-Beatles live moments had been when he and Yoko flew over to Canada for the impromptu and almost totally unrehearsed performance immortalised on the album *Live Peace In Toronto* in September 1969, with a scratch band consisting of Eric Clapton, drummer Alan White (who reappeared on much of *Imagine*) and Klaus Voormann, and three months later at the all-star Unicef "Peace For Christmas" concert at the London Lyceum. Now Nicky Hopkins became part of the projected touring line-up.

In a letter to Eric Clapton in September '71, John and Yoko outlined their Utopian ideas for the Plastic Ono Band, "a circus-cum-carnival with street theatre and local groups taking part" and invited the troubled guitarist to join the enterprise.

"Dear Eric & the Missus,
...after missing the Bangla-Desh concert, we began to feel more and more like going on the road, but not the way I used to with the Beatles – night after night of torture. We mean to enjoy ourselves...
We've asked Klaus, Jim Keltner, Nicky Hopkins – Phil Spector even (!) to form a nucleus group. They all agreed so far and of course we had YOU!!! In mind as soon as we decided.
In the past when Nicky was working around (Stones etc.), bringing your girl/woman/wife was frowned on – with us it's the opposite. Nicky's missus will also come with us – on stage if she wants (Yoko has ideas for her!) or backstage. Our uppermost concern is to have a happy group in body and mind. No one will be held to any contract of any sort.
I consider Jim, Nicky, Phil, Yoko, you could make the kind of sound that could bring back the Balls in rock'n'roll...We can change the world – and have a ball at the same time.
Lots of love to you both from,
John & Yoko'

With Rolling Stones and Harrison commitments looming, as well as nascent plans for his solo outing, Nicky was torn in his loyalties, but luckily found Lennon an understanding employer. The much heralded touring plans never came to fruition.

May Pang: "John was very understanding. He'd say, 'Oh, what a shame, you can't make it? OK'; he'd understand; he was a musician—but everybody made efforts to shift their commitments to other people to be with John."

Nicky Hopkins told *Melody Maker*: "I get along very well with Lennon. John is egotistical to some extent but he's a very honest cat. I told him that if dates started to clash next year, I would have to drop all the other things and work with George and he understood that perfectly. George was in New York when we went there to do Lennon's new single. He played some new songs for us for about two or three hours and they were really incredible."

The single referred to was "Happy Christmas (War Is Over)" (backed with

"Listen, The Snow Is Falling" on the 45) for which—with Christmas specialist Phil Spector still at the helm—John and Yoko reconvened almost all the *Imagine* team at the Record Plant in New York in late October, with the brilliant Jim Keltner on drums.

After his usual piano duties, Nicky added seasonal percussion on chimes and glockenspiel, while Keltner jangled on the inevitable sleigh bells. Work on the A-side was completed quickly and painlessly but a reporter from *Creem* magazine witnessed the more troubled genesis of Yoko Ono's B-side:

Conspicuous by his absence...

"Yoko is telling Nicky to play lighter on the intro: 'Pretend that it's snowing…that snow is melting on your fingertips. Not that banging!' Nicky gets it just right the next time…Klaus and Yoko are into a shouting match about where the chords go at the end of the song. Klaus gets up, unstraps his bass and appears ready to walk out, but John placates both of them and they try it again successfully.

"As (the engineers) are working, Nicky, Hugh and Keltner start playing a blues. 'Oh-oh,' says Phil, 'They've started jamming…let's put a stop to *that*.' He moves to the connecting door, but Yoko pre-empts him. 'STOP JAMMING!' she screams, almost bursting the speakers. As one man, the musicians stop in mid eight-note. Yoko is obviously more than a little tense and confides that she believes the musicians don't take her songs as seriously as she'd like."

May Pang recalled that Nicky was mostly first to leave, seldom staying longer than necessary and, unlike some of his colleagues, almost never hanging around in John's shadow:

"Dolly and Nicky were always off in their own world. Jim hung around us a lot and so did Jesse, but Nicky—not at all. John was always concerned for his health. He loved Nicky and one time, when he couldn't open the studio door, John leapt up and said, 'Let me open it for you, Nicky.'"

Despite his insane schedule, Nicky found his way onto the inseparable John and Yoko's next release, the politically charged (if musically questionable) *Some Time In New York City*. His contribution consisted of an electric piano overdub, to replace Billy Preston's organ part on the raunchy "live from the Lyceum" version of "Cold Turkey," which had somehow been lost between the recording of the show and the mix-down. Nicky solos over the grinding guitars in the song's instrumental

173

part and is left riffing over an interminable fade-out, pulling out every trick in his book, while Lennon howls and moans at the microphone.

His participation in the Yoko Ono screamfest, "Don't Worry Kyoko," that follows, appears to be limited to joining in with the lengthy tune-up at the beginning. He is rewarded with a credit on the sleeve, among a list of unlikely schoolboy-ish pseudonyms, as "Sticky Topkins."

By the time John was ready to start his next opus, *Mind Games*, Nicky was knee-deep in his own album plans and other clients' demands. Until he began working with George, the nearest to the Beatles he came was in March 1972, when he recorded the wildly eclectic and eccentric *Son Of Schmilsson*, at London's Trident Studios, with Fabs' favourite Harry Nilsson. Producer Richard Perry's usual assembly of star sessioneers included Peter Frampton and the ill-disguised drummer "Richie Snare" and guitarist "George Harrysong."

These sessions were filmed for a feature on the reclusive Nilsson, who had never played live, but the project never made it to theatres and only became visible when, years later, a fan put the footage up on the internet—a grainy black

and white glimpse into a twilight world of booze and excess, with Nicky, as ever, sitting impassively at his piano.

Peter Frampton: "He and I hit it off instantly. You gravitated towards Nicky because he was a very bright, sensitive man and you could tell by his playing that his heart was enormous. Harry stayed pretty loose and had us in hysterics all the time."

Nilsson was another favourite among Nicky's many clients and his performance on "Remember Christmas," alone at the piano, apart from a bouzouki and string quartet, is as popular with Nilsson devotees as "You Are So Beautiful" would be for Joe Cocker fans.

In 1974, after extensive touring with the Stones, Nicky was back in Manhattan with Lennon, to record *Walls And Bridges* with the rhythm section of Voormann and Jim Keltner, percussionist Arthur Jenkins, a full horn section led by Bobby Keys, Jesse Ed Davis taking George Harrison's place on guitar, and Ken Ascher, who specialised in orchestration and arrangement, as second keyboard player.

Rehearsals began on July 13th, in a large upstate New York house rented for the purpose by John, followed by a civilised and highly disciplined five-day week at the Record Plant: noon to 10pm daily, with weekends off. John was focussed entirely on the work in hand, gave short shrift to latecomers and was adamant that the sessions remain free from drugs or drink.

May Pang: "John's work ethic was amazing. One time I think Jim Keltner was late; he overslept and John was furious. He'd called a seven o'clock session and you can't start without the drummer. He had been out having a late night and John doesn't take that very lightly. Jim apologised profusely and it never happened again. When John went into the studio he wanted to get the work done."

Coming immediately after John's famous "lost weekend," when he separated from Yoko and spent months carousing in Los Angeles with Nilsson, Ringo and Keith Moon, the temperance regime at the sessions is understandable, but, as May Pang pointed out, for someone who the press insisted had spent months in a permanent haze of alcohol and drugs, Lennon managed to produce some fine music and release several different albums during his "lost" period.

On its release *Walls And Bridges* was rightly greeted as a return to form. Nicky is present on eight of the twelve tracks (Elton John taking the keyboard honours on the Number One single "Whatever Gets You Thru The Night"), though his role is far less prominent than on *Imagine*. The piano is lower in the mix, often drowned out by strings and horns and mostly functions as part of the band rather than as a soloist.

His workmanlike but unspectacular performances would be Nicky's last sessions for Lennon. His absence on *Pussy Cats*, John's L.A. production for Harry Nilsson, and on the sessions for *Rock 'N' Roll* (released a year after *Walls And Bridges*, though recorded mostly before it), was almost certainly down to a conflict of schedules.

Nicky may have crossed paths with John in California when Lennon helped out on Ringo's *Goodnight Vienna*, soon after his own sessions in New York were done, but the reason Nicky never worked with Lennon again was that, as far as the outside world was concerned, at this point John Lennon ceased working. He had reunited with Yoko after his year and a half of enforced bachelorhood, and following the birth of his second son Sean, he entered his period of reclusive domestic bliss at home in the Dakota building.

Nicky mentioned more than once in interviews that he wished he could work with John again, but all such hopes were dashed when Lennon was shot, just two days after giving that interview. Nicky was one of the celebrities asked to comment by CBS News the following day, and he seemed to display a coolly unemotional response:

"Unlike most people, I believed it as soon as I heard it; anything that definite, it just seemed that it was so and it was very sad and everything. It really increases my dislike for living in the States a lot."

Of all the solo Beatles, Nicky's greatest affinity was with George Harrison, with whom, however, he did comparatively little work. Having been, in his own words, "the only man in England who didn't play on *All Things Must Pass*," working closely together on Lennon's music in '71 reminded Harrison of his talents. He wasted no time in involving Nicky in some tracks he was producing for Badfinger (two of whom had played rhythm guitars on *Imagine*), and in discussing future projects of his own. Nicky particularly loved working with "the quiet Beatle":

"The first time I met him it was like meeting my brother. Our birthdays are very close—his is February 23rd and mine's the 24th—that might explain it. We seem to understand each other on a personal level."

In late 1972, Nicky was down in Apple's basement studios, to record the follow-up to George's immensely successful triple album and working back to back with sessions for his own album, *The Tin Man Was A Dreamer*. Peter Frampton, a regular studio guest of both men, described Nicky at the piano:

"He was a smoking fiend; you always knew when Nicky was on a session, because even if there were no musicians in the room, all you had to do was look on top of the piano; it's a flat surface where the music stand is; he would light up a cigarette and they would say, 'OK, let's do a take,' so he'd put it end up, balance it and, if the take was not a long one, he'd have a cigarette to finish; by the end of the session (laughs), there were so many butts that had gone out, propped up on top of the piano and they just stayed there. No one would touch them—it was, well—Nicky!"

Percussionist Ray Cooper also fondly remembered the gravity-defying cigarette ends:

"They never fell over! He would sometimes be playing the piano and this ash would get longer and longer and it's distracting you; you're playing, but you can't help but watch and finally, normally at the end of the song, it would go 'pop' onto his lap; skyscrapers at various stages..."

The early seventies were an incestuous time for the select "A" team of players, who would find themselves, again and again, working in the world's top studios, on projects involving one or another of the ex-Beatles. Musical skills were occasionally bartered in kind rather than with money changing hands. For Nicky, it was the "golden age" in his career.

Peter Frampton: "I met him on *Son Of Schmilsson* and that was my entrée to the small clique of people who seemed to turn up on high-priority sessions; I was

just a single scale session guy and I remember that the session fee went up with the price of hashish. If it was fifteen pounds for a lump that was the session fee; if it was sixteen or seventeen-fifty it went up—there always seemed to be a link."

Nicky began a mutually beneficial relationship with George Harrison (involving musical exchange rather than hashish), with George adding commercial clout to Nicky's solo project and Nicky enhancing *Living In The Material World*.

After his Spector-produced breakthrough album, *All Things Must Pass,* and his headline-grabbing charity Concert for Bangladesh in August 1971, Harrison was on a confident high when he returned to the studio. Most of his songs reflected his spiritual beliefs and though the lyrics are sometimes heavy-handed, the music has a delightful clarity and lightness of touch, with characteristic Harrison chord sequences and gorgeous melodies.

The album's hit single "Give Me Love (Give Me Peace On Earth)" epitomises all that is best about George Harrison's music: the harmony slide guitar sound that he made his own, unusual timing in the vocal and a great tune. Nicky's descending piano part carries the song's bridge section. Nicky plays acoustic piano throughout the record and parts of *Living In The Material World* sound almost more Lennon than Harrison—not surprising, since it is almost the same band as on *Imagine*.

The fold-out cover depicts the key players outdoors with George at a "Last Supper" sized table, groaning with wine, champagne, fruit and food, while in the background a nanny and chauffeur stand in front of Harrison's imposing house,

with luxury cars parked in the driveway. The 2006 re-release of the album includes a set of pictures that eloquently conveys the atmosphere of camaraderie that made the music sound so effortless. George is resplendent in dog collar, bishop's hat and dark glasses, cracking open a bottle of champagne, while the musicians look on in various fancy dress outfits. Nicky looks characteristically uncomfortable, his skinny frame draped in someone else's outsize coat, though one picture captures him in a more relaxed pose, camera in hand sitting cross-legged on the lawn.

On its US release in May 1973, the album joined the single at number one but came in for mixed reviews. In September, *Circus* magazine in the States gave it almost unqualified approval:

"Nicky Hopkins, Gary Wright, Klaus Voormann etc. all help to make a tight, highly pleasing, sometimes slick set. The single has done remarkably well. Use it as a measuring stick for the rest of the album…it's all of equally high calibre."

In the UK a more cynical *NME* writer pronounced it "so damn holy I could scream."

Nicky Hopkins was one of a few westerners invited by George to take part in a production for Ravi Shankar and his family of musicians, released in 1974 on his own Dark Horse label. *Shankar Family & Friends* was recorded in three days at A&M studios in Los Angeles and can best be described as a well-intentioned but ultimately pointless experiment, with awkward English lyrics making for an uneasy clash of cultures. Nicky only appears on the opening track "I Am Missing You."

If *All Things Must Pass* had been his high point and *Living In The Material World* a worthy and still successful follow-up, George Harrison's muse seems to have steadily abandoned him, as he became increasingly more involved in other areas of his life. He carried on making solo albums throughout the seventies, though with diminishing returns both in artistic terms and in sales. Nicky is credited on both his next releases, but only for one track on each.

He can be heard on 1974's *Dark Horse*, largely recorded at George's home studio, Friar Park Studios Henley-On-Thames (FPSHOT), on the song "So Sad," a leftover from the *Material World* sessions. Despite Harrison's twelve-string acoustic and the double drums of Ringo Starr and Jim Keltner, the track never quite catches fire.

Extra Texture, which hit the shops the following year, was an even weaker album and Nicky's one contribution, to the lacklustre "Can't Stop Thinking About You," is sadly his last appearance on a George Harrison recording.

From the moment they split up, any collaboration involving the ex-Beatles, whether on stage or in the studio, was greeted by an explosion of press speculation that they might be about to get back together. The closest they came was on

Ringo Starr's 1973 release, simply titled *Ringo*. *Rolling Stone* magazine led the frenzy of excitement:

"*LOS ANGELES – Three ex-Beatles played together recently at Sunset Sound Recorders and it was enough of an event to launch 'reunion' rumours from coast to coast, cause L.A. pop stations to issue daily 'bulletins' and move a national newspaper to write it up under the headline, COME TOGETHER.*"

As producer of the typically glossy all-star extravaganza, Richard Perry can take credit for bringing in an incredible array of talent on Ringo's behalf and making the best use of the drummer's limited vocal abilities, helping him to score two number one hit singles ("Photograph" and "You're Sixteen") in quick succession.

Ringo's album certainly features all four Fabs, but, alas, not at the same time. John played piano and sang on his own composition "I'm The Greatest" and told *Playboy* magazine that he enjoyed working with George and Ringo again but was embarrassed "when George and Billy Preston started saying 'Let's form a group.'"

Harrison contributed three songs to the project as well as guitar and backing vocals, while Paul and Linda McCartney played and helped sing their song "Six O'Clock." It fell to Nicky Hopkins to dispel the rumours in his own *Rolling Stone* interview, which, with a subtle plug for his own solo album thrown in, he did.

Nicky only played on four songs, sharing keyboard duties with Lennon, McCartney, Larry Knechtel, Billy Preston and James Booker, but did manage to end up on the album's two most successful cuts. He is in right at the start of "Photograph," written by Ringo, with a little help from George Harrison (or vice versa), playing an almost formal solo piano part in the vein of Abba and returning strongly over the fade-out.

On golden oldie "You're Sixteen," Ringo shares drums with Jim Keltner, as well as delivering a surprisingly strong lead vocal, with Nicky's perky piano again in at the top. After Paul McCartney's "mouth sax solo," Nicky can be heard right up to the fade, rocking away with syncopated licks over the straight-ahead rhythm section.

During the album's final cut, "You And Me Babe," (another Harrison collaboration, this time with Beatles friend and roadie, Mal Evans), Ringo thanks the lengthy list of collaborators who have helped him on "this wonderful record"—including Nicky! Apart from this unusual spoken accolade, Nicky is credited, again courtesy of CBS, on the inside of the album's elaborate sleeve and is pictured in the "cast-of-thousands" cartoon that graces the front cover, sharing a snaking keyboard with Billy Preston.

He popped up again a year later on Ringo's *Goodnight Vienna*, but this time only on one of the eleven tracks, Hoyt Axton's somewhat unconvincing anti-drugs and drink opus, "No No Song," which was again picked to be a single and charted in America at a healthy Number 3. Nicky plays electric piano and signs off with a ringing chord, courtesy of his new company, Mercury Records.

A postcard he sent to his mother from the L.A. Beverley Wilshire hotel on June 6th, may explain his brief appearance on the album: "I came over to do some sessions for Ringo, but he & his wife had a big row. I'm staying on to set up a new record deal."

By 1974, the year he recorded his own *No More Changes* album, Nicky was already on a slippery path to increasing drug and alcohol abuse and correspondingly poor health. The period between his first Beatles session in 1968 and his (for the moment) last Beatles-related release (Harrison's *Extra Texture*, from 1975), covered the years of his greatest visibility and success as a player. Whether the downward slide in his personal life affected his reliability, his personality or his ability to play, all elements vital to life as pianist to the stars, the fact is that his work with "A" list celebrities began to dwindle in the mid-seventies.

He was by no means unique in partaking of life's temptations and mostly seems to have maintained his usual impeccable standards in the studio. Richard Perry certainly had no recollection of any deterioration, even while working with the notoriously wild Harry Nilsson:

"I don't have any memories of Nicky abusing himself with alcohol or drugs. (Of) the later years I spent with him I have nothing but fond memories and I don't remember seeing him go down. The Nilsson stuff was fantastic; there's nothing he couldn't play. I really miss him tremendously and it was one of the great thrills of my career to have worked with him."

Peter Frampton, on the other hand, hesitantly admitted to experiencing some problems with Nicky during his sessions from the same era:

"It started around the time that he wasn't playing with the Stones any more. I forget which track it was he played on, but he had this bracelet thing on his left wrist and it used to pop open and there was a pot-pourri of pills in there. I never knew what he was actually taking, but we did have to drive him home one day. We never spoke about it and I don't know whether it was because of the pain he was in or what; the last session we did together for my music we couldn't use; but everyone's allowed a moment. I knew he was not a well person and then, on top of that, to take whatever it was…I don't even know and don't want to know…It was the seventies and we all went there."

Nicky didn't work for a Beatle again until latecomer Paul McCartney contacted him in 1987. Nicky's own notes place him with McCartney for the first time, on March 24th to record the song "Same Love," which waited ten years for its release as a B-side. In the autumn, he was back in Paul's home studio in Sussex, to play on the McCartney/MacManus composition "That Day Is Done."[37] Nicky was brought in to try a pass on the song, when others had failed, though details are hard to come by; every musician who works with McCartney is sworn to total secrecy concerning all aspects of their work together, making it very difficult to gain clear information. Gray Levett was co-managing Nicky at the time:

"McCartney's manager rang me and said that Paul was doing an album. I think Elvis Costello was producing it and was using his keyboard player from the Attractions; Paul didn't want to tread on any toes, but I don't think he was particularly keen on some of the keyboard parts and wanted Nicky. I think he just said, 'What would you do?' The third time he played it, McCartney turned with a big smile on his face and said, 'That's why he's Nicky Hopkins.'"

Nicky's wife Moira accompanied him to the studio:

"When we came in the door, Paul hugged him, looked over Nicky's shoulder

---

[37] The "MacManus" in question—better known as Elvis Costello—co-wrote a batch of songs with Paul around this time, four of which ended up on *Flowers In The Dirt*.

and said to me, 'We've known one another a long time.' He was very pleased to see him and was very affectionate and hospitable. I met Linda, went off to Hastings and at the appropriate time came back and we all sat in the kitchen and had pizza."

Nicky's part, played on an unnaturally bright-sounding electronic keyboard masquerading unsuccessfully as a grand piano, apparently hit the spot. It remained his only appearance on the album. Another song, "The Confessed," which Nicky described that year to *Music Connection Magazine* as "one of those incredible ballads only Paul can write," stayed on the cutting-room floor. There were encouraging signs that Nicky was under serious consideration to become a member of McCartney's touring band and, in November '87, he joined Paul for the first time in public on the BBC's prime-time talk show *Wogan*, accompanying him on "Jet" and "Listen To What The Man Said."

Nicky wrote a poignant message to himself in his notebook under the heading "Ideal Scene":

"Being part of Paul McCartney's band, (as full a member as anyone else in it), doing tours and records and TV appearances, press etc. with them and the band being well-respected, liked and successful."

Having known Paul for twenty years or more, he was upset by what he perceived as a humiliating request from McCartney to audition for his touring line-up. Moira Hopkins knew that Nicky badly wanted the job, because it would allow him to stay in England, but his tenacious loyalty to the acoustic piano meant that he had fallen behind on newer developments in the keyboard world and his unwillingness to embrace synthesiser technology probably cost him his place in Paul's band.

Nicky played his last session with an ex-Beatle almost exactly a year later,

Pupils strike a TV record

CHILDREN from a local school have become little starlets — by making a Christmas record with some super local celebrities.

Youngsters from Forest Row's Greenfields School were chosen to sing alongside the stars in this year's theme song for BBC's Children in Need Campaign.

The song is entitled "Children in Need" and is produced by songwriter and singer extraordinaire Paul McCartney.

More than 20 youngsters from Greenfields, aged between 10 and 18, were chosen because Paul McCartney's keyboard player Woody Woodmansey has two sons who are pupils at Greenfields.

Music teacher Veronica Tupholme said the kids worked very hard for

three days with professional musicians to get it right. But despite the hard grind, they were very excited at the thought of recording the song in Paul McCartney's studio!

And afterwards there was an even bigger surprise! The pupils appeared last Friday night on Terry Wogan's Children in Need show.

There they sang the theme tune with special

celebrities Kevin O'Dowd (Boy George's brother), Michael Jackson's keyboard player Rory Kaplan and pop singer Sinitta.

"This was a real high-light for the girls," said Veronica.

Light show

● CARING STARS: East Grinstead's singer songwriter Craig Mathieson and keyboard player Mickey Hopkins who wrote the song, and Woody Woodmansey, who plays the keyboards in Children in Need.

when McCartney, perhaps with a twinge of guilt, lent his studio, his bass-playing, his production skills and an uncredited backing vocal to "Spirit of Play," a song that Nicky had co-authored with singer Craig Mathieson for 1988's BBC *Children In Need* appeal. Drummer Woody Woodmansey completed the group.

Paul's undiminished admiration for Nicky's playing was obvious, and after tracking was completed, Paul asked if the musicians would carry on for a while, just for fun, and recorded the blues and reggae jam session that subsequently took place.

Only Paul McCartney knows what became of the tapes, but unfortunately his enthusiasm did not extend to the tune they actually came to record. Like most songs of its kind, the sentiments expressed in 'Spirit Of Play' are worthy but sugary and self-evident. Nicky's music and performance stand up well, but the instrumental B-side sounds considerably better than the vocal version. The original trio of musicians is pictured on the single sleeve, having adopted the song title as a group name. Despite his extensive input, McCartney is only credited for his bass playing.

The record was publicised with an appearance on the BBC's charity TV show (with twenty children borrowed from a local school), and a small notice in the local press. It failed to make any impact on its release and rapidly sank without trace, providing a curious finale to Nicky Hopkins' work with the Beatles that began with a revolution twenty years earlier.

Dreamer
The Hopkins Solo Albums

"After albums with the Airplane, the Who, Jeff Beck, Fats Domino, John Lennon and the Rolling Stones, where can you possibly go?"

– CBS Records Publicity

The idea of Nicky Hopkins taking centre stage as an artist in his own right had first occurred in 1966. Shel Talmy had secured a three-album deal with CBS in London and encouraged his favourite studio pianist to step out and record his own instrumental LP. It was never destined to be a straightforward collaboration as Nicky was, from the outset, an uneasy front man.

54. *The Revolutionary Piano of Nicky Hopkins*

The Revolutionary Piano Of Nicky Hopkins is an uncomfortable mix of cover versions, chosen by the artist and producer (with additional input from arranger David Whitaker), ranging from contemporary hits such as "Yesterday," "Satisfaction" and "Goldfinger" to established standards like Ketty Lester's "Love Letters" and Duke Ellington's "Don't Get Around Much Anymore." Nicky came up with four original compositions, two written by himself and two with David Whitaker, the wistful "Jenni" being the most memorable. "Mr. Big," which was chosen as a first single, was described in the press as "a beat version of Chopin's Revolutionary Study."

The album was recorded live at Pye Studios in early 1966, with a full orchestra. The reluctant star must have arrived well prepared since, according to Whitaker's sleeve notes, the combination of "Nicky's precision and the great team spirit at the sessions," meant that they had "five numbers recorded after two and three-quarter hours." Nicky displayed a staggering degree of versatility

55. Promotional photo for *The Revolutionary Piano of Nicky Hopkins*

184

and played his inventive arrangements with exemplary skill ("Satisfaction" starts like a country hoedown), but ultimately, it is hard to imagine at whom the album was aimed. Stylistically light years away from the hip contemporary pop that Nicky was already familiar with from his sessions and from his own roots in rock'n'roll and R&B, it was nevertheless too upbeat and quirky for the "easy listening" instrumental market.

Shel Talmy gushed effusively on the sleeve, describing the twenty-one year old Nicky as "the most promising pianist-arranger on the music scene today – on either side of the Atlantic" and stating categorically that "it's the most enjoyable and exciting LP I have ever had the good fortune to cut."

Forty years later his recollections were more measured and Talmy cheerfully admitted that *Revolutionary Piano* had been totally out of step with the times:

"I thought it would be good fun to do something that Nicky had not done and neither had CBS and I was hoping that it would sell enough to be able to make another one. I didn't think that it was going to be instantly in the top ten, but I did think that it would do better than it did. A lot of it was just not where he was at and I had to really work with him to get it done. I think the results are good, but they could have been better. It really came down to a lack of confidence."

CBS took out ads in the music trades grouping Nicky's record with Charles Lloyd, Lefty Frizzell and Winifred Atwell, under the all-encompassing banner "The Sound Of Entertainment." Though *Melody Maker* reviewed it as "Excellent, exciting and imaginative" and *New Musical Express* gave it three stars, the general reception was lukewarm, from both the press and the public when it hit the racks in May. Nicky discussed its progress and his battles with CBS in letters to his sister Dee in New York:

"I'm glad you like my single. It's funny – most people, like 'Jenni' best. It's so long since I wrote to you that my L.P. has come out as well! It's getting some fair plugs on the radio, mostly on the pirates.38 It's been played on Radio London, Radio Caroline, Radio 390, Radio Britain and Radio Luxembourg, and good old BBC Light! Even so, it's not really selling a lot and 'Mr. Big' didn't sell a light.'

"CBS (the rat-finks) made me pay for the records they sent to the U.S. I told them they were to help try and sell it, but they said they couldn't afford to let me have them free, as they'd sent so many copies out free anyway! So I paid and sent them an enormous bill for a session on which I helped copying a few chords, (which took me about ten minutes). I charged them for arranging, conducting, playing and copying and got the money from them without a murmur! They're hard up???!!!

"Doing a new single (45) record Thursday week – about bloody time – NOT on CBS. I think the hold up has been so Shel Talmy found a way out of his contract. No label set for it yet. Probably be another smash flop!"

---

38 The sixties was the heyday of the mostly offshore pirate radio stations

Their first collaboration having failed so spectacularly to set the world on fire, Shel Talmy made two further attempts to sell Nicky as an instrumental star once he had extricated him from his CBS deal: a version of the Kinks' "Mr. Pleasant," followed by a six-track EP with another mix of current hits and standards, which appeared on MGM under the cheerful moniker *Nicky Hopkins and his Whistling Piano*. Neither release fared any better than the CBS venture. Whether these commercial failures were due to shortcomings in the music is a matter for conjecture, but Shel Talmy put the blame firmly on his protégé's total lack of performing ego:

"Unfortunately Nicky was not great at promoting himself. I kept trying to encourage him into being more upfront and I think it was almost too much for him."

After his discouraging first experiences as a solo act, Nicky returned quietly to his accustomed role as sideman and didn't venture back into the limelight under his own name for another six years, when *Jamming With Edward* was released in 1972.

56. *Jamming With Edward*

Edward was never strictly a Nicky Hopkins solo album, but a collection of rough studio jams, recorded at Olympic Studios with the remaining Stones and guest guitarist Ry Cooder, when Keith Richards briefly went missing in May 1969, during the sessions for *Let It Bleed*.

Nicky Hopkins: "We were right in the middle of doing a track and Keith had to go back to his house because Anita was sick. So I thought 'Fuck it, let's play for a while until Keith gets back,' which is just what we did."

The Stones had recently unveiled their own Rolling Stones record label and Nicky had no objections when it was decided that the "glimpse behind the scenes" resulting from the impromptu sessions was worthy of release as a budget album. The fact that his was the first name that appeared on the front cover, next to the cartoon he had drawn himself, boosted public awareness of his talents considerably, though at the same time causing confusion among Rolling Stones fans and some grief to Nicky himself, who was uncomfortable with star billing on what he considered an inferior product.

Nicky Hopkins: "The name came from some banter between Brian Jones and myself. He was fooling around on bass for some reason and I was at the other end of the studio playing piano. He called over, 'Give me an E, Nicky,' but I couldn't hear him so he shouted, 'Give me an E for Edward.' It all developed out of that and I drew the front cover to look like a page from a Beano comic. We thought people might like to hear what goes down between actual recording proper, but it's not a serious album by any means and I'd hate anyone to say, 'Is this the best Nicky Hopkins can do?'"

One reviewer at the time put the album in its true context:

"Mick, Bill, Charlie, Ry Cooder and Nicky Hopkins, along with the evasive Edward, have devised an album that is a rock enthusiast's dream. It is a jam in the truest sense, totally unrehearsed and spontaneous—five friends rejoicing in themselves and their music. Nicky Hopkins' unrestricted piano playing is astounding."

The rambling blues improvisations captured on *Jamming With Edward* are fine examples of Nicky's extraordinary grasp of American piano styles. The song medley and twelve-bar jam that mutate out of the "Highland Fling" on side two reveal both the light-hearted fun that he often brought to the studio and his incredible deftness as a player. The high level of interest in all the Stones' activities ensured the album a three-week stay in the charts, where it peaked at Number 33 in February '72. The world would have to wait until the following year to hear what a true Nicky Hopkins solo offering would sound like.

In the intervening years, his compositions had been released on records by the Jeff Beck Group, Quicksilver and Steve Miller, and Nicky's profile and confidence had grown immensely as had his expertise, honed by countless hours on stage and in the studios.

The sixties and seventies were a time of enormous growth and change in the record industry. The arrival of rock radio had prompted a shift from a market dominated by singles to full-length LPs, whose sleeves allowed for imaginative and sometimes extravagant cover artwork, as well as longer songs and more involved, album-spanning themes. More importantly for Nicky, it became commonplace for the musicians involved in recordings to receive well-earned credits. This in turn led to an elite of session players, who in some cases became almost as well known as the bands and artists they were playing for.

Nicky's name showed up prominently on more albums than most. His most famous quote to date had been on the Stones' *Beggars Banquet*, but he could now boast "special thanks" name-checks from a wide variety of artists, including the Kinks, Ella Fitzgerald, Mark-Almond and the Easybeats ("We would like to thank Nicky Hopkins for the exciting piano playing, his invaluable suggestions and enthusiasm").

Nicky Hopkins (1971): "I've never thought about a band of my own. I never could see a 'Nicky Hopkins' band or whatever and I don't think I could settle into a band permanently either,' had mellowed to a more hopeful: '...perhaps I could go out once or twice a year—just very rarely. The piano is pretty popular right now, probably more popular than it's ever been, with Elton John and Leon Russell. But it's so hard getting a band together...'"

Long-time friend and collaborator Pete Sears, who followed Nicky into the ranks of the Jefferson Airplane/Starship, narrowly missed joining him for ex-Blue Cheer guitarist Leigh Stephens' first solo album. Pete remembered Nicky asking him to help form a new band as early as 1971, an idea that was dropped, due to extreme road weariness following his subsequent tours with the Rolling Stones.

Though Nicky's ambivalence towards fronting his own line-up remained, he was astute enough to grasp the opportunity afforded to players like himself, Bobby Keys and Jim Price, to take a large and freely available record company budget for his own ends and try another solo album. He was well aware of his own strengths and weaknesses, and planned to rely on outside help for lyrics and lead vocals.

Dolly Hopkins: "We had a lot of money when we were young; Nicky wanted to put in Jerry Williams as singer.[39] CBS threw money at him and Nicky stepped out as a frontman, because he wanted *lots* of money. In the seventies, record companies were giving it away to anyone with any talent and his name was really big back then."

Some of Nicky's associates at the time insist that the real impetus to step forward as a solo artist came more from Dolly than from Nicky himself.

Ray Cooper: "She was very, very strong and was really pushy. When you meet your colleagues' wives, it's always difficult when you realise, 'Whoops! There's something going on here' and you worry about your mate and the music, but in a good way; she was determined to make him a star. Determined."

Nicky signed once again with CBS, but this time in America. After the collapse of the Nicky Hopkins version of Quicksilver, manager Ron Polte remained close with John Cipollina and Nicky, and had a hand in negotiating new deals for both of them:

"I helped them both get connected for their next record contracts, which advanced them a hundred thousand each, I think. Clive Davis gave it to them and then got in a whole bunch of trouble and got fired from CBS. I wasn't directly involved in (Nicky's) deal, but I connected him with the people they finally negotiated with."

The contract Nicky Hopkins signed on June 1st, 1972 guaranteed him two album releases with options for three more; typically for the times, the artist's royalty was frighteningly small while, more unusually, Nicky held on to his right to appear on sessions with other artists.

---

[39] Texas-born Jerry Lynn Williams had played with Little Richard and later found huge success as a songwriter; Nicky Hopkins played on his debut album.

Thirty years later, Nicky's then attorney, Los Angeles based Herb Dodell, emphasised that for an artist known only as a sideman (albeit to some of the most famous names of the time), and with no proven track record, the CBS deal was quite a coup. Nicky was due an advance of $110,000 for the first release alone (half payable at the commencement of recording and half on delivery of a master tape), with additional amounts becoming due if sales exceeded certain targets.

Herb Dodell: "He had the potential of earning a million dollars. That was a hard contract to negotiate but I remember getting a lot of very good concessions from them. One thing that was a big stickler, was a billboard on Sunset Boulevard, which Dolly wanted because somebody else had one; Nicky didn't have the same kind of ego demands, but they made a big deal of putting up a sign on Sunset, guaranteed for at least a month."

The most unusual feature of the contract was that it was actually signed by his wife, as president of the "Edward Music Company," a corporation set up by a previous lawyer in Mill Valley to accommodate Nicky's copyrights and publishing, while Nicky signed an additional agreement as an employee of his own company.

Appalled by the couple's inability to handle money and complete lack of basic skills such as drawing up a budget or paying bills, Herb introduced Nicky and Dolly to Stan Levine, who became their business manager during the good years, taking care of all their paperwork for a percentage of the income.

Herb Dodell: "Nicky never knew how to drive: I always laughed at the fact that when he got all this money, Dolly talked him into buying an Excalibur car and he didn't have a driving licence! She was omnipresent and was actually the one that really pushed all the buttons. In a positive way, she got a lot of things done, because she was so aggressive; you knew she was in the room and she didn't take well to being slighted. It's a personal opinion of course, but I think ultimately Nicky's ability to reach the next level was compromised by her attitude and what she wanted. But I always got along well with her and I found her a lot of fun."

Dee Hopkins: "I think she hung in because he had money at that point. I'm being quite honest with you; she came from nothing anyway and Nicky really didn't care. All he cared about was his music, so the money used to go pretty fast."

It was now Nicky's turn to call in some favours from his celebrity friends. With plenty of material written in the previous months, he arrived back in England on September 5th, 1972 with a worldwide, five-year, eight-album deal with Clive Davis under his belt (announced in the trades with a photo of the artist with his lawyer and the CBS boss), but no studio booked, no musicians contacted and no firm plans for how to proceed.

As luck would have it, George Harrison had time blocked out at Apple Studios for his *Living In The Material World* sessions, on which Nicky was a key player, so he started out working five-day weeks there with the ex-Beatle and went straight to his own project at the weekends. When George suddenly needed to go abroad for two weeks, he offered his studio time to Nicky; after some hurried phone calls, a band was assembled, consisting of Mick Taylor, the ever-present Klaus Voormann, percussionist Ray Cooper and Tubes drummer Prairie Prince.[40] The fledgling drummer, who had known Dolly when she was still with John Hun, received a phone call out of the blue, saying that Nicky Hopkins, her new husband, would love to meet him and have him come and play on his album in England.

Prairie witnessed first-hand the healthy state of the Hopkins's finances, when Nicky bought him a brand new drum kit and had it shipped over to London. He followed with his girlfriend in tow and moved in with Nicky and Dolly in the house they had rented near the racecourse in Epsom Downs. After a few days spent recovering from jetlag, Prairie recalled his first day at Apple with mixed feelings. He recognised producer/engineer Richard Perry in the control room next to the unmistakable figure of Mick Jagger but, before he had even set up his new drum kit for the first time, there were problems. The petulant voice of the Stones' boss came over the intercom:

"Is the drummer ready yet? What's taking so long?"

Prairie broke out into an immediate sweat, but was reassured by Nicky, who told him to take his time and not to worry; when they began checking individual drums, Mick didn't like the way they sounded or what was being played:

"Is there maybe something else the drummer could play, like tambourine or something?"

Again Nicky stepped in and suggested Mick should come back the following day when things had settled in. Herb Dodell was visiting and recalled the tense atmosphere in the studio:

"Richard Perry was the producer there and Jagger came in and wanted to play around with the dials and everything else; they were recording and re-recording over and over and over again and it was late. There was a little Italian restaurant around the corner from the studio and I went over there with Jagger; I'd met him but I didn't know him and I had no reason to talk to him. I had heard complaints about how badly Mick was treating Nicky, but it wasn't my role to be a mediator. If there were issues, I spoke to the group's lawyers. We sat down, had something to eat and he told me that he had graduated from the London School of Economics and was going to stay with the Stones one more year. When the check came—I love to tell the story—he said, 'You had the soup' and actually split the check according to what we ate!"

Mick never returned and Richard Perry only re-surfaced much later at the disc-cutting process in the USA. Nicky was left with only *Imagine* engineer Phil McDonald at the console, but once the musicians were left to themselves, the session soon came together, with Nicky's immaculate timing serving as a metronome.

Ray Cooper: "Nicky was such a wonderfully rhythmic player, so really you ac-

---

[40] Charles "Prairie" Prince is a real person and not, as often misconstrued, simply a pseudonym for Ringo Starr. He later went on to be the drummer for The Tubes.

companied him. Good rhythm is the appreciation of the gaps between, but the cleanliness of that gap is what creates that tension—and he was masterful at that."

Memories differ as to how long backing tracks took to record; some participants said only eight days, while Prairie Prince remembered the process as taking "at least a few weeks":

"I know we took a couple of weeks off at some point and then went back and did more."

The longer time seems more likely, as Nicky would sometimes take thirty or forty versions of the same piece back to Epsom and listen all night, over many cups of tea and many tins of biscuits, only then deciding whether to re-cut a track or move on to a new one. All the songs were recorded as instrumentals and none of the players had a clue as to what might eventually be recorded on top of the basic tracks; Prairie was quite shocked when he first heard Nicky's singing voice.

There followed a succession of cameo appearances by star guests, including Nicky's mentor George Harrison on four songs (billed on the LP sleeve as George O'Hara). Nicky never claimed to be a wordsmith but, under pressure from his wife's ambitions and possibly from his label, he planned to feature vocals on more than half of the record. He confessed to one reporter:

"I'm no lyricist at all. I don't listen to words. I even hear the vocal as part of the music."

Ray Cooper: "I always felt that he was pressured into that album and that he was uneasy—not with the music, but that he had to sing and didn't feel he could do it; suddenly the dynamic was going to change. If it had been a completely instrumental album it would have been wonderful."

Chuck Leavell: "I remember us talking about *Tin Man With A Dream* (sic) and I told him how glad I was he'd done a solo record and how much I enjoyed it and he said, 'Sorry about the vocals.' I said, 'Hey, shit, I thought it was great. Don't be afraid to sing! I'm not Mick Jagger either!'"

Jerry Williams was brought in to cover for Nicky's limited abilities on the raunchier tracks, but with the listener's attention naturally drawn to the lead voice, his appearance led to confusion about whose record this was—and there still remained the acute problem of what to sing. Inspiration came in the form of the wisecracking Harry Nilsson, who was a benign presence in the control room during the album's tracking sessions. His gags provided the (uncredited) seeds for some song lyrics, while Dolly's role in the proceedings now extended beyond taking care of business matters to providing titles and lyrics for many of the remaining songs.

Nicky immortalised his partner with "Dolly's Song" and dedicated "Lawyer's Lament" to Herb Dodell, while "Pig's Boogie" was for his "big orange cat named Pig, who also plays piano":

"Nobody believes me, but he'd climb up and sit on the music stand, which was flat, and watch the hammers going up and down and me hitting the keys. After a couple of days he figured it out, got up on his hind legs on the piano stool, and by God, if he didn't play a bloody tune!"

"Edward" was a remake of the dazzling piece that had already become a favourite with Quicksilver's audience and was almost Nicky's signature tune, "re-cut properly this time as I always wanted it to sound. It's much more compact and makes more sense."

The album's lyrics could be described as clumsy and pages of re-writes in Nicky's red school exercise book testify to the perspiration that accompanied any initial sparks of inspiration. They concern themselves mostly with mundane aspects of Nicky's life in the session world ("Speed On" and "Waiting For The Band"), or downbeat musings on life, love and loss that make Leonard Cohen seem cheerful by comparison.

Not content with her role as co-writer and "executive producer," Dolly was also responsible for the concept behind the album's striking front cover painting, depicting Nicky with piano keys for fingers playing a keyboard made of pink and

57. Nicky with his business manager/lyricist

black human digits, while the back cover depicted part of his collection of vintage tins, which gave the album its title. Dolly brought in her ex-boyfriend John Hunt for the artwork, while Ethan Russell's inner sleeve photo was taken in the fields behind the house in Epsom.

In a May 1973 *Sounds* interview, Nicky freely admitted that work would never have even been started if it weren't for his wife's encouragement:

"She's got a good business head and I don't have, she remembers things and I don't. I play piano and she doesn't. She can write the words and I can't...it's perfect. She handles everything for me."

192

He explained the absence of any acknowledgement of her input, as a desire to avoid the "Paul and Linda McCartney" syndrome, but sneaked her picture into the album's artwork and included the line "Special thanks and love to Dolly" in the credits. His much-maligned partner definitely had the last laugh. Her contribution to so many aspects of *The Tin Man Was A Dreamer* later received the ultimate payback when the royalties from the album were awarded to her as part of her 1986 divorce settlement.

58. *The Tin Man Was A Dreamer*

Nicky decorated his personal notebook with a sticker bearing his name and the album title in Gothic script. The lined pages are full of fascinating peripheral details such as studio dates, fees paid to musicians (£75.00 to horn players Jim Price and Bobby Keys and £300.00 to Del Newman for string arrangements), studio costs, addresses and phone numbers of friends including Harry Nilsson, Jim Horn and vocalist Jerry Williams. There are trial running orders for the songs, suggested aliases for some of the star guests ("Nicholas Q. Maylor" and "George Harrysong" on guitars?) and a Rolling Stones rooming list from the Beverley Wilshire hotel, complete with each musician's "on tour" cricketing alias: (Jagger – Grace, Richards – Truman, Wyman – Hutton, Watts and Taylor – both Bailey and Marshall—presumably Chess—bringing up the rear.)

When Nicky finished work on Harrison's *Material World* album, he already had an invitation to join the Stones in Jamaica and to take part in their upcoming dates in the Far East. He had already survived their gruelling seven and a half week US marathon earlier in the year. The Stones record was completed in London in December, and it was January 1973 before Nicky was finally able to finish his own work. He jetted back and forth between live dates with the Stones, to mixing and mastering sessions at Wally Heider's in Los Angeles, and San Francisco. The legendary David "be great or be gone" Briggs was in the engineer's chair and is credited as co-producer for "vocals and mixing." The pace was exhausting; Nicky was at a mix session in L.A. the night before the Stones' opening gig in Australia.

59. *Tin Man* photo shoot

In early February *The Tin Man Was A Dreamer* was finally finished. However, as every recording artist knows, the completion of an album is the beginning rather than the end of the story. Success and ultimate sales to the public are dependent on record company support and enthusiasm, publicity, radio airplay and the critics' response. Nicky was understandably nervous of the reception his first real self-produced solo album would elicit from the rock press and from the audience he had built up through his activities to date:

"I'm not into any particular set style, which is why the album is so varied. I don't think anybody knew what to expect."

Initial reactions were indeed mixed, to say the least. *Billboard* headed its appraisal *The Tin Man Was A Drummer* (sic) and mentioned some of the players, including one "Laus" Voormann:

"Long awaited solo set from one of the top session musicians of our time, featuring his vocals as well as his virtuoso keyboard playing. Aided by an all-star cast including Mick Taylor, Laus Voormann and a mysterious George O'Hara. Though Hopkins does not have the world's greatest voice it is sufficient, particularly on the rock material. The best cuts here are his instrumentals, which are truly exceptional. All in all, the LP is far above most initial solo efforts. Dealers: the young buyer knows him well."

In England journalist Steve Clarke gave the album a glowing review, while Bud Scoppa in *Rolling Stone* gave a more cautious but accurate assessment. He praised the care and precision of Nicky's playing and approach, but rightly commented on the strange absence of a strong central figure in the "well-made but essentially character-less music," and described Nicky himself as "an almost invisible figure, lurking just on the edge of the spotlight" with the orchestrations and the virtuoso performances of his star guests threatening to drown out his "endearingly fragile voice." In his review, the three instrumental tracks fare slightly better, but even these are criticised, perhaps unfairly, as "routine performances." "It was," Scoppa wrote, "as if Nicky Hopkins is a session keyboard man on his own album!"

Even the most hardened Hopkins fan must admit that, while Nicky flourished when given free rein to embellish the work of others, his second solo album was at best a brave attempt. It underlined Nicky's unease in the spotlight and his lack of strong ego, things that no amount of superstar companions could disguise. One reviewer's retrospective assessment of the record as "a fine early example of power-pop" is probably the most generous description it received.

Whether CBS realised they had a tough sell on their hands or were discouraged by a poor reaction from key press people, their initial efforts on behalf of *Tin Man* were not extensive. There was some advertising in trade magazines such as *Billboard* with the inner sleeve photo appearing under the ironically appropriate byline:

"*After albums with the Airplane, the Who, Jeff Beck, Fats Domino, John Lennon and the Rolling Stones, where can you possibly go?*"

A CBS press insert, titled "Nicky Hopkins Walking Keyboard" failed to mention the album at all, concentrating instead on the standard list of Nicky's guest appearances from Lord Sutch to the Stones. In early May, he dutifully travelled America, as a double-act with the more forceful Dolly, giving interviews to radio stations, the rock press and regional papers. David Spero, who remained friends with Nicky and part-managed him in later years, met him in Cleveland:

"I was disc jockey at radio station WMMS, which at the time was one of the number one FM stations in the country. For some reason, we really hit it off and ended up spending a couple of days together. I showed him around, we went to hear music in some of the clubs and from that point on we always stayed in touch. I know we smoked a joint during that interview…"

Nicky handed out promo items, dreamed up by someone at CBS, of individual piano keys with his name and album title emblazoned on the sides; he gave one to David with the instruction "Build your own piano!" and the personal inscription, "This key will self-destruct in about thirty minutes."

Rock magazine *Crawdaddy* printed a somewhat idealised portrait of the artist and his muse in their hotel room:

60. Nicky with David Spero

"A low-key dude, Hopkins sat in his room like a china figurine contemplating the delicate patterns of his own musical inspiration. While his lady made phone calls and travel arrangements in a corner of the room, Nicky talked dreamily of his Mill Valley hideaway, where he and Dolly have been spending the past couple of years, living the life, making music, writing songs with a cassette player atop his piano and collecting old tins."

David Spero's recollection of Dolly's part in their interview was rather less romantic:

"She sat right next to him the whole time and he didn't answer a question without looking at her; she was involved in every aspect of his life."

Despite all efforts, airplay remained negligible and Nicky was cursed by the fact that most interviewers wanted to talk about his experiences with his star clientele, rather than focus on his own effort. At this point, Clive Davis, his champion at CBS, who was renowned for the muscle he could put behind an act once he was committed, called a special singles meeting for Nicky, which led immediately to Columbia making the single "Speed On" "push single of the week nationwide." The results were instantly noticeable when the album entered the U.S. Top 200 and started climbing thirty places a week.

Nicky Hopkins: "Three days later, the phone rang at 10.00 a.m. and someone from CBS in L.A. woke me up, informing me that Clive was no longer president of CBS Records. I said, 'Do me a favour and call back in three hours.' At one, the phone rang again and he repeated the news. I said, 'That's what I thought you said.' The next week the album disappeared from No. 80 right off the charts!"

An obvious means of promoting his efforts would have been to go out and play live, but the extensive delays in the release date had been due to Nicky's already overcrowded date-sheet. Finding a gap for a "Nicky Hopkins Band" to take to the road was just as hard. Herb Dodell is convinced that Nicky was terri-

61. Nicky with David Spero

fied at the thought of having to front his own project and cites the lack of touring as another major factor in the album's poor performance. A note among Nicky's personal effects mentioned a November 14th sales figure of 73,907 albums in the USA (excluding tapes and eight-tracks), a flop by US standards.

Herb Dodell: "It came out strong, but there were a lot of returns and they only did a second album because they were obligated."

An unlikely compliment was paid to Nicky's songwriting, when crooner Andy Williams recorded "The Dreamer" on his *Solitaire* album, with Nicky on piano. Contemporary interest in keyboard players was at an absolute high point, but Nicky's personality was totally unsuited to the "show" aspects of the business, utilised so effectively by Elton John, whose onstage antics left Nicky unimpressed:

"He's a good songwriter, but he put me off so much when I saw him. Someone like Mick can come off very cool, but with Elton it just looks silly. When is he going to grow up? Star-spangled hot pants, six-mile diameter shades with white rims and dyed hair–I just can't get behind all that."

Tens of millions of Elton John albums sold tell their own story.

Soon after plans for an April tour were abandoned, autumn dates were announced with the original studio quartet of Mick Taylor, Klaus Voormann, Prairie Prince and Ray Cooper (subject to their other commitments). This tour also failed to materialise, and instead most of the same musicians were booked for a new set of sessions in the UK for another recording.

Nicky believed that all his problems were due to Clive Davis' sudden departure from CBS under a cloud of financial scandal, at the end of May 1973. In an interview with England's *New Musical Express*, he insisted that he had delivered a good and very commercial album, but that CBS had simply stopped promoting anybody signed by Clive. David Spero felt that Dolly was the major stumbling block in Nicky's relationship with CBS:

"There was obviously something he needed in that relationship, and if he was happy with it, then who is to judge, but career-wise, her ego got in the way of him moving forward. I know that the relationship he had with Columbia was tainted by having to deal with her. I think it was easier not to be a hit, because, if it had been, who knows what she would have been like afterwards?"

Nicky was understandably bitter about what he perceived as a lack of support. Communications soon broke down completely and he left CBS, totally disillusioned, with *Tin Man* having failed to set the world alight and a second Columbia-financed (and to date still unreleased) album recorded and ready to go but with its original street date of January 1974 having been unceremoniously scrapped.

The only print reference to Nicky's projected follow-up album *The Long Journey Home* appeared in the March issue of *Rolling Stone* in the Random Notes section; because it was subsequently withdrawn, speculation as to its contents has always run high among fans. Recordings found among Nicky's effects finally reveal the hitherto buried piece of work.

He had amassed enough material prior to the *Tin Man* sessions to be able to go straight back into the studio in July 1973. Tracks were recorded at Mick Jagger's "Stargroves" home near Newbury and at Columbia's own London facilities, with many of the same musicians, but without Jerry Williams or Klaus Voormann (replaced on bass by Steve Thompson and the Faces' Ronnie Lane) and this time with Dolly a featured vocalist. Nicky had the use of a "full-size Moog synthesiser" to add to his arsenal of keyboard instruments.

Peter Frampton found Nicky's music "very involved and unique and not straightforward at all" and his friend firmly in control of proceedings.

Fans of *The Tin Man Was A Dreamer* would have found plenty to like on *The Long Journey Home* but, if released, it would not have been destined to cause much of a stir in 1974. The star guests again acquitted themselves well, with George Harrison and Mick Taylor augmented on guitar by Peter Frampton, Ronnie Wood and Jimmy McCullough and the finished work was mixed and mastered by Phil McDonald at Apple. A cover was even designed by drummer Prairie Prince (who led a double life as an airbrush artist), but when Nicky's relationship with CBS broke down, the LP was put on ice.

Correspondence in the early nineties between Herb Dodell and the CBS lawyers sought to establish that by CBS's failure to support the previous album and refusing to release its follow-up, all rights to *The Long Journey Home* should revert back to its author, raising hopes that it might at last be heard by the public. The dispute was never resolved during Nicky's lifetime and the vital reply to a letter seeking to establish ownership of both Nicky's CBS records was missing among his correspondence.

In 1974, with interest in Nicky's brief solo foray already waning, he initially returned to his busy calendar as a session man, leaving his second contract album to languish on the shelf. After the latest round of recordings, yet more touring plans were announced in the press, this time with fellow session aces Jim Keltner and Jesse Ed Davis supposedly forming his backing band along with ex-John Mayall bassist Steve Thompson. Nicky claimed that he needed experienced players, firstly to cope with the complexities of the music on his record, but also to avoid the danger of younger musicians drifting off mid-project to other bands. This potentially exciting line-up unfortunately proved just as hard to pull together, and again no tour took place.

Nicky had been partially resident in the artists' and musicians' enclave of Mill Valley for four years now, but, just as with the scene in San Francisco before, the atmosphere in and around his adopted home had taken a steady turn for the worse with an influx of drug dealers and an ever-increasing level of violence. Ever the conservative, Nicky had already become disenchanted with the local scene:

"I thought that sound was going to evolve out from all the psychedelic bullshit into something really valid, but it never did; it died. Mill Valley's changed; it used to be almost an artists' colony and now it's half commuters and half freaks who don't do anything but hang out and panhandle. It's going to turn into another Haight-Ashbury pretty soon if it keeps going down the way it's been going."

When a multiple shooting in a nearby house coincided with the windows of the Hopkins' truck being blown out by a shotgun, Nicky thought it was time to quit, and the couple decided to head back to England. The move involved a considerable step down in their lifestyle, exchanging a ten-room house in the woods with hardwood interiors and a view over the mountain, initially, for a flat in London's Holland Park that Nicky described as "freezing cold and so leaky that you don't have to switch the shower on, you just stand there." Subsequently the couple found a more comfortable and rural address, west of London: Crown House, Englefield Green, Egham, Surrey. House guest, guitarist David Tedstone described the Hopkins' lifestyle at home:

"He had it all there—his furnishings, his antique furniture, his record collection, the grand piano, a hi-fi system and a housekeeper. He was living quite a grand existence."

Nicky found the state of the UK music scene equally depressing and complained in an interview that the upheavals of moving had meant having to miss out on some valuable studio work. (During that year, however, he still managed to guest on tracks for the Rolling Stones and Harrison, as well as Donovan, Carly Simon and Harry Nilsson, Joe Cocker, John Lennon, Ken Russell's *Tommy* extravaganza and Ringo Starr's lavish self-titled release. A "low-key" Hopkins year was still more than most musicians achieve in a decade.)

Plans for a solo career had not been abandoned entirely, despite Nicky's battering experience with Columbia. His relationships with managers and accountants were complex and mostly short-lived, but did lead to a new deal with Chicago-based Mercury Records, again for two albums with further options, though by now the numbers had shrunk considerably, with $35,000 on offer for the first recording. Contracts were again signed by Dolly, on behalf of "Edward Music."

The failure of *Tin Man* to garner bigger sales was one obvious reason for his next record company's more cautious attitude. However, Herbert Dodell's later correspondence with CBS specifically referred to the fact that Nicky had been sober for over a decade, suggesting at least the possibility that his earlier drug and alcohol use was another significant factor in the breakdown of his dealings with Columbia—and a reason for Mercury's more limited financial investment and insistence in their contract that Nicky commit to at least six weeks of U.S. touring in support of his upcoming album.

Having experienced the difficulties inherent in trying to keep an "all-star" line-up together outside the studio, and with a much smaller budget this time around, Nicky set his sights somewhat lower and hired a group of mostly lesser-known musicians to help record and tour his next album, avoiding the risk of disappearing under the combined weight of his superstar friends. Unfortunately, a combination of exhaustion and depression meant that Nicky—an unwilling front man at the best of times—was in very poor spirits and even poorer physical condition as he embarked on his third solo recording inside a year.

Bass-player Rick Wills was a veteran of various British bands and had already worked with Nicky on albums with Peter Frampton, Duster Bennett and Alexis Korner around this period,[41] while guitarist David Tedstone and drummer Eric Dillon had both toured extensively with Savoy Brown. American Michael Kennedy came in on rhythm guitar and was apparently untroubled by previous fame.

Conversations with three of the musicians revealed different recollections of Nicky as a person, but all agreed that he was at a very low ebb during the recordings and that Dolly's presence was, at the very least, a mixed blessing.

Rick Wills had just been fired from Peter Frampton's band:

---

[41] Wills later went on to play with the enormously successful Foreigner

Nicky Hopkins

Recording Exclusively For

Jmercury

A product of Phonogram, Inc.

62. Promotional photo for *No More Changes*

"Two days later I got a call from Nicky, asking if I'd like to help him make a solo album. I admired his playing and thought he was a really nice person, but he was very fragile, terribly thin and very gaunt and drawn. He and Dolly were bad together and there was a constant flow of illicit things going on between them. I don't know what medication he was on, but he was taking a lot of different things, though his playing didn't seem to be affected in any way. He was worried about doing vocals and wasn't terribly confident, but we started knocking some ideas around."

Recording began at the Who's Ramport Studios, where Nicky particularly loved the piano (a Bösendorfer that apparently went all the way down to a bottom F). He had recently recorded there with British band Coast Road Drive, whose drummer, Steve Chapman, found the situation quite intimidating:

"Ramport was a funky location in Battersea; we had 'early sessions' booked, with eleven or twelve o'clock starts, and had four songs that needed keyboards. Mick Weaver did two and Nicky was booked for the others; we were totally jazzed that he was coming in, but when he arrived he was shaking and looked like he'd been on an all-night bender. We were incredibly disappointed, until he played. He was insanely good."

The original 2-inch tape boxes for Nicky's *No More Changes* note studio dates between 6th and 29th of November 1973, with additional work at Wessex Studios in London and subsequent mixing in Los Angeles. The album went through no less than three producers, with Nicky's role limited to leading the players through the changes, for which he awarded himself a co-producer's credit. Though obviously debilitated by health problems and his diet of sleeping pills and downers, his biggest handicap was a visible lack of enthusiasm for his own project.

Dave Tedstone lived with Nicky and his wife throughout the recording period:

"We'd drive down in Dolly's car from Epsom having arranged to start about six o'clock in the evening, but Dolly would take three hours to decide what to wear and get made up, so we'd arrive about nine or ten, get there late and have to rush through whatever Nicky had decided to do that day. Often there were no finished lyrics or melody lines, so we had to play to a song that didn't really exist and imagine what it might be like when it was finished, which is not a good way to focus people. Sessions generally ran from the evening until as late as possible. It was terrible."

63. Nicky at home with Dave Tedstone

Rick Wills: "Nicky would come in with a vague idea and we'd learn it in the room together and have a go at it. There was never anybody there to say, 'That's really not good enough, let's find a different arrangement.' I think he was more or less in a mist, which was sad, because his playing never failed."

Mike Kennedy: "Nicky was a lot like 'Rainman'—almost autistic. Whether it was just easier for him to deal with things that way, I don't know, but he deferred to everyone on all matters and lived in his own very childlike world, in a trusting and needy way. He never took control and never thought of himself or his needs first. He seemed to need direction in all things."

Dave Tedstone shared the general feeling of frustration:

"We had to really push him to do the album. He had no songs and he kept avoiding it; we'd do a couple of days here and there and then have a break of a few weeks because he'd keep going off, doing sessions with other people. (Mick & Keith called the house every week for one reason or another). One minute he'd want it to be a cohesive band, the next it was to be his solo album and we were just backing musicians; we never knew where we were and there was very little rehearsal. He sometimes brought chord charts into the studio and it was the first time we'd come across the song. Actually he was doing the album as a session musician himself rather than really being a solo artist. I think it was just to fulfil a financial contract."

The guitarist was better placed than anyone to reveal the day-to-day events surrounding the sessions and to offer an explanation for the dispiriting atmosphere, since he was conducting an affair with Dolly that lasted throughout the recordings and for several months afterwards. The experience left him with scars that he still feels today. He described in harrowing detail the routine of home life in Epsom with the Hopkins:

"The only person that could really handle him was his wife. No one liked the fact that she had to take care of him and see he got things done. They all thought she was using him, but I think she had to do what she did, because he needed looking after. He took legitimate medication, but he also took other things recreationally. He just wanted to be out of it all the time. We lived off frozen food out of a supermarket-sized freezer.

"We were having an affair under his nose, but Nicky knew and to some degree gave his permission as if it were the norm, or that he couldn't be bothered and had better things to get on with. It's my biggest regret, because I always thought that if that hadn't happened, we would have had a far better relationship as musicians.

"He would take sleeping pills and crash out on the sofa, we'd carry him to bed and then Dolly would creep into my room. I didn't even particularly fancy her but I found myself 'magnetised' by her and Nicky was often away on sessions. He kept giving me horrible glares over breakfast and I was always saying to him, 'Look, Nicky, I don't want to be doing this' and he would just glare back as if to say, 'I can't stop her doing what she wants to do.' It was never a direct confrontation. There were arguments between them, probably about me a lot of the time.

Nicky looked evil and drawn, with a scary look in his eyes, and I think the songs on that album reflect the break-up of their partnership, ending with 'Lady, It's Time To Go.' It's a bad concept album."

The further he retreated into the twilight zone of his dysfunctional lifestyle, the more room there was for a strong personality such as Dolly to take up the slack. Rick Wills believed that she controlled Nicky by feeding him drugs, and all the musicians had stories of her aggressive and controlling behaviour.

Mike Kennedy: "One night we waited over two hours, while studio time was ticking away, for Dolly to dress in a gypsy outfit and, as she stormed out of the house, she slammed the door, smashing a large glass panel. She was a New Jersey groupie who had bagged a Rolling Stone, was a hundred per cent in control of him and his career and did her best to wreck everyone's spirit. She was an absolute disgrace."

No More Changes was, if anything, even more eclectic than its two predecessors and suffered badly from lack of focus. Workmanlike covers of "Sea Cruise" and Jackie De Shannon's "Hanna" were well executed but unlikely to set pulses racing, and the original songs suffered from the ever more dominant presence of Dolly, who this time around not only was responsible for many of the lyrics but sang them too. Publishing was assigned to "Dolly Publishing."

With the painful process of tracking at last completed, proceedings moved to Los Angeles, where Nicky and Dolly rented an apartment and where the darkness and mayhem intensified.

Kathi McDonald was brought in at the mixing stage to add some welcome vocal muscle. She was joined by Doug Duffey, a friend who moved in the same circles as Nicky during that era of heavy drug use in L.A. Doug offers a scary, but probably accurate portrait of the degree of insanity prevalent in his and other people's lives:

"I met Nicky and Dolly through Backstage Management, who 'mismanaged' Nicky, P-Funk, Bootsy Collins, Martha Reeves, Rare Earth and others at the time. Backstage was made up of Cholly Bassoline, Ron Strasner, and Robert Mittleman—I'm not sure if any of them are still alive. I say 'mismanaging,' but they did help to make George Clinton and Bootsy into major stars and kept Rare Earth and other acts afloat; I have no idea what they were doing with, for or to Nicky.

"I did a lot of house and cat sitting for Nicky & Dolly when they went out of town, which gave me access to his grand piano, the only object of 'furniture' in a huge room with a huge window and great acoustics in a building called 'the Castle,' right under the Hollywood sign. Nicky was like the living dead when I knew him, too many brain cells already destroyed and he and Dolly destroying what was left. Of course everyone in 'El Lay' was doing the same thing at that time.

"As for Dolly: what a piece of work *she* was! Heavy drugs and 'wannabe' witchcraft was not really a good mix. I remember him coming to me at Cholly's house, to try and get me to reverse some voodoo he thought Dolly was doing, because I am from Louisiana. I gave him some plastic trinket and told him it would work.

"The last time I saw them was in the '70s, in Hollywood, in Ralph's Grocery on Santa Monica and neither of them recognized me because they were so wasted,

64. "The Castle"

which was bizarre, considering they knew me well and vice versa. The man deserves recognition for his talent and work rather than for all the tragedies that befell him. He was really childlike and sweet, which was probably his downfall.

"I sang backups on the album with Kathi and Leah Roberti and also 'doubled' some of Nicky's vocal tracks. Due to a printing error I was wrongly credited; instead of my name, they accidentally added a comma, and put 'Doug, Duffy, & Dolly,' which sounds like a law firm. They spelt my name wrong too!"

It is astonishing that, even at his worst, Nicky almost never let his work suffer as a result of his personal problems. Apart from the one occasion mentioned by Peter Frampton, when Nicky was in no fit state to work and apparently had to be taken home, there is not one Hopkins performance, on any of the hundreds of records on which he played, that is anything less than excellent.

65. *No More Changes*

No More Changes can boast at least two decent melodies: the twin piano pyrotechnics of "The Ridiculous Trip" and the stately "No Time." Despite the dreadful state of his health, Nicky plays throughout with his usual taste and timing. The lyrical content, however, is so weak and his plaintive singing so unconvincing, that the whole album has a lacklustre feel, right down to the black and white cover concept, with Nicky on the front and a vamped-up Dolly on the back, both standing on a giant keyboard. Ethan Russell, who was called back to shoot the cover in Los Angeles, remembered the experience as "desperately sad" and recalled Dolly intruding into the business side as much as the creative areas of Nicky's life:

"She was a nightmare. She was like the caricature in *Spinal Tap*. Show business is not a friendly place, and he was being put up in something like the Holiday Inn on Vine. She was on the phone, screaming at the record company, saying that what they were doing wasn't good enough and that kind of thing. To a certain level it wasn't, but she was just making it worse—and he was being Nicky; he was kind of sweet about it, but she was playing it like Nicky was Mick Jagger. And Nicky's not Mick Jagger."

The sleeve credits include a touching dedication to his mother: "God bless her for having a piano when I was a kid!" Mike Kennedy sometimes witnessed Nicky playing at home in England and wished that what he heard in private, could have found its way onto tape:

"I can attest to his genius, because I heard it daily in the guesthouse on his grand; his left hand changes and haunting melodies were from beyond this dimension and just poured out, hour after hour; but ninety-nine per cent of those pieces were one-offs and lost forever. Nicky loved to play, alone or with one person there, just for the fun of it, and his best was never heard by the public."

There is no record of how Nicky felt at the time, but he later admitted that the album didn't measure up to his previous release, initially blaming the fact that rock producers tend to give the piano less prominence than drums and guitars. By 1989 he had disowned it completely:

"No More Changes was terrible. I was too heavily into drugs by that time. I really can't remember a lot of the middle to late seventies. I was stoned most of the time and can't bear to listen to it these days. I didn't realise it at the time, but it was awful—no creativity at all."

Billboard surprisingly described the album as "more varied and better put together than his Columbia LP of some years back, with the instrumental work, as might be expected, the best…" and added somewhat generously that "the vocals sound good on the slower numbers." Other critics mostly agreed with Nicky's own opinion, with reactions ranging from "not particularly exciting" to "complete mediocrity." In retrospect, these are harsh verdicts on an undistinguished but solid album.

Mercury's in-house promotion concentrated predictably on Nicky's past and didn't discuss the new recording at all. His contractual obligation to tour behind his record became the prime means of promoting it. A band consisting of most of the studio players (the absent Rick Wills' position being taken by Jim Leverton from Fat Mattress) and with Dolly as featured vocalist, rehearsed in May for a summer visit to the USA—Nicky's first ever concerts under his own name. Dave Tedstone lived through the chaotic end of the Epsom era:

"We were forced to move into the housekeeper's house when the money ran out, while arrangements were made to get over to the USA on tour; though when I say 'tour,' it was really about half a dozen gigs."

Kicking off at the end of July 1975, the ramshackle line-up managed club gigs in Atlanta (with an up-and-coming Bruce Springsteen's *Born to Run* tour booked at the same venue two weeks later[42]) and in Washington, before the star of the show fell over on stage in a self-confessed state of advanced drunkenness and sprained his wrist. Though in fact only slightly injured, Nicky grasped the excuse to obtain a doctor's letter and cancel the tour, which was losing money anyway, despite mostly positive audience responses. The arrival of some celebrity guests must have underlined the appalling chaos of his situation.

Dave Tedstone: "At one of the first gigs we did, the Rolling Stones came along to see us because they were doing a gig of their own down the road somewhere. That was the night Nicky collapsed at his piano. They came into the dressing room afterwards and I was chatting to Mick Jagger, when I was unceremoniously dragged off by Dolly to have sex in a toilet cubicle. Dolly said that Mick was terrified of her!"

A surviving review singles out songs in the setlist ranging from Jim Reeves' "He'll Have To Go" to Nicky's own "Pig's Boogie" and of course "Edward The Mad Shirt Grinder." "Refugee Blues" and "Lady Sleeps" from the new album came in for praise, as did most of the instrumentals, but to the disappointed writer, Nicky's vocal sounded at best "charmingly vulnerable" and at worst "alarmingly frail."

An already advertised 18th August double-bill with Nils Lofgren at New York's Bottom Line was

THE BOTTOM LINE

NOW
THRU WEDNESDAY JULY 23
ELVIN BISHOP
JOHN SHINE

THURSDAY JULY 24
thru SUNDAY JULY 27
THE
ELEVENTH HOUSE
FEATURING
LARRY CORYELL
JACK DE JOHNETTE'S
DIRECTIONS

MONDAY JULY 28
ONE NIGHT ONLY
MARY TRAVERS

TUESDAY JULY 29
thru SUNDAY AUGUST 3
RAHSAAN
ROLAND KIRK
SONNY TERRY
AND
BROWNIE McGHEE

MONDAY AUGUST 4
thru WEDNESDAY AUGUST 6
ERIC ANDERSEN
ED BLUESTONE

WEDNESDAY AUGUST 13
thru SUNDAY AUGUST 17
BRUCE
SPRINGSTEEN
AND THE
E STREET BAND
SOLD OUT
ALL SEATS $5.00
STANDING ROOM ON
SALE NIGHT OF SHOW

MONDAY AUGUST 18
thru WEDNESDAY AUGUST 20
NICKY HOPKINS
NILS LOFGREN

---

[42] Alex Cooley's Electric Ballroom

pulled at the last minute and ticket stubs for the show, with Nicky's name still on them, have appeared in recent years for sale on eBay.

For someone in Nicky's fragile state of health, the travelling, combined with the responsibility of having his own name on the Marquee, must have been gruelling. Worst of all, his efforts had no effect whatever on the dismal sales of the album.

David Tedstone: "He didn't mix with us as a band. Nicky spent most of the time with Dolly, because she was acting as his manager, so on the road she was the one who took care of his needs. He was obviously present, but I always recall him as being a bit vacant and he certainly wasn't the extrovert that was needed to lead a band. I was 'out of it' myself by that point and didn't know or care; I just wanted to get back to England and I didn't know how I was ever going to do that. Eventually someone gave me the airfare, because things were going nowhere. Their marriage was on the rocks and he didn't know what he wanted to do. He was running away and hiding, trying to get out of his contract."

Mercury predictably declined to pick up their option for another record and Nicky seems to have, literally, exhausted his need to be centre stage. From this point on he would return to his role as sideman to the stars and never attempt another solo album.

Where Am I Now
The Wilderness Years – Part 1

"Nobody's a real victim in life; they choose their situations; I guess he got something out of it."

– Julia Brigden

The autumn of 1975 found Nicky Hopkins bruised from his disastrous band tour and suffering the effects of a lifestyle that he, of all people, was ill-equipped to deal with. His relationship with Dolly, originally borne out of necessity, had become increasingly destructive. Friends and colleagues had seen Nicky's personality change from his characteristic gentleness and good humour to a state that veered from catatonic inactivity to unpredictable bursts of anger. Worst of all, his erratic behaviour was beginning to affect his professional life.

The show business cliché that "cocaine is God's way of telling you that you have too much money" certainly rang true for Nicky, although Kathi McDonald laid much of the blame for the downturn in his fortunes squarely at Dolly's feet:

"I'm a Libra—a real peace loving, sixties type—but I found her overbearing, unkind, cold and selfish. And Nicky could never say no; she helped him spend his money, let's put it that way."

However many of Nicky's friends may have disliked or mistrusted Dolly and wondered what he saw in her, at the beginning they had made a handsome couple. Like anyone else, they made the most of their limitations and must have had some reason for remaining together as long as they did. At this time, Nicky began throwing his money around in a totally irresponsible fashion, as if this way at least his wife wouldn't spend it all.

In the space of a few months, with his earlier love affair with California over,

Nicky had exchanged his luxurious house in the exclusive haven of Marin County for comfortable but rented accommodations in England. The end of his solo ambitions then saw the collapse of even this retreat and left him floating undecidedly between London and Los Angeles, without a firm idea of where he was going next. As usual, it was an offer of work that ultimately determined his next move—from Hollywood back to Mill Valley.

Ever since his-much heralded arrival in the Bay Area back in 1969, his pedigree and brilliance had made him a welcome guest on many local productions. Clients had included Blue Cheer guitarist Leigh Stephens, folk-rock duo Brewer and Shipley, one-time Grateful Dead offshoot New Riders Of The Purple Sage, Pamela Polland, David Hayes, Chet Nichols, Terry Dolan and, in Los Angeles, even comedy duo Cheech and Chong.

Singer-songwriter Pamela Polland, now resident in Hawaii, had once been with CBS as part of the folk-rock group "Gentle Soul" and was then re-signed by Nicky's mentor Clive Davis, in a bidding war with David Geffen's new Asylum Records. Her memories of Nicky at her 1972 session show a marked contrast to his later behaviour:

"I was a big fan of his so I probably asked for him and the record company provided; he was a superstar to the rest of us and everyone went for their personal best because Nicky was there. He was easy to be around, very unassuming and of course, a monster player. As an associate of the Stones, we were prepared for a real 'prima donna' type and instead we got a fun and down-to-earth fellow. Although I wrote all the songs, I didn't have a hundredth of his chops, so he took my songs to a higher level."

An astute engineer's decision to hit the red button at the right moment ensured that Pamela's self-titled album is distinguished by being the only one to preserve Nicky's rendition of that Hopkins favourite, "The Teddy Bear's Picnic."

One of Nicky's longest-running California associations was with the loose conglomerate known as Terry and The Pirates, a Quicksilver offshoot that gigged and recorded for two decades in and around Marin. His connection was through John Cipollina, who described the band philosophy to a journalist in the eighties:

"It's just for fun: musicians get off the road with other bands, still wound up from touring and want to go out and play more gigs. Terry couldn't afford me or the others if he had to keep us together."

Part-time Pirate David Hayes (also Van Morrison's longest-serving bass-player), explained the band's complex history:

"Terry Dolan wrote the songs and held it all together. It would never have gone on for all those years if it hadn't been for him; he was the guy with the station wagon (laughs). He wrote good vehicles for all of us to play on, so when I was off the road with Van I played with them. Nicky was allowed to float in and out more than any-body and we were always honoured to have him. When he was coming in, we all just moved over, gave him space and off he went; there was never any rehearsal involved. There were times when there were people booking us and taking care of us and there were other times when it was strictly just 'throw the shit in the car and get to the gig!'"

Guitarist Greg Douglass, who put in more "Pirate" time than most and later also played with Nicky in John Cipollina's Raven, remembered him from way back when Terry's band was working under its original name Country Weather:

"Nicky had agreed to produce Terry's first album for Warner Brothers Records. At that point the Rolling Stones were gigantic and to me Nicky was a huge star. Quiet as he was at times, he was still bigger than life."

An album deal was drawn up based on initial demos and conditional on Nicky producing—the only time that he ever took on that role for another artist.

Greg Douglass: "In retrospect it was not something he was really comfortable doing, because after the demos, Nicky kind of dragged his heels; he was working on his first solo album and in fact some of the intros to Terry's songs ended up on Nicky's record. Terry finally got a little upset, so Nicky said, 'OK, we'll get started.' I walked in and there's Lonnie Turner from the Steve Miller Band, Prairie Prince on drums and of course Nicky on piano, so I was more than a little intimidated! Nicky was wearing a green velvet cape, which was heady stuff, and wanted everything really slow. Terry seemed to think that he may have been tak-ing some sort of tranquilliser at that point, though it wasn't anything I noticed.

"Nicky went out of his way to make me personally feel comfortable, but I think that he had spent so much time as a sideman, that he was never really comfortable in the role of leader, even as a producer. He would make suggestions but would very much let you have your own head. We completed half an album at Wally Heider's and then Nicky just got too caught up in his other commitments and couldn't finish the record, so the album was completed but never released; the Nicky produced side was more polished. It's another lost San Francisco classic.

"The longest I associated with Nicky was in the band Raven, which unfortunately was during the dark time of Nicky's life. Things were getting pretty ugly between him and Dolly and apparently there was another guy living at the house, that was Dolly's boyfriend. Nicky was drinking an enormous amount of tequila and he would come to rehearsal, learn the songs, play them brilliantly, then the next night he would have completely forgotten and we'd have to re-learn everything—it was frustrating.

"The other thing I remember from those sessions was Nicky's belt. Nicky would do these wonderful glissandos, but was drinking so much that he would sometimes get to the end of the piano, keep going and fall off the stool! It was getting to the point where he was hurting himself, so we finally had to rig up a canvas belt to attach to the keyboard. Nicky was wearing a seatbelt during rehearsals! It was actually pretty funny, because he'd be doing this wonderful run, then he'd jerk right back, so it worked beautifully.[43]

"Nicky was very unhappy at that point in his life and very upset about the situation with Dolly—a lot of self-recrimination, a lot of shame—and John, who was very close to him, felt helpless."

Both musicians appeared on several Terry and The Pirates releases, though not necessarily having recorded at the same time. Their contributions were spread over four albums, most of which were released on European labels.

Despite his many connections in the incestuous world of the San Francisco scene, it was not until 1975 that Nicky got a call from the crown prince of the Marin set, Jerry Garcia.

Not content with his extraordinary workload as a member of the Grateful Dead, Garcia had, since the sixties, involved himself with a number of casual side projects: country rock with the New Riders Of The Purple Sage, bluegrass with Old And In The Way, electronic experiments with Howard Wales and Tom Constanten and funky soul with organist Merl Saunders in the Legion Of Mary, the line-up that immediately preceded his invitation to Nicky Hopkins. In September 1975, Nicky moved back to Mill Valley and joined Elvis Presley's ex-drummer Ron Tutt and bass-player John Kahn in the Jerry Garcia Band, the introduction having come via his friend Dan Healy.

One lady friend, who chooses to remain anonymous and will be referred to as "D," formed a close bond with Nicky after having initially met him at Woodstock when she was just fifteen, and saw him play dozens of concerts with Garcia and others.

After Woodstock, their paths didn't cross again until early 1972, when "D" moved to the west coast and was "nannying" for a local San Francisco band. Nicky was in the meantime installed in his own house, had joined and left

---

[43] Greg's confirmation of the legendary seatbelt was the first eyewitness account of something this author had begun to believe was an apocryphal story. Amusing as such moments may have been, they disguised an underlying sadness.

Quicksilver and was moonlighting with various groups of musicians in and around his home, north of the Golden Gate Bridge. "D" lived with her sister on a houseboat in Sausalito, with neighbours Dino Valenti and Shel Silverstein (in a "big, creaky, scary garbage barge") and moved with her to downtown Mill Valley:

"Nicky was not in very good shape physically at all. He was drinking really heavily and needed and wanted some help that he wasn't and should have been getting at home. I think he sussed out fairly early on that I was essentially fearless and he had no clue how young I was. I wasn't telling him."

For a few months "D" became a fixture in Nicky's life and a bolthole at times of particular stress. She was by no means his only extra-marital "friend":

"We stopped happening there for a bit because of Dolly...I don't think that she ever knew. Nicky did cat around a bit, there's no two ways about it. I don't want to upset her or anybody else, but it was the defining event and relationship of my life—the first half of it—and mattered to me enormously."

When quizzed about Nicky's condition during this period, "D" revealed an otherwise undocumented chapter in Nicky's slide into substance abuse. Their relationship began shortly before the notorious Rolling Stones tour of 1972 and picked up again when Nicky returned to Marin:

"He came off the road with an addiction to 'snowballs'[44] he hadn't had when he left. I think Dolly was down in Los Angeles and he came up here and was just a wreck, a complete mess, I held his head in my lap and watched him go 'cold turkey.'"

Despite this episode, "D" agreed that Nicky was more drawn to alcohol than to heroin:

"That was his big weakness, but he certainly availed himself of the darker, nastier side effects of that kind of tour."

Just as Kathi McDonald before her, "D" felt that it was largely Dolly's influence that led to Nicky's increasing dependence on booze and the subsequent damage to his career.

"The impression I got was that Dolly was not content to be married to the premier session keyboard player of his generation. She wanted a rock star and that was never going to happen. I didn't have the courage to tell him he didn't have the voice or the entire vibe. Dolly talked him into thinking, 'Yeah, we'll do albums and we'll write songs together and you'll be the next great thing.' By 1975, when he came back to Mill Valley, he was desperately unhappy because, with all the good will in the world, with George Harrison giving him the studio time and a raft of friends and people who loved him, he had failed."

John Goddard, Mill Valley's legendary purveyor of vinyl through his now sadly departed record store, Village Music, remembered seeing Nicky "do drugs that would kill anyone else: bottles in rows under the bed and heroin and cocaine taped to sliding cupboards so they were hidden..."

Nicky was still drinking hard when he joined the Jerry Garcia Band in the au-

---

[44] also known as "speedballs"—a cocaine and heroin cocktail

tumn of 1975, having moved with Dolly to a considerably less sumptuous rented house on Erica Road, off Mt. Tamalpais.

"D" : "I don't think he ever stopped. He'd been off in Surrey for two years, trying to do the rock'n'roll thing and the drinking got worse. He'd been down in Los Angeles and hated it. Marin County was home. Mill Valley was home. The house up on Erica Road was home. He was really happy to be back up in northern California, working with Jerry and they had a really good little band."

Nicky played on half of Garcia's album *Reflections*, much of which became the new band's live set-list. The line-up played its debut show at Sophie's in Palo Alto on September 18th, mixing Jerry's original material with his usual wide variety of covers, mostly drawn from blues or country and western sources, and with the spotlight strongly on Garcia's singing and guitar playing. Bay Area journalist

66. Nicky and his cat Pig, at the house on Erica Road

Joel Selvin's review of the band's show at the Keystone in Berkeley, gives a good description of their live activities:

"Sharing lead instrumental chores is pianist Nicky Hopkins. The band's repertoire mixed rhythm and blues oldies such as a slowed-down version of Junior Walker's "Roadrunner" or the ten-minute-plus rendition of Fats Domino's "All By Myself" with Dead-sounding originals like "Mission In The Rain." Hopkins kept up a dry banter with the crowd between numbers, acting loosely as the host, a cigarette constantly dangling from his lips. Garcia has developed into a distinctive vocalist and the band's spare arrangements gave him comfortable room in which to sing. His extemporaneous skills on guitar are well-known...Hopkins, easily Garcia's equal on grand piano, was the bonus. His swirling, melodious and tinkling keyboard work was full of brilliant surprises and twists.'

Alcohol seems to have helped Nicky come out of his shell on stage. When the power failed at the Concord Pavilion at the start of a warm-up show for the band's east coast tour, Nicky (again described as compere alongside his keyboard duties) stepped in before even the first note was played:

"Hopkins supplied a marvellous improvisational piano solo, using only his vocal mike over the piano. Certainly the most talkative member of the band, Nicky had to stick his head inside the piano to talk to the crowd."

Charlie McCollum in the *Washington Star* drew a somewhat cruel comparison between Nicky's previous appearance two months earlier with his own band and his performance as a Garcia sideman:

"Garcia...drew a packed house at Constitution Hall and received a thunderous response from the crowd. For once, the Dead freaks, who have never been accused of being musically discriminating, were right. Garcia did his usual impeccable job on lead guitar...Hopkins, whose work with his own band two months ago at the Cellar Door was less than stimulating, proved again that he is one of the better keyboard men around and really shone on 'Pig's Boogie.' An exemplary evening of rock."

When the band hit New York, Nicky's niece Alix, now eleven years old, witnessed the on-the-road circus at the Beacon Theatre:

"Everybody was passing joints back and forth and my mother smacked my hand when it came near me. I remember Nicky dedicating a song to each of us and going backstage before and after. The Hell's Angels were doing the security and Vinnie, the head of that particular chapter, had a beaver hat, big motorcycle boots and a huge belly covered in tattoos and a leather jerkin, but he was very nice. Nicky had a solo spot in the show and played 'Edward,' 'Pig's Boogie' and one more after that."

Nicky's uncharacteristic assumption of the role of master of ceremonies underlines the shift in his personality and was probably the result of a drink-inspired recklessness, combined with Garcia's total lack of showmanship. His habit of barking like a dog during and after solos is clearly audible on live recordings and was picked up on by audiences too, as a novel way of demanding an encore.

In the circumstances, the collaboration was not destined to last for long and after one studio album and thirty-six shows in four months, Nicky bowed out on New Year's Eve 1975, at another Keystone gig. Grateful Dead magazine *The Golden Road* summed up Nicky's time in the band:

"The Hopkins-model JGB was not universally well received. Many people were used to Merl Saunders' organ and Hopkins' airy piano was a big change and there was also a big change in the repertoire. Hopkins talked to the audience a lot, and while he could be witty, he seemed to be going through a difficult period and his stage chatter could turn into depressing monologues about, say, how somebody killed his cat. This had a tendency to cast a pall over otherwise merry proceedings."

"D" : "Toward the end Nicky became unreliable and sometimes wouldn't even show up. At the New Year's Eve show he was, to use his own phrase, 'pissed as a rat's nightmare!' and could barely get it together to play the first set. That was the last time he ever played with the Garcia Band and after that it got even worse. In February or thereabouts he went back to L.A. because there was no work up here for him."

Nicky later succinctly described touring with Garcia as "rather boring": "Jerry's a real nice guy, but a whole show of Jerry singing and playing guitar was a little bit much."

He returned to Los Angeles in total disarray and "D" didn't see him again until the following winter.

Jon Mark had, in the meantime, settled in the beautiful coastal town of Carmel, and having employed Nicky on Mark-Almond's album *73*, for a while lost touch with his London colleague:

"When (Quicksilver) finished I was stuck in the middle of California, touring with the band and I bumped into some friends who said Nicky was in trouble in San Francisco. I got his phone number and gave him a call to ask what was happening and he was in very bad shape. Dolly was calling us and saying, 'Please help me, he's gone crazy! He's selling all the furniture!'

"I know it got to the point where he sold his piano and one night I got a call saying, 'He's gone downtown to score and I don't know what to do, because he's crazy, he's taken a knife with him.' I said, 'Well, what can I do? I'm a hundred and twenty-five miles away' and after a long conversation, I said, 'Well, let me know what's happening when he gets back' and that was the night he got stabbed. He'd got involved with some people, drew a knife and they stabbed him and cut his artery or his leg or something. It was a nightmare, and a day or two later, he got back to me and said 'Help me Jon, help me!'

"All of us had run-ins of some kind or another with alcohol, drugs or a combination of both, so I knew that he was in really deep shit. I said, 'Come down here for a break, we'll look after you,' but he said, 'No, I've got to do this, I've got to get it together.' We arranged to meet up but that never happened. He'd gone his other way.

"Past a certain age and popularity, America could be absolute hell. You'd be having success, making lots of money, with roadies and crews and buying big homes, but the moment you passed a certain point...I had a roadie called Keith Robertson and his favourite quote, when dealing with record companies was, 'Thank you very next!' and Nicky went through that too.

"There came a point when 'I used to be in Quicksilver Messenger Service,' didn't work any more, just like 'I had Mark-Almond, I know everyone there is to know,' didn't work for me. That's when lots of English musicians, who'd lived there for so long, started to troop home, because ultimately you go back to England, to your local pub, where your Mum remembers you and there's still something substantial, whereas in America, once you're out of fashion or too old, nobody wants you.

"Nicky went to hell and back. We all did. We were kids from the suburbs of London, that grew up during the post-war years and were doing music because we loved it, suddenly getting shoved into America, being made famous, being successful on a level that we couldn't understand—and then losing it."

Unfortunately for Nicky Hopkins, the USA remained the place where he could most easily find work. It's astonishing to realise that even in the early part of his most troubled years, Nicky's satisfied customers still included Ringo Starr, Harry Nilsson, Carly Simon and Martha Reeves (all with Richard Perry producing), as well as Donovan, Joe Cocker, Art Garfunkel—and David Soul.

Jon wasn't the only one to notice the change in his behaviour.

Ron Polte: "We lost touch for a long time and one day I was driving to Sausalito in heavy traffic and I saw him coming out of a liquor store. I blew the horn and he looked at me, looked away and just kept going. I don't know if he recognised me; he had something else on his mind and was walking real...seriously."

Paul Hopkins, now living abroad, helped Nicky out of various financial scrapes: "It must have been 1975-76 when he came to Luxemburg with Dolly and it was quite a weekend. That's where it really came home to me that he'd changed. The old Nicky didn't re-appear until much later."

Back in Los Angeles, Nicky did his best to establish a foothold in the studio scene. Trevor Veitch was a guitar player and contractor (the American version of a London "fixer") in L.A. and used Nicky on many sessions from the late seventies onwards. Trevor's first e-mail stated, "I knew him from Dolly to Moira, from drunk to sober":

"I'd play on the records and hire all the musicians and I had a great deal of power, because I was doing it for (producers) Giorgio Moroder, Bob Esty, Quincy Jones, etc. Nicky had gone away for a while and in '76 or '77 he'd come back to town; I was thrilled to hear from him again because I really liked him and because he played so well. So I started hiring him, and it wasn't just a professional thing, because I'm from Canada, so we both grew up on the Goons."

Trevor knew about Nicky's heavy drinking but said that, in his experience, it seldom intruded into the workplace:

"He was a very benign drunk; he wasn't mean or nasty; he would just sit there with this silly grin on his face making parrot sounds from Monty Python; it was really quite sweet. The biggest problem from a professional standpoint was that he didn't drive, probably for damn good reason, because he would have killed himself. He'd rely on the kindness of strangers to get him to the studio and I'd sometimes drive him home. He worked both with me and for me until his move to Nashville: Donna Summer, Barbra Streisand and a lot of movies. The list is quite long.

"We were all making way too much money for our own good and everybody was either drinking or doing drugs or both. It was the era of pop and disco and for good

67. Drinking with the Boyd Albritton Band

or bad, it meant live bands and orchestras, which is something we all miss now. Giorgio Moroder and Pete Bellotte would record at a studio in Hollywood called Rusk and it was pretty much like a factory over there. We had the damn thing going fourteen/fifteen hours a day and Nicky did a bunch of that stuff.

"Los Angeles is not a place that you move to for the fun and the sun! If you have a thriving career it's a wonderful place, but in harder times, it can get pretty lonely and it's very much 'Out of sight, out of mind.' It's probably fair to say that eighty per cent of all the music done in the United States is done in L.A. Don't leave!"

Richard Perry was another U.S. based producer who was massively successful in the seventies and used Nicky on a regular basis. They had first worked together in

1969, just before Nicky left London, on a session with jazz diva Ella Fitzgerald.

Richard Perry: "I remember that Ella Fitzgerald session very well because I was doing the entire album with her in five days that she had off, in the middle of two months of one-nighters throughout Europe. For some unknown reason, I didn't bring any musicians or an arranger with me, but I knew of Nicky's reputation. He held the whole session together for me—and this was with a live rhythm section and with strings."

Soon after Nicky's arrival in the States, Perry brought him down to Los Angeles to record with Fats Domino, one of Nicky's all-time idols who, due to complications related to unpaid alimony payments, was unable or unwilling to enter California to record. Nicky had the curious task of impersonating one of the great piano players in history on two of his own tracks, an achievement of which he remained inordinately proud.

His connection with the producer came to the rescue again in 1976. One of Richard Perry's most successful clients at the time was diminutive British singer Leo Sayer and the two had recently completed Leo's *Endless Flight* album. Nicky Hopkins was not available for the record, but when the time came to put together a touring band, he was one of the top-level players chosen, along with bassist Reggie McBride, drummer Alvin Taylor and…Bobby Keys:

"Leo Sayer's manager wanted to take him out on the road and he hired all the musicians that were on the album. He was this old English manager that used to take care of one of the very first English soloists; I think it was Tommy Steele; he would come into the dressing room before the gig and give all of us this pep talk. 'We've got to go out there and do this for the kid.' He always referred to 'the kid'…We were a bunch of gritty old veterans that were pretty set in our ways, drinking and snorting and smoking and waving our dicks in the air whenever we wanted to and somehow this seemed to really irritate Nicky.

"He'd started drinking, and Nicky was one of those people that alcohol had a very quick and very drastic effect on. A couple of drinks and all of a sudden he was not cognisant of where he was or what he was doing. The first couple of times I just thought, 'Ah, the guy's finally becoming one of the boys,' but it escalated and he was starting to get a chip on his shoulder and an attitude. He'd get belligerent with people in airports and hotels."

"D" caught the tour in San Francisco:

"Nicky came through town in Leo Sayer's band at the Boarding House. He was apparently living down in L.A. and there was very definitely a wall up; he was with somebody, which was expected, but he was very wary and a little shaky; he and Dolly were still married but she was not who he had with him."

When the tour continued to the east coast, *The Boston Globe* of Tuesday, December 7th, 1976 reported the following, under the headline "Leo Sayer group triumphs over odds":

"His present band is of awesome pedigree, but one of its key members, pianist Nicky Hopkins, who has played with the Rolling Stones, had a bad accident at 2 a.m. Sunday morning. Hopkins was entering the elevator at the Parker House and slipped back-

wards, banging his head on the metal floor, where the doors slide shut. He needed twenty stitches at MGH, where he is listed in good condition and should be well enough to leave by mid-week and will miss the last two gigs of the tour, both in Canada. Interestingly, one of Sayer's best-known songs is 'The Show Must Go On'!"

Of all the stories that surfaced on the subject of Nicky's self-destructive seventies, that told by genial poet and singer Pete Brown takes the prize for the most bizarre. Having written lyrics to some of the most famous Cream songs, Pete was understandably close to Jack Bruce, the band's one-time bass player and lead singer. He dated the following events to the summer of 1976 or thereabouts:

"I did a project with Jack in San Francisco. A very wealthy guy, who was supposedly one of the heirs to the Ticketron Agency, had fourteen cars and three motorbikes, was a huge fan of Jack's and appeared to be latently in love with a childhood friend, whom he was trying to promote as a singer. He was a very good-looking guy but not a singer. Jack was going through a bit of a quiet time and asked if I wanted to go over and do this project, so they flew us over first class and Nicky Hopkins was going to be the keyboard player.

"When we arrived, we were met by a group of people at the airport and they said, 'There's a problem. Nicky Hopkins has been kidnapped by these rivals of ours and he's trapped in a studio and is being forced to play music for some black magic ceremony.' I said, 'What can we do?' 'Well, we'll have to get the guns and go and liberate him' and I thought, 'Oh fuck, I've walked straight into a bloody gang war!'

"Somehow Nicky got out and we were staying and rehearsing in Sly Stone's old house, which he had recently vacated. He had panthers and a crocodile, which he used to let loose to deter trespassers. The animals had gone, but there was a very strange vibe about the place. We must have been there a few weeks working on that project, which never became a record and in the end we had to flee. Luckily we had our tickets."

Whether Pete's memories of the events are accurate or not, his description vividly conveys the kind of people with whom Nicky was sharing his days—and nights—and the utter confusion and decadence that surrounded him in that bleak era.

His next employer was a living legend—but only just.

Gimme Shelter
The Wilderness Years – Part 2

"We turned around and the plane had gone. They took off without us, so that was a bad start."

– Joe Cocker

Ever since his breakthrough show at Woodstock, Joe Cocker had remained a major draw in America. A year later, with Leon Russell as ringmaster, he snatched triumph out of disaster with the *Mad Dogs & Englishmen* tour. *Time* magazine described him as "the most popular white male blues singer in the U.S."

It had taken only two years to transform a Sheffield pub singer into one of the most successful rock acts in the world, but the he paid a high price. His life became a spiral of increasing drug and alcohol abuse that would have killed most people, and left the singer both physically and emotionally drained.

The following years of touring, recording and occasional disappearances had more downs than ups. The accompanying chaos of drunkenness, cancelled shows, legal disputes, drug busts and a heroin habit had, by the mid-seventies,

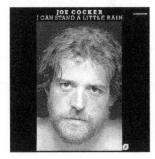 left Cocker's professional reputation in tatters. In the industry, he was considered unmanageable and a likely candidate for the next celebrity obituary.

Nevertheless A&M Records in the USA had stuck by him and was rewarded in the mid-seventies with two accomplished and successful albums, *I Can Stand A Little Rain* and *Jamaica Say You Will*. Cocker's audience was both patient and extremely loyal.

Trumpeter Jim Price lured Joe back into recording in 1973, bringing with him a simple demo of a Billy Preston ballad. Having worked together extensively with the Rolling Stones, Price planned to replace his own basic piano part with the best player he knew: Nicky Hopkins.

Joe Cocker: "I'd been living in London and was a bit disillusioned with the whole business when Jim Price came and played me that song, 'You Are So Beau-

tiful,' which got me back in the studio; it was originally a gospel tune, but Jim kept saying, 'When I get Nicky Hopkins on this track, you'll understand what we're talking about' and of course, when he finally played it to me that way, I couldn't believe this piano part; that's when I did the vocal that stayed on the record; I sang it to wrap around that piano line. It would not have been that song without that piano part. Nicky's thing and the vocal just kissed each other; it was special. I was a late-

comer on the scene and I kind of knew Nicky, but it wasn't like we did that session together. I'd still never met him at that stage."

Nicky consistently picked "You Are So Beautiful" as one of his all-time favourite performances, and when the album was released in 1974, the American public agreed by putting both the LP and later the single into the upper reaches of the charts. The song soon became an anthem to Cocker's fans all over the world, to rival his breakthrough Beatles cover, "With A Little Help From My Friends."

Nicky Hopkins appeared on both those Cocker albums without actually meeting the wayward star. Promotion for the first one began with a legendary performance at the Roxy Theatre in Hollywood, with record company executives, the press and a star-studded audience in attendance. Cocker turned up too drunk to perform and ended up, three songs into the set list, curled up foetus-like at the foot of his own microphone.

The mayhem continued on tour, where there was a strong feeling that part of the audience was only there to watch Joe Cocker falling apart. A follow-up album in 1976 (*Stingray*) failed to match up to its predecessors' sales.[45]

By the time Joe went back to England for Christmas '76, he was deep in debt to his record company and entirely without management. He ended up doing a show in Birmingham to an audience of only two hundred diehard fans. Promoter and manager Michael Lang had remained a fan of Cocker's ever since booking him at Woodstock, and stepped in to rescue what looked like a terminal decline in the raw-voiced singer's fortunes.

Michael described Joe as "near dead" when they started working together,

---

[45] Ironically, his highest profile moment in 1976 was appearing on the hit comedy show *Saturday Night Live* in a duet with comedian John Belushi, who had made a name for himself by doing an uncanny impersonation of Joe Cocker.

with the singer drinking a fifth of booze in the morning and another in the afternoon. Having secured an agreement that if Joe took a drink before any show it would immediately be cancelled, Lang set about systematically re-building Cocker's shattered career, settling his enormous debts at A&M and persuading them to let the singer go.

With so many bridges burned in the U.S.A., Lang planned to start the ball rolling in mid-1977 with a visit to Australia, where Cocker still had a faithful audience. With finances tight, he needed to find a cheaper touring band than the top-level studio cracks Joe had become used to. Lang found a perfect candidate in the workmanlike American Standard Band, a five-piece outfit from near Boston. He added Bobby Keys and Nicky Hopkins to the line-up for additional musical muscle, and to help Joe Cocker feel more comfortable. Since one of the prime objectives was to keep Joe away from obvious temptation, the addition of the two star players to the touring party was an invitation to disaster.

Michael Lang: "Nicky and Joe were soul mates but unfortunately also drinking mates. I didn't realise that I should have made the same deal with Nicky as I had with Joe. He was a bad drunk and we had to have security with him to prevent fights."

THE AGE, Thursday, June 23, 1977

Mad Dog Joe for 12 cities

Joe Cocker: "Talk about people being incorrigible! I mean, we all like to drink, but Bobby and Nicky! I remember they booted us off the plane when we got to Fiji. We flew Air New Zealand from L.A. and it was in the days when they used to have a keyboard and all sorts of things in the top of the airplane and we were playing 'Derek & Clive' (Peter Cook and Dudley Moore's hilarious but filthy taped studio conversations) and of course they came over, 'Mr. Cocker, it's very funny, but would you mind, you're offending the other passengers.' We were so roasted we didn't give a damn, so in Fiji they fooled us into getting off the 'plane to go to a bar. We got out there, but it was midnight and the bar was closed. We turned around and the plane had gone. They took off without us, so that was a bad start."

Michael Lang de-planed with the miscreants, but added that Nicky had actually threatened the life of one of the stewardesses before they were ejected. They caught up with the tour in time for the first show in New Zealand the following day. Cocker mostly stayed to true his pact with Michael, limiting his drinking to after the shows. Reviews for the New Zealand leg of the tour were almost universally positive, and in many papers Nicky was singled out for particular praise:

"It is doubtful that Cocker would have got across to the crowd without the backing of the legendary keyboardist Nicky Hopkins and Texas saxophonist Bobby Keys. These two exceptional artists certainly held the band together. Cocker received an ecstatic response for 'You Are So Beautiful.'"

Quite how Nicky was able to hold the band together is open to conjecture, since he had great difficulty in keeping himself together. In fact, he'd achieved

223

the distinction of out-drinking and out-misbehaving his boss, whose own exploits had become the stuff of legend.

Joe Cocker (from *With a Little Help From My Friends* by J.P. Bean): "He'd had terrible stomach problems all his life so the doctors used to give him Valium. He'd take loads of Valium before a show and then drink Triple White Russians—vodka with cream in it—and be absolutely legless. You'd have to help him up on stage, but sit him down at the keyboard, man, and it was magic, even when he was blitzed. He didn't know any of the titles of the songs: 'What is it—I Can Stand A Little Rain? Oh, you mean G flat!'"

Nicky was beyond caring what the world thought and only made intermittent sense in an interview he gave to one Nevin Topp of *The Press* in New Zealand:

"I managed to get a few sane words in edgeways with Nicky, nine floors up in Noah's Hotel, while competing with the 'Albatross' track from the Monty Python album, Live At Drury Lane. *There was a Beano comic lying on Nick's bed and he suddenly clutched it like it was Linus's security blanket. 'I used to collect these,' he says, 'In fact in my home in L.A. I have Beanos I collected between 1947-53. Really dug the Bash Street Kids and was sorry when they took Biffo the Bear off the front page. I want to be loony! You can quote me on that.' Then the phone rings. 'Happy asylum, good morning.'*

"He says he has done three tours with the Stones and one with "the Midget" (Leo Sayer) and in answer to the question why he hasn't formed his own group answers, 'I need an albatross transplant—badly.'"

The Python-inspired madness continued when the entourage arrived in Australia, where a live show was traded with local airline TAA for a week at the idyllic Keppel Island resort. An exceedingly drunk Cocker was described by Rhonda Plune in *Juke* magazine, as sitting cross-legged, "beer in hand, well advanced on the road to oblivion, lacing his conversation with four-lettered expletives."

Within a day or two, Joe was making the front page of Melbourne's *Truth* (Victoria's top-selling weekly equivalent of the *Sun* or *National Enquirer*):

"COCKER'S OBSCENITY SHOCKS TOURISTS."

"Joe Cocker shouted four-letter words before and after a mock gay dance with former Rolling Stones keyboard player Nicky Hopkins. The dance climaxed with both crashing to the floor at the feet of an attractive blonde waitress. He and his band had earlier been drinking heavily in the sun at the TAA-operated island resort. Most guests clapped and cheered as the Mad Dog and his Englishmen raged on the upper level, but a grey-haired man and his two elderly female companions were visibly upset by the performance and stormed past the heavy drinking entertainer to the poolside exit door."

Joe managed to keep a lid on his excesses when concert time came around, though Nicky later remembered (from *Sonics* magazine, 1989):

"He was drinking so much he had to go offstage and throw up, so he announced, 'And now Nicky will keep you all entertained, while I go off for a quiet spew!' I had to do a couple of Monty Python routines, which didn't go down too well. I remember yelling 'Albatross!' and everyone looking round for it!"

Joe Cocker: "The guitarist would say, 'Oh God, we're in trouble tonight,' when Nicky would be doing his 'Gumby' (another Monty Python reference). If we saw that coming, 'Oh boy!' But the Aussies loved it. They love somebody who is off the wall and I don't think it was so much Monty Python, they just thought, 'Who is this guy?' He was a comedian as well."

Most of the concerts during the two-week visit, billed as "The Return Of The Mad Dog," were sold out and all went down a storm, with mostly positive reviews, blemished only by Cocker's unfortunate lapse on arrival in Perth, where he stepped off the plane and promptly vomited on the tarmac. The subsequent roasting by local reporters at a press conference was nevertheless aimed at his offstage behaviour, not his performances.

In Australia, Nicky somehow found the time and energy to record with a local band, The Ferrets. A new generation of musicians was arriving in the wake of the UK punk explosion and Nicky's credentials, particularly with the Rolling Stones, made him a popular choice for local bands and producers wherever he travelled.

The next destination in Michael Lang's strategy was South America, a territory often neglected by rock bands in the seventies. The touring began in August in Brazil, with shows in Rio, Santos and Sao Paulo. The lunacy continued unabated, with Nicky still a main offender, though here the stakes were considerably higher than just a bad headline in the papers. The Brazilian promoters provided a security guard armed with a machine gun to stand guard outside each band member's room—and this time Dolly came along.

From Brazil the band continued to Buenos Aires and on to Mexico, where the already haphazard concert arrangements became even more chaotic. Nicky was banned from flying altogether after a falling-out with one promoter, which made the whole band late for the next gig. In front of a baying crowd, they discovered that the promoter had only provided one instrument for the two keyboard players, and that didn't work. After a half hour of playing, with firecrackers raining down on the stage, the band ran for the shelter of the tour bus.

Both Cocker and Bobby Keys separately recalled the night of the August 6th, 1977:

Joe Cocker: "It was one of those hotels where the bar stays open all night. We were in Argentina or somewhere daft and everyone had to go to bed and we didn't want to, because we were all sparked after doing a show. I got a huge knock on my door and it was Nicky, in tears, saying that Elvis had died and he was saying, 'Nobody cares!' He'd seen some of the band and he said, 'Nobody gives a -----. Elvis is dead and nobody cares.'

Bobby Keys: "He and Dolly had a big fight—it was the day Elvis died, I'll never forget that—and he came over to my room and was crying and everything. It really bothered me deeply because this guy was going to pieces, man. I mean he was beyond having just a little drinking problem. He had some very serious issues and was starting to piss off a lot of people in the business. It's one thing to be 'rock'n'roll' colourful, it's another thing to go beyond colourful to unreliable and damaging. The manager would say 'Bobby, look after Nicky. You're a big guy and he listens to you.' Because I'd tell him, 'Nicky, if you don't shut up I'm gonna sit on you till you quit wiggling!'"

The final destination was Venezuela, where the appalling organisation at the shows finally led to a total breakdown between Michael Lang and the promoters. After protracted financial negotiations, it was discovered that the promoters held the airline tickets, and it was only after some hair-raising moments that the party made it back to American soil in San Antonio, Texas.

Cocker went back in the studio with New Orleans legend Allen Toussaint and the Crusaders backing him for his album *Luxury You Can Afford*, while Nicky stayed in L.A. making his own studio appearances with Rod Stewart (twice), Jennifer Warnes, Lonnie Donegan, Eddie Money, Carole Bayer Sager and the otherwise forgotten Hollywood Stars.

His touring stint with Cocker was over, but in an attempt to separate Joe from the dealers and hangers-on that flocked to his home, Lang had the idea of moving the singer out to the calmer environment of Woodland Hills, with Nicky and Bobby Keys and their respective wives in one house, and Joe and his partner in another. The ever-optimistic manager hoped that the surroundings would prove conducive to songwriting.

Bobby Keys: "Nicky and myself were residing somewhere out in the San Fernando Valley and Nicky would take pills, for the pain nobody really knew he had, and booze. He'd get completely spaced out, totally unaware of what he was doing and I'd try to look after him some, but hell, I wasn't the best influence or the best watchdog 'cause I was getting boxed myself.

"I didn't get real close to Nicky till we all lived together, when his health and his drinking problem were getting worse. I loved that boy like a brother, but God, he could be a handful to deal with when he got roaring. You'd almost have to knock him out to shut him up. On the next day he wouldn't remember and he'd be back to the shy, retiring and sweet guy again—with a hangover. I'm sure that a lot of that was brought on by medication—it was a real Jekyll and Hyde…"

Obviously writing songs never came high on the agenda.

Joe Cocker: "We lived next door to each other for months in this place with a swimming pool and hardly ever spoke. Nicky gave me a tape with about ten songs on it, but he didn't think like a singer. I think we lived there for about eight months and we never once got round the piano."

When the time came in October 1978 to go out and

promote Joe's latest offering, Bobby Keys was still on board, but Nicky was not. Years later Cocker obviously thought of him with respect and a lot of affection:

"Nicky's personality was very childlike in many ways; he could be almost like a schoolboy, which is probably why he was so talented. He collected stuff in the most bizarre manner. You'd be walking with him through a hotel room and see a sign on somebody's door and the next minute he'd say, 'Cover me, Joe' and he'd have a screwdriver out! An ashtray would be gone as he walked past it. It used to crack us up. It wasn't thievery, he just couldn't resist.

"He had those big, dark smiling eyes. When you saw him with his shirt off, he had a big gut from drinking, because he was always sat at the piano and never exercised. It was scary, because he must have had six operations, where they'd

68. Nicky in 1978

done these huge sewing up jobs on him. He would always be showing you, as if he'd been in battle. So he was a tough guy too.

"You've got to remember that in the seventies a lot of us really didn't know where we were going. The music scene had changed so much since Woodstock. There were new bands coming on the scene like the Eagles and the Police. It was a different sound and I think the drinking was part of feeling like we were on the way out. The memories I have of Nicky were just of that talent, all wrapped up in this very confused ball."

Nicky hated Los Angeles. With his finances depleted, he and Dolly were now living in the humdrum surroundings of Sherman Oaks.

Jon Mark: "Somebody said that Nicky had been asking after me, so I got in touch and he was obviously overjoyed to hear from me and I was overjoyed to hear from him. I drove out to find him, and it was in an area where you wouldn't think he would be. It was smog-ridden, the curtains were drawn and it was perpetually dark inside. I knocked on the door and Nicky threw his arms around me and said, 'Jon, great to see you' and he looked absolutely ravaged; but not like he was out of control. I said, 'Why all the blinds?' 'Oh, because it's too hot.' He had the air conditioning on, but didn't open the curtains. He said, 'It's too bright out there.' The house was much more modest than you'd think a star of his magnitude would have lived in."

Nicky's sister Dee stayed with Nicky and Dolly for several weeks while job and home hunting and shared the living space with seven cats:

"There wasn't much work going on at that time, because when I did get a job, very unusually for him, he asked me to help with the rent. I'm sure she was behind it. There were tremendous fights there. She was very loud and all seven cats would come tear-arseing into my bedroom; they were frightened to death. Nicky and I were real cat lovers."

Nicky's niece also came to see him in California and found Nicky very close to what Alcoholics Anonymous refers to as "rock bottom."

Alix Ninfo: "Just after my fourteenth birthday I went out with my Dad to visit him. Dee was living with them and it was really weird, because he'd changed. He was not the uncle that I remembered; he was very puffy and kind of round and didn't move very fast—Dolly too. It was like they'd aged tremendously in a couple of years. I didn't understand what was going on, until I saw the empty boxes of wine; there were boxes and boxes, so I knew that there was a big drinking problem and there were pills around too.

"There was a lot of weirdness and tension between Dolly and Dee, while Nicky was kind of oblivious; he seemed like he was in his own world and really wasn't talking much. And it was so peculiar that he wasn't skinny any more, but puffy; he was like a big potato. The curtains were always drawn, so it was always dark and we spent all our time in the kitchen, because I was always having cups of tea.

"I didn't stay there; my Dad and I were in a motel. I was really shocked. It was wonderful to see them, but it was so awful that, later on, when my mom told me that he had been going to Narconon and was much better, all I could think was,

'That's great!' I didn't want to see him like that any more."

Not surprisingly these were not bumper years for recording sessions.

In *Still In The Nick Of Time* (Mark Bego's biography of blues singer and guitarist Bonnie Raitt), original Three Dog Night keyboard player Jimmy Greenspoon recalled the chaotic sessions that led to Little Feat leader Lowell George's one solo album *Thanks I'll Eat It Here*. Nicky was one of a long list of musicians that contributed during the almost two years of studio time that went into the record:

"If 'something' ran out in the studio, Lowell and I would go up the hill and get some more 'stuff.' He'd get a case of cognac, drop it off and we'd go up and score some more coke. We'd get back and he'd say, 'OK, where were we?' At one point we left Nicky Hopkins slumped over the piano and went to get another case of cognac. He was still passed out when we returned, so we just recorded without him. Everybody was still in the studio, recording, singing and playing and he'd be slumped over the keyboard—out cold!"

In early 1979, the ever-faithful Richard Perry threw another lifeline in Nicky's direction. After an extraordinary run of success with his various star clients, Perry had finally taken the not unusual step of starting his own label, coincidentally sharing the name Planet with Shel Talmy's earlier sixties imprint. Like his predecessor, he used his favourite keyboard player on most of his productions, with the Pointer Sisters, on film soundtracks such as *The Champ* and with a new signing from England, a band named Night.

Fronted by the double vocal powerhouse of Manfred Mann's Earthband vocalist Chris Thompson and his partner Stevie Lange, the band had started as a part-time fun project in London clubs, with the unpromising name of Filthy McNasty until they found management with aspirations to greater things. Having made a deal with the freshly minted Planet Records, the whole band decamped to California, picked a new name out of the dictionary and lived in hotels until Chris bought a house in Woodland Hills, which they all shared.

Chris Thompson: "We actually went to Los Angeles with a keyboard player, but he wasn't up for all the waiting around that went on while recording with Richard and went home. We used Michael McDonald for a couple of things, and then on 'Hot Summer Nights' Richard said, 'I think we should get Nicky Hopkins." and I said, 'Man, isn't that going to cost a lot of money?' I think triplescale was the term being bandied around. Nicky played something on everything after that and never left us. Richard had it all ways, because he was the record company as well as the producer and it was his studio. It was a great studio but he wasn't budget conscious, let's put it that way.

"I ended up with the job of getting Nicky to the studio, because we were in Woodland Hills and he was in Sherman Oaks with Dolly, so it was on the way in. At first he was getting limousined in by Richard and then we realised that was ridiculous. A couple of times when we went round to pick him up for rehearsals, we heard unbelievable screaming arguments. We'd bang on the door and they wouldn't hear us, so we'd have to wait outside for an hour. The two of them were outrageous. Nicky would eventually hear us and go (adopting soft voice), 'Oh, hi Chris. I'll be out in a minute. I'm just finishing up with Dolly.'

"One night at about eleven o'clock, two taxis rolled up and Nicky got out and banged on the door saying, 'I've left Dolly!' The cab drivers were bringing his LP collection into the house. I said, 'What are you doing Nicky?' He said, 'Well, I'm coming to live with you.' I think I had him for a couple of days and then Dolly came and got him back. That was during the record."

Once in the studio, Chris remembers Nicky's piano transforming the Marvin Hamlisch/Carole Bayer Sager song "If You Remember Me," very much as he had  earlier made "You Are So Beautiful" his own. It became a top ten single under Chris' name and was added to a re-issued version of the Night album.

As recording progressed, Elektra Records, who distributed Planet product, were looking for ways to promote the upcoming release. They put the newly christened Night on the road with the Doobie Brothers; Richard Perry suggested getting Nicky in as a full-time member. The band decided to look for a permanent drummer back in England and Nicky went with them, always glad of a chance to go home. Once there, he realized he was out of step with the changing times.

Nicky Hopkins: "Not only have the fashions and styles changed, so has the music. Everyone is into 'New Wave' and punk rock in England. I felt like a freak walking around, whereas five years ago I would have fit right in."

Night found their drummer Peter Baron in London, and rehearsed for a month in Los Angeles, before joining the Doobie Brothers tour, which ran from May to November of '79.

Chris Thompson: "Nicky agreed to a band split and I think he signed a contract as a band member, because he got included in for the magical royalties that would appear after we sold two million records."

69. Promotional photos for Night

Peter Baron: "We did all the Doobie Brothers dates, but they would stop every two or three weeks and have a week off and then carry on again. More often than not we'd then go and play clubs and smaller venues like the Bottom Line or go and support someone else like Kansas."

Chris Thompson: "Nicky was quite enthusiastic about going back on the road because he was the guy that played with the Rolling Stones and the Beatles, and he knew he had lots of fans out there; I think it appealed to his ego. At the beginning he really felt part of things; he'd say, 'It's great being in a band, I really feel good about this, really love Stevie, love the guys and they're great players.' I think he really saw it as doing something with his career. He loved dressing up to go on stage and pulled all these jackets out; he always wanted to come along and talk to radio stations and was good in those circumstances. Richard felt it was a plus for us to have him, an icon of rock'n'roll! I think he was trying to get away from Dolly as well."

A journalist from *Keyboard World* described Nicky at the time as "clad in a satin blue and yellow flowered shirt, thick corduroy pants, dark blue boots with silver studs, blue sequinned socks and a Rolling Stones 'Sticky Fingers' charm around his neck. He looked as if he was ready to make a guest appearance on the old sixties Sonny and Cher Show." Nicky confessed to Boston's *Messenger-Press* that it was a strange feeling to be on a tour and not be playing with the headliners:

"I'm getting a totally different view of it. The earlier shows we did, people didn't know there was a band called Night opening for the Doobies. They also didn't know that I was going to be in the band. I think we're correcting that now."

Michael McDonald was with the Doobie Brothers and the shared tour gave the two keyboard-players ample opportunity to socialise:

"Night was a collection of extremely talented musicians and writers; I think Nicky was genuinely excited about the group's prospects and was thoroughly enjoying the music he was involved with."

The band's first single, Walter Egan's "Hot Summer Nights," received enough airplay to send it into the top twenty on the *Billboard* charts. Once out on tour, however, it became noticeable that all was not well with their star pianist.

NIGHT, the stunning new group featuring Chris Thompson, Stevie Lange, Nicky Hopkins, Billy Kristian, Robbie McIntosh, and Peter Baron. NIGHT, the album featuring the new single, "COLD WIND ACROSS MY HEART."

NIGHT, currently on tour with the Doobie Brothers.

9/21	Roanoke, VA	9/27	Richmond, VA	10/3	Augusta, ME	10/9	Nashville, TN
9/22	Greensboro, NC	9/28	Hampton, VA	10/4	Boston, MA	10/11	Dallas, TX
9/23	Atlanta, GA	9/29	Largo, MD	10/5	Providence, RI	10/12	Austin, TX
9/24	Lexington, KY	9/30	Syracuse, NY	10/6	Suffern, NY	10/13	Baton Rouge, LA
9/26	Huntington, WVA	10/1	Buffalo, NY	10/7	Philadelphia, PA	10/14	Houston, TX

Produced by Richard Perry. On Planet Records and Tapes.

Management: Raywood and Abraham Agency: Monterey Peninsula Artists

Chris Thompson: "The studio environment was where Nicky felt most comfortable, and I believe it's where he excelled, because he was able to control his environment. He wasn't a well man. The first time he took off his shirt in the dressing room everybody took a sharp intake of breath. We realised that Nicky was drinking and doing Valium, although we didn't figure out the Valium thing until we were actually on the road and he became less reliable and his playing fluctuated."

Peter Baron: "He took a lot of pills, did a lot of coke…"

Nicky had his own brief spot in the show, playing part of "Edward, The Mad Shirt Grinder" as an intro to one of the band songs, described by Peter Baron as "a sort of piano cadenza."

Chris Thompson: "He went from being a genius to fumbling a bit. I was in the middle of Manfred Mann's Earthband at the same time and I was very tired, so for me, as soon as the gig finished, I'd go to bed. I didn't really know what was going on until one of the Doobies came to me and said, 'You really need to find out what's going on with Nicky, because he just turned into a monster last night!' He was drinking with them and he just suddenly turned into this other person and they had to carry him off to bed. It was my job to go and get him out and get him on the plane the next day and he had completely annihilated a hotel room, but had no memory of it. In fact when I opened the door, he said to me, 'Something terrible's happened. While I was asleep somebody came in and smashed my room to pieces.'

"We found out that he needed the Valium to go on stage because he was so nervous, so our job was to keep him off alcohol, because alcohol and Valium are the worst things that you can possibly do together. He and Dolly had had a huge bust-up and he was with a woman photographer, who was very good for him, because she calmed him down.[46] When Dolly found out, there was a big ruckus and the next minute she came out and was on the road for three weeks, until they had another argument and she went home.

"We were running out of money, so we went to the Doobies and told them we weren't able to continue with the tour and, bless them, they had a meeting and decided they would pay us and fly us around on their plane. Actually they had two: a 'Doobie liner' and a 'Crewbie liner' and we flew with the crew. Nicky was a real liability at that point and I have to say that the stress of it all got to me. I was too tired and was trying to do too much. I was always worried whether Nicky would make it to each gig.

"When Dolly came out, he realised he loved her and the photographer girl had to leave; they would be holding hands and walking around, 'Fantastic, found Dolly again' and the next minute the owner would be calling me saying, 'You've got to do something with that couple. It's three o'clock in the morning and they're waking the whole hotel!'

"The whole band was partying too much, but when Nicky was stoned he had no idea of what appropriate behaviour was. We were doing two songs on the Dinah Shore show, which is nationwide television: 'Hot Summer Nights' and the old Freddie and The Dreamers song 'If You Got To Make A Fool Of Somebody,' which started with the piano in F. The camera was locked on Nicky's fingers and I'd tried to keep him straight but hadn't managed to, and it was live! I didn't notice, but the camera guy was going to Nicky's hands and he was moving them down the keyboard, because it was uncomfortable for him and the camera would

---

[46] Photos of Nicky and Michael McDonald, taken by one Elvira Myers on the Doobie Brothers' airplane, were featured in *Rock Scene* magazine in May 1980.

move down as well. They counted down, "10-9-8-7-6-5-4-3-2-1 – Go Nicky!" He had to start it and he just played where his hands were, in the wrong key, and Robbie McIntosh looked at me and said, "He's in the wrong key!" So I had to stop on live TV and say, 'Hey Nicky, it's in F' and Nicky went, "Yeah I know, but the camera man was pushing my hands down the keyboard.' We're having an argument on live TV!

"We did talk to him about his behaviour: 'Nicky, you can't drink too much.' 'Yeah, you're right, I can't drink too much, but I'll just have one Valium, because I need to calm down or maybe I'll have a joint.' So he started having a joint before he went to play and one time, just for a joke, the guys made up a gaffa tape joint and stuck it on top of the piano. Nicky spent the whole of his solo with the joint in his mouth, lighting it with one hand and playing his featured bit with the right hand. I'd cringe sometimes. Generally he was fantastic, but it got worse the longer the tour went on."

Nicky's behaviour became more and more outrageous and surreal. One musician, who preferred to remain anonymous, remembered Nicky walking down the aisle of a commercial airliner, tapping his nose suggestively and asking complete strangers if they had any cocaine to spare.

Chris Thompson: "I think Nicky was a very mild and lovable person until he drank or did Valium or smoked a joint or did some blow. He was one of those people that changed, and Dolly was not innocent either. She drank and did tons of drugs as well. The two of them together were catatonic and I've never heard such arguments in my life. The thing about Dolly was, she really did care about Nicky and I believe that they did love each other, but it was like *Who's Afraid Of Virginia Woolf?*"

Ironically Nicky was the only member of Night with the experience to carry off the stadium-sized venues they were playing with the Doobie Brothers.

Chris Thompson: "We were crap; just not enough experience. You've got to know how to adjust and not get too excited, so that you overplay; you've got to create atmosphere while people are still shuffling in. We were playing those sheds where the first three thousand seats were empty until about three quarters of the way through our show, but you've still got to reach out. Stevie had no experience at all and no experience about when to go to bed either, and the other guys were out every night and just got tireder and tireder and tireder as the tour went on and played worse and worse.

"I was dealing with Nicky, so it was a terrible time for me. The Doobies weren't exactly saints at that point, so nobody was really looking after him, and in the end I remember telling him he had to go home. I don't recall parting bad friends, but it's never nice to say that to somebody."

Peter Baron: "I remember it being at Los Angeles airport that Chris Thompson told him we didn't need him anymore. Nicky felt he was a member of the band and got really pissed off, like anyone when they get fired. I don't have anything bad to say about him musically, but at that time he'd lost his way, not just musically but mentally as well. I remember times when we'd be on the whole floor of a hotel somewhere and you could hear him ranting and raving in his bedroom, talking to himself and shouting. He had a glazed, haunted look on his face, like a bloke who wasn't quite with us."

Chris Thompson: "Night went on to record a second album which I thought it was a much better record, but it didn't have a hit on it and we got dropped almost immediately it came out."

Thompson confessed that, after all his trials, he made no attempt to stay in touch with Nicky after the tour was over. However, he was able to shed light on the next phase in Nicky's life, one that turned his career around and without a doubt saved his life:

"We had a guy called Bob Fisher, who was involved right from the beginning of Night. He was into Scientology and worked at the Celebrity Centre as well as doing cartage. He wasn't somebody who used to shove Scientology down your neck, but if you wanted to talk about it, he would. I think that Nicky did talk to him a couple of times. I've always kept in contact with Bob and I'm fairly sure that he was responsible for actually sticking Nicky in a car and taking him down there.

"I know he was still going downhill after he left us. He was a total mess."

Your Saving Grace
Recovery

"He showed me a letter that he'd got from L. Ron Hubbard and Hubbard described him as the greatest rock keyboard player in the world. I said, 'That's not bad, is it Nick?'"

– Gray Levett

By entering Narconon, a Scientology-affiliated drug addiction recovery programme, Nicky had embraced one of the world's most controversial belief systems. This book is not the place to debate Scientology's methods, its philosophy or its work, but a trawl through the internet reveals as many websites attacking "the church" as in-house sites to promote it. The indisputable fact is that it was through Narconon that Nicky Hopkins found a way out of what seemed to be his insoluble problems.

His life, both professional and personal, had spun wildly out of control. With his long history of illness and medical treatment, a decade of drug and alcohol abuse had brought him very close to the end of his rope. In a hospital visit shortly before he embarked on his rehabilitation and recovery, doctors had given him two weeks to live.

The exact circumstances of Nicky's arrival at a treatment centre are unclear, but an earlier meeting with jazz pianist Chick Corea, himself already a committed Scientologist, played an important part in convincing him that Narconon could rescue him from his downward spiral.

Nicky Hopkins (*Freedom* magazine, July 1979): "In 1977 I saw a late Sunday night interview and music show that featured Chick Corea. I had no idea what he was talking about, but I found out later that he wasn't coked out of his head,

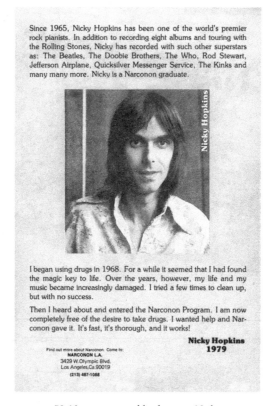

Since 1965, Nicky Hopkins has been one of the world's premier rock pianists. In addition to recording eight albums and touring with the Rolling Stones, Nicky has recorded with such other superstars as: The Beatles, The Doobie Brothers, The Who, Rod Stewart, Jefferson Airplane, Quicksilver Messenger Service, The Kinks and many many more. Nicky is a Narconon graduate.

I began using drugs in 1968. For a while it seemed that I had found the magic key to life. Over the years, however, my life and my music became increasingly damaged. I tried a few times to clean up, but with no success.

Then I heard about and entered the Narconon Program. I am now completely free of the desire to take drugs. I wanted help and Narconon gave it. It's fast, it's thorough, and it works!

Nicky Hopkins
1979

Find out more about Narconon. Come to:
NARCONON L.A.
3429 W.Olympic Blvd.
Los Angeles,Ca.90019
(213) 467-1088

70. Narconon pamphlet featuring Nicky

he was doing it all without drugs. He was a student of Scientology. It was a revelation to me, because at the time I couldn't do anything without drugs.

"I kept having the feeling I wanted to stop taking them, yet at the same time I had the feeling that I couldn't. It was hell. I remember one day when I arrived at the recording studio and began setting up and the next thing I knew I was packing up to go home. I felt terrible because I wasn't able to play and had let everyone down. I later discovered I had actually been playing, but didn't remember doing it. That's scary. I'd be sitting watching the TV cartoons in the afternoon; it was about the only thing I could focus my attention on, but I wouldn't even know what I was watching. It was a zombie-like state!"

Nicky again, in *Sonics* magazine, 1989: "I met Chick and he told me about Dianetics and I felt like I had nothing to lose, so I gave it a try. And I tell you what—it saved my life. It got me off drugs, where nothing else had."

The origins of The Church of Scientology are well documented. Lafayette Ronald Hubbard launched it in 1950, with the publication of his best-selling book, *Dianetics: The Modern Science Of Mental Health*. Hubbard admitted that his ideas drew inspiration from a variety of sources, "Euclid, Pythagoras, Jesus of Nazareth, Lao Tse, Plato and countless other philosophers and thinkers." Contemporary Scientology literature offers this summary of its services and intentions:

"…religious services and materials by which the individual can pursue his own personal route to spiritual freedom, either at home or within his local church. This path is clearly delineated within the scripture of the Scientology religion, works encompassing more than 500,000 pages of written material, 3,000 recorded lectures and more than a 100 films, all authored by the founder of the Scientology religion, L. Ron Hubbard.

"Hubbard once said, 'The world is carried on the backs of a desperate few.' Unfortunately, it is these desperate few who are often the most neglected. It is for this reason that L. Ron Hubbard saw to the formation of a special church, which would cater to artists, politicians, leaders of industry, sports figures and anyone with the power and vision to create a better world. That Church is Celebrity Centre International."

With a complex set of different "levels" to be attained and what, to outsiders, seems an impenetrable array of strangely named activities and jargon, Hubbard's system lent itself from the start to scepticism from non-believers. By the early sixties it had attracted the attention of the U.S. Food and Drug Administration, who claimed that the church's electronic "E-meter" device was "misbranded," with its extravagant offers of "diagnosis, prevention, treatment, detection and elimination of all mental and nervous disorders such as neuroses, psychoses, schizophrenia, and all psychosomatic ailments" and, just for good measure, "most of the physical ailments of mankind, such as arthritis, cancer, stomach ulcers, radiation burns from atomic bombs, polio and the common cold."

The organisation nevertheless grew rapidly, with its ready solutions to the apparent chaos and negativity in the world particularly attractive to young people.

Nicky Hopkins was brought to the enormous Celebrity Centre on Franklin Avenue in Hollywood. Built in 1929 by Eleanor Ince, the widow of a leading producer in the silent film era, the "seven-storey replica of a 17th century French castle" was christened "Chateau Elysee" and was originally conceived as a haven for actors and writers arriving in Hollywood to partake of the boom that accompanied the arrival of the "talkies." Errol Flynn, Humphrey Bogart, Clark Gable and Ginger Rogers all had regular rooms reserved, and the building was a favourite venue for glittering social events and celebrity parties.

When it was converted to its new role for a different generation of "celebrity" Scientology clients, the building lost none of its glamour or luxury.

The Narconon programme was a later addition to Scientology's affiliated services, though not officially part of the organisation itself. It was founded in 1966 by William Benitez, who came across one of L. Ron Hubbard's books while serving time in Arizona State Prison and was inspired by its contents to start a drug rehabilitation programme to cure his own and other prisoners' heroin addictions. Since then, Narconon has grown to become, in its own words, "a worldwide network of over a hundred and twenty rehabilitation centres, educating hundreds of thousands of people each year."

A typical treatment would last on average from three to six months and entail rapid withdrawal from drug use, through "proper nutrition, vitamins and care" and a "new life detoxification procedure," through a regime of exercise, sauna and nutritional substitutes, ridding the fatty tissues in the body of drug residues. The "individually tailored vitamins, oil and multi-minerals, with special attention to magnesium and calcium and closely supervised dosages of niacin" would be followed by "training routines" to prepare the subject for re-entry to normal life.

Narconon claims a uniquely high success rate in weaning its "graduates" off drugs. Though some of its figures have been disputed, it was certainly a success for Nicky Hopkins, and inspired him to pursue Scientology further. He rented a simple apartment close by the Celebrity Centre and enrolled as a student. One Scientology insider (hereafter referred to as "J") met and made friends with Nicky at the Celebrity Centre shortly after his emergence from Narconon:

"At any one given time, there were probably about five or six hundred people at the Centre. Nicky was so unpretentious, that it was a while before I even knew who he was; he didn't walk around flaunting himself."

To an outsider, the very term "Celebrity Centre" implies a curious kind of privilege. Scientology's own literature professes that celebrities are "subject to burdens others can't imagine and the unusual pressures that come with prominence and responsibility." "J") explained that—while in no way exclusive—the churches in entertainment cities such as Los Angeles, Las Vegas or Nashville were specifically tailored to cater to "celebrities, entertainers and their entourage."

"J"): "You don't have to be a famous person to go there. If Nicky wanted to bring a friend, then great; we didn't care if they were a housekeeper, it didn't matter. But the people that work in the 'Celebrity Centres' are artists themselves so they can relate."

"J") remembered Nicky as being in an upbeat state in his newly achieved sobriety. Soon their relationship became close enough for them to be socialising outside of the Centre:

"He was enthusiastic and he wasn't fragile any more. I didn't go through the Narconon programme, because I didn't have a substance abuse situation, but I knew a lot of people that did and he was doing great. The purification programme digs down at a cellular level and gets toxins out; that's why it works so well. It saved Nicky's life, because he had so many drugs deeply embedded in the cells of his body, it was affecting his reaction time and everything else; so when all that comes out, you feel like a million bucks."

"J") took strong issue with Dolly Hopkins' and some other people's recollections of the events that surrounded Nicky's recovery. Dolly insisted that she had been totally resistant to any involvement with Scientology and indeed told this author that church members handcuffed her to the bed, emptied their apartment, abducted Nicky and hid him for six months.

"J"): "That is ridiculous, because she did some courses as well.[47] I hate talking badly about people and I didn't consider myself close to her, but when I started hanging out with Nicky, he was living in the valley and married to Dolly and I thought, 'What the hell is he doing with her?' I never understood that relationship, so I was delighted when he got divorced and delighted when he got married (again)."

Nicky's character, and the degree to which his and Dolly's relationship had deteriorated, was well illustrated in a conversation with Dino Valenti's son Joli:

"I was aged seventeen, living in LA and I was looking for my Dad; I thought Nicky might know where to find him, so I called and got Dolly at home. Nicky was with Chick Corea on some Scientology undertaking, but she said to come over and she could tell me where to find him. One thing led to another and I stayed the weekend. She was stunning and to my seventeen-year old self it was a major event. Nicky was a powerful presence.

"Years later, when I was about thirty, we were both at a show and Nicky called me over and said, 'I think we need to talk.' He took me to a room backstage and said, 'I expect you know what this is about.' I said I had a pretty good idea and that I was very sorry, but after all I was only seventeen. He said, 'I feel much better now we've had this little talk' and after that we were fine."

Several witnesses agree that Nicky made every effort to bring his wife along with him in his recovery, but that Dolly was resolute in her refusal.

Dee Hopkins: "He paid for her to have sessions—counselling or whatever they call it, but she hated it and wouldn't go. He told her that it would be the break up of them unless she straightened herself out, because he had."

Nicky confided in fellow Scientologist Gray Levett:

"I think he found Dolly a strain, but he would never criticise her to me, saying there were faults on both sides and that he couldn't blame anyone but himself for his behaviour. Once he'd emerged and realised that, for the first time in his life, he was free of the harmful effects of drugs and drink, he said, 'The interesting thing is, I could take a drink now, but I don't want to.'"

One of the greatest joys that Nicky experienced with his return to health, was the feeling that his music had come back to him. "J") recalled him playing her a piece he had just composed that "floored her," and she was subsequently instrumental in introducing Nicky to the team behind the ambitious, jazz-orientated soundtrack album, designed, together with a feature-length film, to accompany L. Ron Hubbard's book.

---

[47] Dolly's name appears (along with Nicky's) on several of Scientology's published "Service Completion" lists from 1981 and 1982, and is included on their "All Clears in the United States" list published in 2006.

The grandiose press kit that accompanied BPI Records' 1982 release claimed, "L. Ron Hubbard does not follow trends, he makes them." Initially, and misleadingly titled *Space Jazz*, the album was given a re-release in 1984 under its new name, *Battlefield Earth*. Nicky's contributions were fairly minimal; he added a few standard honky-tonk licks added to "The Mining Song" and joined Chick Corea, his vocalist wife Gayle Moran and bassist Stanley Clarke on "The Banker" (proba-

bly Nicky's first brush with the CMI Fairlight synthesiser). Despite *Battlefield Earth*'s celebrity cameos, L. Ron Hubbard's schoolboy poetry and derivative melodies failed to generate much interest outside of the "church" and the book was a much greater success than the album.

Attending Scientology courses is an expensive process, and most celebrity clients are expected to pay considerable sums for the training they receive. Fees for a three or four month stay in a United States Narconon facility vary, but can involve a fee ranging from $10,000 to $30,000. As a reward for his contribution to *Battlefield Earth*, Hubbard personally awarded Nicky some free courses (considered a high honour in Scientology circles), at a point in his life when, for obvious reasons, his finances were in almost as much turmoil as his emotions. (Nicky later estimated to fellow Scientologist Woody Woodmansey that he had spent more than a million pounds on drugs).

Gray Levett: "He was in correspondence with Mr. Hubbard for a number of years. He showed me a letter and Hubbard, from what I remember, was praising him to the skies for his ability. I think he described him as the greatest rock keyboard player in the world and he smiled and said, 'I wouldn't have minded if he'd described me as competent.'"

During and immediately after his recovery, Nicky had been unable to keep up any kind of a normal schedule as a session musician, though he still found time for some bookings.

In a March 1980 birthday card to his brother Paul (still signed by both him and Dolly), he chose to paint an upbeat picture of "business as usual," with no mention of any ongoing problems or of his involvement with Scientology:

"I left Night in December and have been doing lots of recording sessions. At the end of January I went to New York to do an album with Graham Parker, ran into Mick and overdubbed on some tracks for the forthcoming Stones album. Last week I did five days recording demos with Donna Summer and the week before a couple of movie sessions. Tomorrow I'm going to New York again to do an album with Meat Loaf, so things are finally going well."

In the years following his return to health, out of gratitude for his new lease on life and—according to his sister Dee—partly as a way of paying his debts to the church, Nicky gave up considerable amounts of his time to making personal appearances in bookshops and record stores all over the USA and giving interviews to local newspapers, radio stations and in-house Scientology publications. With his connections to rock royalty, he was an effective advertisement for the Narconon method and he had, by then, become a committed and enthusiastic believer. The trips were organised and expenses paid by the church. His soon-to-be wife, Moira, later explained:

"Nicky disseminated for Narconon to help people that wanted to be drug free, because he had experienced it first hand."

Interviews he gave during 1983 and '84 dwelt evenly on the *Battlefield Earth* project, his own star-studded history, recent recording projects and his drug experiences and subsequent treatment. Some appearances were accompanied by "a thirty-foot-tall alien creature," which stood menacingly outside the appropriate venue. In some towns he lightened up his routine by sitting in with club bands in between commitments. Video footage on the Internet shows him in Charlotte NC, with local heroes The Spongetones, playing a ragged but enthusiastic version of "Revolution," with Nicky taking the piano break to considerable applause.

Singer-songwriter Bill Lloyd was working in a record store near Nashville when Nicky came through in 1984:

"He was in town was to promote *Battlefield Earth*. I now know about L. Ron Hubbard's sci-fi work, but at the time I was just thrilled to meet the guy who had played on so many of my favourite records. The radio hype for Nicky's in-store was already being screamed over the airwaves from our local rock station, WKDF and our Sound Shop staff had earmarked a section of the store to sell the albums and for Nicky to shake hands, sign vinyl and chat with fans. When he arrived, he was all smiles and I learned the distinction between rock stars and professional musicians; he was part of an entourage of two, with Fred Jacobs handling all the detail. Nicky seemed happy to say hello to anyone who wanted to talk, but we weren't getting throngs of patrons. Some fans (obviously liner note readers) showed up with Stones, Kinks, Who and Quicksilver albums, but if truth were told, it was like the scene from *Spinal Tap*: a typical example of the record biz in the eighties!

"He expressed genuine interest when I let him know I was a musician and songwriter trying to make my way and added that he'd be in town for a couple of days and that he and Fred were interested in going to see some music. I suggested John Jackson's band, The Rhythm Rockers and Nicky made it out to the show and I introduced him to the band.

"During our conversations, I'd mentioned that I had a good many of the records he had played on and that if he liked, I could make a compilation tape for him to play before his next gig. Next day, I had a 90-minute Maxell cassette, packed to the brim with classic rock, all featuring Nicky on keys; he and Fred were very grateful and went off to Atlanta that night. Before they left, Nicky graciously signed my copy of *The Tin Man Was A Dreamer*, we exchanged addresses and I took the liberty of giving him a cassette of my own music. I thought that would be the last I'd see of Nicky, but it was not. What an amazing surprise when I received a letter from him a month or two later."

Dear Bill,

Thanks so much for getting the tape made up. The compilation was great; you really made an amazingly good choice and included one song I'd almost forgotten – 'Let's See Action' by the Who. We used it in the Cayman Islands before I played; then Rick from Telluride, (the band I played with), announced that I'd played on all those records.

I enjoyed the tape you gave me too. You've got a lot of talent as a writer, Bill – keep it up. I've got a few days off back here in L.A. then on July 16th Fred and I go to Amarillo then Denver.

Hi to everyone at the store,

All best wishes, Nicky

Bill Lloyd: "The sad part of the story is that when Nicky moved to Nashville nearly fifteen years later, I got his number through Julian and called him. He remembered me after all that time and congratulated me on my own navigation through the business. We made plans to write a song together and set a date for the next month, but he passed on only a couple of weeks later."

One aspect of Nicky's hard-won sobriety was a determination to avoid the temptations afforded by the rock and roll lifestyle still led by many of his former associates:

(From the *Sunday Press*): "Nicky Hopkins won't be playing piano for the Stones on their mooted Australian tour. 'No, I've had enough of all that sort of lifestyle for a lifetime, I think.'"

He was not one of those converts that forced their new convictions onto those around them, and examples of him attempting to persuade anyone else of his beliefs are rare. One of those very few he did try to persuade was Herbie Flowers, with whom Nicky reunited in April 1985 when he joined the highly successful session-players' band Sky, filling the gap left by classical guitarist John Williams.

Herbie Flowers: "Much as I love Nick, I spent quite a bit of time with him on tour with Sky, when I drove him around for two lots of three weeks. In the end I had to tell him to stop doing the Scientology trip. We talked about lots of other nice things, and it was great to see him fall in love and wonderful to go to his wedding…"

Dolly insisted that his changed personality and occasional tendency to preach cost Nicky some session work, citing Pink Floyd's *The Wall* and Pete Townshend as two examples. (The latter seems unlikely, given Pete's own ties to spiritual leader Meher Baba). Nicky's immediate family had varying memories. I asked his sister Dee if he talked about Scientology:

"No. He said, 'If you want to know, call them.' I know my sister and Alix went in New York. I only know it got him off drugs and alcohol. I met a lot of his friends in California and they were the nicest people I've ever come across."

Julia Hopkins said that Nicky didn't push Scientology, apart from unsuccessfully trying to get his Mum to read the books. She and her daughter tried to find out what Nicky found so appealing.

Alix Ninfo: "He encouraged my mother and I to take a look at the Centre in Manhattan, because he really wanted us to understand what he'd been through. It's a brownstone on 82nd Street and is really for the celebrities of the Scientology world. They were very happy to see us, but my mother and I were kind of freaked out; it was interesting, but we weren't into that whole thing; we said we would

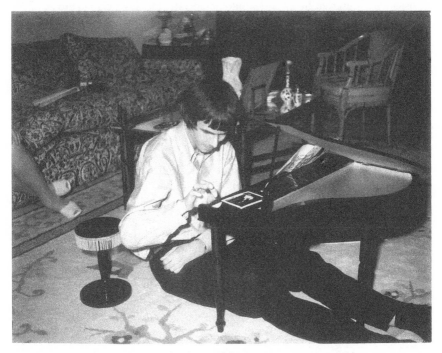

71. Nicky playing Alix' miniature piano

'audit' and were taken around by a young man and introduced as Nicky's sister and niece. I felt they were pushy; they hook up a machine to you, give you a questionnaire, ask you things and monitor your wavelengths or something—just bizarre. I didn't like it. I felt creeped out—but it was interesting."

Even though she was so young, Alix noted big changes in Nicky:

"Whenever he came to town he always stayed with Scientologists and he was always doing something to do with Scientology, in addition to a session or whatever, so half the trip was taken up with that. He didn't really talk about what he was doing because he knew I wasn't interested.

"It was a stumbling block at first, when he was newly out of Narconon and was really paying his dues there and getting back on his feet, but after a couple of years, he was more focused on his career and was on the straight and narrow. When he would come and see us, he was like his old self. We'd giggle and laugh and be really rude and silly."

Nicky chose one of the few professions where growing up is not a necessity and, despite never having kids of his own, he retained an engaging childlike quality and sense of fun that made him very popular with other peoples' children.

Alix: "I remember being given a tiny toy piano and Nicky plonking away on it. He would send me wonderful birthday and Christmas cards, chock-a-block with fun stuff and always brought me strange pins and pussycat things when he came to visit—silly stuff that he knew I would appreciate. He was a big kid anyway."

Over time, the intensity of Nicky's commitment to Scientology gradually softened. He appeared on one further L. Ron Hubbard recording, *The Road To Freedom*, released in 1986, but only on one track, the generic and overblown big ballad "The Way To Happiness," sung as a duet by fellow believers Gayle Moran and eighties pin-up Leif Garrett. Picked as a single, it made little or no impact on the outside world.

If he had failed to bring Dolly into the fold, Nicky had more success with Van Morrison.

"J"): "Nicky and I got Van into Scientology! Nicky had done some recording with him and Van had asked questions about it and Nicky didn't know what to say, so he called me up. 'I've got Van Morrison here; what do I tell him?' I said, 'Just tell him I'll contact him and take care of it.'"

Nicky had joined Morrison for a song, produced by Robbie Robertson, for the soundtrack to the film *The King Of Comedy*. Bassist David Hayes remembers  being sent, in a torrential rainstorm in his old VW camper van, to pick up the volatile singer from San Francisco airport. Once installed in the studio, work came to an abrupt halt when there was a power cut right in the middle of a take:

"It went dead black to where you couldn't even see your hand in front of your face. The engineer or Robbie said, 'Everybody stay where you are and don't move!' So of course Nicky and I and the drummer just sat there; about ten minutes went by and then the lights came on…and Van's gone (laughs). He's disappeared. He went to a restaurant!"

"J") picks up the story: "I went up and saw Van, took an auditor and got him in session and he goes, 'This is great stuff;' he did quite a bit and I believe Van still listens to L. Ron Hubbard lectures."

The cantankerous singer has always been known as a seeker but never seems to have been a long-term convert to any one discipline. In Steve Turner's Van

Morrison biography, sources from the Scientology headquarters in England offered the following statement on Morrison's involvement:

"Van wouldn't be someone who we would term a Scientologist. He liked what he heard but he wasn't that smitten that he wanted to do it full time. He only came down to East Grinstead once and he eventually finished what we call 'fourth grade,' which is about three-quarters of the way to being a clear."

David Hayes: "When the Scientology thing happened, Nicky was always onto Van to try to do something to help them, but Van was not into doing that at all. Nicky felt indebted to the Scientologists and he was always pursuing ways to help their situation. Van was fascinated with religion, so he did dabble in it and he said there were some positive aspects to it, but as far as being one of the soldiers, he would have no part of it."

Morrison's 1983 album *Inarticulate Speech Of The Heart* included, "Special thanks to L. Ron Hubbard" among the credits, while its follow-up was tellingly titled *No Guru, No Method, No Teacher.*

Nicky Hopkins' talents and temperament would seem to have made him a perfect accompanist for Van, and Nicky's diaries reveal that he had previously worked with Morrison in July 1981 on an album project that was subsequently aborted. Nicky's old friend Hugh Murphy had called him in L.A. to book him for a session at the Record Plant in Sausalito, near his old stamping grounds in Mill Valley.

He arrived to find Dire Straits guitarist Mark Knopfler already at the studio. The two musicians ran down a song with a bass-player and drummer only referred to as "James and Darnell." Van Morrison himself later joined the proceedings but left abruptly after only two run-throughs. Apparently the rhythm section was not to his liking and Nicky was left hanging around with the producer until the early hours of the morning.

When work recommenced the following day, Van still wanted the two unfortunate musicians to be replaced and was only persuaded to persevere by the personal intervention of Nicky Hopkins and Mark Knopfler. After a long day's work routining some of Van's material, followed by a half-hour jam session at the end, the next morning brought a phone call from the unpredictable singer that he wasn't coming down to the studio anymore, a turn of events that was too much for Knopfler, who decided to leave for New York immediately. When Morrison then changed his mind yet again, it was too late and the "almost" session was over.

Scientology actively promotes networking between its members. A short time after his treatment in 1980, Nicky moved into an apartment in Los Feliz with fellow Scientologist Jodi Mekler. Through her marriage to producer Gabriel Mekler (Steppenwolf, Three Dog Night), Jodi was a well-connected music industry figure and in fact, managed Nicky until he was introduced to Ron Moss (immortalized on Nicky's incredible calling card from this era). The job consisted mostly of taking calls for sessions and handling financial matters, two tasks to which Nicky had a pathological aversion. Having finally separated from Dolly, Nicky clearly needed someone to act on his behalf.

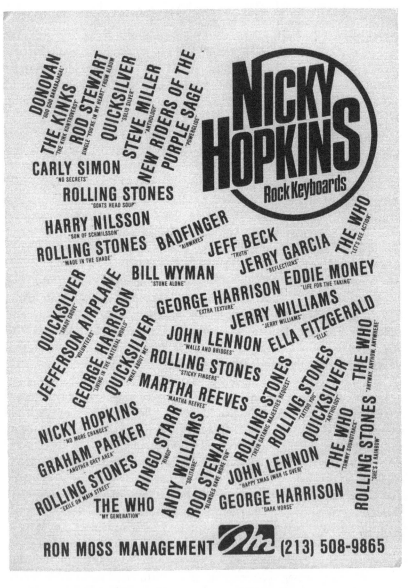

POINTER SISTERS
"PRIORITY"

HARRY NILSSON
"SON OF DRACULA"

BREWER & SHIPLEY
"WEEDS"

JOE COCKER
"I CAN STAND A LITTLE RAIN"

EASY BEATS
"VIGIL"

STEVE MILLER
"NUMBER 5"

STEVE MILLER
"BRAVE NEW WORLD"

JEFF BECK
"BECKOLA"

BAY CITY ROLLERS
"STRANGERS IN THE WIND"

ROLLING STONES
"EMOTIONAL RESCUE"

SHANKAR FAMILY
& FRIENDS

NILS LOFGREN
"NIGHTS FADES AWAY"

QUICKSILVER
"JUST FOR LOVE"

JOHN LENNON
"SHAVED FISH"

STEVE MILLER
"YOUR SAVING GRACE"

JOE COCKER
"JAMAICA SAY YOU WILL"

FATS DOMINO
"HAVE YOU SEEN MY BABY"

MARC BOLAN
"THE BEGINNING OF DOVES"

NICKY, STONES,
RY COODER
"JAMMING WITH EDWARD"

DUSTY SPRINGFIELD
"DUSTY DEFINITELY"

MARK-ALMOND
"MARK-ALMOND '73"

ROLLING STONES
"LET IT BLEED"

ROLLING STONES
"BEGGARS BANQUET"

PETER FRAMPTON
"SOMETHING'S HAPPENING"

JACKIE LOMAX
"SOUR MILK SEA"

CAROLE BAYER SAGER
"CAROLE BAYER SAGER"

ROLLING STONES
"BLACK & BLUE"

ROLLING STONES
"WE LOVE YOU"

RANDY MEISNER
"RANDY MEISNER"

JACKIE LOMAX
"IS THIS WHAT YOU WANT?"

BOBBY KEYS
"BOBBY KEYS"

ROLLING STONES
"JUMPIN' JACK FLASH"

MEATLOAF
"DEAD RINGER"

DONOVAN
"ESSENCE TO ESSENCE"

CLIMAX BLUES BAND
"FLYING THE FLAG"

THE STRAWBS
"THE STRAWBS"

McGUINNESS FLINT
"HAPPY BIRTHDAY RUBY BABY"

DAVID SOUL
"DAVID SOUL"

ROLLING STONES
"IT'S ONLY ROCK & ROLL"

THE WHO
"WHO'S NEXT"

THE BEATLES
"REVOLUTION"

RONNIE WOOD
"1234"

JOE COCKER
"GREATEST HITS"

JENNIFER WARNES
"JENNIFER WARNES"

JOE COCKER
"YOU ARE SO BEAUTIFUL"

THE WHO
"THE WHO BY NUMBERS"

GRAHAM PARKER
"THE UP ESCALATOR"

ROLLING STONES
"THROUGH THE PAST DARKLY"

THE END
"INTROSPECTION"

THE KINKS
"SUNNY AFTERNOON"

SWEET THURSDAY
"SWEET THURSDAY"

THE KINKS
"FACE TO FACE"

NICKY HOPKINS
"THE TIN MAN WAS A DREAMER"

JOHN LENNON
"IMAGINE"

ROLLING STONES
"TUMBLING DICE"

"J"): "Ron was connected to the church and was also Chick Corea's manager. I remember the *Imagine* film came out, with footage of Nicky and John Lennon messing about at the piano, and I wanted to make sure Nicky went to the movie. I called him and he wasn't even aware the movie was coming out. Normally when people are in major films, you have to get their permission, and that's when I realised, 'Damn, he just doesn't have any representation. This is so bad.'"

The efforts of Nicky's various church-related managers in the mid-eighties, however, weren't able to prevent a gradual slow-down in his career. By 1983 his workload had fallen dramatically and in 1985 he made only three appearances on record, one for his old touring partner Rod Stewart. Much of his time was spent touring, with Sky in 1985 and the Gene Clark/Michael Clarke Byrds tribute line-up he joined in 1986.

It was obviously time for a change of plan. During a Christmas 1986 visit his to mother back in England, he decided to move home again. Freda said, "I've got my Nicky back" and his Scientology contacts helped soften his landing.

The church regularly hosted music and arts events to commemorate important dates such as the founder's birthday, New Year's Eve or the release date of *Dianetics*. At one such gathering at the Hollywood Palladium, Englishman Gray Levett was in the audience and the two ex-pats quickly became friends:

"Wherever you were in the world, if you were a dedicated Scientologist, you'd be invited and then, like now, Los Angeles had a huge Scientology population. Suddenly they announced that the entertainment was going to be Nicky Hopkins and he came out and played with a band.

"I had recognised him at the Celebrity Centre because he had a packet of Dunhills, and when there was break, I saw him reach for them and he looked over and smiled, because I'd done the same thing. I thought, 'It must be an Englishman.' Later I visited his apartment, which was a fairly utilitarian place he was sharing with someone who was managing him at the time. It looked a bachelor apartment to me.

"I think he was glad to meet someone from England of a similar age and background and we knew some of the same people, because I was friends with Robin Williamson of the Incredible String Band and he and Robin had bumped into one another at Scientology events. We would mostly complain about what we didn't like about Los Angeles!"

Considering how many years Nicky Hopkins spent in and around the city, it is remarkable how consistently he expressed his loathing for L.A. He had been homesick for a long time and once back in the UK, his first refuge was a small rented flat in London's Belsize Park. From there he was able to renew his friendship with Gray, a relationship that soon led to a formal business agreement and to Gray joining the long list of those that helped manage Nicky's affairs.

Gray Levett: "I was working for a small indie label called Plezure Records and the chap who owned it (Scobie Ryder) also owned a keyboard hire company called Tickle Them Ivories, just down the road from Primrose Hill. Nicky used to spend the afternoons using the keyboards at the hire company. I think he must have been here about six months or so."

Nicky didn't stay long in London and Scientology dictated his next move to the quieter surroundings of East Grinstead in the suburban Sussex countryside, home of the church's UK headquarters. Fellow Scientologists Woody and June Woodmansey, whom Nicky had previously met at a Scientology musical event in the USA, became his temporary landlords in what seems at first an unlikely place for a working musician. Gray visited him in his new surroundings:

"I think Nicky enjoyed the anonymity of suburbia and the fact that he could disappear into this house. The place was stacked floor to ceiling with books and tapes of radio shows, he had a piano and he started working with Woody, so I think it made sense for him to be down there. It was cheaper and he had a bit more room."

Woody Woodmansey: "I was asked to audition with Edgar Winter for a big open-air festival in Portland, Oregon, with Isaac Hayes, Al Jarreau and a whole bunch of artists. There were tons of drummers, all waiting to audition, but I got the job, which was cool after flying all that way. Nicky played with Edgar, and when they asked him to do his own set, he asked me to play drums. I'd been a fan since the *Truth* album, so there was a quick rehearsal and we tried to encourage Nicky to feature himself. I don't know if he was comfortable, but he played brilliantly.

"He was trying to pick up his old contacts in England, which was hard at first, because he'd been out of the country for quite a while and there wasn't a session scene here any more. I remember a woman came up to him and said, 'Do you know, you remind me of Nicky Hopkins' and he kept a straight face and said, 'Do you know, I sometimes feel like Nicky Hopkins.' He liked being back."

June Woodmansey: "He was going to stay for a few days and ended up with his own room. His library started to form…Shelves and more shelves! He had a copy of every play, comedy or show that the BBC had ever put out on the radio. We'd go in and he'd be there documenting it all. I said to him, 'When are you ever going to listen to all this stuff?'"

Returning to a post-punk England after more than a decade away proved more daunting than Nicky expected, and while his new friendships helped both practically and emotionally, it was another Los Angeles connection that would have the most significant effect on his life and wellbeing.

The inevitable and long overdue parting from his first wife had at last became official on January 14th 1986, when the Hopkins' marriage was dissolved in the Superior Court of California, with Nicky listed as petitioner (represented by one Laurence A. Rose), and Dolly, listed as resident in San Diego, as respondent. The couple were certainly not unique in their battles with addiction or in their inability to bring their relationship to an end in a timely fashion. Their last years together showed the classic signs of a co-dependency and, after years of great unhappiness, Nicky's discovery of Scientology finally helped him to make the break.

Apart from an enjoyable but short-lived romance with an actress named

Vanna Bonta, with whom Nicky was seen at a number of events around Los Angeles, he remained more or less on his own for the first years of his recovery, until the day Moira Elizabeth Buchanan came to visit.

Moira Hopkins: "I went with a friend round to Jodi Mekler's in November 1986. It was the first time I met her and we were sitting having coffee when, all of a sudden, Nicky came into the room, in search of a cup of tea. He sat down at the table with us and we started talking about Scotland and England, we had a laugh and got along really well right from the beginning."

Nicky noted the new arrival in his diary entry of December 5th: "A girl called Moira came over with Nancy Gordon this morning and came back again later by herself."

Fashionably thin, good-looking, prone to outbursts of cackling laughter and with a striking shock of red hair, Moira was another Scientology graduate who had been

72. Nicky Hopkins and Moira Buchanan

living in Los Angeles for some time and was currently working as a waitress. Five years younger than Nicky, she too had a previous marriage behind her and a son living in Florida who worked for the church of Scientology. Nicky, though obviously intrigued by his newest acquaintance, didn't make any immediate effort to see her again. Moira had Jodi to thank for bringing her and Nicky closer together:

"Jodi was instrumental in inviting me places he was going to be. I remember a club somewhere on the way to Santa Monica, in early December where Nicky was playing with a native-American poet called John Trudell; Jesse Ed Davis was in the band and I could tell that they really loved Nicky being there."

Moira was born in Scotland and though she had spent her teenage years as part of the then thriving Glasgow art and music scene, she was not otherwise particularly familiar with musicians, nor aware of Nicky's illustrious history:

"Jodi called me one night because Nicky had to do a recording for the Beat Farmers out in Malibu Canyon and she hated to drive the canyons. I had a four-wheel drive pick-up truck, so I offered to drive. I felt a bit shy, but Nicky had me sit down beside him while he wrote out notes on some music paper. They were doing a run-through of one song and he wrote so quickly, I thought, 'This is serious.' The song said, 'And I know that God is here tonight' and he wrote something down and handed it to me and I thought, 'What's he handing it to me for? I can't read music;' I saw that he had written 'God and Chips'! Then he got up and knocked off his part.

"There was a Christmas party and Jodi said, 'Nicky wants you to go.' He made me laugh so much and then dropped the bombshell that he was going home for Christmas, to see his mother. He went to England and I got a letter saying he'd decided to stay."

Soon, Nicky was installed as houseguest with the Woodmanseys, so through the spring the two had to rely on the post to stay in touch.

"We had stories going in our letters; Nicky started it; he had this character, an old man who had a butler; I introduced the Duchess and we had a cook. We used to write these off-the-wall letters with Nicky pretending to be the butler. (Assumes butler voice), 'Oh sir, I've had the same suit for fifteen years, that you purchased for me at Dr. Barnado's. Don't you think I could have a new one?' It changed to a village and cook was an enormously large person who wore enormously large knickers (laughs), which she used to hang on the washing line to blow dry in the breeze…and the Duchess would come round for tea and the old man didn't like her, so he used to throw buns at her…that was Nicky's world. I don't think I'd ever met anybody that I could have so much fun with—and who released my own creative sense of humour.

"There was an understanding there because I knew about Narconon. I loved him already really; I did when I first met him, and in April I called him and asked how he was doing and he said, 'Oh well, I've been seeing this violinist.' After he said that, there was about three seconds of silence while I digested that and (he later told me) that he thought, 'Oh, I think she actually likes me' (laughs). It never occurred to him that I might have seen him as more than a friend."

They were still living and working on two different continents.

Moira continues: "I thought it was great actually, because we were friends before anything else and got to know one another. I liked that. In June there was a phone call to say that he was coming to L.A. to do the Johnny Carson show with Art Garfunkel. I came home one day to a message from Nicky saying, 'I'm here, I'm jetlagged out of my tree and I'm coming round to see you,' and we went out for our first real date to a pizza place on Los Feliz Boulevard, where people who'd probably sung in the chorus, pretend to play opera music; it was pretty bad. There was a little Italian-looking man, with a very serious face and a black beret, who played for the singers on an upright piano and these strangely dressed, very eccentric looking women, with big hats and beads sang opera, while Nicky and I tried to eat a pizza. We were dying with laughter.

"He stayed for about three weeks, at first with Jodi and then with me. A friend had lent him a Fairlight synthesiser and Nicky hadn't been feeling well. He had neuralgia and a doctor had given him some shots, but it made him very nervous and he wanted absolute peace and quiet, so he came and stayed at my house. I wasn't there a lot of the time; he had the Fairlight delivered and sat there during the day, trying out all the sounds. I came home one day and he flipped some switches and all of a sudden there was a barking doggy chorus!

"After that date, we went out another time or two and he said, 'When I go back to England, there's somebody who's been chasing after me; I have to tell her that I have a fiancée, but I don't have one. How do you feel about marriage?' I said, 'I think it's a good thing' and he said, 'Oh, so would you like to get married?' and I said, 'Yes' and he said, 'I suppose I'd better ask you properly then. Would you like to marry me?' and I said, 'Yes.'

"He had to go back because he was auditioning with Paul McCartney, but I couldn't leave, because first I had to sell all my things. I had wanted to go back to Britain anyway and he's the one person that I've met in this lifetime that I didn't have any doubts about whatsoever."

After their lightning courtship, Moira joined Nicky as quickly as possible and they spent Christmas and Boxing Day that year with Woody and his wife. Woody recalled:

"They were both quirky and they complemented each other; it just seemed to fit. We have three boys and Nicky seemed to enjoy having a family."

Still unmarried and still in East Grinstead, the couple soon moved into their own rented accommodation. Rhoda, an actress acquaintance of the Woodmanseys, offered them the use of the top half of her house, where they happily settled in.

Moira Hopkins: "All he wanted to do was hibernate. He wanted to curl up in his room with Kit Kats and cats, go to the bookstores, listen to classical music and BBC plays on the radio. He loved East Grinstead, but I would have preferred to be in Brighton."

They remained at Rhoda's for more than a year and in 1988 took advantage of their host's part-time job as a tour guide at nearby Hever Castle and asked permission to be married there. Three weeks after a civil ceremony in Crawley, Nicky Hopkins and Moira Buchanan were married in the historic surroundings of Anne Boleyn's birthplace on August 25th 1988. He was forty-four and Moira thirty-nine. "Nicky looked at me and said, 'Hmm! It's the new Mrs. H.'"

Guests at the quaintly old-fashioned and formal ceremony included Nicky's family, a handful of old friends from London and newer friends they had made through Scientology. Gray Levett was Best Man, and Moira—matching the traditional top hats and tails worn by Nicky, Gray and Woody Woodmansey—dressed like an Edwardian heiress, in a wide-brimmed hat and full-length white dress. A tartan-clad Scottish piper in a kilt played in the background. May Pang was a last-minute surprise guest:

73. The wedding at Hever Castle, with Art Garfunkel

"I have a picture of him on his wedding day in the back of the car—a totally different Nicky. It was weird because Craig Mathieson, from the Church of Scientology, who married them, was the lead singer in a group called Bananas that I managed in New York. I arrived into London and got this call, 'We'd like to invite you tomorrow; you've got to come to Nicky's wedding,' so I jumped on a train to East Grinstead, with no idea that Craig was the officiating minister. Scientology is not my thing and the people that were running it knew that.

74. Newlyweds Nicky and Moira Hopkins

"Nicky was playing with Art Garfunkel at the time and though Artie didn't sing, he did attend the wedding. I was surprised to see how much healthier Nicky looked than when I had seen him last. He had fattened up a lot; it was a complete turnaround from the frail rock'n'roll guy with stringy hair."

Moira: "It was a fairly big do but not as big as we'd have liked; we had to live within our means at that point and everything was so expensive. We didn't have the Scottish dancing I'd have liked and we didn't have all the people that we would have liked to invite. We went up to Scotland and spent the first night of our honeymoon in a wonderful castle just outside Edinburgh, where Mary, Queen of Scots had stayed. Except for the day my son was born, it was THE best day of my life."

The period of darkness and confusion he went through during the seventies looms large over Nicky's life story, but if one had sat down to design the perfect companion for him, that person would have looked and behaved exactly like Moira. Nicky was finally happy, in a relationship with someone who loved him, understood him and supported him in every way. Her resilience would help to face the challenges that lay ahead.

Violinist Helen O'Hara first made her mark in Kevin Rowland's band Dexy's Midnight Runners, and, having joined Gray Levett's management roster, went on to a solo career playing instrumental music for the budding "new age" market. She brought Nicky in to play piano on two of her CD projects (1990's *Southern Hearts* and *A Night in Ireland*, released in 1998):

"I'm not a Scientologist and I had no idea that Nicky and Gray were. Nicky was quite keen to introduce me to Scientology, but I didn't want anything to do with it, to be honest. He was very involved in it and needed to talk to people about things. That was the only time we clashed. It wasn't really awkward, because Nicky was someone who was very sensitive to other people and sensed that there was no point pushing it. I made it quite clear and we certainly didn't fall out. Robin Williamson came along as well; all Gray's connections were happy to help out—it was really sweet—and all Scientologists!"

Gray Levett said that Nicky "did a huge amount of work" for "the church" and Nicky remained committed to his beliefs. When Art Garfunkel hired him as his pianist of choice and bandleader, he saw to it that Woody Woodmansey became Art's drummer. Nicky took advantage of his world travelling to support Scientology, giving interviews, playing occasional concerts and helping out other church members with their music. Australian Scientology publication *Sonics* had Nicky in their Q & A segment in November 1989, during a Garfunkel visit:

"Hopkins is an ardent Scientologist – indeed he was in Australia to help promote Hubbard's book Dianetics, *and anxious to make sure it gets mentioned in any story about him. Later in his visit he would sit in with Kate Ceberano (herself a Scientologist) and steal the show – not with flashy pyrotechnics, but sheer musicianship."*

A set of large colour photos taken during the same visit showed Nicky striking strange poses that obviously held significance for other believers. The last example of his direct involvement in a Scientology-related musical venture was the McCartney-backed charity single "Spirit Of Play," which Nicky had co-authored with singer Craig Mathieson.

75. The "Spirit of Play" team

In 1991 the available work in England failed to sustain him and Nicky was obliged to make his final return to the USA, where he continued to be dogged by recurrent medical problems and occasional crises, which often clashed with his Scientology convictions.

Moira Hopkins: "There were quite long stretches where he didn't take medication. He only took that when it became too much; he wasn't supposed to with the Scientology. If you needed to see a doctor because of physical illness and take something, yes, but otherwise it would interfere with the counselling."

Despite such contradictions, Nicky's faith remained for the rest of his life and he seems to have found almost as much support from his religion as he did from his immensely happy and successful marriage. Moira Hopkins asserted that Scientology was "pretty much part of Nicky's everyday life right to the end."

The Up Escalator
Later Years

"Playing with Nicky was a lot like playing with Clarence White; you're lucky to be standing next to him and just want to hang on and try to play along."

– John York

After the turbulence and unhappiness of the 1970s, Nicky entered the '80s in a positive state of mind, but with a lot of lost ground to make up in his professional life. Nashville studio legend Charlie McCoy once detailed for me the four phases of a session man's career:

    1) Who is Charlie McCoy?
    2) Get me Charlie McCoy
    3) Get me a young guy like Charlie McCoy
    4) Who is Charlie McCoy?

Nicky had already achieved legendary status through his previous associations, but, as Jon Mark pointed out, there came a point where past glories ceased to have the power to influence present activities. The marketplace had changed irrevocably; by 1980 punk, glam-rock and disco had all been and gone, leaving their mark on the harder-edged, often machine-based sound of what the rock press christened "New Wave"—actually little more than revved-up pop music with attitude.

For better or worse, technology had also taken huge leaps forward, forcing "dinosaur" bands like the Rolling Stones to adapt to survive in the new climate. With synthesised keyboards, sequencers and drum machines dominating the studio scene, for the first time in his career, Nicky found himself no longer at the cutting edge of recording and often marginalised by his dedication to the acoustic piano. His previously immaculate reputation had taken a considerable battering due to his unreliability and occasional lapses during his own ten-year "lost weekend" and many of his previous clients were themselves struggling to maintain their hold on success. Some had died.

John Lennon's decision in 1980 to record his comeback album *Double Fantasy* with a completely new set of musicians mirrored the problems Nicky faced. He was left feeling like yesterday's news, and any chance of recreating the magic of the *Imagine* era died with Lennon on December 8th.

Luckily, the Los Angeles music scene was broad enough to contain dozens of different styles of music. In the first years of the new decade Nicky was still kept busy with a mix of previous clients such as the Rolling Stones, as well as younger bands, keen to soak up some of the glory of the classic era by having a genuine Stones and Beatles sideman guesting on their albums. New areas of work in the film world were also opening up for Nicky, following his contributions to *The Champ* soundtrack in 1979 and the earlier *Tommy*.

Nicky's friend and fellow keyboard player Scott Matthews found himself in much the same predicament:

"It was a wild era. We were both 'dime a dance' session whores—and I use the rather harsh term in a derogatory fashion, because we both had aspirations far and above answering the phone and agreeing to play on people's records that we had never even heard of. All we needed to hear were the words 'double scale' and we were there. On the first session we did together, I asked why in the world he was working on this dreadful record and he told me it was because I had agreed to it; whether he meant it or not, it was what I needed to hear and it was very Nicky to be sweet in the face of sour situations. Lovely man."

Nicky returned occasionally to Northern California to help out old friends like John Cipollina, David Hayes and Terry and The Pirates, while international clients came from as far away as France, Japan and Australia looking for the signature Hopkins touch. Thankfully, some successful contemporary performers and producers were smart enough to recognise that quality never goes out of fashion, and

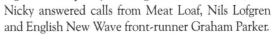

Nicky answered calls from Meat Loaf, Nils Lofgren and English New Wave front-runner Graham Parker.

Nils Lofgren: "I did a record, which Jeff Baxter produced, called *Night Fades Away*. I was living in LA and Jeffrey knew pretty much every player in town, so we had a whole cast of characters come and play on the record; Nicky played most of the piano and was a mainstay on the record. There were times when rather than going off to get a coffee or a sandwich, Nicky would play and I'd sit there and noodle with him, on guitar or maybe on the piano; we didn't just practise what we were doing, we'd go off and do other things.

"Most of the recording was done live and Nicky would go in and overdub, so he was around for most of that project. He seemed pretty happy and very into it.

I went over to his apartment one afternoon and we jammed on his thematic piano ideas and talked about having me assist him in making an instrumental record. He always seemed to be positive and he not only used the gift he had, but seemed to be humbled by it and share it in a real positive way."

Graham Parker's soul and R&B leanings meant that keyboards played a vital part in his sound. After a steady run of albums with the Rumour, he and the band found themselves in the bitter cold of a New York winter, at the Power Station studios with producer Jimmy Iovine—and one keyboard player short.

Nicky Hopkins: "I didn't know Graham until I worked with him in New York on *The Up Escalator* album. May Pang said that Jimmy Iovine, who was the engineer on *Walls And Bridges*, was trying to get hold of me."[48]

Longstanding Rumour member Bob Andrews had left after a 1979 tour of Australia and New Zealand, and Nicky's name came up as a replacement. Both Graham and guitarist Martin Belmont were immediately impressed with their new piano player.

Martin Belmont: "He played on all the basic tracks with us. The fact that he was English and could fit in with that English sense of humour helped. The unusual thing was that he only played piano; even though I'm sure he could have played any sort of keyboard, he wouldn't. He always said. 'I am a piano player, that's it.'"

Graham Parker: "It was always a nightmare getting the Rumour to pay attention to the subtleties and nuances of my new tunes, but Nicky just needed me to run over them once or twice, and he had them down; even little riffs I wanted him to incorporate were right there on the first run through and I never had to remind him to play them by the time we came to record. He was that good.

"I became quite firm friends with him around that period and used to hang out with him and his then wife, Dolly, in Los Angeles, where he lived. We'd lounge by the pool, go out to eat or mess around at his place playing darts. He always had some fine Monty Python gags going and could do sketches word for word! An Englishman through and through, I remember he wasn't mad for fancy Californian cuisine, but liked to go to the English shop there and keep a good supply of 'bangers' (sausages) handy.

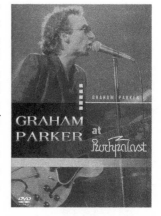

"*The Up Escalator* was the final GP and The Rumour album and Nicky also performed on the very last GP and the Rumour gig, a TV event in the Grugahalle in Essen, Germany called *Rockpalast*;

---

[48] Iovine would also use Nicky on Meat Loaf's *Dead Ringer* album in 1981.

© m. becker

N. HOPKINS   G. PARKER   © m. becker

76. Rockpalast with Graham Parker

the bill also featured Jack Bruce and the Police. That was his only live perform-ance with me, but he did appear in videos for 'Stupefaction' and 'Love Without Greed,' both made in L.A. and both from *Escalator*."

Martin Belmont: "We did a couple of TV shows in America to promote the sin-gle from the album, then two nights at Hammersmith Palais (in London) as a warm-up for the German show; both nights were sold out and both were fantastic.

We did quite a lot of stuff from the album, but he had a huge backlog of other stuff to learn. Looking at the DVD today, it's one of the best gigs we ever did, if not THE best. Graham may have felt it was going to be the last gig, but we didn't know that. It wasn't like, 'this is the end' or anything like that.

"We all got on really well; Nicky would tell jokes and get into that thing that bands get into on the road, where you have little sayings, word games or lines from films, so it was seamless the way he fitted in. He was teetotal and didn't do any chemicals. He had two or three blank years where he couldn't remember anything he had done and I think after that, he decided to pack in everything—and he did."

House photographer Manfred Becker took some wonderful shots of Nicky for the *Rockpalast* archives, looking relaxed and healthy at soundcheck, during the electrifying live show (cigarette dangling characteristically from his lips) and backstage with his new employer.

In a poignant pre-Christmas letter from Los Angeles, Nicky shared some of his thoughts and plans at the end of 1981 with his brother Paul in Austria, who, due to financial constraints, had been helping him with an overdue storage bill:

"Things are a bit tight at present but should soon pick up...I'm getting homesick again. I might do a tour of Europe and the USA with Graham Parker from late Janu-ary to the end of March, but I don't know if he can afford my price. We'll see...

"I don't know if I told you, but about ten minutes drive away is a shop called the 'Cambridge Cupboard' run by English people and they sell lots of English bits and pieces like the Sunday Express, Marmite, Bovril, tea-bags, loose tea, Weetabix, Robert-son's jam, marmalade, Huntley & Palmer's biscuits, Milk Tray chocolates, books, magazines, barley water – they even have sausages and steak & kidney pies made up by an English butcher who lives over here, so that makes life a bit more tolerable.

"I would still love to move back to England, but I'd have to be very rich to make such a move again, as by all accounts things are a lot harder there than here at present.

But then it gets confusing, as I have to remind myself that it's the England of the late '60s I miss..."

Graham Parker disbanded the Rumour after the stunning Grugahalle per-formance. Although the projected touring never took place, he retained Nicky's services for his first album without the band—again recorded in New York—in 1982. The two stayed in touch and later re-connected when Nicky eventually did make it back to England.

Graham Parker: "*Another Grey Area* was recorded at the Power Station, but Nicky also visited my wife and I in our London flat for dinner, both on his own and with Moira, his second wife. He could do a fine dog bark when the mood struck him, which seemed to be most of the time. I think if you listen closely to the fade on 'Big Fat Zero' on the *Grey Area* album, you might hear Nicky in the background, barking madly."

The work he did with Parker ushered in a new, though less glamorous, era of trans-Atlantic travel for Nicky, with stage and studio work on both sides of the ocean allowing him at least occasional visits home. Survival dictated that any potential source of work needed to be pursued, and the following months were distinguished by the variety of different jobs he took on. He even found time to take some lessons and at long last pass his driving test.

Both *Variety* and the *Hollywood Reporter* of July 1982 carried an advertisement, from producer David Courtney (previously involved with Leo Sayer) and his partner, veteran music biz figure Eddie Kritzer, for a "rock'n'roll orientated lead singer" to front a "new supergroup called Stable Force" with players including Earl Slick, Philip Chen, Frankie Banali and...Nicky Hopkins. Since the right vocal candidate could not apparently be found, this project went no further, though Quiet Riot drummer Banali described the band as "sounding fantastic, like a cross between the Rolling Stones and Led Zeppelin."

Later that same year, Nicky was back on German television for another *Rockpalast*, this time taped in Hamburg following a handful of dates with Terry and The Pirates in Holland.

77. Terry and The Pirates in Holland

I had a poignant meeting with Terry Dolan in his apartment in an assisted housing project in Novato, California. The years had left their mark on Terry, but he was still feisty, full of fun and good company. He explained how he kept Terry and The Pirates going for thirty years:

"I sold cocaine. We all did, that's how I financed the group until I was busted in a motel room with 9/10 of one gram and 9/10 of half a gram (the standard measurement for short-changing the customer). I did a month in jail and then I stopped. All those European shows were sold out. I played with two Hall Of Famers and I'm proud of it!"

Bass player David Hayes noticed that Nicky's sense of humour had returned with his sobriety: "He switched as soon as we crossed the border and spoke to me in a very low voice with a German accent he kept up the whole trip."

Such flying visits (Nicky returned to the USA the following day via New York) made no significant contribution to the Hopkins household budget. Nicky's activities on behalf of Scientology were mostly only expenses-paid, so he remained based, still with Dolly and their various household pets (including Floyd the Dobermann), in a modest house in Chula Vista Way in the Hollywood Hills.

After all his previous successes, Nicky explained to *Keyboard World* magazine that he still harboured unfulfilled ambitions:

"Years ago I imagined how exciting it would be to associate with big-name rock and roll bands. I've been lucky to fulfil that dream, but Bob Dylan is one whom I've never worked with and I hope that someday I'll get the opportunity."

Not long after, a call did come to join Dylan's touring band, but Nicky lost his place in a stripped-down line-up that included his old friend Mick Taylor, to the irrepressible Ian McLagan:

"Well, he didn't audition. He was probably Dylan's first choice, or at least Mick Taylor's first choice, but he's not an organ player, and Bob particularly wanted a B3 and didn't want me to play piano. I actually did the first half of the tour with just a B3, but Mick Taylor, bless his heart, rooted for me and they brought a piano in and Bob eventually liked that too. That's why Nicky didn't get the gig and I did."

Not all his clients registered as highly as Dylan on the "hipness" scale, but Nicky's training and classical background still made him first choice for a wide variety of recordings. Richard Perry brought him in to join the cream of the L.A. session world, on the key tracks he co-produced for the 1984 Julio Iglesias album *1100 Bel Air Place*. Nicky came away with the curious credit of "basic arranger" on the Iglesias/Willie

Nelson duet single "To All The Girls I've Loved Before," notable more for its chart success than for its musical qualities. There is no acoustic piano to be heard in the sickly-sweet production of the Spanish crooner's best-known ballad, as by now Nicky was reluctantly coming to grips with recent keyboard technology and playing his parts on a synthesiser. This served him well in early 1985, when he was offered an guest spot on tour in the UK with session band Sky, giving him a golden opportunity to "test the waters" back home. The tour programme for *The Great Balloon Race* listed the group's own Steve Gray on grand piano

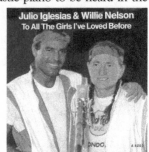

and Nicky as playing only "additional keyboards."

Touring with a currently successful outfit such as Sky was certainly perfectly legitimate employment, but, considering Nicky's past, one can only speculate as to his feelings on reading, in the tour programme, that he had "made the transition from acoustic keyboards." Sky founder member Herbie Flowers recalled the events that led to Nicky's inclusion:

"He was invited in because (guitarist) John Williams decided he didn't want to do it anymore. Nicky was a good reader and everything in Sky was pretty much written out. Before each show I used to have to say, 'Ooh, you've probably noticed that there are a couple of changes in the band; just give us half an hour to prove our point and if at the interval you want your money back, please go to the box office and we'll oblige.'"

Nicky's passport shows at least one more trip back to the UK in the summer of 1985, during which he gave an interview to the local *Express* newspaper, while visiting his mother in Frinton-On-Sea. By October he was back in L.A., where one time Wings guitarist Laurence Juber remembered Nicky taking part in a blues jam at the Central Club in Hollywood, with Knack drummer Bruce Gary and bassist Tim Bogert. Such informal gatherings are the lifeblood of musicians who are not solidly employed, and during the same time period, both Nicky and Bogert joined Laurence in the studio for sessions with New York singer and songwriter Buzzy Linhart.

Another casual meeting led to his next touring and recording involvement and a lasting friendship with Byrds alumnus John York:

"Jodi Mekler was a mutual friend and we wound up having dinner together and Nicky and I happened to be sitting really close to each other; I was asked to start the salad, so I lifted the bowl with my left hand and with my right made a turning motion, as if I were starting a pinwheel; I passed it to Nicky and he looked at me and said, 'We're going to get along great, mate' and from that moment we were friends."

A growing nostalgia for the sixties meant that the surviving members of once illustrious groups were taking advantage of their past glories by going on the road as a tribute band, rather than struggling to establish a new persona. With two original members on board, the Gene Clark/Michael Clarke Byrds tribute originally billed itself as a "20th Anniversary Tribute to Mr. Tambourine Man," but promoters inevitably accentuated the Byrds connection by simply ignoring all but the original name. When it became clear that the undertaking was unlikely to lead back to the big time, drummer Michael Clarke departed in November 1984, leaving the volatile Gene Clark, struggling constantly with his own demons, with an ever-changing line-up to represent the Byrds legacy in clubs, hotels and casinos.

John York: "I was playing with Gene, Michael and Blondie Chaplin and we sometimes had Rick Danko, Richard Manuel and Rick Roberts, but I really wanted to get Nicky in. I knew there'd be no resistance on a musical level, but I was worried Michael would say that we couldn't afford another guy. We were playing at the Trancas in Malibu, so I went in the afternoon of the gig and asked if they had a piano and they said, 'Sure, it's in one of the back rooms and hasn't been used in years.' So I tuned it up, put a pick-up on it and put the thing up onstage. When we showed up for the gig, Michael said, 'Hey, Johnnyboy, what's the piano for, man?' I said, 'Nicky Hopkins is going to sit in with us tonight,' and he said, 'No way!' So from the opening, Michael was blown away and basically fired one of the road managers, so he'd have the money to hire Nicky. I think he stayed six months—maybe a little longer."

John witnessed occasional scenes of music industry indifference to Nicky that shocked him:

"He was the most famous sideman in the world, but in terms of an individual career, he was having a great deal of difficulty. Nicky didn't like to drive, so he would occasionally ask me to bring him places and we went to see Peter Asher, who at the time had Linda Ronstadt and maybe James Taylor. Nicky and I sat on one side of the desk and Peter on the other and I knew these guys had known each other since Beatle days. I couldn't figure out if they were just being terribly British or if Peter was being incredibly rude to Nicky, because he was just telling him, 'I'm sorry, there's really nothing I can do.'

"I've never had the money to invest in anybody, but if I did, I would look for talent like Nicky. He had focus. He knew what he was doing. He had vision. He wasn't someone who had thrown his talent away with drugs and alcohol."

Life on the road with "The Byrds" was a far from luxurious experience. The band travelled by bus more often than by plane and, for the first time since the sixties, Nicky experienced the lower end of the musician's life-style:

John York: "It was physically really demanding, because it wasn't high-end touring by any means, but he never complained about the gigs, even where people didn't treat the band very well or where the guys that do the monitors are not very good. There was no need for him to carry anything as there was a piano at each gig and I carried a tuning gavel just in case. They were almost always electric pianos and I think he was just happy to be playing."

The two friends became roommates on the road and managed to keep the boredom factor at bay with typically incomprehensible touring rituals.

Moira Hopkins: "John told me that they were in a hotel and it was pouring with rain so, to pass the time, they had everything in the room placed half on and half off something—if there was a telephone, it would be half on and half off the table, the lamp on the edge of the bedside table…"

Since the original Byrds sound was almost exclusively guitar-driven, a keyboard player seems an unlikely choice to recruit, but John York explained:

"We made an agreement that we would back off on our parts so we would not cover up anything that Nicky did, and it was fun because things became so orchestral. We didn't realise how far we had gotten into that until the first gig when Nicky wasn't there and we had to automatically re-think every song, because all that orchestration was gone. Playing with Nicky was a lot like playing with Clarence White, where you know you're in the company of someone who is so 'connected' that you're lucky to be standing next to him. You just want to hang on and try to play along."

A January 1986 show, from "Doc Severinsen's Music Showplace" in Oklahoma City, was recorded for DVD release and reveals a hoarse but sober Gene Clark, with John York and Rick Roberts as occasional lead singers and a repertoire made up of new material, Byrds originals and a few covers. The rigours of touring at that level are brought home in John's introduction to Gene's first Byrds songs: "This legend rode seven hundred miles to get here tonight!" Nicky fits seamlessly into the folk-rock style of the band and lifts what are otherwise fairly pedestrian versions of the hits to a new level when he steps up for a solo. His break on "Eight Miles High" is astonishing.

An interview with a Canadian journalist that same month (recalled by York as the unfortunate Stones fan whom Nicky eventually set on fire for asking one too many Mick Jagger questions) was recorded in a typical after-show club atmosphere and revealed Nicky's ambivalent attitude to his first experience with an "oldies" band. The interviewer pointed out that many in the audience were there to see him (some shows were billed as "The Byrds featuring Nicky Hopkins"). When asked how long he would be staying with the band, Nicky's reply, "As long as it feels right" could easily be interpreted as "until something better comes along." The question, as to whether he had anything to do with the original Byrds when he first hit California, was met with a firm "No!"

One incentive for him to stay longer, apart from his fee,[49] was that parallel to their road activities, Gene Clark, John York and guitarist Pat Robinson were working on a second project, recording and writing under the acronym CRY. Pat had even deeper connections to Scientology than Nicky—being personally acquainted with L. Ron Hubbard and his family—and had met Nicky while working as an entertainer at the Celebrity Centre. He was already a successful songwriter, with covers by Joe Cocker, Laura Branigan, Moon Martin and others.

With a number of demos in the can and Gene's then manager representing the trio, attempts to secure a recording deal were already underway when Nicky entered the picture. The obvious benefits of adding his name and expertise to the project soon persuaded all parties to add one more initial to the group name and turn CRY into CHRY, though most of the writing credits were confined to

---

[49] a two-week hotel residency might net about $2,000 for each musician after agent's fees were deducted

the prolific team of Clark and Robinson. John later recorded one Hopkins/York collaboration, "Heartache Susanne" on his *Claremont Dragon* CD, which he dedicated to Nicky.

John York: "Nicky gave me a lot of music that he wanted me to write lyrics for, but at the time I was so in awe of him that it never happened. Recently I was moving my studio and I found those tapes and I'm entertaining the idea of pursuing that again."

Despite strong interest from CBS and others, the undertaking was cursed from the start by the industry's perception of Gene Clark as a solo performer rather than part of a band and one who had, by his drug and alcohol-fuelled behaviour, burned more bridges than even Nicky had.

John York: "Sometimes Gene was sober and sometimes he wasn't. We had to do some shows without him when he was really sick, and that was uncomfortable for me, because I had to front the band and I always felt that my participation in the Byrds was not enough to be legitimate in that stance. CHRY never panned out although all the ingredients were there. It could have been an amazing group if the right business-person had been there at the right moment."

The surviving recorded material, including Nicky's keyboard contributions, remained under wraps until 2001, when Pat Robinson leased enough tracks for a  double CD (under Gene Clark's name) to a German record company, but otherwise there were no takers. CHRY quietly disbanded, though Nicky and John continued to tour with Gene, despite the singer's increasingly unpredictable behaviour. John couldn't recall one specific incident that brought Nicky's tenure with the Byrds to an end, but knew that the travelling was physically draining for him. Nicky remained in contact with both ex-Byrds even after he left L.A., and when Gene Clark's lifestyle inevitably caught up with him and he died in May 1991, John York saw Nicky for the last time at a wake held for the troubled singer.

1986 commenced with Nicky's divorce from Dolly and by November he had met Moira. With no indication that his prospects in the USA were likely to improve any time soon, Nicky decided to follow his heart and make the risky but long considered decision to try his luck again back in England.

Once established back in Britain, Nicky signed a formal contract with P.R.A. (Personal Representation for Artists), the management company Gray Levett formed with his partners Nick Wynne and Scobie Ryder.

Gray Levett: "Nicky said, "I absolutely hate talking money. Would you mind representing me? At least I could say, 'Talk to my manager.'"

Scobie Ryder: "P.R.A.) was set up just to get him back on and get his rates up and when I said, 'We're going charge you out for a lot of money,' it really did bring back his confidence.'

Nicky was given the freedom to use the facilities at Scobie's hire company to familiarise himself with some of the new keyboards. Gray recalled an incident one afternoon, when a currently popular American band were visiting during a break from touring, an event he felt underlined Nicky Hopkins' dilemma arriving back in eighties London:

"Nicky was there being unassuming, a constant cigarette on and staring at the Kurzweil piano, and this young blond, peroxide poser was showing off to the other musicians. He'd modelled himself on Duran Duran—hair teased up and very camp and was looking at Nicky, obviously considering him very unfashionable.

"The American was banging away and asked Nicky if he played, to which he replied, 'A bit,' which was true, because he didn't have a keyboard at home at the time. The guy said, 'Would you like to attempt something?' All the musicians present obviously knew who Nicky was and were laughing, so the guy thought

78. With Scobie Ryder and Gray Levett, celebrating Nicky's signing with P.R.A.

they were joining in on his joke. Nicky said, "'I don't know what to play' and Scobie leaned forward and said sotto voce, 'Why don't you play that piece from Quicksilver?' Nicky goes, 'I don't know if I can remember it; hang on.' He went into it and you should have seen the look on this guy's face! His eyes seemed to move out of their parent sockets and all he managed to get out was, 'Who is he?' Scobie leaned forward, in his Glaswegian way, and says, 'It's Nicky Hopkins. I bet you feel like a cunt now' and at that point the guy passed clear away and everybody cheered. Nicky was going, 'Oh, is he OK?' because it had all been over his head. He was completely unaware that this guy was trying to set him up, because he took people at face value."

There unfortunately remained a rather large gap between Nicky's financial expectations and eighties reality. Helen O'Hara, another of P.R.A.)'s clients, described Nicky at this juncture as "a bit lost."

Gray Levett: "He was keen to make a start, but the music business had changed so radically that the sort of fees that he wanted weren't available from young acts with no money, so it wasn't terribly fruitful."

P.R.A.) oversaw negotiations for the work Nicky did with Paul McCartney, but when this failed to lead to a full band membership, Art Garfunkel became his most significant employer during the during the time he spent in England. Their paths had crossed briefly in the mid-seventies, when Nicky made a fleeting appearance on Garfunkel's most successful post-Simon album *Breakaway*, on the single cut "I Only Have Eyes For You," which satisfyingly went on to spend two weeks at the top of the UK charts.

In 1987 Garfunkel began work on his album *Lefty* in his hometown of New York, with Beatles engineer/producer Geoff Emerick and a small but illustrious team of players, including drummer Steve Gadd, bass-player Joe Osborn, guitarist Hugh McCracken and Nicky on keyboards. The resulting record could not be counted among Garfunkel's successes, but he fell in love with Nicky's piano work and invited him to become his musical director as well as piano player, a role Nicky performed very successfully.

Art leaned heavily on him and soon refused to go on stage without him. The extent to which he had begun to rely on Nicky became apparent during negotiations for a one-off trip from London to L.A. to do Johnny Carson's *Tonight* show, a performance that only involved miming!

Nicky's understandable response was that he would only do it if he was well paid, as the three-minute appearance would take several days out of his schedule. Gray Levett found himself haggling with an old-school American manager:

"Art over-ruled his own manager, even though the poor man was genuinely trying to save him money. He said, 'There are lots of piano players in the world. Goddamit! We're even paying him when he's in the air!'"

Garfunkel had acquired a reputation in certain quarters of the industry as a demanding and easily riled taskmaster, a condition apparently unaffected by his fondness for smoking pot. Luckily Nicky's innate "seen-it-all" ability to remain unruffled by his many employers' eccentricities, helped him in his role as musical director, despite the many challenges that came his way. Psychologically resilient he may have been, but long stretches at the keyboard during Art's lengthy tour rehearsals (at Scobie Ryder's Clink rehearsal facility near London Bridge) aggravated a recurrent physical side effect of Nicky's ongoing medical problems and caused his back to go into agonising spasm. Gray Levett's role sometimes included hands-on as well as business management:

"I'd have to go down every day that he was rehearsing with Art and pop his back in and it was a visible relief to him; he was ready for his day."

Ironically, with all the free benefits of the National Health Service available to him, Nicky's few years in England were otherwise almost trouble-free, apart from an incident that same year with a painful kidney stone, which landed him in the Kent and Sussex hospital in Tunbridge Wells. His niece Alix was living in England with her mother, who, after her marriage ended, had left New York and also made the move back home:

"Nicky was in a huge men's ward and before I went to see him I asked what I should bring and he said, 'I want some fags!' so I bought him a pack of Dunhill's, some music magazines and some chocolates. He was in agony and he only had the one kidney. He wasn't in for long, but it was a hard year.

"Christmas 1987 was the first time for years that the entire family was together for Christmas—obviously without my grandfather, and that vacation in Frinton exposed a lot of the family problems. We rented the flat upstairs from my grandmother, and were all there: Nicky, Mummy, my Uncle Paul and his wife Iris and me; there was a lot of squabbling and a lot of crap came out. Christmas is always a dodgy time. The boys were totally oblivious and were just happy to be together, so it was great for them, but it was not fun for the women; my grandmother was a real instigator; she liked to play the girls off on one another."

Tensions at work were no less demanding.

Woody Woodmansey: "It was Nicky's job to get the band ready because Art was a bit funny. The whole thing relied on feel, because sometimes your parts were so chopped down. We used to play in front of 18,000 people and he'd say, 'I don't want you to play the hi-hat on this track,' so you couldn't play with your right hand, but you had to keep perfect tempo and it was painful. You couldn't relax for one minute and it was the same for Nicky; move the piano lid down half an inch and it was perfect for Art. Nicky was good at seeing what the artist wanted and with Art it was low volume. They'd recorded the albums louder than we played, but he wanted to hear it like the album, so we rehearsed a few numbers before Art came in and Nicky kept saying we were still too loud. 'Let's do this one quieter than the last one,' and eventually we got used to playing at that volume and feeling it, so when Art came in it was spot on and he just nodded at Nicky, 'Yeah, I like this.'"

Despite Garfunkel's occasional petulance, touring with him was the antithesis of Nicky's experiences with the Byrds the previous year. Travel and accommodation were at a comfortable, often luxury level, and the singer's worldwide stardom meant that Nicky played a variety of highly prestigious venues in the four years he spent as Garfunkel's MD.

The Johnny Carson Show was followed by a *Night Of The Proms* in Antwerp, backed by the Belgian Royal Philharmonic Orchestra, and in December by an appearance at the London Palladium, in the presence of Prince Charles and Lady Diana, for the Prince's Trust. (During rehearsals Special Branch officers tried to eject Gray Levett, while Nicky cheekily played "I Do Like To Be Beside The Seaside." Gray also remembered Nicky greeting Elton John backstage with a cheerful "Hi Reg" and the two pianists embracing warmly).

Woody Woodmansey: "We did three numbers: 'Bridge Over Troubled Water,' 'The Sound Of Silence' and 'Bright Eyes' and we were going to meet Lady Di, but there were too many bands, so it was just Art who did"

Another highlight was a three-day stint at the Albert Hall, during a UK tour in early 1988. Nicky was given a solo spot to perform a new Hopkins composition, appropriately titled "The Homecoming," which he played to tremendous applause from an audience that included his mother, his friends and family.

The Garfunkel band played all over Europe and visited Australia and the Far East, a tour which included an appearance alongside other CBS acts—Boz Scaggs, Billy Joel and the Hooters—at a music festival at the Tokyo Dome in Japan. A highlight of the summer of 1990 was a concert for an audience of almost a million and a half in the Bulgarian capital, Sofia.

Nicky Hopkins: "It was an anti-communist rally and over a million people showed up. It felt similar to what was happening in the States back in the sixties. Somebody told us that they used to lock people up for listening to Rolling Stones records."

On tour, the daily task of fixing Nicky's troublesome back fell to Woody:

"He showed me how to do it. You had to hold him and pull him over your back and you could hear it go (sound effects of cracking) and then he was fine; the minute it was in he was firing on all six again."

Garfunkel's name may not have carried the same prestige as the icons with whom Nicky had worked in the sixties and seventies, and after his disappointments with Bob Dylan and Paul McCartney, may have seemed a poor substitute, but Nicky's tenure as bandleader came at a critical time in his life and he was treated extremely well. His position effectively made it possible for him to remain in the UK for as long as he did, whilst still allowing him time to pursue other less lucrative projects—and Garfunkel took every opportunity to praise Nicky's talents.

Woody Woodmansey: "I remember Art coming up and saying, 'That's the best version of "Bridge Over Troubled Water" I've ever done.' He didn't have to say that and I'm sure those kind of compliments are rare and a lot of that was Nicky's due. He gave it more than the record."

Both Nicky and Woody being based in Sussex, the two musicians occasionally socialised with Garfunkel in between concert dates, taking him to visit nearby antique shops, and he repaid Nicky's attentions by coming over from the States specially to join his wedding guests at Hever Castle.

Playing Art Garfunkel's anodyne versions of his hits was not where Nicky's heart lay. During this time period, with considerable encouragement from those around him, he embarked on his first attempt in more than a decade to record again as a solo artist. His increasing grasp of current keyboard technology had opened up previously unheard of possibilities for a solo musician to conjure up filmic textures and orchestral arrangements. Nicky's management were convinced that his particular talents were perfectly suited to both the burgeoning "new age" market, as well as what Scobie Ryder disparagingly described as "pseudo-classical crossover stuff," already championed with huge success by performers such as Richard Clayderman.

Shortly after they'd met, Scobie and Nicky had collaborated informally on a Christmas single, "Dance Away, Christmas Day," which was released to zero response under the band name The Present, on Scobie's own Plezure Records. When Scobie bumped into industry veteran Denis Knowles in the south of France at the MIDEM music business conference in Cannes, he saw a chance for Nicky to pursue his forays into "classical crossover" with someone who had a history of success with pianists and knew the marketplace inside out.

Denis Knowles: "My background goes right back to the sixties with CBS, then United Artists and Arista. I was involved with breaking Richard Clayderman in Britain; I recorded Jacques Loussier's *Best Of Play Bach* and later managed a Chinese concert pianist. I was a fully-fledged consultant when Gray hired me for three months, at my usual monthly fee, to look at Nicky's situation and I came to the conclusion that to try and market him as a solo artist would be difficult, because Nicky wasn't an extrovert. What was clear was his gift for composing.

"I did a deal with Doug Hopkins at Advision Studios, who was a close friend, and he gave Nicky free time in the studio and use of the instruments, to record an idea we had to take things like 'A Whiter Shade Of Pale' and do a 'Moonlight Sonata' approach to it, or 'Nights In White Satin' opening up with a classical arrangement. Because we were both classical buffs, he also did one of the movements from Beethoven's 7th Symphony, opening up in the very sombre slow movement and then going straight into pure Nicky Hopkins; we did the same thing with 'Mars' (from Holst's *The Planets*). We christened the new versions 'Mars, The Bringer Of Chocolate Bars' and 'Beethoven, 7 Not Out,' so all that essential humour was kept in there. I've still got the recordings and they've never been exploited."

Scobie Ryder: "We were taking classical pieces and slowly but surely moving them into the rock area; we had Mitch Mitchell and others on it and it was beautifully done."

Denis' subsequent attempts to sell the concept to the leading "new age" label Windham Hill and other companies proved fruitless. In addition to "The Homecoming," which Nicky had premiered in the Garfunkel shows, he had also composed a more ambitious piece of music in three movements, christened, at Denis Knowles' request, "The Sussex Suite."

"I tried to get Clayderman to record it, because every year I used to come up with a concept for his albums. I wanted to put another slant on him, because actually he is a very good pianist, and get him associated with Nicky Hopkins, the world's greatest session piano player, but unfortunately that never came about. There was also a TV series called *Chancer* and Jan Hammer had co-written a fantastic theme tune, which I got Nicky to record and in June 1990 I sent a letter to Jan to see if he would agree for Nicky to do it."

Nicky was extremely grateful for Denis' active pursuit of such commercial channels and soon asked him to take on his full-time management, an agreement based purely on a handshake. It is unclear exactly when the changeover took place, but Gray and his partners bowed out gracefully, happy that their cli-

ent and friend would be in good hands. Denis' involvement with Nicky's life and work soon transcended just business, as he and his wife became almost surrogate parents to Nicky and Moira, with the younger couple often taking advantage of his invitations to share "the best roast dinners in England."

Aside from his work with Art Garfunkel, Nicky had continued to do occasional sessions for younger bands such as Diesel Park West and the Stones-influenced Dogs D'Amour, whose *Errol Flynn* album was recorded at Maison Rouge in London. Lead singer Tyla e-mailed a thumbnail sketch of his impressions of Nicky:

"He came to the recording studio, played on a few tunes, smoked about 100 cigarettes, got his money and left. When he walked in, I thought he was some tramp who had wandered in off the street in Fulham. He was such a quiet, unassuming person. I didn't want to ask him about the Stones, as I thought he must get sick of it, so we concentrated on the songs we were doing and he quite enjoyed it."

Whether working for the hottest new band on the block or for established names like the Jefferson Airplane (whose reunion CD Marty Balin described as a hideous experience, done just for the money), Nicky's effortless brilliance in the studio never failed to leave a strong impression on those he worked with. Later clients included Gary Moore, Roger Chapman and again Jack Bruce. Jack and Nicky—in his best Otis Spann mode—made a one-off appearance alongside Albert "The Iceman" Collins on Bruce's *Question Of Time* album, delivering an incendiary version of Willie Dixon's "Blues You Can't Lose."

John York: "I gave him a ride to a Jack Bruce session and when we got there Ginger Baker was just leaving. The engineer asked him to go in and get a sound and Nicky started playing. The engineer turned to the rest of us and said, 'I can't hit that button' and we all sat there and listened to him playing. It was when he was working on music for films and it was like listening to Rachmaninoff or something; at a certain point Nicky stopped, took a last drag on the cigarette, put it out and said, 'OK mate' and then started playing like some 65-year old black guy from the Delta. It was unreal!"

Since his recovery, he had regained his reputation

for never delivering anything less than excellence. Moira recalled one rare occasion in England, when he was unhappy with his own performance:

"He did a session for Gary Moore, but for some reason wasn't happy with it and when he came home, it was preying on his mind. The next day he called Gary up and said, 'I'll come all the way back up there and do it again if you like, because I feel like I could do better.' He was very tough on himself."

It is worth remembering that Nicky's workload and the calibre of his client list, even in his less busy times, would constitute success for most musicians, but with no back-up in terms of property or savings, he was still living very much day to day. The impression from his time in England is of an increasing inconsistency in his work: he appeared on television with Irish singer Feargal Sharkey, and guested on various projects, both live and in the studio, with his old friend Bill Wyman, including a charity concert in February '89 in Southampton for the Kampuchea ferry disaster, with a cast including Andy Fairweather-Low and Gary Brooker. Moira remembered several visits to Wyman's country house in Suffolk, and had vague recollections of an offer to join melodic post-punk combo Prefab Sprout and of another unsuccessful audition, this time for progressive rockers Jethro Tull.

After four years in his home environment, Nicky was forced to admit that, much as he loved the suburban atmosphere of East Grinstead, the BBC and the familiar food and weather, England was, if anything, a harder place to survive in than the USA.

Gray Levett: "We never made anything out of it, that's for sure; we did it for Nicky and he did make some serious money at that time, but I had always thought that he was best known in L.A. and that was Catch 22. Had we been in Los Angeles, I think anybody competent and ethical could have looked after him and he would have made a decent career and probably have got into the film or jingle work that appealed to him."

Moira recalled discussions for another solo album while still in England, though not necessarily in the classical vein:

"I said, 'Why don't you do just an amazing rock album.' We even got him a red jacket at John Richmond in London; it was like a Teddy-Boy drape jacket and from the cuffs going upwards towards the elbows, in black embroidery it said 'Destroy' and 'Killer'—a real piano player's jacket. We talked about a solo record, but survival comes first. You've got to have money to put food on the table and somewhere to stay."

Having shared Nicky's ups and downs and disappointments at close quarters, Moira was the pragmatic voice that eventually persuaded her husband that they would be better off back in America:

"He had actually missed a lot of work by not being in L.A., but when I brought up that I thought we really needed to go back, Nicky replied, 'I hate, loathe and detest L.A. I won't go back and I SHAN'T!' I started laughing and I said, 'I guess we won't bring that subject up again for a little while!' He wanted so much to remain in England, but it wasn't to be. After about a week he agreed to it."

Denis Knowles' attempts to sell Nicky as a classical performer may have failed, but one major coup he achieved before Nicky left the UK was tying up his first publishing deal for more than a decade. To this day Denis remains convinced that Nicky took a wrong turn when he abandoned the classical field to join a rock'n'roll band:

"If he had gone straight into composing, when he left the Royal Academy of Music, he would not have gone on the drugs path and all that scene. They (Hamstein Publishing) wanted him for movies."

Nicky's transition back to California was eased considerably by his being in possession of an agreement with U.S. publishing company Red Brazos, a division of Hamstein, which guaranteed a five-figure sum and a comparatively generous royalty rate for the first year of a potential five-year contract. The terms were harsh by British standards, although Nicky was already acquainted with his new partner Richard Perna:

"I had a writer, who has since passed away, by the name of Jerry Williams who was working on some demos in his studio in Tulsa, Oklahoma. Nicky was passing through and ended up on the demos. I happened to talk with Jerry on the phone and he told me that he had Nicky Hopkins there. He spoke about his pedigree as a session player and touring musician and it sounded very interesting, so I met Nicky there and between the sessions he would sit down and play various themes that he had composed. I was really intrigued by his musicality; it was so broad. I was working for Bill Ham's company at the time, and after thinking it over a month or two, with Jerry prodding me, I called Nicky and we worked out a deal. It came together rather quick.

"His track record as a composer at that time was not that great and as a song-writer he would always be an incomplete package, because he didn't write lyrics, but what he did musically was really impressive and he had tremendous access to great lyricists and other songwriters. I thought it would be interesting to see what we could put together."

Moira Hopkins: "Jerry was one of their top songwriters and made a lot of money for Hamstein—he was also a larger than life character and used to getting his own way, but he loved Nicky. In fact, I think he was like hell on wheels—a bit hard to handle. He was a rich man, could do whatever he wanted, could say whatever he wanted and Richard would bow and scrape to him a bit."

Denis Knowles: "My agreement with Nicky was that I would only earn money off things that I generated, so I only took my 20 percent share of the advance and everything else was his. I did the deal through John Cohen at Clintons, who are probably *the* top lawyers in the business. When we got the contract back, it was a typical American contract—very, very heavy—and John rang me and said, 'Denis, this contract is really diabolical and totally unfair and I suggest that we sign it because it wouldn't stand up in court!'"

Denis' involvement in Nicky's career effectively ended when he went back to America. Once the decision to leave was made, the couple shut down their household in East Grinstead, put their possessions into storage and, with heavy hearts and taking only what they could carry in a suitcase, left England in May 1991. Nicky would never see his home country again.

Long Journey Home
L.A. To Nashville

"Nicky was on the up and was happier than he'd been in years, writing his own music and creating soundtracks. He was so happy and so fulfilled."
 – Moira Hopkins

Nicky was used to the schizophrenic and nomadic lifestyle of a travelling session man, but having to uproot again this time was hard. For the first ten months back in L.A. he and Moira stayed with friends in Silver Lake. Trevor Veitch described his accommodation as "a garret in somebody's house." It was not until February 1992 that they eventually found their own place, referred to in a letter to his brother Paul as "*a little guest house in a nice quiet part of L.A.*" and next door to Tom Petty in the central district of Encino. The first weeks in town were particularly bleak, with the usual tedious task of calling round to announce his return.

Moira Hopkins: "There were lean periods when people didn't know Nicky had moved. He narrowly missed doing an album with Alice Cooper; we would bump into people and they'd go, 'Oh, we wanted you for a session, but we didn't know where to find you.'"

Gene Clark was one of the first friends he contacted, and Nicky was devastated when he was told of Gene's untimely death less than three weeks after his arrival.

Moira: "They had become very close friends and were going to work together again. Nicky had been on the phone to Gene a couple of times and they were arranging to meet; then, out of the blue, Gene passed away. It was very shocking for Nicky."

There was little indication that the session situation in Los Angeles was any more vibrant than the scene he had just left behind him, but Nicky made an effort to renew old contacts, visiting Joe Cocker backstage at the Greek Theatre. Nicky had already written to Cocker in an effort to mend the bridges burned when both men were in the grip of their alcohol addictions.

Moira Hopkins: "Joe hadn't received any of the letters and we realised that Cocker's wife, Pam, probably stopped them. She wasn't to know that Nicky had been clean for years; all she had to go on was what Joe had told her about the wild times they used to have. She was there when Nicky asked him about his letters. We were pretty aware of where people were coming from…"

Ian McLagan was appearing locally and invited Nicky to sit in at a gig:

"I was at the Mint and half way through the show I hear this voice from the back of the club, 'Stupid person!' I said, 'Ladies and gentlemen, Mr. Nicky Hopkins,' but because I had the piano on top of the B3, we'd have been sitting in each other's pockets, so I let him take over and he freaked the place out, he just played so beautiful."

English refugees, such as Mac and Rod Stewart, had always huddled together in little enclaves, playing football and frequenting the English shops and pubs. Nicky was only occasionally sighted at such gatherings. Moira recalled somewhat drily:

"Nicky never played football. Kim Gardner ran the Cat & The Fiddle on Sunset Boulevard and Nicky and I went there a couple of times, or we would go to Andy Johns' house, maybe for Thanksgiving dinner, but Nicky didn't want to go out much."

Peter Frampton: "The British contingent was in Santa Monica and I saw him at a party with his Scottish wife and I was thrilled to meet Moira, because you could tell she was like Nicky's fairy godmother. We had a really good evening; we went out on the balcony and probably smoked twenty cigarettes."

Nicky had a good reason to stay home, as expectations for him at Hamstein were high.

Trevor Veitch: "He'd seen the writing on the wall and decided to go after the composer thing; he really surprised me, because I didn't think he had those chops. One of the first things he did when he got a new Korg workstation was to make up a little Irish track that I wrote a lyric to, called 'Wild Irish Rose'; I took Nicky's track to Tom Rush and we added his voice. There are two versions of it: one is cranky and guitar heavy—a loud wall of Marshall's—and the other somewhat more folky. Rush of course opted for the folky one; Nicky and I liked the one with the bad attitude."

Tom Rush: *Work in Progress* was a self-funding demo that didn't land me a label deal, but did turn a profit; it was issued on cassette only because I didn't want the expense of pressing LPs, and CDs were still pricey in small lots; I did a numbered edition of 7500 and it sold out. My recollection is how still Nicky sat with only his hands moving and, of course, how absolutely *right* every note felt, even playing synth penny whistle."

Nicky was a great admirer of John Williams and other contemporary film composers. To prepare for his own entry into the film world, he bought a number of soundtrack albums. Having carefully studied the competition in Hollywood, his first real opportunity came unexpectedly from outside the USA.

Richard Perna: "Hamstein had a sub-publishing deal with FujiPacific for Japan and there was a gentleman working there named Akira Tsukahara, and Akira was really impressed when we signed Nicky Hopkins. The Japanese are probably the biggest music fans in the world, know every  detail on the back of a record and can tell you who made tea at the session! Akira came to me with a Japanese film project for Nicky. We didn't have any, quote, 'film composers' at Hamstein, but Akira brought in several motion pictures and a very successful television series, and Nicky not only wrote the music, but orchestrated it, performed a good portion of it and conducted the orchestras for the recordings. It was something that really expanded his career."

An early morning telephone call with Akira Tsukahara gave me the full story of Nicky's adventures in Japan:

"The release date of the first soundtrack we did was August 1992, so it must have been late '91 that we started representing Hamstein in Japan and Nicky was one of the artists featured on Hamstein's sampler. It featured a number of instrumental pieces Nicky had produced, which I thought would be perfect for Japanese TV. FujiPacific is the publishing subsidiary of Fuji television, so we have a TV division and I played his tape for one of the drama producers, who immediately fell in love with the music and decided to go with it. That resulted in a soundtrack album to a drama series called *The Fugitive*.

 "The project, released through EMI Japan, did very well, so we brought Nicky and Moira over to Japan, which is one of my fondest memories of Nicky. The producer took us out to a location where they were filming the series; Nicky was brought to the set outdoors in the evening and the producer organised photographers and press people; all of a sudden he was the target of flashes and cameras, which I could see was something he was not used to, but he looked very happy.

"A movie called *Patio* was next, and as you can tell from the music, those projects were very different from one another. *Patio* was the most memorable, because we were allowed to hire a large philharmonic orchestra. I was particularly pleased with the main title theme. He was amazing, because not only was he able to write, play, produce and arrange, but he was so versatile. When he was asked to come up with a big John Williams-style Hollywood piece it was there, and when he was asked for something in a Nino Rota vein, he immediately had it. *Patio* was not received very well by the critics, but was a huge, commercially successful project."

Nicky did all the work in Los Angeles, using favourite studios and, when necessary, particular session musicians. The first project, recorded entirely on a Yamaha SY77 keyboard, testified to the progress Nicky had made in using technology to achieve his aims. He completed the album in a month and a half, and fittingly, he is prominently featured with a photograph on the sleeve to the soundtrack CD.

On the more ambitious *Patio*, he used flute and oboe as additional lead instruments and was aided and abetted by concertmaster Sid Page and his old friend Trevor Veitch as "musical coordinator." Moira helped choose the titles for the many individual pieces.

Nicky had no immediate interest from American film companies during his time with Hamstein, but with two successful works released inside a year, offers from Japan kept coming. His next commission was another television series, made by one of Japan's most highly regarded directors.

Akira Tsukahara: "*The Namiki Family* was produced by Mr. Shigemichi Sugita, a legendary director. He loved Nicky's work on *Namiki Family* and hired him again for *Last Song*, a film project."

The appropriately titled film, apparently concerning the fortunes of a rock band, was the last project Nicky worked on for FujiPacific; this time he was only credited with the film's main theme and the incidental music that linked a number of Japanese songs. Mr. Tsukahara was sure that, had circumstances allowed, his favourite composer would have continued to work successfully in his country:

"I knew that Japanese projects could not help him as much as international projects, but I hoped that the soundtracks he recorded with Japanese money would elevate him to the international level of success he deserved. As an artist you need someone to run around for you placing your music and getting your music heard. I don't know how much he was paid for the projects, but it was a pretty decent amount of money and it was not difficult to find jobs for Nicky, because offers and enquiries came pouring in. It's not that I worked so hard, it just came naturally."

As word spread that Nicky was back and available, bookings came in, though the names that crop up in his nineties discography are, with honourable exceptions, more outlandish and less well known. Glyn Johns' younger brother Andy had known Nicky since the Rolling Stones Olympic Studios heyday and brought him in on a number of band projects, but there are probably not too many who mourn the passing of identikit '90s, big-hair bands such as Nicky's clients Noisy Mama, Faster Pussycat or the Killer Dwarfs, or even worthy songwriters such as Stanley Wycoff, aka "Bierce In L.A."

Nicky had by some accounts risen to the elite group of Los Angeles players able to command triple scale for sessions, though Trevor Veitch disputed this:

"No one was triple scale; that was a myth that Nigel Olsson started. Nicky was certainly double and there were some who could occasionally command triple scale, particularly if the producer didn't know what he was doing; Mac Rebennack (aka Dr. John) would get away with it sometimes."

Either way, the rent always had to be paid and Moira still functioned as chauffeur, though she seldom stayed for the sessions:

"If Nicky did turn down any work, it was only because he couldn't get there. If he could do it he would. I drove him to Izzy Stradlin, Joe Satriani and the *Spinal Tap* guys…"

In the early nineties, Nicky joined the hallowed ranks of those privileged to play with one of heavy rock's enduring legends, on the uncharacteristically jaunty and Kinks-like "Rainy Day Sun" from Spinal Tap's *Break Like The Wind*. Bassist Derek Smalls (a.k.a. Harry Shearer) passed my questions on to his band colleague, referred to as "Mr. Memory."

David St. Hubbins (Michael McKean): "I believe his name came up when we were talking about 'Rainy Day Sun' with (producer) T-Bone Burnett. Whoever

280

suggested Nicky was hailed as a genius by the others; it could easily have been me. We had seen him for the role of Viv Savage in the run-up to the movie. In the studio he was every bit as cool as you wanted him to be. We were all over him, of course, but he withstood the fan-hood and played like a dream."

For this dream date, which any musician would cheerfully have done for nothing, Nicky was not only paid but was given a photo, signed by all three band members, with the dedication *"To Nicky Hopkins! You gotta future in rock!"*

Nicky's own past achievements were honoured when MJI Radio invited him in July 1991 to pick his "Desert Island Discs." He chose a top ten list of favourites, on most of which he had played: "Volunteers," "The Song Is Over," "Jealous Guy," "Revolution," "You Are So Beautiful." "Fresh Air," "We Love You," "Beck's 'Bolero" and "Imagine," with only Procul Harum's "A Whiter Shade Of Pale" and the Small Faces "Itchycoo Park" added on.

A far more extensive overview of his career was promised when respected English author and journalist Ray Coleman—at the instigation of Denis Knowles—flew to Los Angeles to interview Nicky for a potential biography. Coleman, former editor of *Melody Maker*, had written authorized volumes on a host of well known musicians, including John Lennon, Paul McCartney, Eric Clapton and Rod Stewart.

These interviews have never seen the light of day, since Ray Coleman sadly succumbed to cancer almost exactly two years after Nicky's passing, with the planned biography still unwritten. Ray's widow Pamela, for reasons best known to herself, has kept these invaluable documents under wraps. They may one day appear in a volume of her husband's unpublished works but, as nothing has appeared in the years that have elapsed so far, this seems unlikely.

Nicky made a new friend when he met surf original Merrell Fankhauser (who, as a member of the Impacts, claims authorship of the original "Wipeout"). Merrell hosted a satellite television show, *Tiki Lounge*, on the central coast and invited Nicky to make a guest appearance, which involved a brief trawl through some career highlights and a jam session with his host. Nicky subsequently played on stage with Fankhauser and ended up credited on no less than two live releases and one of Merrell's strange concept albums about the lost continent of Mu.

Such moments of recognition were a boost to Nicky's spirits. His niece Alix recalled a New York visit in the nineties:

"My husband Matthew and I went to a party with him at the Record Factory, because he'd been doing some sessions over there, and afterwards to the China Club on 73rd and Broadway, just a couple of blocks away from the Beacon Theatre. It was a big rock'n'roll club and he was a big deal there! They gave him a football jacket with leather on it, that said 'China Club' and he got up on stage and jammed with a couple of people."

Despite the respect that survivors such as Nicky and Ian McLagan received from most musicians and producers they encountered, there were exceptions. In his highly entertaining memoir, McLagan described an unfortunate audition for Lenny Kravitz. The retro-rocker's keyboard-playing producer Henry Hirsch was looking for authentic sixties sidemen to take the music on tour but expected Mac to exactly reproduce the parts Henry had played himself on Kravitz' records. In his book, *All the Rage,* Ian recounts:

"I worked on a Melissa Etheridge session that made me more than I would have earned in two weeks on the road with Lenny Kravitz. (They) called a week later to get Nicky Hopkins' phone number. I told him Nicky would be as insulted as I was (having to play Hirsch's studio parts note for note live), but gave it to him anyway and wasn't surprised when I heard Nicky turned him down too."

Despite turning down Kravitz's offer, in general Nicky liked to keep his hand in by playing live and was rarely averse to earning a bit of extra cash. In December 1991, he began making regular trips up to San Francisco to play with Zero, a loose conglomerate of local musicians put together by drummer Greg Anton, whom Nicky had met through John Cipollina.

Nicky played on song demos, some of which made it onto Greg's CD *Chance In A Million,* and a few months later the floating group booked a three-night

stand at the Great American Music Hall, one of San Francisco's oldest and most elegant venues, to record for a projected live album.

Greg Anton: "Dan Healy set up the Grateful Dead's full 24 track recording studio system in the basement and I think Nicky was there all three nights. We were mixing it up, but there were always two keyboard players, often Nicky and Pete Sears playing together, with one playing organ and one on piano."

Nicky graces the rambling sequence of songs with some elegant blues licks, but stands out most on a killer version of "Mercury Blues," with the two British expats duelling fiercely on twin pianos, taking solo after blistering solo with mounting intensity.

Philip Elwood (*San Francisco Examiner*): "The high point...was a two keyboard, fourhanded bit of boogie-woogie by Sears and Hopkins. Using clever, innovative major-against-minor key patterns, the pair gave me as good a boogie earful as I've had since my Albert Ammons/Pete Johnson records wore out."

Nicky's brief excursion to Florida with Bobby Keys and Mick Taylor is documented elsewhere, but soon after the Zero recording, Nicky joined Andy McCoy (christened Antti Hulkko), a one-time member of glam-rockers Hanoi Rocks, on a pre-Christmas tour of Andy's native country, Finland. Now living there again with his American wife, Andy added his own memories of meeting and working with Nicky:

"After Hanoi Rocks, I had a band going called the Shooting Gallery, but I

79. With Andy McCoy in Finland

wanted to do an acoustic tour in Scandinavia and I asked Nicky to come along. We did mainly cover songs: R&B, fifties rock'n'roll and blues. It was him and me and a guy called David Lindholm (referred to by Andy's wife Angela as 'the Bob Dylan of Finland'), and we played about nine gigs, travelling in a van because they were only two to four hours apart. They were big clubs: five hundred to twelve or thirteen hundred capacity and they filled up, basically on my reputation. No one except the hardcore musos really knew who Nicky was. We flew in, rehearsed for two days and started right away; Nicky was the ultimate professional and he was funny as hell. I think it was the last tour he did."

Despite his longstanding sobriety, Nicky occasionally allowed himself to fall off the wagon, as on a drunken flight back to the USA, where Andy McCoy remembered making full use of the drinks trolley and "quite a lot of G and T going down Nicky's throat!" He got on particularly well with McCoy, thoroughly enjoyed the two week tour and came home carrying bundles of cash, which, times having been somewhat hard, he threw all over the bed, to Moira's great delight.

The success of Nicky's Japanese soundtracks cemented his relationship with Hamstein, and Richard Perna placed Nicky with a number of his other writers in hopes of forging productive new songwriting partnerships:

"We put him together with Frankie Miller, and he, Frankie and Joe Walsh formed a little super-group." Joining the new venture brought Nicky back into close contact with his old friend David Spero from Cleveland:

"I got into management right around the first time I met Nicky. I don't think I was on the radio another four months after that and Joe Walsh was the one who pushed me into it. From the mid-seventies on, Nicky would often call me for

283

advice about things he was doing, but I never felt I could take any money from him; it was like a consultant-type thing. Then in the last couple of years we actually got as formal a relationship as we ever had. He promised to give me one of his sparkling silver shoes from a Stones tour if I'd help him out!"

In the intervening years David's clients had included Harry Nilsson, with whom Nicky had of course worked many times, and later Joe Walsh himself:

"I managed Harry for the last four years of his life and I finally convinced him that he should go out and tour, because he'd never done that. I suggested that we could do it on a small scale, in really cool places, at a good ticket price and make some money—and one of the keys to it was that Nicky would be the keyboard player. Unfortunately it was a tour that just never happened."

David's recollection was that he put Nicky together with Walsh and Frankie Miller. However, an interview for *Rockline Satellite Radio* in Hollywood on 2nd February 1993 gives a different story. Nicky, along with underrated English singer Terry Reid, was part of the Joe Walsh band that played "live on the air." In between taking calls from listeners, Joe explained that the project had grown out of yet another Los Angeles jam session:

"We're starting this band because we're bored. It's just like a Valley Band; we're going to call it 'The Flew.' Nicky and a couple of local musicians set up in my garage and just started to play, feeling each other out, having a great time and making tea in the kitchen; We'd do all the Monty Python bits and laugh. I think we originally called it 'The Balls.'"

Joe had vague memories of meeting Nicky much earlier:

"I knew him for quite a while. We figured out that we had met and one time even hung out, but neither of us could remember it—but we knew that we had. I think I met him in London when we were both nuts; we looked too familiar to each other to be meeting for the first time. I had asked Nicky to play for me before and to work on some string charts when I was recording; he was too busy at the time but we had a bunch of dialogue over the phone."

Joe Walsh comes across as likeable and very funny, both on and off stage, and doesn't suffer from the common superstar tendency to take himself, or life, too seriously. He and Nicky had an instant rapport, both musically and personally, having been through similar experiences with rock music's temptations and survived them.

The glimpse provided on the radio show of the music they made to-

The Huntridge Performing Arts Theatre
Bad Dogz Entertainment
and Miller Genuine Draft Present

THE FLEW

Featuring
Joe Walsh
Terry Reid
Nicky
Hopkins
and Special Guests

Friday
Feb. 26
Saturday
Feb. 27

$ 25.00
Advance

Tickets Available at The Huntridge and Club Rock Call 477-0242 For Information
Tickets On Sale beginning Friday, Feb. 12, 5.00 p.m. Details on KOMP and KFBI

gether, promised a great future, with Nicky channelling Professor Longhair on Joe's song "Dirty Games" and taking a scorching organ break on an impromptu version of Buffalo Springfield's "Rock And Roll Woman." Joe only remembered the band playing one publicised show (under the more poster-friendly name The Flew), at The Coach House in San Juan Capistrano, but the groundwork was laid for his later collaboration with Nicky:

"I met Frankie Miller and he was the singer that every guitar player dreams of. I was a more complete guitar player than he had been used to and had some pretty good studio licks and production credits, so we decided to call Nicky and Frankie brought along his bass player, Chrissie Stewart. This was a new direction and a new band. We all had ideas and we were all going to be involved with each other's stuff."

Spring 1993 found Nicky in an upbeat mood, but just as he was beginning to feel that life had taken a positive turn, with plans underway to begin recording with Miller and Walsh, touring discussions with Harry Nilsson and his own ongoing film projects for Japan, Nicky's schedule came to an abrupt halt on March 16th.

Moira woke up to find Nicky pacing the floor in agonising pain and obviously in need of immediate medical attention. She took him to the nearest hospital in Encino, where they received a crash course in the workings of the nineties American health system. Nicky had no medical insurance, and the scandalous events that followed reflect incredibly badly, not just on one hospital in particular, but on the entire structure of healthcare in the USA.

After the lengthy admission process, Nicky was taken in for examination. The first doctor he saw took one look at his patient's gaunt frame and massive scarring and refused point blank to treat him or administer any pain relief, insisting that Nicky must be a drug user. After his years of taking downers, Nicky had built up a tolerance to painkillers and needed much larger doses than the average patient.

Moira Hopkins: "They sent him home in a terrible condition, saying he was an addict and wanted pain pills all the time. I said, 'Do you know why he wants pain pills? Because he's in pain and because you're not doing anything about it.' I stood up to that man!"

It was only when Moira complained directly to hospital management and threatened legal action that Nicky was allowed back the following day and admitted. The surgeon from the previous day refrained from an actual apology, but was at least polite. Still palpably furious at the memory, Moira Hopkins continued the story:

"There were three doctors and none of them could help him. I didn't like them and he went through hell there; they kept him in for a week and did a variety of tests but wouldn't operate, because they were too scared and because he didn't have insurance. Maybe they felt that they weren't competent enough and he would have died on the operating table and I just might have sued them."

Moira remembered sitting with Nicky early one morning, watching a classic English film comedy, *The Titfield Thunderbolt* on the hospital TV, when he was struck with a bout of such agonising pain that doctors took him up to intensive care—where he was kept waiting for the rest of the day. None of the tests undertaken helped to produce a clear diagnosis. After several days Nicky's condition stabilised to a point where the doctors felt that they could send him home, without having made any real attempt to cure what was probably some kind of blockage related to Crohn's Disease.

Moira Hopkins: "That's how cowardly they were and that's why I took him to another hospital, where a young doctor was courageous enough to try the best he could for Nicky. He was scheduled for an operation at Sylmar, but before they could begin, something went wrong and he had to go to a third hospital to check that his heart was all right."

Moira stayed with him through every agonising moment of these ordeals. At one point she remembered a Scottish nurse holding Nicky's hands and asking him bluntly if he wanted to live, a question he answered with a firm "Yes." At his bedside, the three talked quietly about his music and future plans. Nicky showed his usual incredible courage and resilience until finally—on May 5th—he underwent the major operation that had been necessary from the outset. It appeared to be a success; he stayed in the hospital recuperating till the end of the month, at which point Moira took him to the Celebrity Centre in Clearwater to continue his recovery:

"I moved us temporarily into a hotel because Nicky had to have special food that I couldn't fix for him. He had post-op bladder problems and it was only the attentions of a nutritionist with homeopathic remedies that saved him from going back to hospital. After a couple of days laying in bed, he told me that he wanted his keyboards sent over from home, because he had been working on a project for Japanese television and wanted to get it done. I've got a memory of him—a frail, skinny figure, lost in his music, sitting playing with all this vigour, even though a week before he could barely walk. He loved music so much that it could take him out of himself. I used to have to wait for a break, to stop him and say, 'You've got to take this medicine because, whether you feel like it or not, we've got to get you better.'"

As if all this wasn't enough, at the same time Nicky was fighting for his life, Moira discovered a lump that needed examination. She was so busy running around with Nicky from hospital to hospital, that she kept the fact to herself while he was convalescing, and only later went to have it checked. She was relieved to learn that it was not malignant. It was now a much-weakened Nicky Hopkins' turn to be visiting his wife. He had been on a diet of baby food since his release and during one visit, Moira remembered him going down to the canteen while she was in bed, and enjoying a whole pizza, a sure sign that he was on the road back to a semblance of health.

As soon as the immediate "life and death" crisis had passed came the inevitable financial crunch. The bill for the week in Encino alone came to $28,000, and one can only guess at the combined expense of the surgery, the lengthy stay and the medical treatment that Nicky received in Sylmar.

He had had two very good years prior to his latest bout of illness but had nowhere near the means to pay the vast medical bills that arrived. Frantic attempts were made to contact the Rolling Stones office in England, where Nicky might still have been eligible for insurance coverage; in the meantime, Pat Robinson put up a piece of land as a guarantee against the mounting bills. In the end, the Rolling Stones came through in the nick of time and covered the lion's share of his debts.

Nicky had been frighteningly close to dying and, despite his "staying power," recovery was not an overnight process. The first sign that he was able to go back to work was when he joined Joe Walsh and Frankie Miller in December, to start recording some of the material they had been writing. Walsh was on a long-term sabbatical from his membership of the quarrelsome Eagles, who had parted in an atmosphere of acrimony in 1980:

"There was just talk of getting together at that point. Everybody had their own lives and families; the problem with the Eagles was getting everybody's schedule the same. We all had solo commitments and Don was really involved with Walden Woods, so there was a theoretical deal on paper. In the meantime I was quite happy doing the Frankie and Nicky project."

The new band, with drummer Ian Wallace making up the rhythm section, convened with one-time Eagles producer Bill Szymczyk, in the unlikely location of Lookout Mountain, overlooking Chattanooga, Tennessee, in a small but favourite studio of Walsh's. Moira accompanied Nicky and remembers a particularly relaxed and friendly environment, with the seasoned team of veteran rockers sharing meals together in local eateries and enjoying an easy working atmosphere.

Joe Walsh: "The chemistry was 'just so.' We got five songs done in the studio; Nicky was totally involved with the arrangements and of course the keyboard parts; there were a couple of songs where the keyboard was a feature instrument not just a backing thing and he changed the song around a bit so that it would complement what he wanted to do. We said, 'Hey, we're not going to tell you what to fucking play! You can play anything you want, dude and it'll be just fine with us.' Nicky was at his absolute best and coming up with parts that were so special."

As unofficial manager, David Spero was also party to the proceedings:

"Joe and I joked about (Nicky): 'Tell him to do another take,' even though he'd just done one that you'd never even think not to use. Everyone just wanted him to keep playing!"

The tracks from the Chattanooga sessions took a while to be released. Joe and Frankie's song "Guilty Of The Crime," featuring Walsh's slide guitar and Nicky in New Orleans mode, appeared on the soundtrack to the *Robocop* TV series, and again later on a "mixed bag" release of Frankie Miller demos and outtakes (along with a chugging blues-rock version of the country standard "He'll Have

To Go"). A version of Carl Perkins' "Honey Don't," recorded at the same time, with Nashville resident Steve Earle taking the lead vocal, found a home on the *Beverley Hillbillies* soundtrack.

Any further plans for the line-up were put on hold when the powers-that-be in the Eagles camp decided to bury their differences and make a killing with their *Hell Freezes Over* tour and live album. Walsh could not refuse the opportunity, but bitterly regretted having to abandon the promising partnership with his friends:

"We were ready to go out, play live and knock people's socks off. We knew it was going to be a monster, but we never had a chance to show anybody and I feel like a part of me is missing, I really do. They were such good mates and it brought out amazing stuff in me; I was improvising and putting in spontaneous stuff, bouncing off Frankie. We're not allowed to do that in the Eagles—it's charts. I was really getting my chops together and it just went away."

1994 began badly for Nicky when Harry Nilsson died on January 15th, and things were not about to improve. Just two days after Nilsson's passing, the biggest earthquake Los Angeles had experienced since 1971 rocked the city.

Moira Hopkins: "I couldn't handle the earthquakes. We had the little house in Encino and in January '94 I thought it was going to collapse. I was actually surprised it was still standing once the main 'quake had stopped. I still think it was higher on the Richter scale than they gave it out to be, but they didn't want panic to spread. It was very close to the hospital where Nicky had been just a few months previously and I thought, 'My gosh! If it had happened when Nicky had the operations and was so weak he could barely walk, what then?' If we stayed in L.A. and he had to go back up to that hospital, I'd always be afraid. A whole section of the freeway came down and a motorcycle cop got killed because suddenly the road wasn't there any more!"

The impact at home was terrifying.

Moira: "The wooden tiles on the roof started clattering and everything started falling down. I got Nicky out of bed, to stand under a doorway. There were huge up and down and sideways movements. The house stayed standing but everything inside fell down. We went out and sat in the car to listen for reports on the radio, and being up on a hill, we had a view over the valley and could see fires breaking out. The quake was at 4:31 in the morning and there were lots of aftershocks. We only went back into the house when it got light."

Although the early morning timing of the tremors probably vastly reduced the death toll, the massive earthquake nevertheless ultimately claimed upwards of sixty lives and, depending upon which reports one believes, caused injuries to between seven and nine thousand people and more than thirty billion dollars worth of damage. After the riots of two years earlier, it provided Nicky Hopkins with a persuasive argument for leaving Los Angeles as soon as possible. Having only recently given up on forging a career from a UK base, the big question was, where to go?

Richard Perna: "The earthquake really induced Nicky to think about relocating and we thought that Nashville would be a perfect place for him, for three reasons: It's a great town for recording artists, so we felt he could get a lot of work with his pedigree as a session player; secondly, with his skills, we thought we would be able to plug him in with many different songwriters and come up with some quality copyrights and thirdly, Nashville was a reasonable place to live with respect to expenses—it had a great music community."

Moira Hopkins: "It was Nicky's decision to go to Nashville. I put a new set of tyres on the car and we left two weeks later, stopping on the way in Flagstaff, Arizona. By February 3rd we'd reached Santa Fe, New Mexico and stayed with a friend, Gwen, who worked for Narconon. We spent my birthday there on February 5th."

The next port of call was Tulsa, Oklahoma, home of Jerry Lynn Williams, Nicky's mentor at Hamstein. Williams was in the middle of recording his own versions of hit songs he had written for dozens of other artists, two of whom, guitar heroes Stevie Ray Vaughan and Eric Clapton, also contributed to the sessions. Nicky took the opportunity to return a favour and played on four tracks of what would become a star-studded CD, released in 1996 as *The Peacemaker Private Sessions*.

Moira Hopkins: "Jerry had a condo and we stayed there for about three days; he was really happy to have Nicky on the album. We arrived in Nashville on February 14th, 1994—Valentine's Day!"

Richard Perna saved the couple from having to stay in a hotel by introducing Nicky to songwriter Dan Tyler, who loaned them an apartment he owned on Cantrell Avenue.

Nicky had been a California resident for the best part of twenty-five years, and was delighted by the climate and temperament in Tennessee. Opinions among his business colleagues differed as to whether it was going to be a productive place for him to live and work. While Richard Perna was optimistic, David Spero had strong reservations about the move:

"At the time they went, it was a music Mecca, but it wasn't the right music and it's a very closed town. If you're not in the loop, you're not in the loop and I tried my best to get Nicky involved with some of the things down there, but he was definitely an outcast."

Peter Frampton had already made the move to Nashville and was also sceptical as to whether Nicky would have cracked the country scene:

"We were in Nashville at the same time and didn't know it! He would have had Matt Rollings (then the busiest keyboard player in town) to contend with and wouldn't have been accepted into the country thing—nor would he have wanted to be."

I myself have been making regular visits to Nashville since the late eighties and have seen firsthand how the outside world perceives the town in terms of bible manufacture, hardcore country music and little else. The reality is that, particularly in the early nineties, hundreds of musicians, writers and producers—refugees from music centres like Los Angeles, New York and even London—descended upon Nashville, in search of a quieter, greener and less pressured environment in which to work and bring up their families. The fact that Nashville could boast fifty years as the undisputed capital of country music meant that all the prerequisites for an aspiring incomer were present—there are probably more studios, songwriters, musicians, record companies and music publishers per square mile there than anywhere else on earth.

Many who came from elsewhere had nothing to do with the country music charts. The figures that attracted my attention on my first visits were almost exclusively mavericks and renegades—Dan Penn from Alabama via Memphis, Steve Earle and Lucinda Williams from Texas, Felix Cavaliere, Al Kooper and

80. Nicky in Nashville

Steve Forbert from New York, Springsteen bass-player Garry Tallent from New Jersey and Steve Winwood, Roger Cooke, Tony Newman and Peter Frampton from England. When I recorded there, there were productions underway with Feargal Sharkey, Ziggy Marley and Marie Osmond!

Many of the exile rockers, producer Garry Tallent and writer Bill Lloyd among them, were thrilled to know that Nicky had arrived and were looking forward to working with him. He was perfectly qualified to slot into the country music scene of the nineties, when many Nashville stars seemed to want to sound like a cross between the Eagles and the Rolling Stones.

I met him within his first few days in his new environment. I clearly remember the atmosphere of optimism, relief and contentment that permeated the temporary Hopkins household (a small condo on Blair Boulevard, just down from Nashville's legendary watering hole, Brown's Diner), with a kettle boiling in the kitchen for a cup of tea and Nicky sitting on the sofa, surrounded by his keyboards, cassettes and recording devices. Ian McLagan, who had traded L.A. for Austin, Texas, remembered that Nicky was one of the first people to congratulate him on getting out of California:

"He knew I was in Austin and left a message, which I still have to this day: 'Mac, you bastard, you got out. Fucking right, good for you!' He hated L.A. as much as I did. He also said that he and Moira loved their new environment and were planning to buy a place of their own and settle down after all the upheavals they had been through."

Richard Perna: "Nicky assimilated well. He started meeting people and was making tremendous progress. He was definitely accepted by the local community and of course his demeanour was very special. As gifted as he was, he wasn't stuck up and he got along incredibly well with people and had a great perspective."

Perna suggested that Nicky accompany Jerry Williams to an industry showcase gig at that year's South By Southwest music conference in Austin, and on March 21st Nicky wrote a letter for his brother Paul's birthday:

"Well, here we are in Nashville! We did move out of L.A. fast! So did a lot of others too by all accounts. We took 12 days to drive here (Moi drove) stopping for 3 days in Santa Fe and 6 days in Tulsa. It's really nice to be somewhere where the ground doesn't move around. It really was a scary bugger, that quake. It's very pleasant (ahhh!) here – looks quite a bit like the English countryside and there's not a fucking palm tree in sight, thank God!

"Some nice two-storey houses here too. We went to Austin, Texas last week where I played a show with Jerry Williams who sang on my Tin Man album in 1973. We're still looking for a house, but are quite comfortable staying at a friend's town-house that he only uses occasionally as an office."

Moira Hopkins: "Richard wanted Nicky to help push Jerry's music by playing with him, but he also wanted to introduce them around town."

Even back then, SXSW was a massively popular event in the music calendar and most of the dozens of showcase venues were packed for the evening concerts. As a scheduled performer, I arrived early for my time-slot at the Cactus Café and was staggered to see Nicky there, playing some kind of electronic keyboard on the edge of the club's tiny stage.

Nicky had little time to schmooze on his own or Hamsteins's behalf, as he and Moira returned to Nashville the very next morning. One of his first social visits was with affable guitar legend Duane Eddy, a long-time Music City resident.

291

Duane had met Nicky "through mutual friends"—most probably saxophone player Jim Horn, who was also living in town—and got together with him to socialise and try their hands at the number one sport in the "Athens of the South": co-writing songs. Sadly, Nicky's first collaboration was not a success.

Duane Eddy: "We had a very nice afternoon and put down one or two working sketches on Nicky's recording device, but what can two instrumentalists do when they get together? We were writing "Forty Miles Of Bad Road" sideways. Nicky came back a second time to confirm the feeling that nothing was really happening. People always tried to focus on what I'd done in 1958! I have a tape somewhere of the results. It didn't gel, but I really liked Nicky a lot."

Moira remembered "a couple of meetings to write with other songwriters," but while Nicky was finding his feet, she helped to keep up the family finances by taking temporary jobs as a saleswoman and waitress. With assistance from friends, the couple were soon able to move into their own rented two-storey house on Belmont Boulevard, where Nicky was at last able to unpack all his belongings, some of which had been in storage in the U.K. for more than twenty years.

Once surrounded by his books, memorabilia, records and furniture, Nicky began to feel at home for the first time since leaving England four years earlier.

My own recording date with him took place in the spring of '94. At the time he was busy at home, working on music that may have been destined for a Japanese project or simply as part of his commitment to Hamstein. David Spero was in regular contact with Nicky throughout his first few months as a Tennessee resident:

"We used to talk every single morning on the phone and it wasn't necessarily business. Not that much was going on, because he was in Nashville. You've got to see where music had gone; even the classic artists weren't busy, but I was working on a deal for Nicky to go out with Stevie Nicks."

After the decadence of the Fleetwood Mac years, the popular singer was yet another rock star who had conquered her addictions and was proving to have a resilient solo career well into the nineties. Her latest release, *Street Angel*, was a moderate chart success in the early summer and was to be supported by a lengthy series of live shows. Nicky accepted the offer of a place in her touring band.

Moira Hopkins: "I had put all his stuff in the dry cleaners and gone to pick it up, because he was supposed to get on a plane the next day to go and rehearse, but when I got home Nicky was lying upstairs with a kidney stone, so I had to take him to hospital instead."

This highly uncomfortable reprise of Nicky's experience while in England a few years earlier was not dangerous, but was enough to spoil his chances of taking part in another high profile and well paid tour. A tentative approach to the Stones office to suggest that Nicky might join them on their upcoming dates was met with a polite but firm refusal, on the grounds that he would be too frail to withstand the band's battering concert schedule.

Moira Hopkins: "He wanted to play with the Stones again on stage, just for the hell of it."

With Joe Walsh now tied up indefinitely with the Eagles, Nicky remained at home, composing at his keyboard, browsing in Nashville's bookshops and thrift stores and getting to know the town and some of its people.

An appearance on June 21st at the VIP-attended opening of the Nashville Hard Rock Café, with Bobby Keys and a band made up of local musicians, helped spread the word that Nicky was in town. Part-time journalist and broadcaster Peter Rodman described Nicky on stage in a later article for *Bone* magazine, as "practically disappearing behind a bank of keyboards," with his greying hair tied back in a ponytail and a "matronly profile"—hardly a rock star look! With Keys taking centre stage, the band played through some Stones classics and covers to the delight of the invited crowd, and Nicky later consented to a radio interview with Rodman for his Sunday night show on the *Bone Radio Network*.

A photographer from the *Nashville Banner* captured Nicky on a typical porch-swing, alone and arm-in-arm with Moira, in a set of candid photographs that perfectly convey the contentment and optimism that reigned that summer in the Hopkins household. The article drew attention to the "dozens of new friends they had made in the few short weeks since they relocated" and described the couple as not just settled, but "ensconced." Nicky, a lifetime nicotine slave, had even given up smoking!

Moira Hopkins: "Nicky had come to terms with a lot of things in his life and was really happy. We had a great marriage, we were having a lot of fun together and he was creative and working away at lots of different things.

"On the Friday before the Labour Day weekend, Nicky told me he had some pain in his lower back and asked me to call the chiropractor to see if he could fit him in an appointment. I took him for treatment and I remember (Nicky) saying it was strange, because he didn't usually have a problem in his lower back.

"That weekend, we went to some songwriter's do, an outdoor cookout with a swimming pool and I remember sitting with Nicky and he seemed OK—or if he didn't feel well he wasn't saying. Then on the Monday evening, we were watching a film with Anthony Hopkins, where a famous writer's wife dies of cancer. I was holding his hand and thinking, 'That poor man; he's lost his wife; I don't know what I would do if I lost Nicky.' I leant over and hugged him, then it was about 12.30 and he was sitting at the kitchen table reading and had a packet of potato crisps and I said, 'I'm going up to bed to read for a bit.'

"I went upstairs and I read for probably about ten minutes, but I was very tired and I must have fallen asleep. I woke up and heard Nicky yell out to me and I could hear him groaning. I went downstairs, took one look at him and he said, 'Call an ambulance!' I did and then called a doctor who had been recommended to Nicky as a specialist in internal medicine and said, 'Call Nicky's doctor for me, please. I've got to take care of him right now.' I called Bobby Keys' partner and said, 'I am going to the hospital with Nicky' and then instead of an ambulance, a fire truck arrived! It was the fire department! It was so distressing, because I knew that Nicky was in such pain that he couldn't bear it and I didn't know what to do. I couldn't do a thing for him. He was swearing and this fireman said, 'Please sir, don't take the Lord's name in vain.'"

Completely distraught and lost for words at the tragicomedy of the moment and the incredible stupidity of the man's response, all Moira could think was, "You don't know this man; he's a very mild-mannered man but he's in such pain!" After what seemed like an age, an ambulance did arrive:

"They put Nicky in it and I got in my car and followed. I'll never forget that drive as long as I live. Then in the emergency room, he was screaming for them to give him some pain medicine, but they wouldn't; they thought that if they did, it would deaden the pain so they couldn't tell what was going on. How could they be that inhuman?"

Nicky Hopkins died in hospital in the small hours of the morning of September 6th, 1994.

Richard Perna: "The day before Nicky died, I was in Nashville and had dinner with him and Moira and Ralph Murphy. We were going to Harlan Howard's birthday party that evening, which was a big annual event, and earlier in the day I stopped by Nicky's house on Belmont; he was in good spirits and we sat there, talking and joking with one another. After dinner he wasn't feeling well, so he went home from the Harlan Howard thing and I flew home, got off the plane from Nashville around midnight, unpacked and went to bed.

"Frankie Miller had just had a stroke and was on the critical list in New York and at about two or three in the morning, I was woken by a phone call from Dan Tyler, who said he wanted to let me know my writer was dead and I said, 'You mean Frankie died?' 'No, Nicky.' It was a total shock. I flew right back the next day to help Moira."

David Spero: "I put 'Guilty Of The Crime' on the soundtrack for *Robocop* more as a tribute to Frankie and Nicky than anything. Frankie has never been able to sing since and I was with him when it happened. He was visiting Walsh and I in New York at the Riga Royal Hotel when the Eagles were playing at the Giant's Stadium and we were discussing whether we could get the record finished or do some live dates, because there was a break in the Eagles thing. I left (Frankie) about 3.30 in the morning and everything happened about 5.30. I haven't spoken to him for a couple of years now, though I know that he has made great strides."

Joe Walsh: "I still hurt; I still hurt and I've never gotten over it. I had no idea that Nicky was that sick. I knew he was frail and we ran things accordingly, and of course when that happened with Frankie, it was—excuse the language—a complete mind fuck. He (Frankie) was at an Eagles show, we went to the bar afterwards and I went to bed because we had another show next night and that was that; I heard later that he'd gone to hospital. We had great plans for that group, because we could back it up live."

Ralph Murphy, who had looked out for Nicky ever since his arrival in Nashville, stepped in to deal with the unavoidable paperwork, giving permission on

Moira's behalf for an autopsy to be performed. The day before the tragedy, he had made two of Nicky's favourite "shepherd's pies," and after the shock of the sudden turn of events, had the surreal experience of eating them with Nicky's friends but without him.

Moira Hopkins: "Even at the hospital they never actually called it by name, but they did diagnose it on the death certificate. It said Crohn's disease. They did the best they could in Nashville and I think Nicky knew that. If anybody was to blame, I felt it was the doctors at the first hospital he went to in Encino, who did nothing. The operation in '93 obviously hadn't been successful, because internally it hadn't mended properly, but we didn't know. We had tried different things to help Nicky get better and stronger and I'm now resigned to knowing that it was his time to go. I wouldn't have wanted him to live in pain. He suffered a lot and I think he'd had enough."

Word of Nicky's death went out on the news wires early the following morning, and by that afternoon tributes were pouring in from friends and colleagues and obituary notices beginning to appear.

Moira Hopkins: "A lot of people sent me messages and flowers and said some wonderful things about Nicky; that they had loved him as a person and as a musician and that it was going to be a great loss to the music world. Rod (Stewart) had his assistant call and I was supposed to call back; I can't remember if I did or not—but he cared."

Tony Newman had been resident in Nashville for some time when Nicky landed there and the two had been able to renew their friendship, though not for very long:

"We'd speak to each other in a gruff voice like a dictatorial school master and he left me a ridiculous message: 'Far from straight Newman, straighten up your act, laddie!'—and then he was dead."

Richard Perna stayed in Nashville to help organise the funeral details with Moira. On the day, the cremation was followed by a ceremony in the peaceful surroundings of the Radnor Lake nature reserve outside Nashville, and Richard recalled that even these sad proceedings had humorous moments:

"The turnout for his funeral was quite amazing. There were a lot of people there and it was a great event. During his life, Nicky was historically late and when we got to the lake, everyone realised that we had forgotten to bring Nicky's ashes with us, so in true fashion he was late for his own funeral.

"There were probably over a hundred guests and I made a speech. One of the telegrams from someone who had worked with him talked about how at the end of recording, he would bark, so I thought, in tribute to Nicky, everybody at the funeral should do the same and the whole crowd burst out barking like dogs. It was a beautiful setting and Nicky played at his own funeral, because we had his music there."

Wreaths, flowers and tributes continued to arrive from the famous—including Paul and Linda McCartney—and not so famous; Carlo Little went to the nearby florist in Harrow but didn't know where to send his flowers:

"I knew the funeral was in Nashville and I thought there can't be more than three or four cemeteries; the American operator was trying to help; She said, 'Leave it with us' and amazingly Moira confirmed later that the flowers got there."

Chuck Leavell: "It was a great blow for all of us when he passed on; Bobby (Keys) was the only one of us that could make the funeral; I felt compelled to do something, so I wrote a letter about how we met and the heavy influence that he had on me and so many other piano players and I was proud that Bobby was able to read that to the group."

There were obituaries in all the major music publications and in most of the better quality newspapers and magazines:

Rolling Stone considered him to be "the best and busiest studio pianist in rock & roll...who leaves behind a musical legacy unparalleled by any keyboardist in rock."

Billboard included a lengthy and erudite Ray Coleman piece, ending with the fact that the two had been collaborating on Nicky's biography.

MOJO carried a piece by American journalist Dave Marsh who wrote that Nicky would be remembered "for establishing the British approach to rock'n'roll keyboards...playing with sophisticated swing and authentic rock power."

Ray Davies was quoted at length in the *New York Times'* "Lives Well Lived" segment and, alongside Pete Townshend and others, in Britain's *Independent* newspaper. The London *Times* and the *Guardian* contented themselves with career summaries and a seventies-era photo.

The cliché that "today's newspaper is tomorrow's fish and chip wrapper" is regrettably true and once the frenzy of attention died away Moira was left, along with Nicky's friends and associates, to come to terms with the loss of a good friend and an irreplaceable talent.

Richard Perna: "Nicky wrote a tremendous amount of music and after he passed away (and before Bill Ham sold Hamstein Music), we catalogued over fifteen hundred pieces. Nicky may still be unrecouped at Hamstein, but we looked at him as a long-term prospect and had he lived, his career would have progressed with respect to soundtracks. He left behind some spectacular melodies, but they will go nowhere unless somebody works with them and gets them out there. Mosaic Music who bought Hamstein, probably didn't know they existed and they were then sold to Stage Three, a London-based company. I doubt seriously if anyone in that company knows about them either."

Any songwriter will testify that it is hard enough to keep tabs on publishing royalties during one's lifetime and next to impossible afterwards. Although Nicky was a prolific composer during his later years, the majority of his work was as a sideman and his death was an object lesson in how swiftly and relentlessly the industry moves on and how quickly the great are forgotten. The life of the session musician is even more precarious than that of writers and composers, whose work is at least under copyright protection. The hired hand lends his talents for a one-off fee.

In recent years there have been great advances made in the payment of players, for their contributions to works that have gone on to sell millions of copies for the artists whose names appear on the label, but gave nothing to the brilliant studio musicians who actually made the records. (Remember Nicky's six pound ten shilling fee for "Revolution"?) Nicky's widow Moira had a steep learning curve, unravelling the arcane structures of the various music industry factions, who control and distribute the financial side of show business, from the unions and copyright societies to publishers and record companies. The fact that his wife still needs to work to make ends meet, despite a lifetime of playing at the top level with some of the greatest artists of our time, speaks volumes.

Moira mentioned some unfulfilled plans Nicky had when he died: a house of his own, a last tour with the Stones and a film score for a British-made movie (he was a great admirer of David Puttnam and hoped to work with him one day).

"There were things he would still like to have done. I think he would have had a fabulous time with all the new keyboards that are out now and with the changes in technology since he's been gone. He would have loved it."

In the years since Nicky's death, the internet explosion has meant that there are now platforms for devotees of almost any imaginable subject to meet and discuss their hobbies and passions. Nicky Hopkins fans are no exception.

While researching this book, I received e-mails from fanatical collectors of Nicky memorabilia, with detailed discographies, listings, obscure information (often subsequently proven to be wildly inaccurate) and many helpful leads.

His recordings are well represented on eBay, with annoyingly regular appearances of that misprinted sixties single, "High On A Hill" by Nigel Hopkins, still erroneously believed to be Nicky's work.

In 2006 his friends and fans were delighted when an independently produced one-hour programme dedicated to Nicky went out nationwide in the UK on BBC Radio 2, with well respected broadcaster Bob Harris presenting interviews and music clips from some of Nicky's better known clients and performances. The show was repeated in September 2008, on the anniversary of Nicky's death and this time was made available on the Internet. Both broadcasts produced a flurry of e-mails from listeners, some of whom knew Nicky or had stories about him, that were of great assistance in completing this book. With few exceptions, all the members of the music fraternity who contributed loved Nicky, loved his music and were thrilled that, at last, he would be receiving some overdue recognition.

Since then, Nicky has been represented with his own pages on MySpace and Wikipedia, with video clips on YouTube and on dozens of other websites honouring one or other of the bands or artists with whom he played. Some of these sources have a tendency to recycle the same inaccuracies, but equally often they display incredible dedication and an obvious love of the subject.

An internet-based petition has circulated, so far unsuccessfully, to get Nicky nominated to the Rock And Roll Hall Of Fame in Cleveland.

There are session men who might claim to have played on more individual records than Nicky: Charlie McCoy in Nashville, Clem Cattini in London and Hal

Blaine in Los Angeles come to mind, but for sheer variety and quality, Nicky's extraordinary achievements stand head and shoulders above any other musician in rock history. He lived and worked with most of the great artists and bands of his era, but has remained obstinately hidden and is in danger of becoming a forgotten footnote in pop history.

Success is hard to define. In a business where everything is measured in dollars, cents and column inches, a musician like Nicky cannot be said to be up there with Elvis or the Beatles, and yet he represents the armies of gifted and hard-working players, who seldom make it to the red carpet, but make indelible contributions to the songs that provide the daily soundtrack to our lives.

In the end, the most important legacy of his troubled and too short life is in the grooves of the hundreds of records he played on.

The day after Nicky died, Ian McLagan and his wife Kim were shopping in Austin and stopped to have a drink in Nicky's honour. They chose a weirdly appropriate bar, with church pews as benches and coffins for tables and ordered a round of beers. They were amazed when, without them lifting a finger, the Rolling Stones' "Street Fighting Man" came on the jukebox. That first song was followed by an unbroken succession of Nicky Hopkins performances but when Mac asked the barmaid if she knew who Nicky was, she said she'd never heard of him and that if nobody put money in the machine, it played its own random selections. The couple decided that Nicky would have liked "that silly touch" and drank a toast to his memory.

All the best.
Nicky Hopkins

Discography

Albums

Nicky features on 43 albums in the Billboard book of US Top 40 Hits

1965

Chris Farlowe and The Thunderbirds	Chris Farlowe and The Thunderbirds	Bellaphon CR 3016
The Kinks	The Kinks Kontroversy	Pye NPL 18131
The Who	My Generation	Brunswick LAT 8616

1966

Chris Farlowe	14 Things To Think About	Immediate IMLP 005
The Who	The Who Sings My Generation	Decca DL 4664 (USA)
Andrew Oldham Orchestra	The Rolling Stones Songbook	Decca LK 4796
Nicky Hopkins	The Revolutionary Piano Of Nicky Hopkins	CBS BPG 62679
The Creation	We Are Paintermen	Hit-Ton HTSLP 340037
The Kinks	Face To Face	Pye NPL 18149
Chris Farlowe	The Art Of Chris Farlowe	Immediate IMLP 006
Twice As Much	Own Up	Immediate IMLP 007

1967

Rolling Stones	Between The Buttons	Decca LK 4852
Alan Tews Orchestra	This Is My Scene	Decca LK 4865

Brian Jones	Mord Und Totschlag (A Degree Of Murder) (soundtrack)	(never officially released)
Cat Stevens	Matthew And Son	Deram DML1004
Mark Wirtz / Derek Lawrence	Mood Mosaic	Columbia SX 6153
Soul Survival	Soul Sounds	Columbia SX 6158
Yardbirds	Little Games	Epic BN 26313
Mike Vickers	I Wish I Were A Group Again	Columbia SX 6180
The Kinks	Something Else By The Kinks	Pye NPL 18193
Cat Stevens	New Masters	Deram DES 18010
Rolling Stones	Their Satanic Majesties Request	Decca TXS 103

1968

Amory Kane	Memories Of Time Unwound	MCA MUPS 348
Billy Nicholls	Would You Believe	Immediate IMCP 009
Tony Hatch & Jackie Trent	The Two Of Us	Pye NPL 18214
Jimmy Page et. al. (aka Gerry Temple)	Burn Up	Stateside CSSX 240777 (France)
Jimmy Page, Nicky Hopkins, John Paul Jones, Albert Lee, Chris Hughes, Keith David De Groot, Clem Cattini And Jim Sullivan	No Introduction Necessary	Spark SRLM 107
PP Arnold	First Lady Of Immediate	Immediate IMCP 011
Twice As Much	That's All	Immediate IMCP 013
Anita Harris	Just Loving You	CBS 63182
The Move	The Move	Regal Zonaphone LRZ 1002
PP Arnold	Kafunta	Immediate IMCP 017
The Scaffold	The Scaffold (Live At Queen Elizabeth Hall)	Parlophone PMC 7051
Jeff Beck Group	Truth	Columbia SCX 6351
Duncan Browne	Give Me Take You	Immediate IMCP 018
Giles, Giles & Fripp	Cheerful Insanity Of…	Deram SML 122
The Easybeats	Vigil	United Artists ULP 1193
The Iveys	Maybe Tomorrow	Apple SAPCOR 8 (export)
Dusty Springfield	Dusty…Definitely	Philips SBL 7864
Kinks	The Kinks Are The Village Green Preservation Society	Pye NPL 18233
Beatles	The Beatles	Apple PMC 7067/68
Rolling Stones	Beggars Banquet	Decca SKL 4955

1969

Nick Hopkins Caravan	Hammond On The Rocks	Volksplatte SMVP 6132 (Germany)

Rock-A-Fellas	Rock 'N' Roll Happening '69	Columbia SMC 74423 (Germany)
Family	Family Entertainment	Reprise RSLP 6340
Leigh Stephens	Red Weather	Philips SBL 7897
Poet and the One Man Band	Poet And The One Man Band	Verve Fortune SVLP 6012
Jackie Lomax	Is This What You Want	Apple APCOR 6
Roy Harper	Folkjokeopus	Liberty 21888
Strawbs	Strawbs	A&M Records AMLS 936
Ella Fitzgerald	Ella	Reprise RS 6354
The End	Introspection	Decca SKL R 5015
Jeff Beck Group	Beck-Ola	Columbia SX 6351
Sweet Thursday	Sweet Thursday	Tetragrammaton T 112
Donovan	Barabajagal	Epic BN 26481
Steve Miller Band	Brave New World	Capitol E-ST 184
Jefferson Airplane	Volunteers	RCA LSP 4238
Steve Miller Band	Your Saving Grace	Capitol E-ST 331
Brewer & Shipley	Weeds	Buddah Records KSBS 2016
Quicksilver Messenger Service	Shady Grove	Capitol SKAO-391
Rolling Stones	Let It Bleed	Decca SKL 5025
Girls Together Outrageously	Permanent Damage	Straight STS 1059

1970

Crispian St. Peters	Simply	Square Records SQA 102
Doris Troy	Doris Troy	Apple SAPCOR 13
Screaming Lord Sutch	Lord Sutch & Heavy Friends	Atlantic 2400 008
Various Artists (Jefferson Airplane)	Woodstock	Atlantic 2663 001
Steve Miller Band	Number 5	Capitol SKAO 436
Quicksilver Messenger Service	Just For Love	Capitol SKAO 498
Quicksilver Messenger Service	What About Me	Capitol SMAS-630

1971

Badfinger	Straight Up	Apple SW 3387
Jim Price	Kids Nowadays Ain't Got No Shame	A&M SP 4321
Rolling Stones	Sticky Fingers	Rolling Stones COC 59100
Donovan	HMS Donovan	Dawn DNLD 4001
Rolling Stones	Get Your Leeds Lungs Out (Live At Leeds, March 13, 1971)	Excitable Recordworks 4511-1 (unofficial release)
McGuinness Flint	Happy Birthday Ruthie Baby	Capitol ST 794
Various Artists (Jefferson Airplane)	Woodstock 2	Atlantic 60 002
The Who	Who's Next	Track Records 2408 102
John Lennon	Imagine	Apple PAS 10004

| The Who | Meaty Beaty Big & Bouncy | Track Records 1406 006 |
| Rolling Stones | Hot Rocks 1964-71 (compilation) | London 2PS 606 |

1972

Carly Simon	No Secrets	Elektra EKS 75049
Bobby Keys	Bobby Keys	Warner Bros. K 46141
Harry Nilsson	Son Of Schmilsson	RCA LSP 4717
Pamela Polland	Pamela Polland	Columbia KC 31116
Nicky Hopkins	Jamming With Edward	Rolling Stones COC 39100
New Riders Of The Purple Sage	Powerglide	Columbia KC 31284
Rolling Stones	Exile On Main Street	Rolling Stones COC 69100
Chet Nichols	Time Loop	Kama Sutra KSBS 2057
John Lennon	Some Time In New York City	Apple SVBB 3392
Jerry Williams	Jerry Williams	Spindizzy Records KZ 31404
Terry Dolan	Unreleased EP (Acetate Only)	Warner Bros.

1973

Cheech & Chong	Los Cochinos	Ode 77019
Jerry Williams Group	Down Home Boy	Columbia C 30279
The Kinks	The Great Lost Kinks Album	Reprise MS 2127
Rod Stewart	Rod Stewart & The Faces	Springboard SPB 4030
Nicky Hopkins	The Tin Man Was A Dreamer	Columbia KC 32074
Mark-Almond	Mark-Almond '73	Columbia KC 32486
Beatles	1967-1970 (compilation)	Apple SKBO 3404
George Harrison	Living In The Material World	Apple SMAS 3410
Ringo Starr	Ringo	Apple PCTC 252
Rolling Stones	Goat's Head Soup	Rolling Stones COC 59101
Andy Williams	Solitaire	CBS 65638
Rolling Stones	No Stone Unturned	Decca SKL 5173
Donovan	Essence To Essence	Epic EPC 69050

1974

Duster Bennett	Fingertips	Toadstool L 35436
Marc Bolan	The Beginning Of Doves (compilation)	Track Records 2410 201
Martha Reeves	Martha Reeves	MCA 414
Shankar Family	Shankar Family & Friends	Dark Horse AMLH 22002
Nicky Hopkins	The Long Journey Home	CBS (unreleased)
Harry Nilsson	Son Of Dracula (soundtrack)	Rapple ABL 1-0220

Joe Cocker	I Can Stand A Little Rain	A&M SP 3633
The Who	Odds And Sods	Track Records 2406 116
Rolling Stones	It's Only Rock'N'Roll	Rolling Stones COC 59103
Peter Frampton	Something's Happening	A&M AMLH 63619
Coast Road Drive	Delicious And Refreshing	Deram SML 1113
John Lennon	Walls & Bridges	Apple 3416
George Harrison	Dark Horse	Apple SMAS-3418
Various Artists (Jimmy Page session)	Rock Roots (compilation)	Immediate C 154 52128/29

1975

Alexis Korner	Get Off Of My Cloud	Columbia PC 33427
Nicky Hopkins	No More Changes	Mercury SRMI 1028
Quicksilver Messenger Service	Solid Silver	Capitol ST-11462
Various Artists (John Entwistle, Alice Cooper)	Flash Fearless Versus The Zorg Women (Parts 5 & 6)	Chrysalis CHR 1081
Ringo Starr	Goodnight Vienna	Apple PCS 7168
Various Artists (The Who)	Tommy Original Soundtrack	Polydor PD 29502
Rolling Stones	Metamorphosis	Decca SKL 5512
Mercury-Vertigo	Mercury-Vertigo Sampler (compilation)	Mercury-Vertigo (promo only)
Joe Cocker	Jamaica Say You Will	A&M SP 4529
Art Garfunkel	Breakaway	Columbia PC 33700
The Who	The Who By Numbers	Polydor 2490 129
George Harrison	Extra Texture (Read All About It)	Apple SW-3420
John Lennon	Shaved Fish	Apple SW 3421

1976

Jerry Garcia	Reflections	Round Records RX 107
Bill Wyman	Stone Alone	Rolling Stones COC 59105
Rolling Stones	Black & Blue	Rolling Stones COC 59106
David Soul	David Soul	Private Stock PS 2019
Various Artists (John Lennon)	All This And World War Ii	20th Century Records 2T 522
Jennifer Warnes	Jennifer Warnes	Arista AL 4062

1977

Fratelli La Bionda	Tutto Va Bene	Baby Records LPX 016 (Italy)
Hollywood Stars	Hollywood Stars	Arista AL 4119
The Ferrets	Dreams Of A Love	Mushroom Records L 36 437 (Australia)
Dingoes	Five Times The Sun	A&M L 36237

Carole Bayer Sager	Carole Bayer Sager	Elektra 7E 1100
Lonnie Donegan	Puttin' On The Style	Chrysalis 51 1158
Easybeats	The Shame Just Drained	Albert Productions APLP 026
Rod Stewart	Footloose And Fancy Free	Warner Bros. BSK 3092

1978

Valdy	Hot Rocks	A&M SP 9034 (Canada)
Bay City Rollers	Strangers In The Wind	Arista AB 4194
Rod Stewart	Blondes Have More Fun	Warner Bros. BSK 3261

1979

David Grusin	The Champ (soundtrack)	Planet P 9001
Eddie Money	Life For The Taking	Columbia JC 35598
Pointer Sisters	Priority	Planet P 9003
Terry and The Pirates	Too Close For Comfort	Wild Bunch
Badfinger	Airwaves	Elektra 6E 175
Lowell George	Thanks I'll Eat It Here	Warner Bros. BSK 3194
Night	Night	Planet P 2
Various Artists (Rocky Sullivan)	City Lights (compilation)	Jupiter Records 2000

1980

Brooklyn Dreams	Won't Let Go	Casablanca NBLP 7226
Climax Blues Band	Flying The Flag	Warner Bros. BSK 3493
Graham Parker & The Rumour	The Up Escalator	Arista AL 9517
Nervous Eaters	Nervous Eaters	Elektra 6E 282
Raven	John Cipollina's Raven	Line Records LICD 9 00053 O
Rocky Sullivan	Illegal Entry	Rag Baby INT 147 405
Rolling Stones	Emotional Rescue	Rolling Stones CUN 39111
Shogo Hamada	Home Bound	Sony SRCL 4601

1981

Margie Jameson & Brian Booker	Jameson – Booker	RCA KKL1-0428 (Canada)
Joe Egan	Map (aka Stay As You Are)	Ariola 203 008
Meat Loaf	Dead Ringer	Epic FE 36007
Bob Burchman	Ritoru Champion (soundtrack)	Orange House
Phantom, Rocker & Slick	Phantom, Rocker & Slick	EMI America ST 17172
States	Picture Me With You	Boardwalk LBW 17010
Tim Goodman	Footsteps	Columbia NFC 37410

Tim Hardin	Unforgiven	San Francisco Sound SF 10810
Pure Prairie League	Something In The Night	Casablanca NBLP 7255
Rolling Stones	Tattoo You	Rolling Stones CUNS 39114
Nils Lofgren	Night Fades Away	Backstreet BSR-5251
Ron Wood	1234	CBS 85227
Climax Blues Band	Lucky For Some	Warner Bros. BSK 3623

1982

Graham Parker & The Rumour	Another Grey Area	Arista AL 9589
Larry Lee	Marooned	Columbia FC 37692
Michel Berger	Dreams In Stone	Atlantic 80029-1
Randy Meisner	Randy Meisner	Epic FE 38121
Rocky Sullivan	Internal Affairs	Rag Baby/Line
Terry and The Pirates	Rising Of The Moon	Rag Baby INT 147 410
Scaffold	Singles As & Bs (compilation)	Charly Records CM 114
Riggs	Riggs	Full Moon FMH 3655
Buzzy Linhart	Four Sides Of Buzzy Linhart	Caromar Records CM 101
Dusty Springfield	White Heat	Casablanca NBLP 7271
L. Ron Hubbard	Space Jazz (Aka Battlefield Earth)	Applause Records APLP 9000

1983

Carl Wilson	Trouble At Home	Target Video Productions
Jon Mark	The Lady And The Artist	Line Records LLP 5240 (Germany)
Patrick Simmons	Arcade	Elektra 60225 1
The Tubes	Outside Inside	Capitol ST 12260
Tim Bogert	Master's Brew	Takoma ST 72805
Various Artists (Van Morrison)	King Of Comedy (soundtrack)	Warner Bros. 9 23765 1
Walter Egan	Wild Exhibitions	Backstreet BSR 5400

1984

Carl Wilson	Youngblood	Caribou CRB 25225
Julio Iglesias	1100 Bel Air Place	Columbia QC 39157
Maggie Lee	White Zone	Columbia 39317
Broken Edge	Time For A Change	Polydor 817 280

1985

Matt Kelly	A Wing And A Prayer	Relix RRLP 2010
Rick Springfield	Tao	RCA AJL 1-5370
Taxxi	Expose	MCA MCA 5580

| Urban Stroll | Urban Stroll | A.M.I. Records |

1986

Belinda Carlisle	Belinda	I.R.S. Records IRS 5741
Bradley Ditto	Check Me Out	High Fire / Clean CR 1000
Rod Stewart	Rod Stewart – Every Beat Of My Heart	Warner Bros. 925 446 1

1987

Beat Farmers	The Pursuit Of Happiness	MCA MCA 5993
Chris Farlowe	Buzz With The Fuzz	Decal LIK 16
Hayes/Springer Brotherhood	Sneaker Waves	Rag Baby RBCD 9 00491
Insiders	Ghost On The Beach	Epic EPC 460123

1988

| Beatles | Past Masters Volume 2 (compilation) | Capitol CDP 7 90044 2 |
| Art Garfunkel | Lefty | Columbia FC 40942 |

1989

Dogs D'Amour	Errol Flynn / King Of Thieves	China 839 700 1
Jefferson Airplane	Jefferson Airplane	Epic OE 45271
Diesel Park West	Shakespeare Alabama	EMI CDP 7 91689 2
Paul McCartney	Flowers In The Dirt	Parlophone CDP 7 91653 2
Jack Bruce	A Question Of Time	Epic 465 692

1990

Helen O'Hara	Southern Hearts	New World Music CD 212
L. Ron Hubbard & Friends	Road To Freedom	BPI Records BPILP 03
Roger Chapman	Hybrid & Lowdown	Polydor 847 117 1 (Germany)
Terry and The Pirates	Silverado Trail	Big Beat WIK 89
Gary Moore	Still Got The Blues	Virgin V 2612

1991

Albert Lee	Black Claw & Country Fever (compilation)	Line Records LICD 9 01057 O (Germany)
Bierce In L.A.	L.A. River	Rococo Records RR 1 D
Terry and The Pirates	Wind Dancer	Rag Baby RBCD 9 00114
The Blessing	Prince Of The Deep Water	MCA MCAD 10070
Noisy Mama	Everybody Has One	ATCO 91399
David Bowie	Early On (1964-1966)	Rhino R2 70526

1992

Spinal Tap	Break Like The Wind	MCA MCA 10514
Shooting Gallery	Shooting Gallery	Mercury 314 512 184 2 (Canada)
Killer Dwarfs	Method To The Madness	Epic EK 47322
Joe Satriani	The Extremist	Relativity 471672 2
Faster Pussycat	Whipped	Elektra 61124
Nicky Hopkins	The Fugitive (soundtrack)	Toshiba EMI TOCT 6640
Jayhawks	Hollywood Town Hall	Def American 512 986 2
Bill Wyman	Stuff	Ripple Records RIP 103
Izzy Stradlin	Izzy Stradlin and the Juju Hounds	Geffen GEFD 24490
Jefferson Airplane	Jefferson Airplane Loves You (compilation)	RCA 61110 2
Nicky Hopkins	Patio (soundtrack)	Toshiba EMI TOCT 6841

1993

Bierce In L.A.	Vale Of Tears	Rococo 002 2
Nicky Hopkins	Namiki Family	Toshiba EMI TOCT 6914
Murray Attaway	In Thrall	DGC / Geffen 24495
Dramarama	Hi-Fi Sci-Fi	Chameleon 61489
Matthew Sweet	Altered Beast	Zoo Entertainment 72445 11050 1
Various Artists (Joe Walsh & Steve Earle)	The Beverly Hillbillies (soundtrack)	Fox 66313
Various Artists (Matthew Sweet)	No Alternative	Arista ARCD 8737

1994

Bang Tango	Love After Death	Music For Nations CDMFN 174
Jono Manson	One Horse Town	Club De Musique (Italy)
Merrell Fankhauser	California Live	Legend LM 9007 (France)
Tom Rush	Work In Progress	Night Light Records
Various Artists (Nicky Hopkins)	Last Song (soundtrack)	Pony Canyon PCCA 00492
Zero	Chance In A Million	Whirled Records WRR 1960
The Move	Shazam (Outtakes)	Repertoire (Japan)

1995

Nathan Sark	Nomad Blues	<private pressing>
Various Artists (Joe Walsh)	A Future To This Life – The Robocop Series Soundtrack	Rhino 71888

Novato Frank	Rock'n'Roll Heaven	Legend Music LR 101 (France)
Julian Dawson	Travel On	Watermelon 1043
Keith West	Sessions 1965-1974 (tracks recorded in 1968)	RPM 141

1996

Freddy Lynxx	The Courageous Cat	Sucksex Records 05
Jerry Lynn Williams	The Peacemaker	Black Mark 30410022
Tamara Champlin	You Won't Get To Heaven Alive	Turnip 9
Rolling Stones	Rock And Roll Circus	ABKCO Records 1268
Mark Wirtz Orchestra	The Go-Go Music Of The Mark Wirtz Orchestra & Chorus	RPM 172

1997

Bill Wyman	The Bill Wyman Compendium: Complete Solo Recordings (compilation)	One Way Records 8056
John Lennon/Yoko Ono	Wedding Album (CD reissue w/ extra tracks)	Rykodisc 10413
John Kay	The Lost Heritage Tapes (recorded in 1976)	Macola Record Group MAC 1201
Luciano Gomez	The Fire Still Remains (recorded in 1982)	Luce Records

1998

Boyd Albritton Band	Prehistoric Raven	Flying Crowbar Music
William Topley	Mixed Blessing	Mercury 314 558 452 2
Helen O'Hara	A Night In Ireland	New World Music CD 450
John Lennon	Anthology	Capitol C2 7243 8 30614 2 6

1999

Billy Nicholls	Snapshot	Southwest SWCD 0004
Doug Fieger	First Things First	Zen Records
Tomorrow	Tomorrow (CD reissue w/ extra tracks)	EMI 498 8192
Bill Wyman & Rhythm Kings	Anyway The Wind Blows	Velvel Records 79768
Majic Ship	Songwaves Project	Gear Fab Records CBM 101

2000

Chris Hill & Denny Laine	Arctic Song	Ribble Records
Various Artists (Matt Kelly)	Dead Delites, Vol. 4	Relix 2101

2001

Adam Bomb	New York Times (recorded in 1990)	Mausoleum 541399 2510153
Kinks	Songs We Sang For Auntie – BBC Sessions 1964-1977	Sanctuary 84504
Chris Farlowe and The Thunderbirds	Dig The Buzz – First Recordings '62-'65 (compilation)	RPM 220

2002

Roy Harper	Today Is Yesterday (Outtakes) (compilation)	Science Friction HUCD 037
CRY	After The Storm	Coyote Records 0000056

2003

Merrell Fankhauser	Merrell Fankhauser And Friends	Altrichter Music 310557 (Germany)
Tony Hatch	The Essential Tony Hatch & His Orchestra: Grooves, Hits and Themes (compilation)	Castle Pulse 33354
Merrell Fankhauser	Return To Mu	Sundazed SC 11088
Mu	The Last Album (recorded in 1974)	Akarma AK 258
Don Fardon	I'm Alive (compilation)	RPM 269
Mike Berry	Don't You Think It's Time: R&R Hits From The 60s & 70s	Castle 811
Gene Clark	Under The Silvery Moon	Delta Deluxe 723839

2004

(Tribute To The) Byrds	The Byrds – Never To be Forgotten (DVD of 8/26/86 show)	Planet Song 8575 (Germany)
Jerry Garcia	All Good Things: Jerry Garcia Studio Sessions (box set - compilation)	Rhino 78603
Bonaroo II	Children Of The Stars	<self-released>
Fats Domino	Sweet Patootie (compilation)	Rhino Handmade 7880

2005

Jerry Garcia	Garcia Plays Dylan (Live Songs 1975)	Rhino 73263

2006

Frankie Miller	Long Way Home	Jerkin' Crocus 9
Buzzy Linhart	Studio	Buzzart Records 2064

Del Shannon	Home And Away (recorded in 1967)	EMI Zonophone 0946 374853 2 3

2007

Terry and The Pirates	Return To Silverado	Evangeline/Acadia ACAM 8132
Quicksilver Messenger Service	Live At The Kabuki Theatre	Snapper SNPZ 803415255627
Vashti	Some Things Just Stick in Your Mind: Singles and Demos 1964-1967 (compilation)	Fat Cat Records 59

2008

Terry and The Pirates	Comanche Boots	Evangeline/Acadia ACAM 8210
Labelle	Back to Now	Verve 001151102

2009

Cliff Bennett and The Rebel Rousers	Into Our Lives (The Joe Meek & EMI Years 1961-1969) (compilation)	EMI 697 3882
Quicksilver Messenger Service	Castles In The Sand (rehearsals, recorded in 1969/70)	Snapper SNAP 297 CD
Rod Stewart	The Rod Stewart Sessions 1971-1998 (compilation)	Stiefel Entertainment / WB Records 19758
Jerry Garcia Band	Let It Rock	Rhino 522469
Beatles	Come And Get It: The Best Of Apple Records (compilation)	EMI 46397

Singles & EPs

1963

Screaming Lord Sutch	Jack The Ripper / Don't You Just Know It	Decca F 11598
Cyril Davies All-Stars	Country Line Special / Chicago Calling	Pye International 7N 25194
Cliff Bennett and The Rebel Rousers	*Everybody Loves A Lover* / My Old Standby (B-side only)	Parlophone R 5046
Neil Christian	A Little Bit Of Someone / Get A Load Of This	Columbia DB 7075
Casey Jones & The Engineers	One Way Ticket / I'm Gonna Love	Columbia DB 7083

1964

Cyril Davies	The Sound Of Cyril Davies (EP)	Pye International NEP 44025
Chris Farlowe and The Thunderbirds	Girl Trouble / Itty Bitty Pieces	Columbia DB 7237

| Lou Johnson | (There's) Always Something There To Remind Me / *Wouldn't That Be Something?* (A-side only) | London HLX 9917 |
| Lou Johnson | A Message To Martha (Kentucky Bluebird) / *The Last One To Be Loved* (A-side only) | London HLX 9929 |

1965

The Murmaids & The Outlaws	To Know Him Is To Love Him / *<unknown>* (A-side only)	Chattahoochee Records (USA)
The Sessions	Let Me In / Bouncing Bass	Fontana F 1529 (USA)
The Who	Anyway Anyhow Anywhere / Daddy Rolling Stone	Brunswick 05935
Vashti	Some Things Just Stick In Your Mind / I Want To Be Alone	Decca F 12157
The Outlaws	Don't Cry / Only For You	Smash S 2025 (USA)
The Who	Anyway Anyhow Anywhere / Anytime You Want Me	Decca 31801 (USA)
Ben Carruthers & The Deep	Jack O' Diamonds / Right Behind You	Parlophone R 5295
Major Rowely	There's A Riot Going On / Do It The Right Way	Stateside SS 438
Ritchie Blackmore Orchestra	Getaway / Little Brown Jug	Oriole CB 314 *(also released in the USA as by The Outlaws, label unknown)*
Adam, Mike & Tim	Little Pictures / Summer's Here Again	Decca F 12221
The Lancasters	Satan's Holiday / Earthshaker	Titan FF 1730 (USA)
Davy Jones & The Lower Third (David Bowie)	You've Got A Habit Of Leaving / Baby Loves That Way	Parlophone R 5315
Gregory Phillips	Down In The Boondocks / That's The One	Immediate IM 004
The Frays	For Your Precious Love / My Girl Sloopy	Decca F 12229
Liz Shelley	Make Me Your Baby / You Made Me Hurt	Brunswick 05940
Factotums	In My Lonely Room / A Run In The Green And Tangerine Flaked Forest	Immediate IM 009
The Who	*My Generation* / Shout & Shimmy (B-side only)	Brunswick 05944
The Truth	Who's Wrong / She's A Roller	Pye 7N 15998

The Who	*My Generation* / Out In The Street (B-side only)	Decca 31877 (USA)
Dave Helling	Christine / The Bells	Planet PLF 101
Dodie West	Make The World Go Away / *Who Does He Think He Is* (A-side only)	Piccadilly 7N 35287
The Kinks	Till The End Of The Day / Where Have All The Good Times Gone?	Pye 7N 15981
The Merseybeats	I Stand Accused / All My Life	Fontana TF 645
The Pretty Things	Midnight To Six Man / Can't Stand The Pain	Fontana TF 647
Tony Lord	World's Champion / *Makes Me Sad* (A-side only)	Planet PLF 102
The Untamed	It's Not True / Gimme Gimme Some Shade	Planet PLF 103
Mike Berry	Somebody Stole My Gal	HMV (unreleased until 2003)

1966

David Bowie with The Lower Third	Can't Help Thinking About Me / I Say To Myself	Pye 7N 17020
The Lancastrians	The World Keeps Going Round / *Not The Same Anymore* (A-side only)	Pye 7N 17043
Dani Sheridan	Guess I'm Dumb / *Songs Of Love* (A-side only)	Planet PLF 106
Jon Mark	Paris Bells / Little Town Girl	Brunswick 05952
The Kinks	Dedicated Follower Of Fashion / *Sitting On My Sofa* (A-side only)	Pye 7N 17064
Anita Harris	Something Must Be Done / Funny Kind Of Feeling	Pye 7N 17069
Nicky Hopkins	Mr. Big / Jenni	CBS 202055
The Who	A Legal Matter / Instant Party	Brunswick 05956
The Who	*Substitute* / Circles (B-side only)	Reaction 591 001
Perpetual Langley	We Wanna Stay Home / So Sad	Planet PLF 110
Ronnie Jones	My Only Souvenir / Satisfy My Soul	Smash S2047 (USA)
The Harbour Lites	Run For Your Life / Lonely Journey	Fontana TF 682

Zuider Zee	(You're My) Soul & Inspiration / Please Don't Call Me	CBS 202062
Perpetual Langley	Surrender / Two By Two	Planet PLF 115
Soul Brothers	Got To Get A Good Thing Going / *Good Lovin' Never Hurt* (A-side only)	Mercury MF 916
Twice As Much	Sittin' On A Fence / Baby I Want You	Immediate IM 033
Lindsay Muir's Untamed	Daddy Long Legs / Trust Yourself	Planet PLF 113
The Creation	Making Time / *Try And Stop Me* (A-side only)	Planet PLF 116
The Kinks	Sunny Afternoon / *I'm Not Like Everybody Else* (A-side only)	Pye 7N 17125
Marc Reid	For No One / Lonely City Blue	CBS 202244
The Who	*The Kids Are Alright* / The Ox (B-side only)	Brunswick 05965
Twice As Much	Step Out Of Line / Simplified	Immediate IM 036
Beverley	Happy New Year / Where The Good Times Are	Deram DM 101
Cat Stevens	I Love My Dog / *Portobello Road* (A-side only)	Deram DM 102
The Creation	*Painter Man* / Biff Bang Pow (B-side only)	Planet PLF 119
The Easybeats	Friday On My Mind / *Made My Bed, Gonna Lie In It* (A-side only)	United Artists UP 1157
The Imagination	Guantanamera / You've Got Your Troubles	CBS 202354
The Who	La-La-La Lies / The Good's Gone	Brunswick 05968
Twice As Much	True Story / You're No Good For Me	Immediate IM 039
Cat Stevens	Matthew And Son / Granny	Deram DM 110

1967

Marc Reid	The Magic Book / My World Turns Around You	CBS 202581
V.I.P.s	*Straight Down To The Bottom* / In A Dream (B-side only)	Island WIP 6005

Marianne Faithfull	Is This What I Get For Loving You? / *Tomorrow's Calling* (A-side only)	Decca F 22524
PP Arnold	Everything's Gonna Be Alright / Life Is But Nothing	Immediate IM 040
Del Shannon	Runaway (1967 Version) / *Show Me* (A-side only)	Liberty LBF 15020
Jeff Beck	*Hi Ho Silver Lining* / Beck's Bolero (B-side only)	Columbia DB 8151
The Easybeats	Who'll Be The One / Saturday Night	United Artists UP 1175 (Germany)
Peter & Gordon	Sunday For Tea / Start Trying Someone Else	Columbia DB 8159
Cat Stevens	I'm Gonna Get Me A Gun / School Is Out	Deram DM 118
Yardbirds	Little Games / Puzzles	Columbia DB 8165
Mike Vickers Orchestra	Air On A G String / Proper Charles	Columbia DB 8171
Twice As Much	Crystal Ball / Why Can't They All Go And Leave Me Alone?	Immediate IM 042
PP Arnold	The First Cut Is The Deepest / Speak To Me	Immediate IM 047
The Kinks	Mr. Pleasant / *This Is Where I Belong* (A-side only)	Pye 7N 17314 (export)
The Kinks	Mr. Pleasant / *Harry Rag* (A-side only)	Reprise 0587 (USA)
The Kinks	*Waterloo Sunset* / Act Nice And Gentle (B-side only)	Pye 7N 17321
The Kinks	*Waterloo Sunset* / Two Sisters (B-side only)	Reprise 0612 (USA)
The Easybeats	Heaven And Hell *Pretty Girl* (A-side only)	United Artists UP 1183
PP Arnold	The Time Has Come / If You See What I Mean	Immediate IM 055
Beverley / *Denny Cordell Tea Time Ensemble*	Museum / *A Quick One For Sanity* (A-side only)	Deram DM 137
Cat Stevens	A Bad Night / *Laughing Apple* (A-side only)	Deram DM 140
Nicky Hopkins	Mr. Pleasant / Nothing As Yet	Polydor 56175

Dave Davies	Death Of A Clown / _Love Me Till The Sun Shines_ (A-side only)	Pye 7N 17356
Keith West / _(Mark Wirtz Orchestra)_	Excerpt From A Teenage Opera / _Theme From 'A Teenage Opera'_ (A-side only)	Parlophone R 5623
Warm Sounds	Sticks & Stones / Angeline	Immediate IM 058
Tony Hatch & Jackie Trent	The Two Of Us / _I'll Be With You_ (A-side only)	Pye 7N 17300
Rolling Stones	We Love You / Dandelion	Decca F 12654
Martin's Magic Sounds	Mon Amour / Midem Melody	Deram DM 141
Biddu	Daughter Of Love / Look Out Here I Come	Regal Zonophone RZ 3002
Duffy Power	Davy O'Brien (Leave That Baby Alone) / July Tree	Parlophone R 5631
Mike Vickers Orchestra	Captain Scarlett And The Mysterians / Kettle Of Fish	Columbia DB 8281
The Kinks	Autumn Almanac / Mr. Pleasant	Pye 7N 17400
The Kinks	Autumn Almanac / David Watts	Pye 7N 17405 (export)
Kippington Lodge	Shy Boy / Lady On A Bicycle	Parlophone R 5645
Keith West / Mark Wirtz' Mood Mosaic	Sam (From 'A Teenage Opera') / Thimble Full Of Puzzles	Parlophone R 5651
Dave Davies	Susannah's Still Alive / Funny Face	Pye 7N 17429
Rolling Stones	2000 Light Years / She's A Rainbow	Decca F 22706 (export)
Bill Wyman / Rolling Stones	In Another Land / The Lantern	London 45-LON-907 (USA)
Arthur Greenslade	Joanne EP	20th Century Fox SR 4202

1968

Chris Rayburn	One Way Ticket / Photograph Of Love	MGM / Music Factory CUB 2
Clinton Ford	Cathy I Love You / American Girl	Pye 7N 17521
Sandie Shaw	Those Were The Days / Make It Go	Pye 7N 17611
Mark Wirtz	(He's Our Dear Old) Weatherman / _Possums' Dance_ (A-side only)	Parlophone R 5668

Gerry Temple	Lovin' Up A Storm / Everything I Do Is Wrong	RCA Victor RCA 1670
Jeff Beck	*Love Is Blue* / I've Been Drinking (B-side only)	Columbia DB 8359
Kippington Lodge	Rumours / And She Cried	Parlophone R 5677
Easybeats	Hello How Are / Falling Off The Edge Of The World	United Artists UP 2209
Paul Jones	*And The Sun Will Shine* / The Dog Presides (B-side only)	Columbia DB 8379
The End	*Shades Of Orange* / Loving Sacred Loving (B-side only)	Decca F 22750
The Bachelors	I'll Walk With God / *I Can't Wish You Any More* (A-side only)	Decca F 22814
The Scaffold	*Do You Remember* / Carry On Krow (B-side only)	Parlophone R 5679
Herman's Hermits	Sleepy Joe / Just One Girl	Columbia DB 8404
The Kinks	Wonder Boy / Pretty Polly	Pye 7N 17468
The Stocking Tops	I Don't Ever Want To Be Kicked By You / *The World We Live In's A Lonely Place* (A-side only)	CBS 3407
Anita Harris	We're Going On A Tuppeny Bus Ride / *Artie* (A-side only)	CBS 3468
The End	Loving Sacred Loving / *We've Got It Made* (A-side only)	Sonoplay SN-20054 (Spain)
Rolling Stones	Jumpin' Jack Flash / Child Of The Moon	Decca F 12782
The Aquarian Age	10,000 Words In A Cardboard Box / Good Wizard Meets Naughty Wizard	Parlophone R 5700
Dusty Springfield	I Close My Eyes And Count To Ten / No Stranger Am I	Philips BF 1682
Nicky Hopkins	Nicky Hopkins Top Pops No. 1 – Medley: Cinderella Rockefella, Lady Madonna, Congratulations/Part 2	MGM MGM 1419
Ray Stevens	Mr. Businessman / *Face The Music* (A-side only)	Monument MON 1022

Spooky Tooth	Love Really Changed Me / Luger's Groove	Island WIP 6037
The Who	Dogs / Call Me Lightning	Track Records 604023
The Who	Dogs / Circles	Polydor 59 210
PP Arnold	Angel Of The Morning / Life Is But Nothing	Immediate IM 067
The Scaffold	1-2-3 / Today	Parlophone R 5703
Sweetshop	Barefoot & Tiptoe / Lead The Way	Parlophone R 5707
The Kinks	Days / She's Got Everything	Pye 7N 17573
Madeline Bell	Thinkin' / *Don't Give Your Love Away* (A-side only)	Philips BF 1688
The Easybeats	Land Of Make Believe / We All Live Happily	United Artists UP 2219
Keith West	On A Saturday / The Kid Was A Killer	Parlophone R 5713
Elmer Hockett's Hurdy Gurdy / Mood Mosaic	Fantastic Fair / Yellow Spotted Capricorn	Parlophone R 5716
Anita Harris	Dream A Little Dream Of Me / The Flying Machine	CBS 3637
Billie Davis	I Want You To Be My Baby / *Suffer* (A-side only)	Decca F 12823
Roger Williams	The Impossible Dream (The Quest) / Dulcinea	London HLR 10214
Kippington Lodge	Tell Me A Story / *Understand A Woman* (A-side only)	Parlophone R 5717
Roger James Cooke	Skyline Pigeon / *I'm Burning* (A-side only)	Columbia DB 8458
Guy Darrell	Skyline Pigeon / Everything	Pye 7N 17586
Symon & Pi	Got To See The Sunrise / Love Is Happening To Me	Parlophone R 5719
The Move	Wild Tiger Woman / Omnibus	Regal Zonaphone RZ 3012
Beatles	*Hey Jude* / Revolution (B-side only)	Apple R 5722
Jackie Lomax	Sour Milk Sea / The Eagle Laughs At You	Apple APPLE 3
Rolling Stones	Street Fighting Man / No Expectations	London 45 LON 909 (USA)

Barbara Acklin	Love Makes A Woman / *Come And See Me Baby* (A-side only)	MCA MU 1038
Dave Dee, Dozy, Beaky, Mick And Tich (DDDM & T)	The Wreck Of The Antoinette / Still Life	Fontana TF 971
Dusty Springfield	I Will Come To You / The Colour Of Your Eyes	Philips BF 1706
Engelbert Humperdinck	Les Bicyclettes De Belsize / Three Little Words (I Love You)	Decca F 12834
Spooky Tooth	The Weight / Do Right People	Island 6046
The Easybeats	Good Times / *Lay Me Down And Die* (A-side only)	United Artists UP 2243
The Hollies	Listen To Me / *Do The Best You Can* (A-side only)	Parlophone R 5733
The Glass Menagerie	I Said Goodbye To Me / Frederick Jordan	Pye 7N 17615
The Scaffold	Lily The Pink / Buttons Of Your Mind	Parlophone R 5734
Tages	Halcyon Days / *I Read You Like An Open Book* (A-side only)	MGM 1443
Together	Henry's Coming Home / Love Mom And Dad	Columbia 8491

1969

Leigh Stephens	Red Weather / Sake Zwadoo	Phillips 40628 (Promo Only)
Spike Milligan	The Q5 Piano Tune / *Ning Nang Nong* (A-side only)	Parlophone R 5771
Small Faces	Afterglow / *Wham Bam Thank You Man* (A-side only)	Immediate IM 077
Roy Orbison	*My Friend* / Southbound Jericho Parkway (B-side only)	London HLU 10261
Barbara Acklin	Am I The Same Girl / *Be By My Side* (A-side only)	MCA MU 1071
Donovan & Jeff Beck Group	Barabajagal / Trudi (*also as Bed With Me*)	Pye 7N 17778
Jeff Beck Group	Plynth (Water Down The Drain) / Hangman's Knee	Columbia 1C 006 90 346 (Europe)
Jeff Beck Group	Plynth (Water Down The Drain) / Jailhouse Rock	Epic 5 10484 (USA)
Sweet Thursday	Mary On The Runaround / Getting It Together	Tetragrammaton T 1512
Jefferson Airplane	Volunteers / We Can Be Together	RCA 74-0245

1970

Ella Fitzgerald	Get Ready / Open Your Window	Reprise R 0850 (USA)
Fats Domino	Have You Seen My Baby / *Make Me Belong To You* (A-side only)	Reprise R 0891 (USA)
Fats Domino	*New Orleans Ain't The Same* / Sweet Patootie (B-side only)	Reprise R 0944 (USA)
Flirtations	Can't Stop Loving You / Everybody Needs Somebody	Deram DM 295

1971

McGuinness Flint	Malt & Barley Blues / Rock On	Capitol CL 15682 (USA)
Rolling Stones	*Brown Sugar* / *Bitch* / Let It Rock (live) (Let It Rock Only)	Rolling Stones RS 19100
Rolling Stones	*Wild Horses* / Sway (B-side only)	Rolling Stones RS-19101
Bill Elliott / Elastic Oz Band	God Save Us / Do The Oz	Apple APPLE 36
The Who	Let's See Action / *When I Was A Boy* (A-side only)	Track Records 2094 012
John Lennon / Plastic Ono Band	Imagine / It's So Hard	Apple 1840
John & Yoko / The Plastic Ono Band	Happy Xmas (War Is Over) / Listen The Snow Is Falling	Apple R 5970

1972

Chet Nichols	Time Loop / *The Offing* (A-side only)	Kama Sutra KA 552
Rolling Stones	Let It Rock / Blow With Ry	Rolling Stones RS 19102 (Germany)
Rolling Stones	Tumbling Dice / Sweet Black Angel	Rolling Stones RS 19103
Rolling Stones	All Down The Line / *Rocks Off* (A-side only)	Rolling Stones SAM 3 (promo only)
Rolling Stones	Happy / All Down The Line /	Rolling Stones RS 19104
Harry Nilsson	Spaceman / You're Breaking My Heart	RCA 2266
Harry Nilsson	Remember Christmas / The Lottery Song	RCA 2300

Harry Nilsson	You're Breaking My Heart / Remember Christmas	RCA 102156
Harry Nilsson	Spaceman / Turn On Your Radio	RCA 102183

1973

George Harrison	Give Me Love (Give Me Peace On Earth) / *Miss O'Dell* (A-side only)	Apple R 5988
Nicky Hopkins	Banana Anna / Pig's Boogie	CBS 1241 (Holland)
Nicky Hopkins	Speed On (S) / Speed On (M)	Columbia 4-45869 (promo)
Nicky Hopkins	Speed On / Sundown In Mexico	CBS 1328 (USA)
Nicky Hopkins	Speed On / Pig's Boogie	Columbia (USA)
Nicky Hopkins	Waiting For The Band / The Dreamer	CBS (USA)
Rolling Stones	Angie / Silver Train	Rolling Stones RS 19105
Ringo Starr	Photograph / Down And Out	Apple 1865
Ringo Starr	You're Sixteen / Devil Woman	Apple 1870

1974

Ringo Starr	*Oh My My* / Step Lightly (B-side only)	Apple 1872
Marc Bolan	Jasper C. Debussy / *Hippy Gumbo* / *Perfumed Garden Of Gulliver Smith* / (Jasper C. Debussy Only) (JCD Recorded In 1967)	Track Records 2094 013
Rolling Stones	*It's Only Rock'n'Roll* / Through The Lonely Nights (B-side only)	Rolling Stones RS 19114
Ringo Starr	Only You / Call Me	Apple R 6000
Joe Cocker	You Are So Beautiful / It's A Sin When You Love Somebody	A&M 1641

1975

Alexis Korner	Get Off Of My Cloud (mono) Get Off Of My Cloud (stereo)	Columbia 3-10166 (promo only)
Ringo Starr	No No Song / *Snookeroo* (A-side only)	Apple 1880

Robin Millar w/ Mick Taylor	Catch As Catch Can / *For My Life* (A-side only)	WEA 821003 (France)
John Lennon	No. 9 Dream / What You Got	Apple R 6003
Rolling Stones	*Out Of Time* / Jiving Sister Fanny (B-side only)	Decca F 13597
Art Garfunkel	I Only Have Eyes For You / *Looking For The Right One* (A-side only)	CBS S 3575

1976

Dane Donohue	I'm Easy / Restless Feeling	Columbia 10333
Rolling Stones	Fool To Cry / *Crazy Mama* (A-side only)	Rolling Stones RS 19121
The Wurzels	The Combine Harvester (Brand New Key) / *The Blackbird* (A-side only)	EMI 2450

1977

Rod Stewart	You're In My Heart / *You Got A Nerve* (A-side only)	Riva 11

1979

Chris Thompson & Night	If You Remember Me / Theme From 'The Champ'	Planet P 45904
Night	Hot Summer Nights / *Love Message* (A-side only)	Planet K 1367
Night	Hot Summer Nights / Party Shuffle	Planet P 45903
Night	Cold Wind Across My Heart / *You Ain't Pretty Enough* (A-side only)	Planet K 12420

1980

Graham Parker	Stupefaction / Women In Charge	Arista AS 0523
Rocky Sullivan	Love Me Just A Little / Shake Your Shake	Jupiter Records DGC 1003
Shogu Hamada	Tokyo / Kayaku No Yoni	CBS/Sony Japan

1981

Rolling Stones   *Start Me Up* /   Rolling Stones RSR 108
                                                 No Use In Crying
                                                   (B-side only)

1982

Space Jazz   Jonnie /   Applause Records
                                                 Alien Visitor's Attack

1983

Carl Stewart   Trouble At Home /   XES Records DST 001
                                                 The Monkey's In You

Ian McCorkle   McCriminal (EP)   Ah Me 00001

1984

Julio Iglesias / Willie Nelson   To All The Girls I've Loved   Columbia 04217
                                                 Before /
                                                 I Don't Want To Wake You
                                                   (A-side only)

Julio Iglesias / Diana Ross   All Of You /   Columbia 04507
                                                 The Last Time
                                                   (A-side only)

1985

The Present (with Scobie Ryder)   Dance Away (Christmas Day)   Plezure Records 844
                                                 (vocal & instrumental versions)

Religious Freedom Crusade   Hey, Bud Clark /   BPI Records
                                                 Battle Of Portland 1985

1986

Rod Stewart   Every Beat Of My Heart /   WEA 8625
                                                 Trouble
                                                   (A-side only)

L. Ron Hubbard   The Way To Happiness /   BPI Records
                                                 <unknown>
                                                   (A-side only)

1988

Spirit Of Play   Children In Need /   Release Records KIDS 1988
                                                 Children In Need (instrumental)

1989

Keith Relf   Together Now /   MCCM 89 002
                                                 All The Fallen Angels
                                                   (A-side only)
                                                   (Recorded In 1968)

Paul McCartney   *This One* /   Parlophone R 6223
                                                 The First Stone
                                                   (B-side only)

1992

Izzy Stradlin and the Ju Ju Hounds	Pressure Drop (EP) (Can't Hear 'Em only)	Geffen GFSTD 25

1993

Joe Walsh & Steve Earle	Honey Don't (Beverley Hillbillies) / *Hot Country Dance Sampler* (A-side only)	Fox Records RDJ 62717-2

1995

Joe Walsh / Frankie Miller / Nicky Hopkins	Guilty Of The Crime	Pyramid PRCD 7118 (CD single)
Bierce In L.A.	Do Some Don'ts / <*unknown*> (A-side only)	Rococo Records 623

1997

Paul McCartney	Beautiful Night / Same Love	Parlophone CDR 6489

1998

Jerry Lynn Williams	*Sending Me Angels* / *What Can I Do* / Running On Faith (Running On Faith only)	Blue Mark Records BLUE CD 1001 (Germany)

Unconfirmed Sessions or Unreleased Material

Papa John Creech, Alma Cogan, Sammy Davis Jr., Lesley Duncan, Adam Faith, Marianne Faithfull, Clinton Ford, Freddie And The Dreamers, Goldie and the Gingerbreads, Neil Christian & The Crusaders, Johnny Hallyday, Tony Hatch & Jackie Trent, Lee Hazelwood, Herman's Hermits, Engelbert Humperdinck, John's Children, Quincy Jones, Ronnie Jones, Tom Jones, Marmalade, Robin Millar (LP or single 1973), Anthony Newley, Peter & Gordon, John Phillips, Rockin' Vickers, Bob Seger (unreleased album), Barbra Streisand, Jim Sullivan, Donna Summer, Soundtracks: Breathless (Richard Gere); All The Right Moves (Tom Cruise); The Right Stuff; Vision Quest.

Bands & Live Appearances

Bands

Nicky was either a full member or as part of the support band for many tour projects. It's impossible to list them all, as many appearances were for single shows or events, and in many cases the "band" was assembled for just the one performance. The following list includes most of the actual bands and artists that Nicky performed with for extended periods.

1960, 1961-62
Screaming Lord Sutch and The Savages

> David "Lord" Sutch (vocals)
> Bernie Watson (guitar)
> Carlo Little (drums)
> Nicky Hopkins (keyboards)
> Rick Brown (bass)

1960
The Saxons

> Bernie Watson (guitar)
> Johnny Jenks (drums)
> Nicky Hopkins (keyboards)
> Rick Brown (bass)

1962
Cliff Bennett and The Rebel Rousers

> Cliff Bennett (vocals)
> Mick Burt (drums)
> Moss Groves (saxophone)
> Frank Allen (bass)
> Nicky Hopkins (piano)
> Bernie Watson (guitar)

1962-63
Cyril Davis & His R&B All Stars

> Cyril Davies (vocals, harmonica)
> Bernie Watson (guitar)
> Carlo Little (drums)
> Nicky Hopkins (keyboards)
> Rick Brown (bass)
> Long John Baldry (vocals) – 1963-67

1968
Poet and the One Man Band[50]

> Albert Lee (guitar)
> Tony Colton (guitar)
> Ray Smith (guitar)
> Pat Donaldson (bass)
> Barry Morgan (drums)
> Nicky Hopkins (piano)

1968-69
The Jeff Beck Group

> Jeff Beck (guitar)
> Mickey Waller (drums)
> Nicky Hopkins (piano)
> Rod Stewart (vocals)
> Ron Wood (bass)

1969
Sweet Thursday[50]

> Alun Davies (guitar, vocals)
> Jon Mark (guitar, vocals)
> Nicky Hopkins (piano)
> Brian Odgers (bass, woodwinds)
> Harvey Burns (drums)

1970, 1975, 1977, 1981-82, 1989
Terry and The Pirates[51]

> Terry Dolan (guitar, vocals)
> Greg Douglass (guitar)
> John Cipollina (guitar)
> Andy Kirby (drums)
> Bill Baron (drums)
> Bones Jones (drums, vocals)
> Buddy Cage (pedal steel guitar)
> Dave Carter (bass)
> David Hayes (bass)
> Greg Elmore (drums)
> Jeff Meyr (drums)
> Lonnie Turner (bass)
> Mark Springer (French horn, vocals)
> Nicky Hopkins (piano)
> Pete Sears (organ)
> Steve Derr (guitar, vocals)

---

[50] Neither Poet nor Sweet Thursday ever played live. They produced one album each.

[51] Hundreds of musicians have played with Terry and The Pirates over the years. Sorting out which ones played at the same time as Nicky is impossible. This short list covers those for whom we can confirm either live or session dates that Nicky played on.

1970-71
Quicksilver Messenger Service

David Freiberg (bass, vocals)
Greg Elmore (drums)
John Cipollina (guitar)
Nicky Hopkins (piano)
Dino Valenti (guitar, vocals) – 1971
Gary Duncan (guitar, vocals) – 1971

1971-73
The Rolling Stones' Touring Band

Mick Jagger (vocals, harp)
Keith Richards (guitar)
Mick Taylor (guitar)
Bill Wyman (bass)
Charlie Watts (drums)
Bobby Keys (saxophone)
Jim Price (trumpet, trombone)
Nicky Hopkins (piano)

1975-76
Raven

John Cipollina (guitar)
Andy Kirby (drums, vocals)
David Weber (drums)
Greg Douglass (guitar)
Hutch Hutchinson (keyboards)
Nicky Hopkins (piano)
Skip Olsen (bass)

1975
Jerry Garcia Band

Jerry Garcia (guitar, vocals)
John Kahn (bass)
Nicky Hopkins (piano)
Ron Tutt (drums)

1976
Leo Sayer's Touring Band

Leo Sayer (guitar, harp, vocals)
Alvin Taylor (drums)
Bobby Keys (saxophone)
Nicky Hopkins (piano)
Don Preston (synthesiser)
Reggie McBride (bass)
Steve Madaio (trumpet)

1977
Joe Cocker's Touring Band

Joe Cocker (vocals)
Bobby Keys (saxophone)
Cliff Goodwin (guitar, vocals)
Deric Dyer (saxophone, vocals)
Howard Hersh (bass)
John Riley (drums, vocals)
Kevin Falvey (synthesiser, vocals)
Nicky Hopkins (piano)

1978
Night

Chris Thompson (guitar, vocals)
Stevie Lange (vocals)
Billy Kristian (bass)
Nicky Hopkins (piano)
Peter Baron (drums)
Robbie McIntosh (guitar)

1979
Rocky Sullivan's Touring Band

Rocky Sullivan (vocals)
John Cipollina (guitar)
Nicky Hopkins (piano)
Greg Douglass (guitar)
Mario Cipollina (bass)
Joey Covington (drums)
Trish Robbins (backup vocals)
Jill Bergman (backup vocals)

1985
Sky (Touring Band)

Herbie Flowers (bass)
Kevin Peek (guitar)
Nicky Hopkins (keyboards)
Paul Hart (keyboards, guitar, cello, etc.)
Steve Gray (keyboards, saxophone)
Tristan Fry (drums)

1985-86
A 20th Anniversary Celebration of the Byrds (Touring Band)

Gene Clark (guitar, harp, vocals)
Billy Darnell (guitar) – 1985-86
Blondie Chaplin (guitar) – 1985
Carlos Burnell (bass) – 1985-86
Greg Thomas (drums) – 1985-86
John York (guitar)
Michael Clarke (drums) – 1985
Nicky Hopkins (keyboards)
Pat Robinson (keyboards)
Rick Danko (bass) – 1985
Rick Roberts (guitar, vocals)

1986
CRY/CHRY[52]

Gene Clark (guitar)
John York (guitar)
Pat Robinson (guitar)
Nicky Hopkins (piano)

---

[52] CRY/CHRY was a studio-only project to develop demo material for eventual recording contracts. Any live work involving the four musicians was done under the "20th Anniversary Celebration of the Byrds" name.

1987-89
Art Garfunkel's Touring Band

Art Garfunkel (vocals, guitar)
Nicky Hopkins (piano)
Simon Nicol (guitar)
Jess Bailey (keyboards)
Woody Woodmansey (bass)
Jeffery Jones (guitar)
Rob Sabino (synthesiser)

1991-92
Zero

Greg Anton (drums)
Martin Fierro (saxophone)
Steve Kimock (guitar)
Lowell "Banana" Levinger (keyboards)
Tony Saunders (bass)
Liam Hanrahan (bass)
Judge Murphy (vocals)
Pete Sears (keyboards, vocals)
Bobby Vega (bass)
Robert Hunter (lyrics)
John Kahn (bass)
Nicky Hopkins (piano)
Kathryn Warner (vocals)

1992
Tumbling Dice

Mick Taylor (guitar, vocals)
Bobby Keys (saxophone)
Nicky Hopkins (keyboards)
Fuzzy Samuels (bass)
John Marr (drums)

1993
The Flew

Joe Walsh (guitar)
Nicky Hopkins (keyboards)
Phil Jones (drums)
Rick Rosas (bass)
Terry Reid (vocals)

Other Live Appearances

Al Jarreau, Andy McCoy, Bob Weir, Edgar
Winter, Feargal Sharkey (TV), Frank
Stallone, John Trudell (w/Jesse Ed Davis),
Lulu, Paul McCartney (TV), Rocky Sulli-
van, The Dinosaurs, The Spongetones,
The Teabags

Film & Video Appearances

Sympathy for the Devil	The Rolling Stones	April 22, 1969 (filmed in June, 1968)	Directed by Jean-Luc Godard
The Rolling Stones Rock and Roll Circus	The Rolling Stones	October 15, 1996 (filmed Dec. 11-12, 1968)	Directed by Michael Lindsay-Hogg
Gimme Some Truth: The Making of John Lennon's Imagine Album	John Lennon	April 11, 2000 (filmed in 1971)	Directed by Jonas Mekas & Andrew Solt
Did Somebody Drop His Mouse?	Harry Nilsson	Never released (filmed in Mar. & Apr., 1972)	Directed by Richard Perry
Ladies and Gentlemen: The Rolling Stones	The Rolling Stones	January 1, 1974 (filmed in 1972)	Directed by Rollin Binzer
Cocksucker Blues	The Rolling Stones	1972 (filmed in 1972)	Directed by Robert Frank
Graham Parker at Rockpalast	Graham Parker & The Rumour	March 24, 2005 (filmed Oct. 18-19, 1980)	Rockpalast Archives
Rockpalast: Rock Palace: West Coast Legends Vol.5	Terry and The Pirates	November 29, 2010 (filmed Dec. 6, 1982)	Rockpalast Archives

Diamond Tiaras
Nicky Hopkins' Piano Style, Influences & Legacy

"A classical pianist with rock'n'roll fingers…"

– Klaus Voormann

Ian Stewart's widow, Cynthia Stewart-Dillane, had a lot to say about her husband's and Nicky Hopkins' time with the Rolling Stones. Both men died too young but one positive memory spoke eloquently of their talents:

"I can remember Nicky coming round to the house where there was a little sunroom and in this tiny space was Stu's old 'joanna' upright piano and a baby grand that the Stones had lent him. I remember Nicky sitting at the grand and Stu at the upright, making unbelievably beautiful music. Stu never read a note of music in his life, whereas Nicky was a classically trained pianist, and I noticed the difference between their hands. Nicky's fingers were long, pale, thin and hairless and Stu's were hairy with strong fingers. Stu did not finger the keyboard the way a proper pianist would, but Nicky changed chords professionally, classically. Their music was very beautiful."

If one thing distinguished Nicky Hopkins from other players in rock, it was his affinity for and lifelong loyalty to the real piano. His recorded appearances on electric keyboards or Hammond organ are few and far between and in later years his grudging conversion to the use of synthesiser technology was out of necessity rather than choice. Not surprisingly, Nicky was featured on countless occasions in musicians' magazines, discussing his early training, his technique, his equipment and his session history.

Nicky Hopkins (*Contemporary Keyboard*, 1976): "You can't replace a grand piano with an electric. A lot of bands make the mistake of recording with an acoustic piano and then go out on stage with an electric instrument. Using the electric is easier than renting a piano at each gig and then spending half an hour putting the pick-up on it, but for me the sound of the acoustic is worth the trouble."

The records in Nicky's own collection reveal his wide-ranging piano influences. Among the hundreds of items he owned (carefully alphabeticised, as with most vinyl junkies) were rock'n'roll and boogie-woogie singles and albums by Albert Ammons, B. Bumble and the Stingers ("Nut Rocker"), Chuck Berry (with Johnnie Johnson at the keys), Booker T & the M.G.s, Dave Brubeck, Floyd Cramer, Ray Charles, Clifton Chenier, Fats Domino, Aretha Franklin, Erroll Garner, Jerry Lee Lewis, Meade Lux Lewis, Ramsey Lewis, Little Richard, Big Maceo Merriweather, Dudley Moore, Garnet Mimms, Randy Newman, Billy Preston, Professor Longhair, Joe Sample, George Shearing, Nina Simone, Otis Spann, Art Tatum and Stevie Wonder. In interviews he added the names of more obscure favourites such as Pete Johnson, "Cripple" Clarence Lofton and Lafayette Leake and recalled "a pile of old '78s" at his parent's house with Chopin's "E Flat Nocturne" and "Liebestraum" by Franz Liszt. Naturally, his tastes also included novelty items such as Ray Turner's *Kitten On The Keys*.

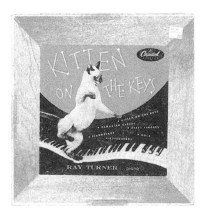

Moira Hopkins: "He got to meet Johnnie Johnson, his No.1 favourite, at the Royal Albert Hall during one of Eric Clapton's blues nights. Chuck Leavell took him backstage and when he came back, I said, 'So, did you speak to Eric Clapton?' He said, 'Oh yes—but I met Johnnie Johnson! When I think of all the licks I've stolen off that man during the years—it's one of the greatest nights of my life!' I've never seen Nicky so star-struck."

He later also professed admiration for jazz players such as Chick Corea, Herbie Hancock, Keith Jarrett and Bill Evans, though never considering them as influences on his playing.

Nicky's instinctive feel for traditional American piano styles and his uncanny ability to assimilate New Orleans, Memphis, Nashville and Chicago-born idioms into his own playing, was further nurtured by his friendships with like-minded souls such as Cyril Davies, John Baldry and Ian Stewart and his voracious appetite for new sounds on record. His classical training gave him the skills to analyse and "get under the skin" of his many influences and, like the Rolling Stones themselves, to re-import them back into the USA in a vibrant new form that was uniquely his own.

Having begun his career in the early sixties, Nicky suffered, along with every other pianist in that era's pop and rock music, from an absence of decent amplification for his instrument. With Screaming Lord Sutch and Cyril Davies he carried his own tuning equipment, often his own microphones and his tiny Hohner Cembalet to cope with the unpredictable situations he found himself in, and the primitive instruments often waiting for him at the venues.

During his years in London studios, limitations in technology presented other hazards:

Nicky Hopkins (*Contemporary Keyboard*): "The arrangers would write out massive reading things, which did me a lot of good, because I was a comparatively slow reader, but most recording was two-track, so if you hit a wrong note, there might be up to a hundred players who had to do the whole song again."

In time, experience led to a considerable relaxation in his approach:

"In general, I just write out the chord changes and work off that. I get the feel of it and play whatever feels right."

Robin Millar met Nicky with the Rolling Stones and used him on a project of his own in the early seventies:

"On the album that he did with me and Micky Taylor, I saw Nicky a lot, because there was only one room in the Apple Studios; He would always focus when it was time to do a take, but he could switch off. The minute you would finish, there would be conversations about how it had gone and what should happen next and you'd look over and Nicky would be leaning back, his feet, usually with what we used to call plimsolls, white trainers, up on the keyboard and the copy of the paper that he'd tucked into the piano lid while we were doing the take; he'd be reading a bit more of the article, but cocking an ear to what was going on, and when it was time for another take, he'd just quietly fold the paper and...three, four, he'd be right on it.

"He was what I would call a figurative player; he would look for little motifs that would highlight, or he would just bed in and support. I play keyboards and was in two minds whether to play myself. Mick Taylor persuaded me that I wouldn't regret getting Nicky in, and within an hour of the first take of the first song he did, these deeply sensitive little parts would come out. Thank goodness I wasn't playing."

By 1968, the choices available to those wanting to use an electric instrument had widened considerably, but for acoustic pianists, nothing had changed dramatically on the live front. When Nicky returned to the stage with Jeff Beck, more often than not he was forced to face sideways or backwards to minimise onstage feedback. The microphones stuffed inside his instrument were the only weapons in his battle with the insane level of volume coming off the Marshall and Orange amplifiers popular at the heavier end of the rock spectrum. The wing mirrors he later added to his grand piano when he toured with the Stones probably don't qualify as a keyboard innovation!

In a *Rolling Stone* magazine keyboard feature in 1980, Nicky was interviewed along with such colleagues as Little Feat's Bill Payne and Booker T. Jones and recalled the magic moment that decent amplification at last arrived for piano players:

"Up until last year, I always used an acoustic grand. Years ago I would use a contact mike through the soundboard to amplify it. Then when I was with Quicksilver Messenger Service, Carl Countryman gave us one of his first pick-ups, and it was amazing to get both the volume *and* the tone through the sound system so well."

81. The Countryman Pickup controller on top of the piano

Gary Duncan: "The Countryman Piano Pick-up was invented for us (Quick-silver). Carl was working on it when I came back to the group. He'd come in every night and screw around with some new thing to see if he could get it to work. He came up with a pick-up that goes into the piano and clips on to the harp and it's got pick-ups that fit across the strings to take a grand piano and make it electric."

Soundman Dan Healy claims to have had a hand in the development of the system:

"The very first piano pick-up ever made was for Nicky Hopkins and was really my idea. In those days you would wrap rags round microphones and stuff them in the sound hole of the piano, which was hardly a way to amplify a piano up to the levels of electric guitars. Nicky was a Baldwin artist, so we always got these beautiful nine-foot Baldwin concert grands on a rock'n'roll stage and there we were putting microphones in with rags round them! Nicky agreed to be my guinea pig and we made a prototype, which a lot of times would blow up in the middle of the show, but in the end Nicky was the first pianist in rock'n'roll who's sound was out there. Fortunately for all of us, he was always game to try ideas, even though they might be hopelessly inadequate and there was never any regret or reprisal."

By the time Nicky was playing with Jerry Garcia in 1975, he had graduated to a Helpinstill pick-up, also designed specifically for the live situation by a Texas manufacturer. Dan Healy elaborated:

"The Helpinstill has much less hum than the Countryman and you can turn it up much louder without getting feedback. It works on a magnetic principle like a guitar pick-up, with six metal bars that you mount as close to the strings as you can. In the old days the bands weren't nearly as loud as they are now."

The enormous strides that were taking place in all areas of music, affected keyboard technology too and four years later, Nicky took his own Yamaha CP 80 electric grand piano on tour with Night, which he said, "reproduces sound like an acoustic—and comes pretty close, the main problem being with the bass end which is almost impossible to keep in tune."

Because Nicky refused to stray from the piano, Chris Thompson brought a younger player into Night's line-up to carry the Hammond parts on synthesiser and Tim Schaefer sparked his colleague's interest in the new generation of electronic instruments. In the meantime, Nicky had relaxed enough to admit to owning a Fender Rhodes and, of course, had often used a harpsichord for studio work.

"There were no synths around when I started in '65. The first time I ever saw one was at Mick Jagger's place around 1969. Mick had just got this big Moog in and he and I spent about three hours trying to get some sounds out of it that made sense—and failed. You could only get one note at a time, so they were a bit boring. I lost interest after that."

This is an unfair dismissal of the inventive Moog parts he created for his own *Long Journey Home* album in the early seventies, but his allegiance to the grand piano remained central, and having once had the use of a Bösendorfer at the Who's Ramport Studios, that became his brand of choice, though he never owned one:

"Every Bösendorfer that I've ever played on has been magnificent. There are some great Yamahas and some bad ones, the same for Steinways and Bechsteins; Blüthner seems to be pretty good, though some are too bassy. Personally I've got a Mason and Hamlin, which is a Boston-made seven-foot grand. It's gigantic and I got it in San Francisco in 1970. They haven't been as good in recent years, but mine is from 1924."

This instrument later had a chequered history and actually appeared for sale on the Internet. Nicky had sold it, during one of his many moves, to Doobie

Brothers member John McFee, with the proviso that he could buy it back at a later date. When that moment came, his wife Moira remembers that the agreement was for some reason not observed and sadly Nicky never regained his favourite piano.

A decade after his passing, in September 2005, a mysterious seller in California, "user ID kept private" offered the Mason & Hamlin for sale on eBay to the highest bidder prepared to beat a $13,000.00 reserve. Apparently nobody stepped forward with the requisite cash and initially the item remained unsold. One person that, for sentimental reasons, considered buying it, was Nicky's anonymous friend from the seventies.

"D" : "My friend Michelle said, 'You know my brother-in-law has Nicky's piano.' When Nicky was going in for surgery, he had borrowed money from John McFee and offered the piano as collateral. When he (McFee) put it up for sale, I talked to my husband about buying it but we had no place to put it. We thought about donating it to the Hall Of Fame, as Nicky is not in there, which is a travesty. There needs to be more of him than a silver jacket, half-buried behind something Mick wore onstage, in the Rolling Stones exhibit. John e-mailed me on the morning of the September 7th and apologised, saying that Benmont Tench of Tom Petty's Band had beaten me to it, the only consolation being that he was a huge admirer of Nicky's."

Benmont took up the story:

"His piano was advertised on the Internet and Rick Rubin saw it; he knew I liked Nicky, but more to the point, he knew that I loved Mason & Hamlin. John McFee had it in a studio in Solvang and I was in Big Sur, so on the way back down, I stopped to play it and wasn't sure; I have an old beat-up 1873 Bösendorfer Baby Grand that I love as well as a Steinway and a Yamaha upright; I thought, 'I don't need another piano.' Then I played it and I thought, 'I need another piano.' They were happy for me to have it, because they'd had offers from people that weren't going to know what they had, or respect it, and might have just used it for decoration.

"I had it refinished, because there were some gouges and some duct tape stuck to it and it's beautiful: you hit a note on the low end and it sounds fantastic. I didn't know Nicky, though I met him once or twice and had a few phone conversations with him, but curiously he called me, just before he moved to Nashville, and said he was selling a piano and wondered if I might want it. I had no room for it, so I had to pass, but I expect it was the same piano, so I wound up with it anyway!"

In 1987 Nicky was interviewed by *International Musician & Recording World* and was obviously doing his best to bury his reputation as "just a piano player," emphasising the work he had done on the *Battleship Earth* album using the Fairlight, as well as his recent conversion to Kurzweil instruments:

"I need to become more familiar with the Fairlight and other electronic keyboards—take six weeks to figure it all out for myself and catch up with the technology. Meanwhile, I have got myself an Ensoniq ESQ 1, which has been a great starting point. I've already outgrown it, but it's been good. It's an all-in-one keyboard unit with a built-in sequencer, takes up very little room and is inexpensive too."

With the arrival of digital technology in the nineties, it became possible to achieve a very close approximation of true sound with synthesised instruments. Nicky tried out both Roland and Yamaha digital pianos while on tour in Australia, announcing that the latter "sounded like a brand new Bösendorfer Grand!"

He had begun to lose work due to his insistence on using just piano, but, more importantly, he was now coming to see his future as no longer simply a session man, but as a composer for films:

"I've been writing since the late sixties, but I was never very good at writing rock'n'roll songs. Around 1980, I realised that my music is very suitable for movies and I put together a film demo, which is getting around. It's just a beginning, but very exciting. I'll be writing on a Fairlight or something similar; it's wonderful for composing; instead of trying to work out what a horn line or string part is going to sound like, you can actually hear it."

Chuck Leavell was another traditionalist who forced himself to embrace the new technology in the early '80s and had several conversations with Nicky on the thorny topic:

"He wasn't interested enough in those sounds and I don't think it was something he really wanted to do. He knew what he was good at and that was the piano, so why mess with a good thing, you know?"

After his move back to England in the eighties, however, Scottish musician Scobie Ryder watched Nicky embrace the latest keyboard developments:

"To be honest I had little or no idea who he was. Despite being in the music industry, I'm not a widely scoped kind of person, so I didn't understand the enormity of the history and the amount of input Nicky had had into modern rock'n'roll. We got him involved with synthesisers and the day we started was the first time I'd ever seen him play. There was a Kurzweil piano in the office and I said, 'You could put some synth strings in this.' He was on it straight away and it was incredible to see him achieving complete oneness with the machine."

When this author met Nicky ten years later, there was a Yamaha keyboard standing in his Nashville apartment and he was already a veteran of several film and TV soundtracks. True as he was to his beloved grand, he was not some musical ostrich with his head in the sand, but kept up to scratch with the latest gear right up to the end of his life and would certainly have blossomed in the era of the Pro-Tools and Logic systems and computer recording.

Though Nicky held an unparalleled reputation among other musicians and in the industry, apart from his brief early success backing Lord Sutch and Cyril Davies, he was largely unknown to the general public until he went on the road with Jeff Beck.

Nicky's presence in the magazines and weekly music papers increased rapidly from then on, spreading to North America when he left for California. In 1970, he made his first showing in the prestigious *Playboy* magazine polls, coming in at

Number 17 in the vote for best pianist; by the following year he had leapt to second place, with only Dave Brubeck ahead of him. In '72, despite recording with various Beatles and touring prominently with the Rolling Stones, competition from, Leon Russell, Burt Bacharach and the more flamboyant Elton John, pushed him back to fourth place. A year later he had overtaken Burt, but still lingered behind the previous top two names at Number 3.

The early seventies were without doubt the most visible years in Nicky's career, but the nature of his role of "sideman to the stars" and his natural reticence meant that Nicky was never destined to become a household name. For serious music fans and the eagle-eyed however, he was a constant presence in the press, if often only by association, and hardly a week went by without his work prominently featured in the music weeklies.

Rolling Stone of December 27th, 1969 carried reviews of *Let It Bleed*, *Your Saving Grace* and a full-page advertisement for *Volunteers*. In February 1970, the same paper offered full-page advertisements for Quicksilver's *Shady Grove*, a full-page Warner's advertisement including the G.T.O.s *Permanent Damage* and a review of Richard Perry's *Ella Fitzgerald* production.

Nicky was an innovator whose talents were appreciated by his colleagues, even if the public remained largely ignorant. Richard Perna, besides being Nicky's publisher in the last years of his life, was himself an accomplished musician and played with Nicky the morning of the day he died:

"He had a couple of keyboards set up and we sat down facing each other and were really having a lot of fun, talking about musical composition and chordal passages; Nicky didn't have the biggest stretch for a keyboard player, but he played internally; if you notice his voicings, he did a lot with bass notes, but with his right hand, he would play his inversions a little differently and get a tremendous amount of colour from them. You could always tell his playing because of that. Very distinctive!"

Chuck Leavell admired Nicky's ability to find the perfect place in the mix:

"I think he understood better than anybody how to be heard but not be in the way. He would find something that would catch everyone's ear."

Robin Millar: "In the three years that I saw quite a bit of him in and out of the studio, I don't remember anyone formally asking Nicky to do anything. He was Nicky Hopkins; its not that you wouldn't have dared to argue with him, it's just that you knew it would be fine. There was no point saying, 'That little figure you played in the second chorus was great, could you play that in all the choruses?' Each take was breathtaking, but different from the last one. Nicky would remember a specific figure, so you didn't need to remind him."

Mill Valley resident Scott Matthews, who worked with Nicky on a number of occasions and whose resume of superstar affiliations almost measures up to Nicky's own, offered my favourite summary of his studio talents:

"It was his sense of economy as well as his flair. He listened well. Musicians aren't taught to do that—they just want to play! It's a gift that he had, to know instinctively when to lay low and when to rise above the maddening din and shine brightly. He had wonderful voicings and inversions that seemingly brought more music out of rather straight-ahead (i.e. borderline boring) guitar-based songs. That guy saved a lot of people's records from sounding mediocre."

Many of those interviewed were quick to praise Nicky, both as a man and as a musician and I have gathered together some of their comments here. But first there is an unsolicited e-mail message from drummer Billy Lee Lewis, who played with Nicky just once, on a session for his friend David Hayes, that provides a perfect portrait of his strange mixture of goofiness and brilliance:

82. Nicky Hopkins

"Nicky was the primary pianist on the date. A few of us were in the control room, while he was alone in the studio and presumably unaware that the piano microphone was live. Nicky pulled out his handkerchief and blew his nose two or three times. He then, with his index finger, went straight to the note his nose had made. He proceeded to alternate between nose and keyboard—"honk, plink, honk, plink"—several times and each time nailing the exact note on his "instruments." He was charmingly oblivious to the fact that his mates, sequestered in the control booth, were falling over themselves with laughter. Minutes later he slipped into an exceptionally beautiful, unidentified, classical piece, that entranced us to the point that we never thought to hit "record." That two-minute incident perfectly encapsulates the slightly nutty, "absent-minded professor" demeanor I perceived in him. I've always considered it an honor to have worked with him and I wish you the best with your book."

"Nicky could play anything. He was a genius."

– Bill Wyman

"He was the guy who basically set the tone; he just had it. It felt so good and it sounded so good; you couldn't help but love what he did. He brought such heart to his playing and every project he touched has a soulful, symphonic feel to it that comes from the way he connected to his instrument. I can hear a piano and know that it's Nicky. I wish he were here right now—it would be so great if he could just walk out on the stage and sit down at the piano."

– Steve Miller

"It was such a thrill to work for him as well as have him work with me. Every time I hear Joe Cocker's 'You Are So Beautiful' I want to cry before Joe's even come in. People try to emulate that piano piece, but there's only one person could have played that—Nicky Hopkins."

– Peter Frampton

"I can't speak highly enough of his piano playing. Most guys who think they can play—let's call it boogie-woogie—none of them can do the right hand like Nicky."

– Rod Stewart

"In my opinion, Nicky was the greatest rock'n'roll piano player of all time. There's nothing he couldn't play. He had superb musicianship and incredible feeling and technique. Whatever the origin of the song, he always seemed to nail it, conveying the roots, but at the same time making it modern."

– Richard Perry

"I worked with Richard Tee—I've even had Ray Charles alongside me and Nicky was up there with all of those guys; he just made you listen. Nicky was a genius, but a lot of the time genius isn't noticed until many years later."

– Joe Cocker

"'Chicago Calling' made me want to play the piano. Neither Ian Stewart nor I could compete with Nicky as a piano player. Our talents are our own, but we couldn't just play something that brilliant after hearing it for the first time. He really was incredibly, annoyingly talented."

– Ian McLagan

"Some of us are fortunate to have our styles, but Nicky was so recognisable. Within four bars of any given song you'd say, 'That's Nicky Hopkins.' You hear people like me today, who were undoubtedly heavily influenced by Nicky, trying to steal his licks. He was just a brilliant, brilliant musician!"

– Chuck Leavell

"It was always a treat to know Nicky was going to be on the session, because you knew he was going to be uplifting—a kind, positive force in the room."

— Nils Lofgren

"He was a rare and truly gifted musician whose love for it seemed to come from an altruistic and humble place within, which always resulted in a passionate and powerful contribution on stage and in the studio."

— Michael McDonald

"Headline words to describe Nicky would be 'breathtaking,' 'superb' and 'supernatural.' With Jefferson Airplane, we cut tracks all together; he would take a few notes and immediately play a perfect pass, but be unsatisfied and do two more. We loved them all and tried at least once using all three takes at once."

— Paul Kantner

"He had this rhythmic way of playing. It was like water; beats that rush over the top of each other and all end up in the same place."

— Gary Duncan

"He was the best 'comping' piano player of that age. He was a great soloist too, but most piano players lack the ability to comp really well. The left hand of the piano can really be a problem, especially for a bass player, if the piano player is not sensitive to leaving space for other people. Nicky never once got in the way of anything and that's genius."

— David Hayes

"Nicky Hopkins was the most important rock'n'roll session musician—ever."

— Dave Marsh

Nicky Hopkins was, as one famous astrologer put it, "one of a kind in his field, and difficult, if not impossible to replace." I am grateful to the ever-eloquent Robin Millar again for the perfect last word:

"I can't think of anyone who recorded before or after him who fulfilled anything remotely resembling the role that a Nicky Hopkins piano part played on a recording. In fact, were I to be in a situation as a producer and thinking in my mind, 'What would be great on this would be a Nicky Hopkins piano part' and wondering who I could get to do it, I have to tell you I can't think of anyone!"

Bibliography

Books

Bacon, Tony

London Live: From the Yardbirds to Pink Floyd to the Sex Pistols: the inside Story of Live Bands in the Capital's Trail-Blazing Music Clubs (Miller Freeman, San Francisco 1999)

Badman, Keith

The Beatles Diary Volume 2: After The Break-Up 1970-2001 (Omnibus Press, London 1999)

Barnes, Richard

The Who: Maximum R&B, A Visual History (Eel Pie, London 1982)

Bean, J.P. / Cocker, Joe

Joe Cocker: With A Little Help From My Friends (Random House, London 2003)

Beatles

The Beatles Anthology (Cassell & Co., London 2000)

Becker, Manfred / Ruechel, Peter / Wagner, Christian

Das Rockpalast Buch: Die Ersten Sieben Jahre (Sounds Verlag, Muenchen 1982)

Beckmann, Dieter / Martens, Claus

Star-Club (Rowohlt, Reinbek 1980)

Bego, Mark

Bonnie Raitt: STILL In the Nick Of Time (Cooper Square, New York 2003)

Bird, Brian

Skiffle: The Story Of Folk-Song With A Jazz Beat (Robert Hale Ltd., London 1958)

Blaney, John

Lennon & McCartney, Together Alone: A Critical Discography of the Solo Work (Jawbone, London 2007)

Bloom, Jerry

Black Knight: The Ritchie Blackmore Story (Omnibus Press, London 2006)

Bockris Victor

Keith Richards (Omnibus Press, London 2001)

Booth, Stanley

Keith: Standing In The Shadows (St. Martin's Griffin, New York 1995)

Booth, Stanley	*The True Adventures Of The Rolling Stones* (A Capella, Chicago 2000)
Boyd, Joe	*White Bicycles* (Serpent's Tail, London 2006)
Bramwell, Tony / Kingsland, Rosemary	*Magical Mystery Tours; My Life With the Beatles* (Thomas Dunne/St. Martin's Press, New York 2005)
Brown, Joe	*Brown Sauce* (Willow Books, London 1986)
Brown, Mick	*Tearing Down the Wall of Sound: The Rise and Fall of Phil Spector* (Bloomsbury, London 2007)
Charlesworth, Chris / Hanel, Ed	*The Who: The Complete Guide to their Music* (Omnibus Press, London 2004)
Coleman, Ray	*Clapton!* (Grand Central Publishing, New York 1988)
Cooper, Michael / Roylance, Brian	*Blinds & Shutters* (Genesis Publications, Guildford 1989)
Cordes, Gerd / Thomas, Wolfgang	*The Rolling Stones Over Germany: Schickt einen Fahrer mit langen Haaren* (Verlag Maria Thomas, Siegen 1998)
Cunningham, Mark	*Good Vibrations: A History of Record Production* (Castle Communications, London 1996)
Dalton, David	*The Rolling Stones: The First Twenty Years* (Alfred A. Knopf, New York 1981)
Dalton, David (editor)	*Rolling Stones: An Unauthorized Biography in Words, Photographs, and Music* (Amsco Music Publishing, New York 1972)
Dalton, David (editor)	*The Rolling Stones: The Greatest Rock 'n 'Roll Band In The World* (W.H. Allen & Co., London 1975)
Davies, Dave	*Kink: An Autobiography* (Hyperion, New York 1997)
Davies, Ray	*X-Ray: the Unauthorized Autobiography* (Viking/Penguin, London 1994)
Davis, Clive / Willwerth, James	*Clive: Inside The Record Business* (William Morrow, New York 1974)
Davis, Stephen	*Old Gods Almost Dead: The 40-Year Odyssey of the Rolling Stones* (Broadway Books, New York 2001)
Des Barres, Pamela	*I'm with the Band: Confessions of a Groupie* (Jove, New York 1988)
Duncan, Shelley	*My Husband the Rock Star: Ten Years with Quicksilver Messenger Service: A Memoir* (Flower Child Books, San Francisco 2002)
Einarson, John / Clark, Gene	*Mr. Tambourine Man: The Life and Legacy of The Byrds' Gene Clark* (Backbeat, San Francisco 2005)
Elliott, Martin	*The Rolling Stones: Complete Recording Sessions 1962-2002* (Cherry Red, London 2002)
Emerick, Geoff / Massey, Howard	*Here, There and Everywhere: My Life Recording the Music of the Beatles* (Gotham Books/Penguin, New York 2007)
Engelhardt, Kristofer	*Beatles Undercover* (Collector's Guide Publishing, Burlington, (Canada). 1998)
Fascher, Horst	*Let the good times roll! Der Star-Club-Gründer erzählt* (Eichborn, Frankfurt 2006)

Fawcett, Anthony

John Lennon: One Day at a Time: A Personal Biography of the Seventies (Grove Press, New York 1976)

Frame, Pete

More Rock Family Trees (Omnibus Press, London 1998)

Frame, Pete

Pete Frame's Complete Rock Family Trees (Omnibus Press, London 1993)

Frame, Pete

Pete Frame's Rockin' Around Britain: Rock'n'roll Landmarks of the UK and Ireland (Omnibus Press, London 1999)

Giuliano, Geoffrey / Giuliano, Avalon

Revolver: The Secret History Of The Beatles (Metro Publishing 2006)

Goodman, Fred

The Mansion on the Hill: Dylan, Young, Geffen, Springsteen and the Head-on Collision of Rock and Commerce (Jonathon Cape 1997)

Gray, Michael

Mother!: The Frank Zappa Story (4th Edition) (Plexus Publishing 2003)

Greenfield, Robert

Exile on Main St.: A Season in Hell with the Rolling Stones (Da Capo 2006)

Greenfield, Robert

S.T.P.: A Journey Through America With The Rolling Stones (Panther 1975)

Harper, Colin

Dazzling Stranger: Bert Jansch and the British Folk and Blues Revival (Bloomsbury 2000)

Harry, Bill

The Encyclopedia of Beatles People (Blandford Press 1997)

Heckstall-Smith, Dick

The Safest Place in the World: Personal History of British Rhythm and Blues (Quartet Books 1989)

Heylin, Clinton

Van Morrison: Can You Feel The Silence (Viking/Penguin 2002)

Hinman, Doug

The Kinks: All Day and All of the Night: Day by Day Concerts, Recordings, and Broadcasts, 1961-1996 (Backbeat 2004)

Hjort, Christopher

Strange Brew: Eric Clapton and the British Blues Boom (Jawbone 2007)

Hjort, Christopher / Hinman, Doug

Jeff's Book: A Chronology of Jeff Beck's Career, 1965-1980 – From the Yardbirds to Jazz-Rock (Rock 'N' Roll Research Press 2000)

Hodges, Chas

The Rock'n'Roll Years of Chas Before Dave (Lennard Publishing, Wheathampstead 1987)

Holland, Jools / Loewenstein, Dora

The Rolling Stones: A Life On The Road (Virgin Books 1998)

Hoskyns, Barney

Waiting for the Sun: Strange Days, Weird Scenes and the Sound of Los Angeles (Viking 1996)

Hounsome, Terry

Rock Record 7: Directory of Albums and Musicians (Record Researcher Publications 1997)

Janovitz, Bill

The Rolling Stones' Exile on Main St. (Continuum 2007)

Jones, Dylan (Editor)

Meaty Beaty Big and Bouncy!: Classic Rock & Pop Writing from Elvis to Oasis (Hodder & Stoughton 1996)

Karnbach, James / Bernson, Carol

Rolling Stones: The Ultimate Recording Guide (Aurum Press 1997)

Kent, Nick — *The Dark Stuff: Selected Writings on Rock Music, 1972-93* (Penguin Books 1994)

Kooper, Al — *Backstage Passes: Rock 'N' Roll Life in the Sixties* (Stein & Day 1977)

Kostelanetz, Richard — *The Fillmore East: Recollections of Rock Theater* (Schirmer Books 1996)

Leigh, Spencer — *Puttin' on the Style: The Lonnie Donegan Story* (Finbarr International 2003)

Lewisohn, Mark — *The Complete Beatles Chronicle* (Pyramid 1992)

Lewisohn, Mark — *The Complete Beatles Recording Sessions: The Official Story of the Abbey Road Years* (Hamlyn/Octopus 1988)

Loewenstein / Dodd (editors) — *According To The Rolling Stones* (Phoenix/Orion Books 2004)

Macdonald, Ian — *Revolution in the Head: Beatles Records and the Sixties* (Fourth Estate 1994)

Madinger, Chip / Easter, Mark — *Eight Arms To Hold You: The Solo Beatles Compendium* (441 Productions Inc. 2001)

Martin, George — *Summer Of Love: The Making of Sgt Pepper* (Genesis Publications 2006)

Matovina, Dan — *Without You: The Tragic Story of Badfinger* (Frances Glover, USA 1997)

McCartney, Mike — *Thank U Very Much: Mike McCartney's Family Album* (Panther 1982)

McLagan, Ian — *All the Rage: A Rock 'n' Roll Odyssey* (Sidgwick & Jackson 1998)

Michaels, Ross — *George Harrison: Yesterday & Today* (Flash Books 1977)

Miles, Barry — *Hippie* (Sterling Publishing 2004)

Miller, Andy — *The Kinks Are The Village Green Preservation Society* (Continuum 2004)

Neill, Andy / Kent, Matthew — *Anyway Anyhow Anywhere: The Complete Chronicle Of The Who 1958-1978* (Sterling Publishing 2005)

Norman, Philip — *Symphony for the Devil: The Rolling Stones Story* (Linden Press/Simon & Schuster, New York 1984)

Obermaier, Uschi — *High Times* (Heyne Verlag, Muenchen 2007)

Oldham, Andrew Loog — *2Stoned* (Vintage/Random House 2003)

Oldham, Andrew Loog — *Stoned: A Memoir of London in the 1960s* (Vintage/Random House 2001)

Pang, May & Edwards, Henry — *Loving John: The Untold Story* (Warner Books, New York 1983)

Peebles, Andy — *The Lennon tapes: John Lennon and Yoko Ono in conversation with Andy Peebles, 6 December 1980* (BBC 1981)

Pegg, Nicholas — *The Complete David Bowie* (Reynolds & Hearn 2006)

Perry, John — *Classic Rock Albums: The Who – Meaty, Beaty Big & Bouncy* (Schirmer Books 1998)

Pythons, The — *The Pythons: Autobiography* (Orion 2003)

342

Rawlings, Terry	*Rock on Wood: Biography of Ronnie Wood* (Boxtree, London 1999)
Record Collector Magazine	*The Rare Record Price Guide 2008* (Record Collector 2008)
Repsch, John	*The Legendary Joe Meek: The Telstar Man* (Woodford House, London 1989)
Sanchez, Tony	*Up and Down with the Rolling Stones: My Rollercoaster Ride with Keith Richards* (Morrow Quill Paperbacks, New York 1979)
Selvin, Joel	*Summer of Love: The Inside Story of LSD, Rock & Roll, Free Love and High Times in the Wild* (Plume/Penguin, London 1995)
Shankar, Ravi	*Ravi Shankar: An Autobiography – Raga Mala* (Welcome Rain 2001)
Shapiro, Harry	*Alexis Korner: The Biography* (Bloomsbury 1997)
Sharpe, Graham	*The Man Who Was Screaming Lord Sutch* (Aurum Press, London 2005)
Sheff, David (interviewer) / Golson, G. Barry (ed.)	*The Playboy Interviews with John Lennon and Yoko Ono: The Final Testament* (New English Library 1982)
Southall, Brian	*Abbey Road: The Story of the World's Most Famous Recording Studios.* (EMI Records 1982)
Spector, Ronnie / Waldron, Vince	*Be My Baby: How I Survived Mascara, Miniskirts, & Madness, or My Life as a Fabulous Ronette* (Macmillan 1991)
Sutch, Lord David / Chippendale, Peter	*Life as Sutch: The Official Autobiography of a Monster Raving Loony* (Harper Collins, London 1991)
Tarlé, Dominique	*Exile* (Genesis Publications 2001)
Taylor, Derek	*It Was Twenty Years Ago Today: An Anniversary Celebration of 1967* (Fireside 1987)
Turner, Steve	*Van Morrison: Too Late To Stop Now* (Viking 1993)
Twelker, Uli / Schmitt, Roland	*The Small Faces & Other Stories* (MPG Books, London 2002)
Unterberger, Richie	*Urban Spacemen and Wayfaring Strangers: Overlooked Innovators and Eccentric Visionaries of '60s Rock* (Miller Freeman, San Francisco 2000)
Voormann, Klaus	*Warum spielst du Imagine nicht auf dem weißen Klavier, John?: Erinnerunger an die Beatles und viele andere Freunde* (Ullstein Heyne List, Muenchen 2003)
Walker, Michael	*Laurel Canyon: The Inside Story of Rock-and-Roll's Legendary Neighborhood* (Faber & Faber, New York 2006)
Watts, Derek	*Country Boy: A Biography of Albert Lee* (McFarland & Co. 2008)
Welch, Chris	*Peter Grant: The Man Who Led Zeppelin* (Music Sales 2003)
Whittaker, Adrian (editor)	*Be Glad: An Incredible String Band Compendium* (Helter Skelter 2004)
Wood, Ronnie	*Ronnie: The Autobiography of Ronnie Wood* (Macmillan 2007)
Wyman, Bill	*Rolling With The Stones* (DK Publishing 2005)

Magazines

Beat Instrumental

Billboard

Bone Magazine

Circus

Crawdaddy

Disc & Music Echo

Eye

Good Times

History Of Rock (Orbis)

Keyboard

Melody Maker

MOJO

New Musical Express

New York Times Magazine

Playboy Magazine

Record Collector

Rock

Rolling Stone

Shindig

Sonics

Story Of Pop

What's New Boston

Zoo

Photo Credits

Many photographs in this edition come from various contributor's personal archives. Whilst the author and publishers have made every reasonable effort to trace the copyright owners of images used in the book, there may be some omissions of credits for which we apologise. We shall be very happy to attribute any such credits in a second edition.

Numbered Photos

© 1979 by Narconon, courtesy of the Nicky Hopkins Archive: 70
© Allan Ballard, courtesy of the Nicky Hopkins Archive: 54
© Boyd Albritton, courtesy of Mike Somavilla: 67
© Chris Ching, courtesy of Gray Levett: 78
© Dominique Tarlé, used by permission: 38-44
© Ed Perlstein, used by permission: 68, 81
© Ethan Russell, courtesy of the Nicky Hopkins Archive: 59, 65
© Günter Zint, K&K Center of Beat, used by permission: 12, 27, 31
© Jim Marshall, used by permission, courtesy of Deborah Grabien & Amelia Davis: 32, 47
© Jon Sievert, Humble Press, used by permission: 66
© Karl Maria Hofer, used by permission, courtesy of the Nicky Hopkins Archive: 24, 52-53
© Len Bunn, used by permission, courtesy of Ken Kirkman and The Old Alpertonians: 8
© Leo Orginos, used by permission, courtesy of Barbara Holden: 34
© Manfred Becker, used by permission: 76
© Mark Mawston, used by permission: 1
© Oswald Baumeister, used by permission: 48, 50
© Pete Dyer, used by permission: 19
© Scott Windus, courtesy of the Nicky Hopkins Archive: 69
© Todd "One Heart", courtesy of Ron Polte: 33
Author's personal collection: 26
Courtesy of Alan Benson: 6

Additional Photos

Index

Christian, Neil, 34, 52, 311

Cinderella Studios (Nashville), 113

Cipollina, Antonia, 117, 121, 128, 131

Cipollina, Gino, 120, 122, 131

Cipollina, Jan, 117, 119–120

Cipollina, John, x, 115–117, 119, 121, 123–124, 126–129, 188, 211, 257, 282, 325–326, *331*

Clapton, Eric, 34, 85, 112, 141, 168, 172, 281, 289, 329

Clark, Gene, 248, 263, 265–266, 276, 310, 326

Clarke, Frank, 54

Clarke, Michael, 248, 263, 326

Clarke, Stanley, 240

Clarke, Steve, 194

Clayderman, Richard, 270–271

Clayton, Merry, 135

Cliff Bennett and The Rebel Rousers, 29–33, 311, 325

Climax Blues Band, 305–306

Clinton, George, 204

Clooney, Rosemary, 19

Coast Road Drive, 201, 304

Cocker, Joe, ix, x, 156, 174, 200, 217, 221–227, 265, 277, 304, 321, 326, 337

Cocker, Pam, 277

Cogan, Alma, 57, 324

Cohen, John, 274

Coleman, Pamela, 281

Coleman, Ray, 281, 296

Collins, Albert, 272

Collins, Bootsy, 204

Colman, Stuart, 161

Colton, Tony, 70, 325

Columbia Studios (London), 198

Colyer, Ken, 34

Constanten, Tom, 212

Cooder, Ry, 186–187

Cooke, Roger James, 290, 318

Cooper, Alice, 28, 276, 304

Cooper, Michael, 93

Cooper, Ray, 176, 188, 190–191, 198

Cordell, Denny, 67, 315

Corea, Chick, 235–236, 239–240, 248, 329

Cosby, Bill, 70

Costello, Elvis, 180

Country Weather, 211

Countryman, Carl, 331

Courtney, David, 261

Covington, Joey, 326

Cramer, Floyd, 22, 54, 95, 329

Cream, 220

Creation, The, 300, 314

Creech, Papa John, 324

Crohn, Burrill Bernard, 45

Crohn's Disease, 45–46, 286, 295

Cropper, Steve, 83

Crosby, David, 115

Cruise, Tom, 324

Crusaders (The), 226

CRY/CHRY (band), 265, 310, 326

Currie, Sylvia, 44, 47–50

Cyril Davies All-Stars, 36–37, 39–40, 43, 51, 311

Daltrey, Roger, 74–75, 84–85, 87

Danko, Rick, 263, 326

Darin, Bobby, 22

Darnell, Billy, 326

Darrell, Guy, 318

Dave Dee, Dozy, Beaky, Mick And Tich, 319

Davies, Alun, 58, 70–71, 325

Davies, Cyril, 34–43, 51, 74, 77, 88, 311, 325, 330, 334, *see also* Cyril Davies All-Stars

Davies, Dave, 78–80, 82, 316

Davies, Ray, *xiii*, 40, 73, 77–83, 89, 296

Davis, Billie, 318

Davis, Clive, 188–189, 196–198, 210

Davis, Jesse Ed, 173–174, 199, 250, 327

Davis, Sammy Jr., 62, 324

Davis, Tim, 112–113

Davy Jones (Bowie) & The Lower Third, 312

Day, Doris, 19

De Groot, Keith David. *see* Temple, Gerry

De Lane Lea Studios (London), 105

De Lory, Al, 127

De Shannon, Jackie, 69, 204

Deborah (hitchhiker), 119

Decca Studios (London), 54

Deep Purple, 28, 70

Delaney & Bonnie, 135

Dennis, Felix, 171

Derr, Steve, 325

Des Barres, "Miss Pamela", 101

Dexy's Midnight Runners, 254

Diana, Lady, 269

Diesel Park West, 272, 307

Dijon, Rocky, 94

Dillon, Eric, 200

Dingoes (The), 304

Dinosaurs, The, 327

Dire Straits, 245

Ditto, Bradley, 307

Dixon, Willie, 272

353

357

About Julian Dawson

Julian Dawson was born in London 4th July 1954, the same day that Elvis first got together with Scotty and Bill to invent rock'n'roll. He is one of seven brothers.

He passed nine misspent years in two Catholic boarding schools and three good ones at Art College, before deciding to take up music full time and playing his first professional jobs for the US army in Germany. After a return to London, he spent the next years on the road all over Europe and the

UK with various band line-ups, playing his own songs from day one and eventually landing his first record deal.

One pub-rock influenced LP was followed by two albums for Polydor, both recorded at the legendary Can Studio near Cologne with Jaki Liebezeit and guests Richard Thompson and Toots Thielemans. *As Real As Disneyland* garnered album-of-month status and sold well in the German-speaking territories, setting a pattern of Dawson having more success abroad than at home that has remained a feature of his career so far.

In the early nineties Julian turned his attentions to the USA, making two albums in Nashville with E Street Band bass-player Garry Tallent producing and a host of local guests, including Vince Gill, Duane Eddy, Bill Payne and Steve Forbert. *Fragile As China* charted in Germany and helped him build a radio presence and a solid following in the USA, where he still tours at least once a year.

Visits to the States, and Nashville and Austin in particular, became a regular part of his life, leading to further recordings (five in all for BMG) and co-writes and collaborations with artists such as Dan Penn, Nicky Hopkins, Jules Shear and Lucinda Williams, with whom he also recorded a lovely duet, "How Can I Sleep Without You." His 1995 album *Travel On* features his collaboration with Nicky Hopkins: "You're Listening Now." In 1996 he produced country legend Charlie Louvin's comeback album *The Longest Train*.

Sharp-eyed music lovers may have caught Julian at festivals such as Newport (USA), Cambridge, Cropredy and Glastonbury in England, on tour with Plainsong, Al Stewart, Fairport Convention and others, on TV's *Later With Jools Holland* (with Richard Thompson) or the Europe-wide *Rockpalast* with his own band.

For several years he kept together a phenomenal live band, featuring guitarist Steuart Smith, now with the Eagles. More albums followed both as a member of Plainsong with Iain Matthews and solo, including *Under The Sun* with Soft Boys Kimberley Rew and Andy Metcalfe; 2002's *Hillbilly Zen* with ex-Byrd Gene Parsons; and *Move Over Darling* with Richard Thompson, Dan Penn and the Roches. After a well-received album of covers of women's songs—*Nothing Like A Dame* in 2006—his CD *Deep Rain* was produced by soul legend Dan Penn in his Nashville studio and is currently available on Blue Rose Records. It was followed in 2010 by *Julian Dawson Live*, with his current band.

What spare time he has is spent with his family, listening to music, collecting vinyl rarities, walking, writing and simply enjoying life.

For more information, look on the internet:
www.juliandawson.com

CPSIA information can be obtained
at www.ICGtesting.com
Printed in the USA
BVHW081928220620
581988BV00001B/35

9 780984 436224